Canada: The State of the Federation 2004

Municipal-Federal-Provincial Relations in Canada

Edited by

Robert Young and Christian Leuprecht

Published for the Institute of Intergovernmental Relations
School of Policy Studies, Queen's University
by McGill-Queen's University Press
Montreal & Kingston • London • Ithaca

Canadian Cataloguing in Publication Data

Library and Archives Canada has catalogued this publication as follows:

Canada : the state of the federation.

Annual.
1985-
Continues: Year in review, ISSN 0825-1207.
ISSN 0827-0708
ISBN 1-55339-016-4 (2004 issue ; bound).—ISBN 1-55339-015-6 (2004 issue : pbk.)

1. Federal-provincial relations—Canada—Periodicals. 2. Federal government—Canada—Periodicals. I. Queen's University (Kingston, Ont.). Institute of Intergovernmental Relations

JL27.F42   321.02'3'0971   C86-030713-1 rev

The Institute of Intergovernmental Relations

The Institute is the only organization in Canada whose mandate is solely to promote research and communication on the challenges facing the federal system.

Current research interests include fiscal federalism, the social union, health policy, the reform of federal political institutions and the machinery of federal-provincial relations, Canadian federalism and the global economy, and comparative federalism.

The Institute pursues these objectives through research conducted by its own staff and other scholars, through its publication program, and through seminars and conferences.

The Institute links academics and practitioners of federalism in federal and provincial governments and the private sector.

The Institute of Intergovernmental Relations receives ongoing financial support from the J.A. Corry Memorial Endowment Fund, the Royal Bank of Canada Endowment Fund, the Government of Canada, the Government of Ontario, and the Government of Manitoba. We are grateful for this support which enables the Institute to sustain its extensive program of research, publication, and related activities.

L'Institut des relations intergouvernementales

L'Institut est le seul organisme canadien à se consacrer exclusivement à la recherche et aux échanges sur les questions du fédéralisme.

Les priorités de recherche de l'Institut portent présentement sur le fédéralisme fiscal, l'union sociale, la santé, la modification éventuelle des institutions politiques fédérales, les mécanismes de relations fédérales-provinciales, le fédéralisme canadien au regard de l'économie mondiale et le fédéralisme comparatif.

L'Institut réalise ses objectifs par le biais de recherches effectuées par son personnel et par des chercheurs de l'Université Queen's et d'ailleurs, de même que par des congrès et des colloques.

L'Institut sert comme lien entre les universitaires, les fonctionnaires fédéraux et provinciaux et le secteur privé.

L'Institut des relations intergouvernementales reçoit l'appui financier du J.A. Corry Memorial Endowment Fund, de la Fondation de la Banque Royale du Canada, du gouvernement du Canada, du gouvernement de l'Ontario et du gouvernement du Manitoba. Nous les remercions de cet appui qui permet à l'Institut de poursuivre son vaste programme de recherche et de publication ainsi que ses activités connexes.

CONTENTS

IV Policy

V   Processes

VI Chronology

FOREWORD

This year's *Canada: The State of the Federation* explores aspects of multilevel governance in Canada. As the introduction explains, it seems time to broaden the scope of intergovernmental scholarship in Canada to provide space for cities and municipalities more generally. The demography of the country is tilting rapidly towards the urban areas, substantial provincial-municipal restructuring has taken place, new global forces seem to be pressing cities to the forefront, and the advocates of city power are pressing for more resources and autonomy, with considerable success. The purpose of this volume is to present new research about these trends and to deepen our understanding of the complexities of municipal-federal-provincial relations in Canada. For those interested in Canadian federalism, some of the material presented here will be unfamiliar, yet the principles and processes parallel those encountered before, and it is appropriate that we become acquainted with a much richer and more complex world than the traditional one of federal-provincial relations.

The contributions presented here originated as papers delivered at the conference on "Municipal-Federal-Provincial Relations: New Structures/New Opportunities," held by the Institute of Intergovernmental Relations at Queen's University on 9–10 May 2003. This conference, and this volume, would not have been possible without the steady support of Harvey Lazar, then the Institute's director. Always keen on innovation, Harvey's encouragement and hard work are deeply appreciated. Thanks are due as well to the other sponsors of the event: the Canadian Network of Federalism Studies, the network of Villes-Régions-Monde, and the Social Sciences and Humanities Research Council of Canada (SSHRC), through the Federalism and Federations Program.

Thanks are also extended to those who served as session chairs and discussants – Naomi Alboim, Rianne Mahon, André Juneau, Alastair Saunders, Geoffrey Martin, Jean-Pierre Collin, Ron Vogel, Enid Slack, Neil Bradford, and Tom Courchene – as well as to the conference organizers, Mary Kennedy and Patti Candido, who handled all the logistics with their usual grace and good humour. Rachel Starr and James Sleeman of PinkCandyProductions developed the conference website.

Converting conference papers into books can be harder than negotiating complex intergovernmental agreements. First, many actors are involved. As always, the Institute's *State of the Federation* owes much to referees – twenty-six of them – who cannot be publicly thanked but who contributed their expertise to improve the work of the authors. We are very grateful to them. The authors themselves endured delays and uncertainty but rose to the occasion of revisions. Mary Kennedy fastidiously kept track of a multitude of files, while Patti Candido handled the accounts. The superb editing of Carlotta Lemieux maintained the Institute's high standard of presentation. Valerie Jarus deserves much praise for her careful work at the publishing end, while Mark Howse contributed the cover design. Kingston Language Services handled the translation of the abstracts. Aron Seal and Stephanie Quesnelle assembled the chronology of major events in Canadian federalism that concludes this volume. It covers the 2004 calendar year and has a useful index.

Conversion of papers into a book also requires financial support. Some was forthcoming from the Institute and some from the Canada Research Chair on Multilevel Governance at the University of Western Ontario. More was supplied by SSHRC through the Major Collaborative Research Initiative on "Multilevel Governance and Public Policy in Canadian Municipalities," with which many of the contributors are involved. This book is the first tangible output of this very large research project. It will soon be followed by another Institute publication, a comparative volume that presents surveys of multilevel governance in some of the world's major federations. The SSHRC support is much appreciated.

Finally, I wish to thank my co-editor, Christian Leuprecht. He was a postdoctoral associate at the Institute and was assigned by Harvey Lazar to chase progress. As it turned out, his efforts and advice and collaboration as a colleague were invaluable.

Robert Young
February 2006

PREFACE

I am pleased to introduce *Canada: The State of the Federation 2004*, edited by Robert Young and Christian Leuprecht. Robert Young has been associated with the Institute for almost two decades and has published three other books with the Institute. He has had a long-standing relationship with the State of the Federation series, having co-edited the 1992 volume. Christian Leuprecht is a research associate at the Institute who, under the auspices of my predecessor, Harvey Lazar, got involved in the later stages of this project to help bring it to fruition. I want to thank Drs. Young and Leuprecht for their professionalism and Dr. Lazar for his leadership in seeing this important project through to completion.

Sean Conway
Director, IIGR
May 2006

CONTRIBUTORS

Loleen Berdahl, Ph.D., is the senior researcher for the Canada West Foundation, a non-profit, non-partisan public policy research institute in Calgary, Alberta. Her research interests include urban policy, federalism, and public opinion.

Julie-Anne Boudreau is assistant professor at the Institut national de la recherche scientifique-urbanisation, culture, et société (INRS-UCS) in Montreal. She holds the Canada Research Chair on the City and Issues of Insecurity.

Thomas J. Courchene is the Jarislowsky-Deutsch Professor of Economic and Financial Policy in Queen's School of Policy Studies and is senior scholar of the Institute for Research on Public Policy (Montreal).

Christopher Dunn is a professor of political science at Memorial University of Newfoundland. His teaching and publishing areas have included Canadian politics, the constitution, public policy, and public administration.

Joseph Garcea is an associate professor in the Department of Political Studies at the University of Saskatchewan, where he teaches courses in municipal government, public policy, public management, and federalism. His areas of research and publication include municipal government, urban reserves, immigration, citizenship, and multiculturalism.

Pierre Hamel is professor of sociology at the Université de Montréal. He has written extensively on social movements, urban politics, and local democracy. His current research includes a comparative analysis of city-regions in Canada.

J. David Hulchanski is director of the Centre for Urban and Community Studies and a professor in the Faculty of Social Work at the University of Toronto. His Ph.D. is in urban planning. His research is focused on social policy, urban housing, and neighbourhoods.

Christian Leuprecht is assistant professor in the Department of Political Science and Economics and the Division of Continuing Studies at the Royal

Military College of Canada. He is cross-appointed to the Department of Political Studies at Queen's University, where he is also a research associate at the Institute of Intergovernmental Relations and a fellow of the Queen's Centre for International Relations.

Melville McMillan is a professor of economics at the University of Alberta. He specializes in the economics of the public sector and has devoted much of his scholarly efforts to the study of local government in Canada and elsewhere.

Christian Poirier is associate professor in the Department of Political Science at Laval University. His research involves interest groups and policy in Canada, Quebec, and comparatively, notably in the cultural and immigration sectors.

Ken Pontikes is a professional affiliate in the Department of Political Studies at the University of Saskatchewan, where he teaches courses in municipal government, provincial politics, and public administration. He has served as a deputy minister for Saskatchewan's Department of Municipal Affairs, Culture and Housing and as director of planning and development for the City of Saskatoon.

Stephanie Quesnelle is a research assistant at the Institute of Intergovernmental Relations and is studying at York University's Osgoode Law School.

Jean Rousseau has a Ph.D. in political science and is currently a researcher at the Conseil de la santé et du bien-être. His interests concern the transnationalization of social movements, the current transformation of citizenship politics, and the impact of globalization on Quebec politics.

Andrew Sancton is a professor of political science at the University of Western Ontario. He was an expert witness on the losing side in the court challenges to provincial legislation for municipal amalgamation in both Toronto and Montreal.

Aron Seal is a Master of Arts student of economics at Queen's University. He is a research assistant in the Institute of Intergovernmental Relations and a teaching assistant in Queen's University's Department of Economics and in the Royal Military College's Department of Politics and Economics.

David Siegel is dean of the Faculty of Social Sciences and professor of political science at Brock University. He has a Ph.D. in political science from the University of Toronto and an M.A. in public administration from Carleton.

Patrick Smith has a Ph.D. from the London School of Economics and is director of the Institute of Governance Studies and professor of political science at Simon Fraser University. His research interests include local and metropolitan governance, global cities, and public policy.

Kennedy Stewart has a Ph.D. from the London School of Economics and is an assistant professor in Simon Fraser University's graduate Public Policy Program. His research interests include cities, research methods, democracy, and democratic theory.

Tom Urbaniak is assistant professor of political science at Cape Breton University. He is a recent Ph.D. graduate of the University of Western Ontario, where his research focused on mayoral leadership, suburban development, and the politics of Mississauga, Ontario.

Robert Young is professor of political science at the University of Western Ontario. He is a fellow of the Institute of Intergovernmental Relations and holds the Canada Research Chair in Multilevel Governance.

I

Introduction

Introduction: New Work, Background Themes, and Future Research about Municipal-Federal-Provincial Relations in Canada

Robert Young and Christian Leuprecht

Ce chapitre présente d'abord une introduction aux articles qui suivent, puisque ce ne sont pas tous les lecteurs qui connaissent bien les différents aspects des relations intergouvernementales lorsque celles-ci incluent les gouvernements municipaux. Puis, dans ce chapitre, on discute de plusieurs thèmes que l'on retrouve sous-jacent des analyses présentées. Ces thèmes incluent les raisons pour lesquelles on s'intéresse de plus en plus aux questions d'ordre municipal au Canada (tels que les changements démographiques, la mondialisation et l'apparition de nouvelles valeurs et de nouvelles technologies), l'impact des nouvelles méthodes d'administration publique, les façons dont la gouvernance à niveaux multiples en Europe a modifié nos idées préconçues, et le rôle de la défense des intérêts des municipalités par des organismes et des individus spécifiques. En dernier lieu, on explore quelques possibilités de recherches éventuelles sur la gouvernance à niveaux multiples, des recherches qui peuvent êtres effectuées dans le but de poursuivre le travail présenté dans ce volume.

INTRODUCTION

To those familiar with the work of the Institute of Intergovernmental Relations and with the *State of the Federation* series, the papers in this volume will represent something of a departure from the norm. "Intergovernmental relations" as normally construed implies federal-provincial relations. But here the emphasis is shifted to include cities, and municipalities more generally, as actors in the intergovernmental matrix. Not only do some of the chapters that follow focus on relations between municipalities and provincial governments in their institutional, fiscal, and political dimensions, but others – the majority of the articles – are concerned with the complexities of municipal-federal-provincial relations. As the ordering in the last phrase implies, matters of special concern here are interactions between local governments and the central government. This is of increasing interest in Canada, though the last survey of the field was done more than ten years ago (Andrew 1994) and the last monograph on the topic dates from the 1970s (Feldman and Graham 1979).

The contributions collected here are ordered into four categories: the background to change in multilevel governance in Canada, municipal restructuring, municipal-federal-provincial policies, and the processes of complex intergovernmental relations. The first section of this introduction provides a brief resumé of each chapter. In the next section are explored more general issues about multilevel governance, ones that form the context for the Canadian case and are illuminated by the works presented here. Finally, there are suggestions for further research and reflection, suggestions that arise both from the wealth of information and ideas contained in this set of papers and from the continued evolution of the Canadian federation.

A caveat is in order first. For several decades, many (but not all) scholars interested in Canadian federalism have sought to affirm a certain constitutional egalitarianism by referring to the "orders" of the federation. This hearkens back to K.C. Wheare's definition of the federal principle as "a method of dividing powers so that the general and regional governments are each, within a sphere, co-ordinate and independent" (Wheare 1953, 22), and the usage may have originated somewhere not unadjacent to the Institute of Intergovernmental Relations – an honest broker in Canadian federalism if there ever was one. Hence, we refer to the provincial "order" of government, emphasizing not so subtly a co-sovereign status for provincial states that is equal to that of the federal order. But when municipal governments are concerned, this terminology breaks down. Under section 92.8 of the *Constitution Act 1867*, municipalities lie firmly within provincial jurisdiction as "creatures of the provinces"; that is, as "simply one of the powers given to the provinces to exercise as they see fit" (Tindal and Tindal 2004, 179). However much their leaders, advocates, and allies strive to win them more autonomy and status, in part through rhetorical spin, this fundamental fact has not changed; nor is it likely to. Moreover, the term is cumbersome when applied to three "orders." Finally, analysts and political actors throughout the world are content to refer to "levels" of government. Discussing government in contemporary Europe (let alone "governance" in that entity) would be frustrating were we not able to speak about the six or seven levels of government operating there. This is especially true with respect to the term "multilevel governance," which is used around the globe. "Multi-order governance" does not work. So here we may speak of "levels" – with no intent, of course, of elevating Ottawa at the expense of the provinces.

THE CONTRIBUTIONS

The first three chapters here provide background for the others. To start, Loleen Berdahl provides an account of recent initiatives Ottawa has made towards municipalities. These began tentatively when Jean Chrétien's government created Infrastructure Canada, set up a caucus task force on urban issues, and then established a cities secretariat within the Privy Council Office. This movement accelerated when Paul Martin took power and inaugurated his New Deal for Cities and Communities. Drawing on the extensive work of the Canada West Foundation, Berdahl outlines some municipal-federal relations in major prairie cities and draws conclusions about how Ottawa might better organize these relationships.

Next, Melville McMillan provides a comprehensive overview of the fiscal position of Canadian municipalities. Local governments in Canada are heavily reliant on the property tax, along with fees and transfers. The great bulk of transfers flow from provincial governments, often with conditions. Municipal revenues have not grown in parallel with those of the federal and provincial governments, and the vulnerability of local governments to exogenous shocks is made clear in the data McMillan provides about Ontario, where the Progressive Conservative government led by Mike Harris conducted a sweeping reform of functional responsibilities and fiscal structures. Overall, provincial transfers to municipalities dropped after 1995 (a consequence, one might argue, of federal cuts in payments to provincial governments) and again after 1999. Transfers to municipalities between 1995 and 2001 fell by about one-third, straining the politically sensitive property tax and setting the context for rising local demands for more resources.

The contribution by Tom Courchene is no doubt the most sweeping piece in the collection. He places cities, especially global city-regions (GCRs), in the context of globalization, a set of changes in the flow of money, goods, services, ideas, technologies, and people. Economic success, he contends, hinges on successful competition in the knowledge-based economy, and since much of this is centred in the big GCRs, they must attract and retain talent. This requires money, and while there is room for more effort by municipal governments to raise revenues, Courchene deploys his expertise in federal-provincial fiscal relations to argue strongly for a rebalancing of resources towards the cities. If competitiveness is imperative, there is no real choice about this.

It is partly in the name of competitiveness that many provincial governments have restructured their municipal systems substantially, and this is the topic of the second section of this book. During the last decade, there were major realignments of boundaries and functions in almost every Canadian province (Garcea and LeSage 2005). Change on this scale had not been witnessed since the 1960s, when very complex systems of government involving counties and other intermediaries were reformed and there were experiments with metropolitan, two-tier, and special-purpose structures (O'Brien 1993; Young 1987). As in that decade, the contemporary restructuring has occasioned much more interest in local government by citizens and scholars alike.

In a comparative chapter, Andrew Sancton plumbs the causes of amalgamation in Halifax, Montreal, and Toronto. His careful analysis shows that these major developments cannot credibly be attributed to global forces; nor did they come about because of the dynamics specified in society-centred theories of structural change. Instead, he argues, provincial governments – indeed, provincial premiers – were able to push through amalgamations because of their relatively autonomous position in the constitutional order.

But these changes provoke opposition, which is the focus of the next two chapters. Pierre Hamel and Jean Rousseau place the Montreal amalgamation within the long history of centre-regional relations in Quebec. This has been marked by contestation for power by the periphery and also by strong citizen demand for greater democratic control over the technocratic and business-oriented Quebec state. The latest amalgamation was an institutional fix, they argue, imposed by the centre, rather than being a more profound change that might have bolstered the participation of the citizenry while securing popular assent.

Julie-Anne Boudreau expands this analysis of resistance, geographically embracing the Toronto case along with Montreal and theoretically aiming to explore the "rescaling" inherent in amalgamations and their politics. At the same time that functions and authority are re-allocated in space, new technologies and mobilization strategies allow for political activity to occur at various scales (or levels of government). In Montreal, part of the resistance to amalgamation involved the anglophone community which, given its weakened linguistic situation provincially, was determined to preserve its autonomy locally. In Toronto, the downtown "urbane" community fought the threatening provincial-driven amalgamation on a variety of scales; one notable counterattack consisted of massive support for the federal Liberal Party.

The repercussions of change also occupy David Siegel, who explores provincial-municipal developments in Ontario more broadly, providing a lucid survey of recent realignments of borders, responsibilities, and finances. The system in Ontario evolves in "fits and starts," he observes, noting that the latest "fit" in the province remains incomplete in important respects. Moreover, the amalgamations, especially in Toronto, are bound to have significant long-term consequences in the political arena.

The last two sections of this book focus directly on municipal-federal-provincial relations. The second of these is mainly concerned with process, while the first explores two policy fields, housing and immigrant settlement. Many other policy fields could have been included. Lacking here is work on hard policy areas, such as infrastructure and property development. Another notable gap concerns Aboriginals and the policies in place (or not) to assist them, especially in the major western cities, where they constitute a rapidly rising share of the population. But fortunately there is a growing body of work on First Nations people in cities generally (Graham and Peters 2002). Many other policy fields are touched on in the four chapters that deal with the processes of multilevel governance.

Christian Poirier's contribution examines the settlement and social integration of immigrants, a hugely important issue in Canada, especially in the metropolises where most immigrants settle. The study compares policy about "the management of ethnic diversity" in Ottawa and Montreal, and Poirier makes two intriguing observations. First, city governments have considerable autonomy in this field, because their administrations are linked into the local immigrant networks and they administer relevant services such as housing, policing, and recreation. Second, and somewhat contradictorily, while the federal government plays an important role in the field, it tends to work in formal partnership not with city governments but with grassroots non-governmental organizations (NGOs).

Housing policy is a field of similar complexity, according to David Hulchanski. He shows that there is a long tradition of municipal-federal relations in housing, dating back to the 1940s. Concluding direct intergovernmental agreements has not been difficult when there is a will to proceed on both sides. But Hulchanski sets changing housing policy within the larger context of the shape and evolution of the welfare state, and he argues trenchantly that dual housing policies exist. There is a policymaking consensus and a continuing pattern to policy such that most effort is directed towards the primary part of the system – owners and higher-end renters – rather than the secondary part – renters, the homeless, and the rural poor. This analysis has sobering implications for those concerned with social inclusion in the neoliberal state, be it federal, provincial, or municipal.

The final section contains papers concerned with the processes of municipal-federal-provincial relations; that is, how policies are formed in complex intergovernmental systems. Smith and Stewart begin with an analysis of Vancouver and focus on two issues. First, they argue that Canadian cities, apparently constrained constitutionally to merely beaver away at service provision, can nevertheless set the policy agenda and lever resources from other levels of government. Second, they are interested in a "whole of government" approach, which means that for hard and complex problems, the resources, expertise, and jurisdictional authority of all levels of government need to be deployed in a coordinated fashion. Studying homelessness and drug policy, they show that determined local leadership can indeed bring about change and intergovernmental cooperation.

Tom Urbaniak's chapter reinforces this point. He examines the goals and strategies of the municipal government of Mississauga, a very large "edge city" of the type that slips under most scholars' radar screens. The mayor of Mississauga, Hazel McCallion, is a uniquely successful and powerful politician who is currently serving her tenth term. Drawing on general theories about the limits to municipal action and the opportunities for leadership, Urbaniak examines the city's manoeuvring with Ottawa on three crucial dossiers: the Pearson airport, the waterfront, and homelessness. He demonstrates that local political pressure and the land-use planning expertise located only within municipal administrations have enabled the mayor to put effective pressure on other levels of government, especially Ottawa, so that they help drive economic development in the city.

Christopher Dunn paints a very different picture of the periphery – Newfoundland and Labrador – and indeed of the deep periphery of the province's rural areas. Local government here is relatively weak, and Dunn shows how the federal government's priorities and programs can shape and reshape the most vital local bodies – economic development organizations – as they struggle to access a wide range of funding opportunities. The provincial government inserts itself into these relationships selectively. It attempts to mediate them when the regional distribution of benefits is visible and salient, as it is in such fields as infrastructure funding and housing.

This demonstration of a widespread federal presence in municipal relations is reinforced by the work of Garcea and Pontikes, who study Saskatchewan. They document a multiplicity of programs that require municipal-federal cooperation, municipal-federal-provincial cooperation, or cooperation between sets of government actors and NGOs or business. In these relationships, the provincial government generally favours "dual bilateralism" so that it can play an important mediating role. However, Saskatchewan governments are resource-constrained and therefore pragmatic. Building on a very rich empirical base, Garcea and Pontikes suggest that there is a range of possible provincial roles, several different approaches to the municipal-federal relationship, and a variety of intergovernmental mechanisms in play. All of the papers collected here point to avenues for future research, but this one offers the most suggestions for scholars interested in pure intergovernmental relations within the complex world of Canadian multilevel governance.

BACKGROUND THEMES

The intent of this section is not to provide a comprehensive analysis of the context for the following chapters about multilevel governance in Canada, a task that would require more space and time than are available. Instead, the aim is to suggestively sketch some developments and forces that illuminate the descriptive and analytic content of the papers collected here. In particular, we focus on features that have augmented the salience of urban problems and municipal governments. We look at four elements: the deep determinants of change, new public management, emerging views of multilevel governance, and the power of advocacy.

DEEP DETERMINANTS

Canada's urban centres are growing. Some increase is at the expense of rural and small-town Canada, where the demographic challenge is to cope with the effects of population decline on tax bases and service provision (Bourne 2003). Between 1996 and 2001, about 712,000 Canadians moved to one of the census metropolitan areas (CMAs) from non-metropolitan locales, a shift of a remarkable 2.4 percent of the population. At the same time, however, 672,000 people moved out of the CMAs to exurbs and smaller centres (Statistics Canada 2002a, 9). Most of the growth in Canadian cities is the result of immigration from abroad. In Toronto, for example, during this same period out-migration was just exceeded by in-migration and natural increase. The real growth came from about 374,000 foreign immigrants (Statistics Canada 2002a, 14–15; 2002b, table 4). And the urban concentration of immigrants is rising. Of those who came to Canada before 1961, 73 percent live in CMAs; but of those who arrived between 1991 and 2001, 94 percent live in CMAs (Statistics Canada 1992, table 1; 2003, 40). As well, there is a very substantial movement of Aboriginal people into cities, especially in the West (Peters 2002).

These flows place tremendous pressure on governments. Overall, rising population leads to environmental stress and pressure on infrastructure. New infrastructure is expensive, and the aging stock costs more and more to maintain. Municipalities must also strive to integrate immigrants into the local labour market and into society in general (Frisken and Wallace 2003), tasks that involve many tools under municipal authority. But the provincial governments are also necessarily involved, through social assistance and education policy and through credential certification, while Ottawa shares responsibility for the level and mix of the immigrant flow and has a pan-Canadian stake in multicultural policy (Jedwab 2001). The sea changes in the ethnic composition of cities make citizens interrogate the essence of their local community and focus attention on the level of government that serves it most directly.

The movement of people is only one component of globalization, which has profoundly affected governments and societies everywhere (Cable 1995; Scholte 2000). Concerns about competitiveness and government deficits have led to service cuts, reduced transfers, and the offloading of responsibilities, with the municipal level bearing the brunt of neoliberal restructuring. Increasing inequality and economic polarization are remarkable in Canada's urban centres (Séguin and Divay 2002). At the same time, the big cities are increasingly regarded as the gateways to the world economy and as the engines essential for growth and competitiveness (Scott 2001; Sassen 2000). National states are constrained in their traditional economic functions by international treaties that pass powers upwards, while the functions exercised at the lower level have become more critical for growth. This is a worldwide phenomenon sometimes called "glocalization" (Courchene 1995). On the one hand, this heightens the importance of municipal efforts to compete on the world stage (Banner 2002). On the other, it provides a strong incentive for national governments to concern themselves with urban performance. In Canada, cities may be creatures of the provinces, but as Courchene puts it in his chapter, "where competitiveness is at stake, Ottawa will become involved, regardless of what the written constitutional word may say ... Ottawa will necessarily become strategically as well as politically involved in city matters."

Along with this, Canadian values are changing. There is good evidence that Canadians, like the citizens of most advanced industrial countries, now evince less deference to established elites and elected politicians (Nevitte 1996). Rather than accepting to be passive consumers of policy, citizens are concerned with democratic participation, and for many individuals this is most feasible at the local level. Indeed, analysts writing from diverse theoretical stances regard municipalities as the prime locale for the creation of democratic structures, the exercise of accountability, and direct engagement in policymaking (Magnusson 2002; Breton 2002; King 2003). Another value change is the rising importance of identity in politics. New dimensions of inclusion and exclusion have become relevant to individuals and communities, and many cultural struggles about identity and rights are fought out at the municipal level (Holston 2001; MacGregor 2002). Finally, there is our changing social capital. At the same time that the traditional sense of national citizenship may be declining and social bonds are weakening, governments have sought to bolster individuals' engagement in collective and voluntary activities (Benest 1999; Veenstra 2002; Phillips 2003). Necessarily, these efforts to reinforce the associational sinews of society have important loci in the neighbourhood and municipality (Forrest and Kearns 2001; Johnson 2003).

A final driver in the context of multilevel governance is technological change. Of particular interest is the dramatic decline in communications costs. The internet and e-mail have made new connections possible for individuals, facilitating the horizontal organization of like-minded people around issues such as parkland, women's shelters, and heritage preservation (Stanbury and Vertinsky 1995). New technologies also open up wider strategic opportunities, for vertical linkages can be formed more easily with groups organized at different scales – at the provincial, national, and global levels (Cox 1993; Deibert 2002). Political contestation is now multiscalar, as Julie-Anne Boudreau shows in her contribution here. But these technologies have also become available to governments, notably municipal administrations, which use them to serve citizens and cement new connections. They have also profoundly affected the conduct of public administration, helping to open new avenues for cooperation in multilevel governance.

NEW PUBLIC ADMINSTRATION

The environment within which public servants function today is very different from that of a mere decade ago. New public management (NPM) principles have profoundly altered the process of public administration. At the federal level, change has been widespread (Pal 2006, 202–25). Less is known about the pattern of reform at the municipal level, but some exploratory work strongly suggests that local public service has changed too (Young 2003; Tindal and Tindal 2004, 287–97). Leaving aside the NPM precepts about privatization, cost recovery, and performance measurement, the relevant innovations are that administrative structures have been flattened, public servants have gained much more discretion, horizontal collaboration is encouraged, NGOs are involved, and the mission is to serve the citizenry through delivering public services thoughtfully (Pal 2006, 76; Rhodes 1996).

With respect to multilevel governance, this makes for a problem-oriented, fluid, entrepreneurial, and collaborative approach. First, as was seen most notably in the Vancouver Agreement (discussed by Smith and Stewart in this volume), public servants from all levels of government can adopt a citizen-centred orientation, identifying the various dimensions of complex problems and cooperatively allocating tasks to those with the resources and jurisdictional authority to accomplish them (Rogers 2004). Such collaborative initiatives require trust and, equally important, shared goals. In effect, public servants now often work in what international-relations scholars call "coalitions of the willing" – networks of like-minded individuals concerned with an issue or sector. In line with a core component of the notion of governance, these networks often include NGOs.

For example, one Ontario municipality has a local Children's Services Funding Group that includes municipal, provincial, and federal officials, along with representatives from the United Way (Young 2003, 4). The networks may be enduring, like this one, or they may coalesce around particular initiatives, such as expositions or industrial developments. As well, new technologies and the liberty offered by NPM make horizontal collaboration across municipalities much easier and more widespread, and these relationships may engender more cooperation with other levels of government. Indeed, a remarkably thorough empirical study of collaborative government in the field of economic development in the United States found that horizontal and vertical collaboration are correlated (Agranoff and McGuire 2003, 99–124). In short, NPM facilitates complex intergovernmental relations. Now, it may be that the collaboration enabled by NPM structures and processes is most widespread in the day-to-day management of minor programs and issues, while more formal mechanisms come into play for major intergovernmental initiatives. But routine matters are the stuff of government that affects many citizens most of the time. And big deals do not get made without lots of cooperative sherpas.

EUROPE AND MULTILEVEL GOVERNANCE

Thinking about complex intergovernmental relations has been greatly stimulated by scholarship about the European experience. In the European Union (EU), powers shift steadily upward to the common institutions; new subnational and supranational regions are created and reinforced, blurring the boundaries of nation-states; and considerable decentralization has occurred in the United Kingdom, Spain, France, and Italy. Hence, the emergence of the term "multilevel governance" (MLG), defined as "a system of continuous negotiation among nested governments at several territorial tiers – supranational, national, regional, and local – as the result of a broad process of institutional creation and decisional reallocation that has pulled some previously centralized functions of the state up to the supranational level and some down to the local/regional level" (Marks 1993, 392).

Leaving aside the intense European debates about identity, citizenship, and constitutionalism, some matters remain relevant to the Canadian experience. One concerns the legitimacy of evolving institutions, a perennial issue in the EU. What forms of democratic participation are necessary to build public trust in new institutions such as our amalgamated cities? In complex MLG systems, can citizens participate effectively or at least hold policymakers responsible? More prosaically, the European experience shows some of the drawbacks of intergovernmental relations. One is the "joint decision trap," which opens up when formal or informal decision rules require unanimity: with many players, *immobilisme* can be a common result. Short of this, it remains true that when the number of actors involved increases, so do transactions costs – the resources expended in negotiating. When it is imperative to reach some form of agreement, these costs can be very high. Such drawbacks may be familiar to those observing the lack of progress on the Toronto waterfront and the negotiations that produced the Vancouver Agreement, for example.

Flowing from the European experience, and informed by the EU debates about community and variable geometry, is a blunt but useful distinction between two types of MLG. Hooghe and Marks (2003) posit a Type I governance, built around stable communities, where powers are bundled and assigned to a limited number of durable governmental levels. Jurisdictions are nested within one another and memberships do not intersect horizontally. This corresponds to most of the Canadian intergovernmental system and to much of Europe, where *arrondissements* or neighbourhoods nest within municipalities, which nest within regions, which nest within provinces, national states, transnational regions, and the EU itself. In contrast is Type II governance, where authorities are designed around specific functions; they proliferate (like American special districts or Swiss intercommunal associations), have non-identical voluntary memberships, and are impermanent and flexible. In the Type II model, government bodies are formed to provide some limited set of services, with an emphasis on efficiency, economies of scale, and externalities, while Type I governments represent communities of interest – groups of people who are somewhat distinct and relatively homogeneous and who share common goals and some sense of identity.

This is a useful framework for thinking about many aspects of municipal governments and their relations with other levels of government (Young 2005, 5–9). In the present volume, it is clear that most contributions are embedded in the Type I model, where municipal amalgamation, for instance, simply creates larger communities of interest (in theory). But the models do help us reflect on government action, especially that of the federal government. First, Ottawa's relations with municipal governments break through the nesting arrangement, bypassing the provincial level. Second, as shown here by Christopher Dunn in particular, the federal government can help form special-purpose Type II bodies. Finally, Ottawa can bypass municipalities as well, within the nesting arrangement, by acting directly upon local communities. It is worth stressing this point once more. As Urbaniak puts it, "an urban agenda is not necessarily a municipal agenda." Both the federal government and provincial governments confront urban issues directly, and they will act to solve urban problems. Despite the emphasis here on intergovernmental approaches and collaborative governance, there are other ways to proceed.

ADVOCACY

Urban affairs are on the policy agenda, not only at the provincial level but, more unusually, in Ottawa too (Andrew, Graham, and Phillips 2002). Some of the deep determinants of this were outlined above, and they are wrapped up pretty comprehensively in Tom Courchene's chapter here. The pressures, he argues, are such that the federal government will "necessarily" become involved in urban matters. But in politics little happens inevitably. For anything to move forward there must be advocacy and pressure by real actors in the political arena. Long ago, Richard Simeon sketched a model of policy formation that emphasized environmental, institutional, and intellectual factors as background determinants; but political actors were crucial: it "is *through them* that the broader political forces operate" (1976, 576).

The cities agenda has had powerful and skilled advocates. Some have been located in think tanks. In particular, as the references in Loleen Berdahl's paper demonstrate, the Canada West Foundation played an early role in researching and publicizing urban issues (see also Gibbins 2004). So did the Canadian Policy Research Networks (Bradford 2002; Seidle 2002). Many academics from a variety of disciplines have contributed to the debate (Wolfe 2003; Boothe 2003). But these were all relative latecomers, attracted to an issue that was rising fast.

Two of the most articulate and influential advocates for municipalities addressed the conference at which the papers collected here were presented.[1] One was James Knight, chief executive officer of the Federation of Canadian Municipalities (FCM). He has "made a career of urging the Government of Canada to take account of municipal and urban concerns and to adopt appropriate policy and program responses." Knight spoke to the conference about demographic and economic pressures and about the central role of cities in the new economy. But he also compellingly outlined the erosion that has occurred in municipal services and intrastructure because of the fiscal crisis created by inadequate resources. This is a note that the FCM has sounded for years, with considerable success. (For a typical position paper, see Federation of Canadian Municipalities 2001.) The organization, Knight noted, is active on multiple fronts, engaging federal agencies that range from the RCMP to Environment Canada, Transport Canada, Health Canada, Industry Canada, and several Crown corporations and regulatory agencies. But it is on finances and municipal services – especially infrastructure – that the FCM has concentrated, mobilizing the political clout of 1,050 municipalities representing 80 percent of the Canadian population.

Determined individuals can also make a difference. One is Alan Broadbent, the second advocate to address the conference. Broadbent is chairman and CEO of Avana Capital Corporation and chairman of the Maytree Foundation, which does practical work in urban community development. A devotee of the work of Jane Jacobs, Broadbent has spearheaded the drive to achieve greater autonomy for Toronto (Rowe 2000; Broadbent et al. 2005), but his efforts have extended to Canadian cities in general. After a meeting in Ottawa where he learned that "the federal government might pay a lot more attention to these issues if there seemed to be some political imperative behind them," he sparked the first meeting of the C5 (the mayors of Montreal, Toronto, Vancouver, Winnipeg, and Calgary) and then worked to broaden it to include leaders of civic and business organizations. Studies and recommendations about urban issues have flowed from private firms and other groups right across the country as a consequence. If the place of municipalities in Canada's system of multilevel governance is strengthening, it is partly because of Broadbent's pressing arguments that "they need more control of their destinies."

FUTURE RESEARCH

The papers gathered here provide a host of insights into complex intergovernmental relations in Canada and point the way towards many avenues for future work in MLG. Concentrating on municipal-federal relations, there is an evident requirement for much basic mapping of relationships. From work like that of Smith and Stewart, Urbaniak, and Hulchanski, we see that these relations are widespread and that cooperation and conflict both characterize policymaking in many fields. But the surface has only been scratched. First, much more information is needed about how these relationships operate in small and medium-sized municipalities; there, it seems likely that elected politicians rather than officials will be more central intergovernmental players. Some policy fields deserve more attention as well; urban Aboriginal policy (including urban reserves), the infrastructure programs, emergency planning, and issues around federal property in municipalities seem to offer rich opportunities. Finally, there are special-purpose (Type II MLG) bodies. Municipal-federal relations involving these deserve study both when they are federal, like the Atlantic Canada Opportunities Agency and the various regulatory agencies, and when they are primarily municipal, like development agencies such as Montréal International, the Greater Vancouver Housing Corporation, upper-tier authorities, tourism and sports organizations, and public-health and other regulatory authorities. The goal here is not only to map relationships but also to correlate the quality of public policy with the structure of interaction that produces the policy.[2]

Another characteristic that needs to be better understood is the policy capacity of municipal governments. At a time when the large cities are pressing for more autonomy and resources, it is important to examine the competence of their administrations. One aspect of this is expertise in intergovernmental relations. There is a growing trend for cities to create positions in this area and to strengthen existing cadres, but more needs to be known. The structural relationships of intergovernmental relations units also deserve exploration. Do they report to the mayor, the CAO, or the council? The more general question of expertise involves normal functional departments. What is the municipal capacity for policy analysis in such fields as tourism, immigrant settlement, and urban Aboriginal issues? Are municipal administrations in any position to deal in a sophisticated way with their federal and provincial counterparts?

Another direction for research is to examine how provincial governments insert themselves into municipal-federal relations. We need to know much more about the situation in Quebec, where there is a statutory provision that agreements between municipalities (or other agencies) and other Canadian governments require prior authorization from the provincial government (Quebec 2002, ch. M-30, s. 3.12). Apparently, this is indeed enforced. More generally, Garcea and Pontikes recognize in their contribution that the provincial role is not part of a zero-sum game; apart from monitoring and regulation, provincial governments can be involved as advocates, mediators, and partners. These authors also classify various provincial approaches to the relationship and mechanisms of interaction, along with some determinants of the overall provincial stance. But other considerations are relevant to the study of these tripartite relationships, including the province's political complexion, its policy capacity, and the nature of the policy in question – its locus of jurisdiction, visibility, stakes, and complexity (Young 2003). This area of research is one that lends itself to comparative work across provinces, fields, and cities, for cases can be carefully selected to control for confounding factors. This last possibility illustrates a general advantage of studying the intergovernmental relations of municipalities: unlike the federal-provincial instance, where the "small-N" problem is acute, there are plenty of cases to work with.

Multilevel governance raises many issues of democracy and power. In complex intergovernmental systems, it is important to undertake some mapping of the participation of organized interests, or "social forces" more generally, in the policy process. In this volume, Boudreau, Sancton, and Hamel and Rousseau describe the failure of powerful citizen groups to counter the forces that were pressing for amalgamation. But Smith and Stewart document much more public involvement in the Vancouver Agreement, and Poirier points to the incorporation of groups in policy implementation. We could use much more information about citizen involvement in various policy fields. The role of business is especially interesting. Local-government scholars worldwide have a long tradition of concern about the power of business in municipal policymaking. Some argue that local politics are essentially pluralistic (Dowding 2001); others hold that business and professional groups can forge alliances with different interests to create durable "urban regimes" (Stone 1989; Logan, Whaley, and Crowder 1997); still others take the view that municipalities, constrained by their small scale and policy impotence, cannot escape from pro-business development policies (Molotch 1993; Peterson 1981). Considerations of multilevel governance inject a new dimension into this line of research. On the one hand, other levels of government, especially Ottawa, can be recruited by social forces to counter local or provincial business influence, as the anti-amalgamationists tried to do in the Toronto case. On the other hand, there is the possibility that decentralization can replicate "market-preserving federalism" at the local level, disciplining policy into an anti-interventionist mold because of horizontal intergovernmental competition and the exit option of business (Harmes 2006).

Accountability also is often raised as a democratic issue when MLG systems become more pervasive. This may seem to deserve some normative reflection, because sorting out what level of government is responsible for policy is very difficult when there are complex arrangements to transfer funds and when authority over programs or projects is diffused among many agents. But is this really a problem? Accountability is often raised as an issue by public-finance economists working with simple models of democracy. Their concern ignores the fact that many voters are rationally ignorant, and, more important, that retrospective evaluation of policy probably accounts for about one-quarter – at the most – of the variance in party choice in advanced industrial democracies. Another perspective is that MLG raises a different criterion by which voters can hold politicians accountable, and easily so: Can they make an intergovernmental deal, and a good one?

The politics of municipal-federal-provincial relations deserves more thought and research. Purely partisan considerations have largely been written out of the study of federal-provincial relations by political scientists, perhaps unduly so. And outside Quebec, partisan politics, in the sense of local politicians' affiliations or alliances with Liberal, Conservative, and NDP governments, remains largely subterranean. But exploring the effects of partisanship in MLG systems could produce interesting findings. It is *terra incognita* in Canada. Beyond pure party relationships lie issues about cooperation and alliances. After all, politicians are elected, and they can throw support to those contesting at different levels in exchange for future beneficial relations. When does this happen? What is the overlap between those who work for candidates at the local, provincial, and federal levels? In office, there are obvious advantages to having reliable allies at the other levels of government. Both electoral assistance and politically advantageous intergovernmental cooperation can flow from them. On the other hand, there are reasons to safeguard autonomy. It may be necessary to cooperate with the rivals of one's "friends" in due course, and there are often advantages to running campaigns against the "uncooperative" (or unpopular) incumbents elsewhere in the system. Too close an association with allies means that blame will spill over from their unpopular decisions. It can also impede productive horizontal relations with other governments at the same level. Sorting out such calculations about costs and benefits could be worthwhile. But this will not be easy. Game theorists often conclude their analyses of simple two-player games with the assurance that generalization to three or more players is straightforward. Well, it's not.

A more tractable and pressing question is "How do cities get more power and resources?" We have already examined advocacy, but this is not sufficient. Obviously, individuals can only get so far, and representative institutions must aggregate many interests, including those of small towns and rural municipalities (with divergences illustrated by the recent disputes between the City of Toronto and the Association of Municipalities of Ontario and by the uneasy coexistence of the Alberta Urban Municipalities Association and the Alberta Association of Municipal Districts and Counties). Comparative work would help here. So, too, could some reapplication of the federal-provincial literature on province building (Young, Faucher, and Blais 1984). We may find that structural factors conducive to city power crystallize into electoral promises made by provincial and federal politicians. Business pressure is clearly a factor as well, though the Toronto experience indicates that politicians' demands for autonomy will not be supported unconditionally by firms entrenched in particular cities (Lewington 2005). As Urbaniak shows here, shrewd political leadership is essential. More important, institutional change may have long-term power-enhancing repercussions. As David Siegel notes in his contribution, "the City of Toronto has twenty-eight members of parliament, twenty-eight members of the provincial legislature, and one mayor. It is not difficult to figure out who will speak with the greatest authority about the needs of the people of Toronto." This raises the question of citizens' identification. We know that the way and degree that citizens identify with European states has a very significant bearing on their support for European integration (Hooghe and Marks 2004). Is it similarly true that citizen identification with their city will ultimately lead to its drawing down more powers? Normally, determinists think that economic forces will drive institutional change, while citizen attachments will follow epiphenomenally. This view may be correct. But it may be that identification can drive the process. We know almost nothing about how Canadian urban residents identify with their cities. It could be worth finding out more, because this might help explain the migration of authority to this country's global city-regions.

But enough of future research opportunities. Let's turn to the interesting research that has already been done by our authors.

NOTES

Thanks for assistance with this introduction are due to Tait Simpson, Ben Elling, Kelly McCarthy, and Andrew Quinlan.

1 Since this is a peer-reviewed volume, their speeches are not published here, but they are accessible at www.iigr.php/conference_archives/papers#conf_1. Quotations are drawn from this source.
2 Some of this work is being undertaken through a SSHRC Major Collaborative Research Initiative on "Multilevel Governance and Public Policy in Canadian Municipalities." For more information, see www.ppm-ppm.ca.

REFERENCES

Agranoff, Robert, and Michael McGuire. 2003. *Collaborative Public Management: New Strategies for Local Governments*. Washington: Georgetown University Press

Andrew, Caroline. 1994. "Federal Urban Activity: Intergovernmental Relations in an Age of Constraint." In *The Changing Canadian Metropolis: A Public Policy Perspective*, ed. Frances Frisken, 427–57. Berkeley and Toronto: Institute of Governmental Studies Press, University of California, Berkeley, and the Canadian Urban Institute

Andrew, Caroline, Katherine A. Graham and Susan D. Phillips, eds. 2002. *Urban Affairs: Back on the Policy Agenda*. Montreal & Kingston: McGill-Queen's University Press

Banner, Gerhard. 2002. "Community Governance and the New Central-Local Relationship." *International Social Science Journal* 54 (172): 217–31

Benest, Frank. 1999. "Reconnecting Citizens with Citizens: What Is the Role of Local Government?" *Public Management* 81 (2): 6–11

Boothe, Paul., ed. 2003. *Paying for Cities: The Search for Sustainable Municipal Revenues*. Edmonton: Institute for Public Economics

Bourne, Larry S. 2003. "Elastic Cities, Inelastic Governments: Urban Growth and Urban Governance in Canada." *Canadian Issues*, February, 14–18

Bradford, Neil. 2002. "Why Cities Matter: Policy Research Perspectives in Canada." Discussion Paper F/23, Canadian Policy Research Networks

Breton, Albert. 2002. "Federalization (Not Decentralization) as an Empowerment Device." Paper presented at C.D. Howe Institute Policy Conference, "Who Decides? Democracy, Federalism, and Citizen Empowerment," held in Toronto, 15 November

Broadbent, Alan, et al. 2005. *Towards a New City of Toronto Act*. Toronto: Ideas That Matter

Cable, Vincent. 1995. "The Diminished Nation-State: A Study in the Loss of Economic Power." *Proceedings of the American Academy of Arts and Sciences* 124 (2): 23–53

Courchene, Thomas J. 1995. "Glocalization: The Regional/International Interface." *Canadian Journal of Regional Science* 18 (1): 1–20

Cox, Kevin R. 1993. "The Local and the Global in the New Urban Politics: A Critical View." *Environment and Planning D: Society and Space* 11: 433–48

Deibert, Ronald J. 2002. "Civil Society Activism on the World Wide Web: The Case of the Anti-MAI Lobby." In *Street Protests and Fantasy Parks: Globalization, Culture, and the State*, ed. David R. Cameron and Janice Gross Stein, 88–108. Vancouver: University of British Columbia Press

Dowding, Keith. 2001. "Explaining Urban Regimes." *International Journal of Urban and Regional Research* 25 (1): 7–19

Federation of Canadian Municipalities. 2001. "Early Warning: Will Canadian Cities Compete? A Comparative Overview of Municipal Government in Canada, the United States, and Europe." Paper prepared for the National Round Table on the Environment and the Economy

Feldman, Lionel D., and Katherine A. Graham. 1979. *Bargaining for Cities*. Montreal: Institute for Research on Public Policy

Forrest, Ray, and Ade Kearns. 2001. "Social Cohesion, Social Capital, and the Neighbourhood." *Urban Studies* 38 (12): 2125–43

Frisken, Francis, and Marcia Wallace. 2003. "Governing the Multicultural City-Region." *Canadian Public Administration* 46 (2): 153–77

Garcea, Joseph, and Edward C. LeSage Jr., eds. 2005. *Municipal Reform in Canada: Reconfiguration, Re-Empowerment, and Rebalancing*. Don Mills, Ont.: Oxford University Press

Gibbins, Roger. 2004. "The Missing Link: Policy Options for Engaging Ottawa in Canada's Urban Centres." In *Reconsidering the Institutions of Canadian Federalism*, ed. J. Peter Meekison, Hamish Telford, and Harvey Lazar, 411–22. Montreal & Kingston: McGill-Queen's University Press

Graham, Katherine A.H., and Evelyn Peters. 2002. "Aboriginal Communities and Urban Sustainability." Discussion Paper F/83, Family Network, Canadian Policy Research Networks

Harmes, Adam. 2006. "Neoliberalism and Multilevel Governance." Forthcoming, in *Review of International Political Economy*

Holston, James. 2001. "Urban Citizenship and Globalization." In *Global City-Regions*, ed. Allen J. Scott, 325–48. New York: Oxford University Press

Hooghe, Liesbet, and Gary Marks. 2003. "Unraveling the Central State, but How? Types of Multi-level Governance." *American Political Science Review* 97 (2): 233–43

– 2004. "Does Identity or Economic Rationality Drive Public Opinion on European Integration?" *PS: Political Science and Politics* 37 (3): 415–20

Jedwab, Jack. 2001. "Leadership, Governance, and the Politics of Identity in Canada." *Canadian Ethnic Studies* 33 (3): 4–38

Johnson, Cathleen. 2003. "A Model of Social Capital Formation." SRDC Working Paper, series 03-01. Ottawa: Social Research and Demonstration Corporation

King, Loren A. 2003. "Democracy and City Life." *Politics, Philosophy, and Economics* 3 (1): 97–124

Lewington, Jennifer. 2005. "City, Province Strike Plan for New Power Balance." *Globe and Mail*, 15 November

Logan, John R., Rachel Bridges Whaley, and Kyle Crowder. 1997. "The Character and Consequences of Growth Regimes." *Urban Affairs Review* 32 (5): 603–29

MacGregor, Sherilyn. 2002. "Bright New Vision or Same Old Story? Looking for Gender Justice in the Eco-city." In *Urban Affairs: Back on the Policy Agenda*, ed. Caroline Andrew, Katherine A. Graham, and Susan D. Phillips, 71–92. Montreal & Kingston: McGill-Queen's University Press

Magnusson, Warren. 2002. "The City as the Hope of Democracy." In *Urban Affairs: Back on the Policy Agenda*, ed. Caroline Andrew, Katherine A. Graham, and Susan D. Phillips, 331–44. Montreal & Kingston: McGill-Queen's University Press

Marks, Gary. 1993. "Structural Policy and Multilevel Governance in the EC." In *The State of the European Community*, vol. 2, *The Maastricht Debates and Beyond*, ed. Alan W. Cafruny and Glenda G. Rosenthal, 391–410. Boulder: Lynne Rienner Publishers

Molotch, Harvey. 1993. "The Political Economy of Growth Machines." *Journal of Urban Affairs* (15) 1: 29–53

Nevitte, Neil. 1996. *The Decline of Deference: Canadian Value Change in Cross-National Perspective.* Peterborough, Ont.: Broadview Press

O'Brien, Allan. 1993. *Municipal Consolidation in Canada and Its Alternatives.* Toronto: Intergovernmental Committee on Urban and Regional Research

Pal, Leslie A. 2006. *Beyond Policy Analysis: Public Issues Management in Turbulent Times.* 3rd edn. Toronto: Nelson

Peters, Evelyn J. 2002. "Aboriginal People in Urban Areas." In *Urban Affairs: Back on the Policy Agenda,* ed. Caroline Andrew, Katherine A. Graham, and Susan D. Phillips, 45–70. Montreal & Kingston: McGill-Queen's University Press

Peterson, Paul E. 1981. *City Limits.* Chicago: University of Chicago Press

Phillips, Susan D. 2003. "In Accordance: Canada's Voluntary Sector Accord from Idea to Implementation." In *Delicate Dances: Public Policy and the Nonprofit Sector,* ed. Kathy L. Brock, 17–61. Montreal & Kingston: McGill-Queen's University Press

Quebec. 2002. "An Act Respecting the Ministère du Conseil Exécutif." *Revised Statutes of Québec,* ch. M30. Quebec: Éditeur Official

Rhodes, R.A.W. 1996. "The New Governance: Governing without Government." *Political Studies* 44: 652–67

Rogers, Judy. 2004. "Remarks" at deputy ministers' and CAOs' round table: "Reflections on Intergovernmental Relations." Institute of Public Administration of Canada, National Conference, held 31 August, Vancouver

Rowe, Mary W., ed. 2000. *Toronto: Considering Self-government.* Owen Sound: Ginger Press

Sassen, Saskia. 2000. *Cities in a World Economy.* 2nd edn. London: Pine Forge Press

Scholte, Jan Aart. 2000. *Globalization: A Critical Introduction.* New York: Palgrave

Scott, Allan J., ed. 2001. *Global City Regions: Trends, Theory, Policy.* New York: Oxford University Press

Séguin, Anne-Marie, and Gérard Divay. 2002. "Urban Poverty: Fostering Sustainable and Supportive Communities." Discussion Paper F/27, Canadian Policy Research Networks

Seidle, F. Leslie. 2002. "The Federal Role in Canada's Cities: Overview of Issues and Proposed Actions." Discussion Paper F/27, Canadian Policy Research Networks

Simeon, Richard. 1976. "Studying Public Policy." *Canadian Journal of Political Science* 9 (4): 548–80

Stanbury, W.T., and Ilan B. Vertinsky. 1995. "Assessing the Impact of New Information Technologies on Interest Group Behaviour and Policymaking." In *Technology, Information, and Public Policy,* ed. Thomas J. Courchene, 293–379. Kingston: John Deutsch Institute for the Study of Economic Policy

Statistics Canada. 1992. "Census Metropolitan Areas and Census Agglomerations: Population and Dwelling Counts." 1991 Census. Cat. no. 93-303. Ottawa: Minister of Industry, Science, and Technology

– 2002a. "Profile of the Canadian Population by Mobility Status: Canada, a Nation on the Move." 2001 Census, analysis series. Cat. no. 96F0030XIE2001006. Ottawa: Minister of Industry

– 2002b. "A National Overview: Population and Dwelling Counts." 2001 Census. Cat. no. 93-360-XPB. Ottawa: Minister of Industry

– 2003. "Canada's Ethnocultural Portrait: The Changing Mosaic." 2001 Census, analysis series. Cat. no. 96F0030XIE2001008. Ottawa: Minister of Industry

Stone, Clarence N. 1989. *Regime Politics: Governing Atlanta, 1946–1988.* Lawrence, Kansas: University Press of Kansas

Tindal, Richard C., and Susan Nobes Tindal. 2004. *Local Government in Canada.* 6th edn. Toronto: Nelson

Veenstra, Gerry. 2002. "Explicating Social Capital: Trust and Participation in the Civil Space." *Canadian Journal of Sociology* 27 (4): 547–71

Wheare, K.C. 1953. *Federal Government.* 3rd edn. London: Oxford University Press

Wolfe, Jeanne M. 2003. "A National Urban Policy for Canada? Prospects and Challenges." *Canadian Journal of Urban Research* 12 (1): 1–21

Young, Robert. 1987. "Remembering Equal Opportunity: Clearing the Undergrowth in New Brunswick." *Canadian Public Administration* 30 (1): 88–102

– 2003. "Provincial Involvement in Municipal-Federal Relations." Paper presented at the conference on "Municipal-Federal-Provincial Relations: New Structures/New Connections," held 9–10 May at the Institute of Intergovernmental Relations, Queen's University, Kingston

– 2005. "Cities: Issues in Demography, Governance and Finance." Background paper for the Ditchley Foundations Conference, "The World's Cities: Can They Take the Strain?" held on 16–18 September at Langdon Hall, Cambridge, Ont.

Young, Robert, Philippe Faucher, and André Blais. 1984. "The Concept of Province-Building: A Critique." *Canadian Journal of Political Science* 17 (4): 783–818

II

Background

2

The Federal Urban Role and Federal-Municipal Relations

Loleen Berdahl

Ce chapitre permet d'explorer la situation de la politique urbaine fédérale et les interactions entre les gouvernements municipaux et le fédéral au terme de l'ère Jean Chrétien en 2003. À cette époque, les questions urbaines constituaient une préoccupation de plus en plus importante en matière de politique, et un des thèmes dominant l'ensemble du débat urbain était que le gouvernement fédéral devrait jouer un rôle explicite en politique urbaine. C'est sous cet effet de pression grandissante que le gouvernement fédéral a renforcé son intérêt dans les affaires urbaines. Ce chapitre soulève trois questions. En premier lieu, quel est le rôle du gouvernement fédéral dans les questions urbaines et est-ce que ce rôle implique des interactions fédérales-municipales? En deuxième lieu, quel était l'état des interactions fédérales-municipales en 2003? Et en dernier lieu, quelle conduite le gouvernement fédéral devrait-il suivre pour améliorer sa capacité d'agir efficacement dans les questions urbaines? On explorera la nature des interactions fédérales-municipales en exposant le cas de cinq villes des Prairies : Calgary, Edmonton, Winnipeg, Saskatoon et Régina. Un addenda conclura ce chapitre en soulignant les modifications apportées aux politiques urbaines fédérales entre le printemps 2003 (gouvernement majoritaire de Jean Chrétien) et l'été 2005 (gouvernement minoritaire de Paul Martin). Les assises de ce chapitre sont fondées sur une étude de recherche pluriannuelle continue, le Western Cities Project de la Canada West Foundation, qui explore une grande variété de sujets traitant des considérations urbaines, fiscales, sociales, environnementales et gouvernementales.

INTRODUCTION

Despite decades of urbanization, Canada's cities, urban policy challenges, and municipal governments have received relatively little national policy attention from academic researchers, policy analysts, and practitioners, and municipal relations with the federal government have largely been ignored.

This was particularly true in the 1980s and 1990s. Debates about the division of political powers were discussions of federal-provincial centralization or decentralization, and discussions about fiscal capacity focused on vertical fiscal imbalance between federal and provincial governments, ignoring the municipalities. While the vast majority of Canadians lived in urban centres – and a solid majority in large urban centres – policy discussions and debates proceeded as if Canada by and large had only two forms of government, federal and provincial, and two sites for policy and programs, Canada as a whole and individual provinces.

Urban issues began to occupy a more prominent position in national affairs in the late 1990s and the early years of the new century. A number of factors converged to raise urban issues (and, to a lesser degree, the role of municipal governments) as a key national policy debate. To provide but a few examples, public backlash to forced amalgamations in Toronto and Montreal raised awareness of the limited powers of cities. The Big City Mayors' Caucus of the Federation of Canadian Municipalities (FCM) began exerting public pressure for greater attention to the needs of Canada's large cities. Independent public policy research institutes, including the Canada West Foundation and the C.D. Howe Institute, published reports on urban issues in large cities. And the research branch of a large private-sector organization, the TD Bank, argued that Canada's large cities were under stress, raising the profile of urban issues to the business sector.

One dominant theme in much of the rising urban debate was an argument that the federal government should play an explicit role in urban policy. The result of this growing pressure was a sharp increase in federal interest in urban affairs. In May 2001, Prime Minister Chrétien appointed the Prime Minister's Caucus Task Force on Urban Issues (hereafter referred to as the Caucus Task Force) to consult with Canadians and key urban stakeholders about a potential federal urban agenda. The September 2002 Speech from the Throne argued: "Competitive cities and healthy communities are vital to our individual and national well-being, and to Canada's ability to attract and retain talent and investment … They require new partnerships, a new urban strategy, a new approach to healthy communities for the 21st century" (Canada 2002). Among the federal initiatives promised were a tripartite "ten-year program for infrastructure to accommodate long-term strategic initiatives essential to competitiveness and sustainable growth," "investments in affordable housing for those whose needs are greatest, particularly in those Canadian cities where the problem is most acute," and programs for homelessness, urban Aboriginal peoples, and immigrant settlement.

This flurry of federal interest in urban issues was a significant step. At the same time, given the current dynamic federal political environment, it is difficult to say if it will be sustainable or if urban issues are a "flavour of the week" policy field soon to fall away without meaningful long-term change. If the various forces raising the profile of urban issues – particularly the FCM, researchers, and business groups – reduce their focus on federal urban engagement, federal interest may wane as quickly as it has emerged.

But the very fact of growing federal interest in urban issues raises at least three questions: What is the federal urban role, and does it imply a federal-municipal relationship? What is the current federal-municipal relationship? And what steps could the federal government take to improve its ability to act effectively on urban issues? This paper will explore these questions in stages, with the current nature of the federal-provincial relationship explored through a brief discussion of the cases of five prairies cities: Calgary, Edmonton, Winnipeg, Saskatoon, and Regina. The research base for this analysis is the Canada West Foundation's Western Cities Project, and thus thanks are extended to the hundreds of researchers and practitioners who participated in the project in various ways over its course.

THE FEDERAL URBAN ROLE

In January 2000, the Canada West Foundation launched the Western Cities Project, a multi-year research initiative to explore the policy challenges faced by western Canada's large cities. What became very clear in the project is that it is impossible to look at urban issues without considering the role of the federal government. Across the considerable range of topics explored – including urban Aboriginal people, urban finance, affordable housing, intergovernmental relations, arts and culture – more often than not there was a federal dimension to the policy issue. This finding was striking because, in a strict constitutional sense, municipal governments are a provincial responsibility. If one assumes strict adherence to jurisdictional boundaries, one might assume little need for a federal role in cities.

However, it is important to recognize the difference between "urban" and "municipal." Municipal *institutions* are indeed solely within provincial jurisdiction, but urban issues simply refer to policy issues of importance in urban areas. As Vander Ploeg (2002, 3) points out, "[w]hile many concerns can be tagged as 'urban issues' it does not logically follow that local governments are responsible for them." The federal government is prohibited from interfering with the structure and operation of municipal institutions, but it faces no such constitutional constraint when it comes to urban issues such as housing, public transportation, infrastructure, or the arts. Furthermore, policy in exclusive or concurrent federal spheres such as immigration, the environment, employment and training, trade, and fiscal policy can and do have a great impact on cities. Thus, it must be recognized that, where the vast majority of Canadians live, federal actions and inaction have a major impact. Federal engagement in urban affairs is unavoidable, a fact of political life.

The federal government is involved in a number of urban issues simply through its own programs, such as immigration, housing, support for cultural institutions, and research funding. This point was acknowledged by the Caucus Task Force, which wrote, "The Government of Canada has always shown an interest and played a key role in urban life ... [It] is a significant investor in urban areas, both in terms of its physical presence and the services it delivers ... Many federal departments have a stake in urban issues through national objectives and international obligations" (Liberal Party 2002a, 8). Urban areas have always been affected by federal policy, even if federal policy takes little or no consideration of its urban consequences.

The federal government has an impact on urban areas not only through its actions but also through its lack of action. Its retreat from policy areas, as was witnessed in the 1990s, can result in urban decline and public pressure for municipal governments to assume these responsibilities. The Federation of Canadian Municipalities (1998) wrote, "It has become common for the federal government to place increased financial pressure on municipal governments. Examples include the offloading of federally-owned and -subsidized airports, marine ports and fishing harbours onto communities, the elimination of funding for new social housing, and increased costs to municipal governments and provinces for RCMP services." It is often because of federal retreat that we see municipal governments becoming highly involved in dealing with issues of homelessness and other social services, and working to promote economic growth and development. As one might expect, these "residual responsibilities" are not accompanied by increased funding. One senior municipal official stated, "In the last couple years, the City has begun to fund emergency shelter and transitional housing projects such as the Salvation Army and the Drop-In Centre. Prior to senior government cutbacks, capital dollars would have been provided by the federal and provincial governments for such projects. The City is now expending significant dollars in an area that was historically a senior government responsibility."

The point to stress is that the federal government does have, and indeed has always had, an urban role. While this role is not always explicitly recognized, it does exist. In addition to affecting the urban areas generally, the federal government's urban actions or inaction can have a significant direct or indirect impact on municipal governments. Calls from researchers, community leaders, and municipal officials for an "expanded federal urban agenda" do not necessarily imply a demand for the federal government to become involved in areas of municipal responsibility or provincial jurisdiction. An expanded federal urban agenda could consist of increased federal action in its existing spheres of exclusive or concurrent jurisdiction. An expanded federal urban agenda could be as simple as having the federal government do a better job at its current urban activities.

Despite the highly urban nature of many of its programs, the federal government has not had a coordinated urban strategy. One often-cited reason for the lack of a coherent federal urban strategy is the federal government's three-decade-old failed experiment with an urban strategy – the Ministry of State for Urban Affairs (MSUA), which operated from 1971 to 1979. MSUA was set up to coordinate federal urban activities, establish agreements among the three levels of government, and conduct research. The ministry failed to meet its goals partly because "the federal policy irritated the provinces, and they became increasingly vocal in their opposition" (Andrew 1994, 431). The legacy of MSUA's demise is that federal governments "continue to have federal policies enacted without regard to their urban impact" (Tindal and Tindal 2000, 231). To this day, MSUA is often given as an excuse for inaction rather than as a motivation to find a better model for managing the federal government's urban role.

However, tentative steps were taken to reopen the door shut by MSUA's demise when in May 2001 Prime Minister Chrétien established the Caucus Task Force to conduct public consultations to find ways in which "the Government of Canada can work more collaboratively, within our federal jurisdiction, to strengthen the quality of life in our large urban centres" (Liberal Party 2002b, iv). The Caucus Task Force released its interim report in April 2002 and its final report in November 2002. The reports acknowledged the federal role in urban areas, and the final report called for an increased federal urban presence in three areas: affordable housing, transportation/transit, and sustainable infrastructure. These recommendations suggested the potential for important expansion of the federal urban policy role, but they did not necessarily point to a more coordinated urban policy framework.

Another potentially important – albeit somewhat subterranean – development at the federal level was the establishment of the Task Force on Canada's Urban Communities within the Privy Council Office (Institute on Governance 2002). As the final report of the Caucus Task Force describes, "Within the Privy Council Office, an internal Task Force on Urban Communities was established to develop a profile of the federal presence in urban centres, research into best practices and to explore ways of integrating federal programs" (Liberal Party 2002b, iv). According to a biography of the PCO task force's director general, Adam Ostry, the task force's mandate was "to develop a vision of the Government of Canada's role with respect to Canada's urban centres as well as a coordinated strategy and action plan on urban issues" (Couchiching 2002). (It is interesting that this description goes beyond urban *issues* to consider urban *centres* as well.) The PCO task force's mandate was to focus on horizontal integration of federal urban interests by bringing relevant departments to the same table. This horizontal coordination could be very important to the federal government's urban strategy in the years ahead.

Does the federal urban role imply a federal-municipal relationship? As will be discussed in the next section, to date the federal-municipal relationship has been informal and limited in scope. The federal government does not have any institutional structures to engage with municipal governments. At present,

there is no mechanism for providing sustainable federal funding to municipalities and no formal mechanism for consulting municipal governments on
urban issues or on the many federal policies that affect urban areas. There is no
federal body to provide a point of contact with municipalities. Communications
with municipal governments tend to be ad hoc, and this ad hockery limits the
ability of Canadian governments to work together to address urban issues.

As part of its consultations, the Caucus Task Force met with municipal
government officials, and in its reports it identified a need for "all orders of
government to coordinate resources, and consult and collaborate on a new
approach to the challenges in Canada's urban regions" (Liberal Party 2002a,
iv). However, the Caucus Task Force did not go so far as to recommend institutional structures (such as a ministry or formal consultation model) to manage
federal urban issues and to allow for tripartite dialogue. Thus, while the Caucus Task Force recommended an expanded federal urban policy role, it did
not recommend expansion of the federal-municipal relationship.

It is interesting to note that federal dialogue on urban issues deliberately
refers to "urban communities" and "urban issues" rather than to "municipalities," "cities," or "city-regions." There are both advantages and disadvantages
to this approach. The advantages are that it allows the federal government to
look at urban communities in a broad sense (in effect, adopting a city-region
model) and, perhaps more importantly, allows the federal government to sidestep the constitutional arguments that inevitably arise; it is one thing for the
federal government to deal with (provincially controlled) municipal governments and quite another for it to examine urban areas. The disadvantages are
that "urban communities" can be an overly broad definition, encompassing
small towns of a few thousand and large city-regions of many millions; also,
the emphasis on "urban communities" risks ignoring the relevance of municipal governments – and, indeed, of provincial governments. Another
disadvantage, of course, to this "urban issues" approach is that at some point
it will become fundamentally impossible for the federal government to effectively address urban issues without also coming to grips with municipal
governments, because municipal governments are, by definition, engaged with
a multitude of urban issues on a daily basis.

THE CURRENT FEDERAL-MUNICIPAL RELATIONSHIP IN
PRAIRIE CITIES

Given that municipalities are a provincial responsibility, one might expect
little formal federal engagement with municipal governments. To a large degree, this expectation has been met. Although the federal government has been
involved in urban issues, this involvement has rarely been within an explicit
urban policy framework that includes a relationship with municipal govern-

ments. (In many cases, the involvement does not even include explicit recognition that the policy field is primarily urban in nature.) Nonetheless, an informal or ad hoc federal-municipal relationship has evolved around three primary points of contact: political interaction, bureaucratic interaction, and joint and tripartite agreements.

There is a modest degree of political interaction between municipal and federal governments. In addition to the consultations associated with the Caucus Task Force, municipal officials report that there is occasional dialogue between mayors and federal ministers – both "ministers responsible" for a given program area and "regional ministers." As one municipal official described it, "The mayors are very prudent in dealing with ministers. They don't want to waste the time of the minister. A mayor meeting with a minister is the first stop in signaling the importance of an issue to the federal government." The importance of regional ministers was raised by a number of individuals. Stated one, "The presence of the Honourable Ralph Goodale as our Member of Parliament and senior Minister has been an immense help – we meet with him regularly." At the same time, one complication that was raised is that there is the potential for pressure for mayors to meet with both the minister responsible and the regional minister – a requirement that could slow the process considerably. (Given that only prairie municipalities were consulted for this paper, it is not clear if this is an issue outside western Canada.) It is noted that city councillors, by and large, do not have relationships with the federal government, unless the city councillor is a member of the Federation of Canadian Municipalities.

The political interaction resulting from the Federation of Canadian Municipalities, and more specifically the Big City Mayors' Caucus, is of particular note. The Big City Mayors' Caucus has become an important lobbying group, and much of its lobbying is directed at the federal government. This is significant, because strong lobbying by mayors is in part responsible for the greater American federal urban engagement.

Another point of federal-municipal interaction is seen at the bureaucratic level. Many municipal officials spoke of the importance of Western Diversification as an important interface and as the first point of contact for general matters. It was also acknowledged that there is occasional (and often informal) contact between municipal governments and specific departments, such as Transport Canada, Infrastructure Canada, Human Resources and Development Canada, Canada Mortgage and Housing Association, and Indian and Northern Affairs. Contact is often initiated because of joint programs (to be discussed later in this section) and because of significant federal structural changes that affect municipal governments, for instance, such as the establishment of airport authorities and the establishment of urban reserves in Saskatchewan.

Both federal and municipal officials are quick to point out the cooperative tone of federal-municipal bureaucratic interactions and the fact that useful work can be accomplished, though municipal officials are more likely to point to the ad hoc nature of these interactions. In addition, both federal and municipal officials raise the issue of differing federal and municipal "organizational cultures." In general, municipal officials see federal action as being extremely slow, while federal officials see municipalities as being extremely impatient for action.

Federal-municipal interaction at the bureaucratic level appears to be growing, often in the absence of the provincial governments. In the recent past, there have been at least three interactions of note:

- In December 2002, the Saskatchewan Council of Senior Federal Officials held a meeting on Saskatchewan cities. Invited speakers included the city managers of Regina and Saskatoon (Bob Linner and Phil Richards, respectively), the vice-president of the Saskatchewan Urban Municipalities Association (Don Schlosser), and the president and CEO of the Canada West Foundation (Roger Gibbins).
- In February 2003, the Alberta Council of Senior Federal Officials dedicated its monthly meeting to "the cities agenda." Invited speakers included senior officials with the cities of Edmonton and Calgary (Bruce Duncan and Brenda King, respectively) and the president and CEO of the Canada West Foundation (Roger Gibbins). The agenda included discussion of both homelessness and urban Aboriginal issues.
- In March 2003, the Institute for Public Administration Canada held an intergovernmental dialogue in Vancouver entitled "Competitive Cities, Healthy Cities: Charting Collaboration." This two-day event brought federal officials together with provincial and municipal officials and local community leaders. According to one participant, much of the discussion focused on "how the federal government can become involved and make a difference."

It is notable that two of the three interactions involved a regional Council of Senior Federal Officials. The regional councils were established in 1982, with one in each province and territory. Council membership typically includes regional directors general and assistant deputy ministers (Canada, Treasury Board Secretariat 2003). In recent years, Regional Councils have been becoming much more engaged across a variety of policy issues, taking on important horizontal integration and regional/local coordination roles. As Juillet notes, "[M]ore people are turning to federal councils for assistance in dealing with the formulation and implementation of horizontal policies. Recently, the federal councils have been asked to play important roles in the management of the government's national homelessness and urban aboriginal policies" (2002). Given that homelessness and urban Aboriginal policies are clearly urban issues, federal councils may play a growing federal role in the years ahead.

The third area of federal-municipal relationship is joint programs and agreements. Tripartite agreements and joint programs are the most formal aspect of the federal-municipal relationship. When the federal government does become formally involved with municipal governments, it is typically through its spending power and often in the form of tripartite agreements. In the prairie context, there are a few noteworthy recent examples of joint and tripartite programs:

- *Residential Rehabilitation Assistance Program* (joint program). Through the Canada Mortgage and Housing Corporation (CMHC), the federal government provides funding support for renovations to homes for low-income, disabled, and Aboriginal Canadians. The federal government provides these funds to the municipal governments, and the municipal governments are responsible for administering the program. (For example, city inspectors conduct the home inspections.) Funding is provided 100 percent by the federal government, and the municipal role is strictly administrative. The provincial government has no role in the program.
- *Urban Development Agreements* (tripartite agreement). Two prairie cities – Winnipeg and Edmonton – have experience with tripartite urban development agreements. The Winnipeg Development Agreement began in March 1995, and between 1995 and 2001 a total of $75 million (equally cost-shared among the three governments) was spent on seventy projects. In January 2003, a memorandum of understanding was signed by all three parties to negotiate a new agreement. The second prairie tripartite urban development agreement was the unfunded Edmonton Economic Development Initiative, which began in 1995 but has since been terminated. (In January 2003, Western Diversification announced $1.5 million in funding over three years for the Greater Edmonton Competitiveness Strategy.) Saskatchewan cities did not enter into urban development agreements, reportedly because of problems regarding the engagement of First Nations communities, but there is still interest in developing agreements. Overall, the success of urban development agreements is unclear. As Gibbins (2004) writes, "It is difficult to determine whether the urban development agreements in western Canada provide a suitable model for a more comprehensive strategy of federal engagement with urban affairs ... [T]he agreements demonstrate a limited willingness and capacity of the federal, provincial and municipal governments to work together. The underlying principles and operating procedures seem to provide a sound tripartite model. However, WD's considerable creativity with respect to urban development agreements was not matched with sufficient resources."
- *Infrastructure Agreements* (tripartite agreement). The Infrastructure Canada initiative, announced in the 1999 Speech from the Throne and in the February 2000 federal budget, is an example of federal involvement in municipal affairs through a trilateral agreement among the three levels of government.

There are numerous examples of programs under the Infrastructure Canada-Alberta Program (ICAP), including city storm sewer improvement in Calgary and a new waste management plant in Edmonton. In Winnipeg, the Canada-Manitoba Infrastructure Program (CMIP) has projects underway to build four ethnocultural centres, as well as a downtown waterfront renewal project. The Canada-Saskatchewan Infrastructure Program (CSIP) has approved projects in both Saskatoon and Regina; however, as one official argued, the tripartite nature of these programs is suspect: "[T]here is a federal-provincial agreement that allocates the federal funds by province and the terms under which they will be distributed. There is no direct municipal involvement in Saskatchewan, at least in those negotiations."

To date, tripartite agreements have had a number of shortcomings. They often have a limited shelf life and a narrow focus, are sporadic and episodic in nature, and fail to incorporate a principled strategy for engaging municipal governments (Wong 2002, 13). Moreover, they impose inconsistent financial demands on municipalities and deliver inconsistent financial resources. Frequently, municipal governments are equal funding partners, responsible for providing one-third of the funding, with the federal and provincial governments each also providing one-third. In other agreements, however, municipal governments have been allowed to participate at lower funding levels. In some agreements, municipal governments are given equal voting rights, while in others they have limited decision-making authority.

The funding structure of tripartite agreements can present a problem in that municipal governments, with significantly fewer fiscal resources than federal or provincial governments, experience considerable financial strain if required to provide a full third of the project's funds. This strain can distort local funding priorities, negatively affect long-term municipal fiscal capacity, and even limit local ability to participate in joint projects. As Wong (2002, 13) writes, "[A]lthough tripartite agreements such as the [Infrastructure Canada Program] are beneficial to cities, equal cost sharing among the federal, provincial and municipal governments [strains] the limited city finances. Some [municipal officials] doubt that cities could handle two IPC-like agreements at any one time." Municipal governments also express great concern (and rightly so) that they are not allowed to participate fully at the decision-making table. This lack of authority undermines the municipality's ability to represent the interests of its citizens and reduces local control over projects. Furthermore, it creates significant differences in municipal voice across the country, since some provinces allow their municipal governments to sit at the table while others do not.

Clearly, the current federal-municipal relationship is limited in scope and weak in respect to institutionalization. Although some tripartite agreements do involve direct federal-municipal relations, the federal government lacks formal mechanisms to receive municipal government feedback on federal action or inaction, and it lacks mechanisms to provide sustainable funding to municipal governments. The municipal representatives whom Canada West consulted indicated that the status quo poses a number of problems for cities. Important urban perspectives, they asserted, are not always brought to bear on federal policies that affect cities; issues of urban finance are ignored at the federal level; and municipal governments are faced with extensive de facto residual responsibilities, because if federal and provincial governments fail to adequately address policy issues in their own domains, municipal governments are left to address the policy gap, despite their lack of resources to do so. For these reasons, it is not surprising that Canada's big city mayors are increasingly vocal in demanding federal attention to cities and urban issues. Of course, attention and action are two very different things. Referring to the federal-municipal relationship, one municipal official commented, "After all is said and done, more is said than done." Considering the barriers impeding a stronger federal-municipal relationship, this may be an apt assessment.

IMPROVING THE FEDERAL URBAN ROLE

What steps could the federal government take to improve its ability to act effectively on urban issues? How can the federal government ensure that its own policy actions – be they explicitly urban policies or not – work for the betterment of Canada's cities? There are at least three options that should be considered:

First, the federal government needs greater coherence and coordination of its own urban policies and programs. Specifically, there is an ongoing need to coordinate horizontally. This may require a single ministry being made permanently responsible to ensure horizontal federal urban policies. Without a single ministry being responsible to coordinate the various federal urban policies, department-specific urban initiatives "might lead to overlapping programs and conflicting criteria for eligibility" (Wong 2002, 10). A single ministry responsible for urban affairs would encourage a holistic federal approach to cities. It must be stressed that the ministry responsible could be an existing ministry, such as the Privy Council Office, and that the scope of the responsibility would need to be carefully defined. A minister responsible broadly for "urban Canada" would have an impossible mandate; indeed, one could argue that this mandate would encompass most of the federal government's activities. The purpose is not to create an urban affairs ministry that would rival the mandate and scope of other ministries but simply to make one ministry responsible to ensure that all federal departments work together to coordinate their urban efforts.

Second, the federal government needs tools with which to evaluate the impact of federal action on urban areas and on municipal governments. One idea that is often raised is the adoption of an "urban lens" to evaluate existing and future federal policy. The Caucus Task Force asserts, "We need to apply an urban 'lens' to all policies and programs, both national and international that are directed at urban regions. An urban perspective will guide future legislation and policies so that programs designed for urban centres can be assessed for both negative and positive consequences" (Liberal Party 2002a, 3). Presumably, an urban lens would operate similarly to the existing federal rural lens, which requires federal policymakers to answer a number of questions before implementing a new policy. Examples of these questions include: How is this initiative relevant to rural and remote Canada? Have the most likely positive and negative effects on rural Canadians been identified and, where relevant, addressed? Have rural Canadians been consulted during the development or modification of the initiative? (Rural Secretariat 2002). Addressing similar questions for urban policy would be beneficial; ideally, municipal and provincial governments would be consulted in answering these questions.

It should be noted that the very need for an urban lens raises an intriguing question: Why is it, in a country where six out of ten people live in large urban areas, that the federal government must be reminded to think about urban issues? Why is it that the federal government had a "rural lens" and rural secretariat long before entertaining questions about urban Canada? (Ironically, the Caucus Task Force notes that the federal government's successful approach to rural Canada should serve as its model for focusing on urban issues.) The answer is likely to be found in the overrepresentation of rural areas and the underrepresentation of urban areas in the House of Commons. Canada's rural areas are continually given greater political weight than their populations warrant. This results in myriad political incentives for governments to focus on rural concerns and to be myopic on urban issues. (It should be noted that urban underrepresentation may be even more acute in provincial legislatures, thereby reducing the provincial incentive to consider, or even tolerate, an expanded federal urban role.) While there are constitutional limits to how strictly the federal government can pursue "representation by population," steps could be taken to make political representation more equitable. For example, seat reallocations could occur quickly after a census, the number of seats in the House of Commons could be expanded, or the electoral system itself could be changed to incorporate proportional representation principles. A variety of legislative tools could be employed to address the issue. The real obstacles in this regard are political, for Canada's rural interests would chafe against the loss of Commons seats.

Third, the federal government needs formal mechanisms to consult municipal and provincial governments on federal urban policies and programs. A common complaint from municipal governments is that federal (and, for that matter, provincial) governments do not adequately consider the impact of their policies on urban areas, despite the fact that many federal policies have significant urban dimensions and ramifications. Because the lack of formal consultation mechanisms, communications tend to be ad hoc, and this limits the ability of Canadian governments to work together to address urban issues.

Some form of federal consultation mechanism – such as the establishment of a federal standing committee on urban affairs – would institutionalize federal consultation with provincial and municipal governments. The mechanism would ensure that the federal government consults with provincial and municipal representatives on a regularly scheduled basis, allowing for a consistent urban perspective in national policymaking. The purpose of the consultations would not be to give provincial and municipal governments a role in federal decision making; rather, it would be to ensure that the perspectives of big cities are taken into account in federal decision making. The regular consultations would also create stronger tripartite relationships, increase the opportunity for vertical policy integration, and address the Caucus Task Force's desire for "all orders of government to coordinate resources, and consult and collaborate on a new approach to the challenges in Canada's urban regions" (Liberal Party 2002a, vi).

One challenge, however, is that while it is (relatively) easy to figure out who participates on the federal and provincial sides, determining municipal participation is not as easy. Assuming a federal "big cities" strategy with the focus on a small number of Canada's largest cities, municipal participation could be limited to those cities. This would help the federal government avoid the pressure to include all Canadian cities, which would result in an unworkable consultation process and a "watering down" of large urban concerns.

Overall, each of these options – greater coherence and coordination on federal urban policies and programs; tools to evaluate the impact of federal actions on urban areas and on municipal governments; and formal mechanisms for the federal government to consult municipal and provincial governments on federal urban policies and programs – would institutionalize the federal urban role. Such steps would likely improve the federal government's ability to act effectively on urban issues and would not necessitate an expansion of federal urban activity.

There are a number of advantages to institutionalizing urban affairs at the federal level: greater federal awareness of urban issues, improved coordination of federal urban programs, and the greater potential for increased federal consultation with municipal and provincial governments on urban issues. Of course, a number of political barriers would surface with any effort to institutionalize urban affairs at the federal level. For instance, could the federal government resist pressures to include all "urban areas," regardless of size, thus weakening the impact of a federal urban strategy? Would a ministry responsible for urban affairs be able to coordinate federal policies effectively? Would institutionalizing the federal urban role create greater pressure for an expansion of the federal urban role, both within and outside federal jurisdiction? If so, would the federal government be extremely reluctant to increase its financial commitment to urban issues? (One can imagine a considerable price tag attached to expanded federal urban engagement!) And, perhaps most importantly, could the federal government create institutional structures without upsetting the provinces?

The provincial side of the federal urban role and the federal-municipal relationship needs to be considered closely, for it is the critical political barrier facing the federal government. In Canada, municipalities are neither constitutionally recognized nor given any specific powers or responsibilities. Instead, "Municipal Institutions in the Province" are assigned as one of a number of provincial responsibilities in section 92(8) of the *Constitution Act, 1867*. As noted earlier, the constitution does not restrict a federal role in urban affairs, just as the constitutional assignment of hospitals to provincial jurisdiction has not prevented active federal engagement in health policy. Nor does the constitution preclude a federal relationship with municipal governments, a conclusion supported by the experiences of two similar federal countries: Australia and the United States (Berdahl and Sapergia 2001). But while the Australian and American experiences demonstrate ample room within existing constitutional frameworks for new innovative relationships among the federal, provincial, and municipal governments, Canadian provincial and federal governments have tended instead to see Canada's existing federal arrangements as a constitutional straitjacket.

However, the real constraints, to the extent that they exist, are financial and political; they reflect more a lack of imagination or political will than black-letter constitutional law. While the constitution itself may be flexible enough to allow an expanded relationship, the political reality is that the federal government has to be aware of provincial sensitivities. Provincial governments rarely see a role for the federal government in urban affairs, and they often guard this policy field carefully.

Evidence of this jurisdictional jealousy is seen in the press releases arising from the annual meetings of provincial and territorial ministers responsible for local government. (These meetings are held to allow ministers to discuss key issues facing municipal affairs ministries.) For example, the 2000 meeting discussed negotiations with the federal government regarding water and wastewater projects. At this meeting, "concern was expressed over federal involvement in local government issues which could override provincial/territorial priorities" (Canadian Intergovernmental Conference Secretariat 2000). The 2001 meeting had an expanded discussion of the federal role, including discussion of drinking-water safety: "[T]he Ministers feel the federal government must be part of the solution by supporting a separate and incremental approach to meeting drinking water safety needs which builds on work already being undertaken by provinces and territories"; similarly, the Caucus

Task Force came under discussion: "While there was recognition among provinces and territories that increased federal involvement was critical to meet the challenges faced by many urban centres, the involvement of the federal government must be based on an approach that recognizes and integrates provincial interests, priorities and jurisdictions" (Canadian Intergovernmental Conference Secretariat 2001). The 2002 meeting had a similarly cautious approach to the federal government: "Acknowledging the federal government's growing interest in financial support for municipalities, the ministers reinforced the importance of respecting the exclusive constitutional responsibility of the provinces and territories for municipal affairs." Instead of calling for funding for municipalities or urban issues directly, the ministers called for a remedy to "the fiscal imbalance between the provincial and federal governments" (Canadian Intergovernmental Conference Secretariat 2002). These positions were restated in the fall 2002 meeting, at which the ministers called for the federal government to increase its health-care funding as a means of reducing the fiscal imbalance.

It is important to note, however, that the provinces are not equal in their opposition to federal engagement. George Anderson, at the time deputy minister of intergovernmental affairs, Privy Council Office, wrote before the 2003 Quebec election: "In this debate on a possible federal urban agenda, it is important to bear in mind that provincial governments have explicit constitutional jurisdiction for municipalities, though provinces approach this differently. The Quebec government will not permit any municipality to enter into a direct agreement with the federal government without authority from the province. In contrast, the new government in British Columbia proposes to give municipalities greater autonomy and has promised new legislation in this regard" (Anderson 2002).

Overall, provincial cautiousness is understandable, but it is a major barrier to institutionalizing the federal urban role. However, should the political will exist, it must be stressed that there are options for federal engagement that include (rather than circumvent) the provincial governments; indeed, a federal urban strategy must engage the provincial governments if it is to be effective (Berdahl 2002). The real challenge is not so much figuring out how such a model might be constructed, but balancing urban issues among the many other areas of federal-provincial strain and conflict. As the provincial and federal governments continue to battle it out over health care, there is limited goodwill left to develop a cooperative urban strategy.

To summarize, there are numerous political barriers to institutionalizing the federal urban role. Getting around these barriers requires, more than anything, political will. This seems to exist among the majors of big cities and the leaders of the federal Liberal and New Democratic parties. However, it is unclear when or if the provincial governments will ever develop the political will to pursue a tripartite relationship on urban issues or to allow or facilitate an expanded bilateral federal-municipal relationship. Indeed, provincial resistance may prove to be the most critical – and perhaps an insurmountable – barrier to institutionalizing the federal urban role and ultimately achieving an effective urban strategy. Since the federal government needs to maintain positive intergovernmental relations with the provincial governments, it is unlikely to risk damaging federal-provincial relations over urban issues. Thus, while the constitution does not restrict a federal role in urban affairs, political realties require the federal government to tread lightly.

CONCLUSION

There is considerable political momentum building behind a federal urban agenda. Urban issues are beginning to attract the attention of Canada's corporate sector and are clearly on the federal political agenda. It is this situation that simultaneously represents the greatest opportunity and the greatest threat for Canada's large cities. The opportunity lies in the federal political will and interest to address not only immediate policy concerns but also structural issues such as the vertical fiscal imbalance and the need for greater federal awareness of urban issues. The challenge is to take advantage of this opportunity but to do so in a way that fosters long-term and sustainable benefits and that includes, rather than aggravates, the provincial governments. The risk is that through impatience, short-term thinking, or lack of creativity, the federal government will cobble together ad hoc relationships that will fail to address structural issues or, worse, will create new urban problems.

At the same time, it is imperative that the federal government take steps to ensure the long-term benefit of Canada's large cities. As Paul Reed, author of a recent statistical study entitled *Metropoles and Peripheries: The Evolution of City-Regions in Contemporary Canada*, states, "Federalism will come to be seen either as irrelevant, or in some radically modified form, as indispensable" (MacGregor 2003). This is one of the greatest challenges before the federal government as it moves forward.

ADDENDUM

This paper was written in the spring of 2003, when Jean Chrétien's majority government was "testing the waters" of federal urban engagement. A tremendous amount of change has occurred between the writing and presentation of this paper and its publication. As was expected, the new Liberal government of Paul Martin began with a strong focus on urban issues. First, Prime Minister Martin created the Cities Secretariat within Privy Council Office in December 2003. Also in December 2003, he created the External Advisory

Committee on Cities and Communities, chaired by former B.C. premier Mike Harcourt (Canada, Office of the Prime Minister 2004). This committee's mandate is to provide advice on federal policies related to cities and communities as they are being developed, to advise the federal government on how to engage provincial, territorial, and Aboriginal governments, and to develop a long-term vision on the role of cities in Canadian quality of life.

In July 2004, Martin moved the Cities Secretariat from the PCO, merging it with Infrastructure Canada (Infrastructure Canada 2005). The former parliamentary secretary for cities, John Godfrey, was made the Minister of State for Infrastructure and Communities. The Cities Secretariat's "New Deal for Cities and Communities" seeks to move forward on three fronts: relationships, funding, and looking at federal policies through a "cities and communities lens."

The Martin government also made a number of high-profile funding commitments to municipal governments. The 2004 federal budget gave a 100 percent GST rebate to municipalities. In February 2005 the federal government committed to providing gas tax revenues to municipalities, to be distributed through bilateral agreements with the provincial and territorial governments. (As of June 2005, agreements have been signed with Alberta, British Columbia, Ontario, and the Yukon, and an agreement-in-principle is in place with Quebec.) The federal government reports that the GST rebates and the gas tax revenue sharing will provide municipalities with $7 billion over ten years.

Certainly, the creation of the Cities Secretariat and the establishment of a minister of state responsible for cities and communities will result in significant changes in the federal-municipal relationship. There is now a federal ministry responsible to examine the urban impact of federal policies, and there is a greater federal emphasis on consulting with provincial, territorial, and municipal governments on urban issues. Time will tell if this new ministry will be successful in creating a coordinated federal urban strategy and the extent to which it will tangibly benefit urban areas and urban residents. Its short-term success will rest not only with the electoral fortunes of the minority Martin government but also with its ability to engage the provincial and territorial governments positively.

REFERENCES

Anderson, George. 2002. "Cities and the Federal Agenda." *Horizons* 5 (1)

Andrew, Caroline. 1994. "Federal Urban Activity: Intergovernmental Relations in an Age of Restraint." In *The Changing Canadian Metropolis: A Public Policy Perspective,* vol. 2, ed. Frances Frisken. Berkeley: Institute of Governmental Studies Press, University of California; Berkeley, and the Canadian Urban Institute

Berdahl, Loleen. 2002. *Structuring Federal Urban Engagement.* Calgary: Canada West Foundation

Berdahl, Loleen, and Sophie Sapergia. 2001. *Urban Nation, Federal State: Rethinking Relationships*. Calgary: Canada West Foundation

Canada. 2002. *The Canada We Want. Speech from the Throne to Open the Second Session of the Thirty-Seventh Parliament of Canada*. www.sft-ddt.gc.ca (accessed 8 October 2002)

– Office of the Prime Minister. 2004. *Prime Minister Names Members of External Advisory Committee on Cities and Communities*. News release, 15 February www.pm.gc.ca/eng/news.asp?id=79 (accessed 28 June 2005)

– Treasury Board Secretariat. 2003. *Regional Councils of Senior Federal Officials: History*. www.tbs-sct.gc.ca (accessed 9 April 2003)

Canadian Intergovernmental Conference Secretariat. 2000. News release: 2000 *Conference of Provincial-Territorial Ministers responsible for Local Government*. Fredericton, N.B., 31 July – 1 August. www.scics.gc.ca (accessed 9 April 2003)

– 2001. News release. *Conference of Provincial-Territorial Ministers Responsible for Local Government*. London, Ont., 13–14 August. www.scics.gc.ca (accessed 9 April 2003)

– 2002. News release. *Conference of Provincial-Territorial Ministers Responsible for Local Government*. Victoria, B.C., 12–13 August. www.scics.gc.ca (accessed 9 April 2003)

Couchiching Summer Conference. 2002. *2002 Speaker Biographies*. www.couch.ca/history/2002/bios.html (accessed 3 April 2003)

Federation of Canadian Municipalities. 1998. *1998 Policy Statement on Municipal Finance*. Ottawa: Federation of Canadian Municipalities

Gibbins, Roger. 2004. "The Missing Link: Policy Options for Engaging Ottawa in Canada's Urban Centres." In *Canada: The State of the Federation 2002. Reconsidering the Institutions of Canadian Federalism*, ed. J. Peter Meekison, Hamish Telford, and Harvey Lazar, 411–22. Kingston: Institute of Intergovernmental Relations, Queen's University; Montreal: McGill-Queen's University Press

Infrastructure Canada. *New Deal for Cities and Communities*. www.infrastructure.gc.ca/ndcc/index_e.shtml (accessed 28 June 2005)

Institute on Governance. 2002. "CityScapes: Federal Perspectives on Urban Communities." Notes on a seminar presentation by Claire Morris, Deputy Minister, Intergovernmental Affairs, Privy Council Office, 18 September. Ottawa: Institute on Governance

Juillet, Luc. 2002. *The Federal Regional Councils and Horizontal Governance*. Prepared for the Regional Federal Councils and the Treasury Board Secretariat, September (accessed 9 April 2003)

Liberal Party of Canada. Prime Minister's Caucus Task Force on Urban Issues. 2002a. *Canada's Urban Strategy: A Vision for the Twenty-First Century*. Chair, Judy Sgro. Interim Report. [Ottawa: The Task Force]

– 2002b *Canada's Urban Strategy: A Blueprint for Action*. Chair, Judy Sgro. Final Report. [Ottawa: The Task Force]

MacGregor, Roy. 2003. "Rise of the Metropolis Suggests Two New Solitudes: Cities – and Everywhere Else." *Globe and Mail,* 19 February

Rural Secretariat. 2002. *Canadian Rural Partnership: Checklist of Rural Lens Considerations.* www.rural.gc.ca (accessed 7 October 2002)

Tindal, C. Richard, and Susan Nobes Tindal. 2000. *Local Government in Canada.* 5th edn. Scarborough: Nelson Thompson

Vander Ploeg, Casey. 2002. *Framing a Fiscal Fix-Up: Options for Strengthening the Finances of Western Canada's Big Cities.* Calgary: Canada West Foundation

Wong, Denis. 2002. *Cities at the Crossroads: Addressing Intergovernmental Structures for Western Canada's Cities.* Calgary: Canada West Foundation

3

Municipal Relations with the Federal and Provincial Governments: A Fiscal Perspective

Melville L. McMillan

Ce chapitre permet d'examiner la situation fiscale des administrations municipales canadiennes et leurs rapports intergouvernementaux, depuis 1988, en ce qui a trait à la fiscalité. Un fait saisissant est la réduction marquée des subventions octroyées aux municipalités durant les années 1990. Ces subventions qui représentaient 25 pour cent des budgets au début de ces années ont chuté par la suite à 17 pour cent, traduisant ainsi la volonté des provinces de rééquilibrer leurs dépenses. La dépendance accrue des municipalités envers leurs propres sources de revenus a fait grimper les taxes foncières à leur plus haut niveau depuis trente ans, en relation aux revenus disponibles des contribuables. Ainsi, la proportion des revenus municipaux obtenue par le biais de l'impôt foncier est passée d'environ 32 pour cent à près de 42 pour cent. Tandis que la nécessité des municipalités de collecter des revenus était définitivement augmentée, il y a peu d'indications illustrant que leurs responsabilités en terme de dépenses aient été augmentées de façon considérable à l'extérieur de l'Ontario. Les compressions fiscales ont touché davantage les municipalités de l'Ontario que les autres villes canadiennes. Malgré la croissance économique et la situation fiscale des provinces, ces dernières, à l'exception de l'Alberta, ont démontré peu d'ardeur à restituer le système de subventions provincial. En outre, les initiatives du gouvernement fédéral visant à octroyer un remboursement complet de la TPS ainsi que les nouvelles ententes avec les villes et les communautés, qui totalisent environ 2 pour cent des budgets municipaux, apparaissent comme des avancées majeures dans le domaine. Il faut se rendre à l'évidence que la grande majorité des villes canadiennes n'auront d'autre choix que de subvenir elles-mêmes à leurs besoins. En définitive, ces municipalités devront ouvrir leurs horizons pour favoriser leur autonomie financière. Pour y arriver, certaines options ont été évaluées, par exemple, les sources de financement locales, les ventes et l'impôt sur le revenu.

INTRODUCTION

Municipal governments have received unusual attention during the past decade. Some significant reshuffling of provincial-municipal responsibilities in Ontario and some high profile amalgamations in Toronto, Montreal, and Halifax have particularly attracted public attention. In their shadow, less obvious changes have also occurred as the provinces have investigated options for the organization, responsibilities, and financing of municipal government.[1]

From another perspective, municipalities, and especially the cities, have been the focus of examinations by various public policy centres. For several years now, the Canada West Foundation has been engaged in its major Western Cities Project.[2] Previous to that, the Institute for Research on Public Policy undertook a project on city-regions (Hobson and St Hilaire 1997). Contributions have come from the C.D. Howe Institute (Kitchen 2000b; Slack 2002) and the TD Bank Financial Group (2002, 2004). In a recent "territorial review" of Canada, the OECD included major sections addressing urban and metropolitan issues (OECD 2002). The Canadian Tax Foundation recently published a series of papers as a symposium on municipal finance and governance reform (Canadian Tax Foundation 2002), and Kitchen and Slack (2003) extended this theme. The Canadian Policy Research Networks undertook a group of studies focusing on the federal government's role in cities (e.g., Seidle 2002). Complementing these independent works, the federal government established the Prime Minister's Caucus Task Force on Urban Issues, which reported in November 2002. There have also been a number of conferences on municipal issues, of which the one leading to this volume, the Institute for Public Economics' conference, Paying for Cities (Boothe 2003), and the September 2003 Strategies for Urban Sustainability conference in Edmonton are examples. As an illustration of ongoing interest, a nationwide academic study into multilevel governance and public policy in Canadian municipalities is underway.

Why this surge of interest and activity in municipal affairs and especially those of urban municipalities? Perhaps an underlying cause is a sense that municipalities are not living up to expectations or to their potential. Perhaps there is a feeling that municipal governments are becoming less able to achieve their goals and meet the needs of their residents. The validity of either of these speculations could be debated.

Addresses on municipal issues are commonly motivated by reference to urbanization, global competitiveness, and the fiscal squeeze. Also important, as revealed by papers elsewhere in this volume, is the municipal lack of voice (which is largely the result of their lacking of constitutional standing and coming under provincial jurisdiction); that is, municipalities are not engaged, or properly engaged, when they are affected by the decisions and actions of the provincial and federal governments. Much of that discussion has been focused on the settlement and integration of immigrants and Aboriginal people, affordable housing, and – more in the provincial context – amalgamation, funding changes, and responsibility realignment. The impact of all these factors could be explored further, but fiscal considerations are the focus here.

Fiscal matters have been a continuing concern of municipal governments.[3] Concerns typically focus on fiscal capacity and on fiscal arrangements with other governments. Matters dominating (but not unique to) recent discussions are the variability and uncertainty of intergovernmental transfers, the costs of offloaded or downloaded responsibilities, new (or the perception of expanding) local needs, a growing infrastructure deficit, and the constraints on own-source revenues imposed by reliance on a single major tax, the property tax.

The objective of this paper is to examine municipal governments' fiscal situation and their intergovernmental fiscal relations. The main directions are to outline what exists, to identify the forces shaping the structure, and to explore what might be. The paper begins with the fiscal picture. Included there is a search for evidence of the seriousness of the municipal fiscal problem. Municipal fiscal arrangements are briefly reviewed in the context of the lessons from fiscal federalism. Various suggestions have been advanced on how municipal finances and intergovernmental fiscal relations might be reformed. A number of these are outlined and assessed. Discussion and conclusions complete the paper. For a summary look ahead, this analysis suggests that the future of municipalities will largely be in their own hands (as it should be) but the municipalities' strength and dexterity could be improved.

THE FISCAL PICTURE

AN OVERVIEW

Municipal government expenditure represented 4.4 percent of GNP in 2001 and about 10.5 percent of total government outlays.[4] This percentage is slightly smaller than the 4.5 percent of GNP that it represented in 1988, the first year that independent municipal government data were available. Despite the slightly lower percentage, per capita real (GDP deflator adjusted) dollar expenditures by municipal governments increased 15 percent over this period.

The per capita levels and percentage distribution of municipal expenditures for 2001 are shown in table 1. The figures are total expenditures, including both operating and capital outlays. The range of per capita municipal expenditure is large – from a low of $378 in Prince Edward Island to $1,948 in Ontario. The (population weighted) average for Canada is $1,545. The provinces tend to divide into two groups. For Quebec and the provinces farther west, per capita expenditures are relatively high (above $1,050) while in Atlantic Canada they tend to be lower (below $1,050). Nova Scotia defines the upper end in Atlantic Canada because its municipal governments, unlike elsewhere, contribute significantly to schooling (14.2 percent of municipal expenditures), and, at 4.5 percent, still finance more than the norm of social services, though that share has dropped dramatically (from 23.3 percent in 1988) and a final reduction was expected to occur in 2003.[5] Ontario municipalities are the highest spenders because one-quarter of their outlays go to fund social services. Otherwise, the Ontario outlay would be second to that of Alberta and its distribution closely parallel to the Canada average. Among the other provinces, the average share of expenditures going to social services is less than 1 percent. Ontario has a tradition of placing somewhat more expenditure responsibilities on its municipalities than other provinces, and the local government "reforms" introduced during the 1990s exacerbated that burden. The province assumed full responsibility for funding schools (with new provincial property taxes to contribute to the cost) and, in exchange with the local level, shifted a variety of responsibilities (notably, all social housing costs, the costs of maintaining previously provincial highways, and half of the cost of land ambulances) to the municipal governments.[6] This reassignment of responsibilities to the municipalities, particularly the social services component, contrasts with the prevailing pattern and is contrary to "best practices" recommended by students of fiscal federalism. There will be occasion to reflect more on this situation below.

Social services in Ontario and education outlays in Nova Scotia are the major anomalies in table 1. To this, only the low share of protection costs in Newfoundland and Labrador might be added. Otherwise, the patterns are quite homogeneous. The major expenditure areas are protection (such as fire and policing), transportation, environment (water and sewerage services, solid waste management, and recycling), and recreation and culture. Together with general services (municipal administration), these categories account for almost 75 percent of municipal outlays Canada-wide and more than 85 percent in most provinces. Debt-servicing costs averaged 5 percent in 2001 but ranged from 1.7 to 11.1 percent. Unlike the federal and provincial governments, municipalities cannot borrow for operating purposes; they can only do so for capital expenditures.

A perspective on the revenue side of the municipal accounts is provided by table 2. There are two major sources of revenue – those from the municipalities' own sources and those from intergovernmental transfers. Transfers, or grants, accounted for 17 percent in 2001 and own-source revenues for 83 percent. Property and related taxes are the main source (63 percent overall) of own-source revenue and represent, across Canada, 52.2 percent of total revenue. Property and related taxes consist of real property taxes and property-related taxes. Real property taxes (those on land and improvements) provide, on average, 41.9 percent of total revenue. Property-related taxes (10.3 percent of municipal revenue across Canada) primarily consist of lot levies and special assessments (usually for cost recovery of specific improvements), payments in lieu of taxes from other governments and their agencies, and business taxes. Business taxes can be levied on a variety of bases (for example, rent, area,

Table 1: Level and Allocation of Municipal Government Expenditures by Province and for Canada, 2001

	Nfld	PEI	NS	NB	Que	Ont	Man	Sask	Alta	BC	Canada
Per capita expenditure (dollars)	767	378	1,020	865	1,284	1,948	1,091	1,141	1,581	1,284	1,545
					Percent allocation						
General services	16.2	12.9	10.4	11.1	12.2	8.9	13.6	12.4	12.2	10.0	10.4
Protection	4.7	23.1	21.1	21.0	16.7	13.4	19.7	17.6	14.3	18.8	15.1
Transportation	28.6	21.5	16.9	20.2	27.2	18.1	23.4	31.7	28.3	16.5	21.4
Health	0.1	0.1	0.1	0.4	0.2	3.5	2.2	0.6	1.5	1.8	2.2
Social services	0.2	0.0¹	4.5	0.0	1.4	24.7	0.3	0.5	1.5	0.2	12.5
Education	0.1	0.0	14.2	0.0¹	0.1	0.0¹	0.0¹	0.0¹	0.3	0.0¹	0.3
Conservation and development	0.7	1.7	0.8	2.4	2.8	1.6	2.4	3.6	3.4	1.4	2.1
Environment	22.1	12.7	16.8	25.3	12.0	13.3	17.4	15.4	13.9	20.4	14.4
Recreation and culture	14.5	21.9	10.7	12.6	12.4	8.7	9.4	14.2	13.7	19.5	11.5
Housing	0.6	0.0	0.2	0.3	2.9	5.0	0.4	0.4	0.7	0.6	3.2
Regional planning	1.2	2.3	1.5	2.0	2.5	0.1	2.3	1.7	3.0	2.3	1.3
Debt charges	11.1	3.7	3.7	4.2	9.4	2.3	8.5	1.7	7.1	6.3	5.0
Other	0.0¹	0.0¹	0.0¹	0.2	0.0¹	0.2	0.4	0.1	0.0¹	2.2	0.4
Total²	100.0	100.0	100.0	100.0	100.0	100.0	100.0	100.0	100.0	100.0	100.0

¹Negligible (less than 0.05 percent)
²May not sum exactly, due to rounding

Source: Data from Statistics Canada, Public Institutions Division, Financial Management System (as of fall 2002); author's calculations

sales), but assessed property value is the most common, and they are levied in addition to real property taxes. Unlike real property taxes, the occupant (not the owner) is liable. Business taxes are not collected in British Columbia, Ontario, New Brunswick, and Prince Edward Island. In fact, municipalities in Prince Edward have almost no property-related taxes and rely on the real property tax. Property and related taxes vary considerably in relative importance – from 44.4 to 73.7 percent of total revenue in Alberta and Nova Scotia, respectively. Because of the pattern of interprovincial revenues, there is somewhat less variation in the actual dollar amounts per capita collected. Revenues from the sale of goods and services, or user charges, are the next most important item, representing almost one-quarter of total revenue. Thus, property and related taxes and user charges account for about 90 percent of own-source revenue and 75 percent of total revenue. Investment income is a more modest source (4.9 percent across Canada), but it is still important, especially for municipalities in Alberta, British Columbia, and Manitoba. Much of this revenue comes from utility ownership. While own-source revenue averages 83 percent of the total, and municipal governments in most provinces are close to the average, it ranges from about 74 to 94 percent. Newfoundland is at the low end and Nova Scotia and British Columbia set the upper level.

The importance of own-source revenue varies with the contribution of intergovernmental transfers. Municipalities in British Columbia and Nova Scotia receive only about 6 percent of their revenue from grants, while those in Newfoundland get about 25 percent.[7] Overall, grants provide 17 percent of revenue. Intergovernmental transfers essentially mean provincial municipal transfers. The federal grants represent no more than 2.9 percent of total revenue in any province, and for all Canada they average 0.4 percent of total revenue (or about 2.4 percent of aggregate transfers to municipalities). All federal transfers are designated for specific (expenditure) purposes. Provincial transfers may be general purpose (unconditional) or specific purpose. Specific purpose grants dominate – 14.2 percent versus 2.4 percent overall – and dominate in all provinces except New Brunswick, though to a lesser extent in Nova Scotia and Prince Edward Island.

To summarize, municipal government represents about 10 percent of total government expenditure. Local expenditures are, with few exceptions, to provide services benefiting local residents (notably, fire and police protection, roads and public transport, water and waste management, and recreation and cultural services). Municipal government relies on own-source revenues for more than 80 percent of revenues. Own-source revenues essentially mean property and property-related taxes and user charges and fees. Transfers, which are almost entirely provincial transfers, now account for 17 percent of total revenue (down from 23 percent in 1988). These transfers are predominately conditional. Readers interested in a more detailed fiscal picture may refer to Kitchen (2003b). While much of the concern expressed about the municipal situation is being focused on cities, there is no uniform and compatible source

Table 2. Level and Allocation of Municipal Government Revenues by Province and for Canada, 2001

	Nfld	PEI	NS	NB	Que	Ont	Man	Sask	Alta	BC	Canada
Per capita revenue (dollars)	704	437	1,013	839	1,293	1,914	1,120	1,062	1,739	1,137	1,513
					Percent source						
OWN-SOURCE REVENUE											
Property and related taxes	54.3	62.3	73.7	55.1	64.3	48.3	46.7	54.3	44.4	53.0	52.2
(real property taxes)	(36.3)	(61.2)	(58.0)	(47.7)	(44.2)	(42.2)	(35.3)	(45.4)	(31.6)	(46.3)	(41.9)
Consumption taxes	0.1	0.0	0.0	0.0	0.0	0.0	1.4	3.6	0.0	0.2	0.1
Other taxes	1.0	0.5	0.1	0.5	0.3	1.3	1.1	0.8	1.6	2.4	1.2
Sales of goods and services[1]	16.4	26.9	16.4	25.3	16.5	23.9	23.4	24.3	26.1	29.3	23.0
Investment income	1.9	1.6	3.5	1.0	2.0	4.1	8.0	4.4	10.3	8.5	4.9
Other	0.6	1.5	0.2	0.5	2.3	1.7	0.8	1.0	1.6	0.6	1.6
Total own source[2]	74.3	92.8	94.0	82.4	85.5	79.3	81.5	88.5	84.1	94.2	83.0
TRANSFERS											
General purpose	6.3	3.3	2.7	12.4	1.9	2.3	7.9	4.6	0.9	1.1	2.4
Specific purpose	19.4	3.9	3.3	5.2	12.6	18.3	10.6	6.9	15.0	4.7	14.6
federal	2.9	0.3	0.5	1.0	0.2	0.3	1.1	2.1	0.5	0.5	0.4
provincial	16.5	3.6	2.8	4.2	12.4	18	9.5	4.9	14.5	4.3	14.2
Total transfers[2]	25.7	7.2	6.0	17.6	14.5	20.7	18.5	11.5	15.9	5.8	17.0
Total revenue[2]	100.0	100.0	100.0	100.0	100.0	100.0	100.0	100.0	100.0	100.0	100.0

[1]Includes user fees, charges, etc.
[2]May not sum exactly, due to rounding

Source: Data from Statistics Canada, Public Institutions Division, Financial Management System (as of fall 2002); author's calculations

of data for different classes of municipalities comparable to the Statistics
Canada Financial Management System data utilized for this paper.

A FISCAL SQUEEZE?

As already noted, considerable concern has been expressed about Canadian
municipalities, especially cities being squeezed fiscally between downloaded
responsibilities, rising expectations, and a slowly growing tax and revenue
base. This issue is examined in this section. Initially, only national data are
considered, but then a revealing subnational perspective is taken.

A National Perspective

Intergovernmental transfers to municipalities have declined during the past
decade as upper-tier governments cut transfers to fight their deficits. Figure 1
shows federal and provincial transfers to the municipalities as a percentage of
expenditures from 1988 to 2001. Transfers declined after 1995 and again after 1999. Between 1988 and 2001, they fell from 22.4 to 16.6 percent of
expenditures.[8] In fact, because of an anomaly relating to Quebec (to be explained below), transfers in the other provinces fell to 14.2 percent or by more
than one-third on average rather than by one-quarter. The actual impact was
even somewhat greater because transfers had amounted to about 25 percent of
expenditures during the first half of the 1990s.

**Figure 1: Intergovernmental Transfers and Debt Charges as a Percentage of
Canadian Municipal Expenditures, 1988–2001**

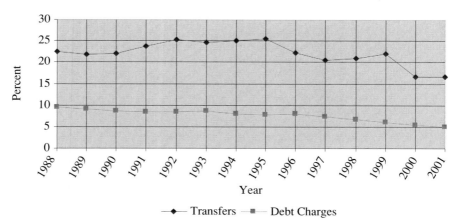

Sources: Data from Statistics Canada Public Sector Statistics, Financial Management System
Basis, Catalogue No. 68-212, various years and parallel data from the Public Institutions Division

Transfers have declined since 1988, but so have the debt charges paid by municipalities. This too is shown in figure 1. Debt charges fell almost continuously from 1988 to 2001, from 9.5 to 5.0 percent of expenditures. To a large extent, the 5.8 percentage point drop in transfers was offset by the 4.5 percent drop in debt expenses. A result of these parallel trends was that, unlike federal and provincial governments, the municipal governments realized no fiscal dividend from declining interest rates. The fiscal flexibility that municipalities might have gained from lower interest rates was largely lost to (or captured by) the provinces through reduced transfers leaving the municipalities no better off.

Are there obvious consequences of these and other developments for municipal expenditures? Various (absolute and relative) expenditure series were calculated for Canadian municipalities over the 1988–2001 period. A review of these indicates that municipal expenditures have kept abreast – but only abreast – of national output, incomes, and other subnational (provincial and school board) expenditures over the 1988–2001 period. For example, see the two series plotted in figure 2. Municipal total expenditure as a percentage of GDP was 4.54 percent in 1988 and 4.4 percent in 2001.[9] In addition (but not shown in figure 2), municipal program

Figure 2: Trends in Canadian Municipal Expenditures, 1988–2001

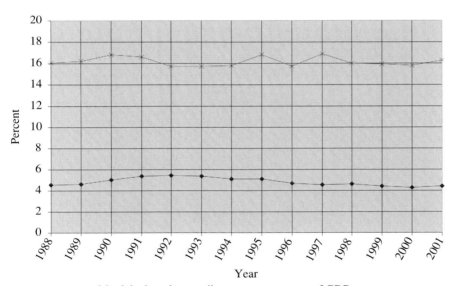

—◆— Municipal total expenditure as a percentage of GDP

—×— Municipal program expenditure as a percentage of consolidated provincial and local government program expenditure

Sources: Municipal financial data from same Statistics Canada source as tables 1 and 2; GDP data from Statistics Canada, CANSIM II; author's calculation

spending also barely changed; as it moved only from 4.11 to 4.19 percent of GDP.[10] Finally, municipal program expenditures as a percentage of consolidated provincial and local (subnational) program expenditures also showed no trend, starting at 16.1 and ending at 16.3 percent. If municipalities have been burdened by downloading and if they responded by spending to meet those new responsibilities, one might have expected these shares to have become larger.

Generally speaking, it appears that municipal expenditures have kept pace with standard economic indicators over the 1988–2001 period. The municipal expenditure burden does not seem to have increased or, at least, to have resulted in larger relative expenditures. At the same time, note that real (inflation adjusted) per capita municipal total expenditures have risen about 15 percent, from $1,262 to $1,453.[11]

What has been happening on the revenue side of the municipal picture? Again, a number of series of indicators were calculated for the 1988–2001 period. Figure 3 shows the trends in municipal revenues. As a result of diminished transfers, own-source revenues increased from 76.9 to 83 percent of total revenues. As a percentage of personal disposable income, an indicator of burden, own-source revenues increased from 5.27 percent to 5.87 percent, an 11.4 percent increase over the fourteen years.[12]

The increase in own-source revenues primarily came from increased real property taxes. Real property taxes rose from 32.2 to 41.9 percent of total revenue – a 9.7 percentage point change representing a 30.1 percent increase in the real property tax share. Meanwhile, property-related taxes grew little over the period and declined from 16.2 to 10.3 percent of total revenue. Sales, fees, and charges increased from 20 to 23 percent; this was the only other major category to show an increase. Other own-source revenue declined. The contribution of transfers declined by almost six percentage points and the decline of property related taxes was of a similar magnitude. Thus, while sales, et cetera, made a contribution to the increase in own-source revenue, the real burden fell on the real property tax.

Between 1988 and 2001, real property taxes increased 26.8 percent as a percentage of GDP, 30.6 percent as a percentage of personal income, and 33.9 percent as a percentage of personal disposable income (PDI). The constant (1992) dollar per capita tax rose from $418 to $544, or by 30.1 percent. These are substantial increases in what is often regarded as a less popular tax.

Events of the 1988–2001 period lead to a number of observations and tentative conclusions. The municipalities managed to maintain their expenditures relative to GDP, PDI, and total subnational government spending. Real dollar per capita expenditures even rose by about 15 percent. Any new downloaded expenditure responsibilities do not show up as higher relative aggregate expenditures. This observation is not to deny their existence. However, downloads may have been small or accommodated by reductions elsewhere, but troublesome nonetheless. Capital spending may have suffered, and deteriorating

Figure 3: Contributions to Canadian Municipal Revenue

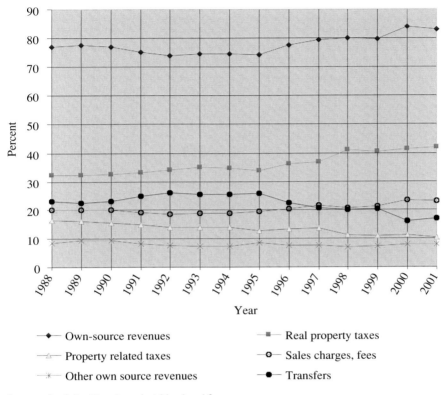

Sources: Statistics Canada, as in tables 1 and 2

infrastructure may be temporarily masking the problems. There is a lack of information on capital spending at the municipal level. For local government in total, however, real per capita capital acquisition held steady throughout the 1990s but continued (as from the 1960s) to decline relative to capital consumption allowances. Furthermore, there is evidence that, over this period, municipal debt was greatly reduced and their financial assets considerably augmented (for example, local government net debt was halved from 1994 to 2001). While more detail is needed, there is not substantial evidence (at least, from aggregate expenditures) of a fiscal squeeze adversely affecting Canada's municipal governments.

The obvious impact of recent developments affecting Canadian municipal government has been on the revenue side. Substantially reduced transfers have been replaced largely by sharply increased property taxes. The main

downloading and the squeeze on municipal government during the past decade or more appears to have been primarily on the revenue side (rather than
on the expenditure side) with municipalities having to support a larger share
of municipal expenditures from their own sources as transfers declined.

The inelasticity of the property tax is a common though somewhat faulty
complaint. Especially in the past, because the period between property tax
reassessments was typically lengthy (every seven years and sometimes longer),
property tax revenues have not automatically increased with property values
or with economic activity but have required (seemingly unpopular) tax rate
increases to maintain real dollar revenues and municipal government purchasing power. Despite this complication, the response of the property tax to the
demands made upon it over the study period has been remarkable. Real property taxes have not only kept up with (as is fairly typical) but have increased
relative to GDP, personal income, and personal disposable income, even during a period dominated by slow or no real income growth and an inhospitable
environment for tax increases in many provinces. This development suggests
that the property tax can be responsive when required. Not to be ignored, the
movement to market value assessments as the property tax base and the trend
to their annual (or at least frequent) adjustments are making the property tax
more elastic. Still, the property tax is for many people a more obvious tax
than many other, often larger, taxes, thus exposing it to greater scrutiny.[13]

Despite the recent success in maintaining municipal expenditures through
property tax increases, Canadians may be pushing the limits of the property
tax. This pressure could be contributing to calls for municipal fiscal reform.
Municipal governments are not alone in their use of this tax. School boards
(notably in Manitoba and Saskatchewan) and most provinces (largely as a
result of provincializing the local school property tax when provincializing
school finances) also impose property taxes. At about 70 percent of municipal
taxes (2.1 compared with 2.96 percent of PDI in 2001), these taxes are significant and, in the case of provincial property taxes, the taxpayers see no
direct local benefit as they do for municipal taxes. The consolidated provincial and local property taxes as a percentage of personal disposable income
have risen from 4 percent to more than 5 percent (as high as 5.7 percent) since
the early 1990s. These levels have not been experienced since the 1960s
(Kitchen and McMillan 1985). During that period, the stress which the baby
boomers put on local school financing prompted school finance reform, with
greatly expanded provincial grants yielding notable reductions in the overall
property tax burden. With those lower levels behind us, the return of potentially critical levels of property tax burdens may press for further reform.
Perhaps economic growth and growing PDI will lessen the pressure. However, a logical change in the circumstances would be for the relevant provinces
to reduce their property taxes and fund schooling entirely out of general revenues, leaving the property tax field entirely to municipal government.

A Subnational Perspective

Nationally aggregated data can be helpful, but because municipal affairs come under provincial policy, they can mask as much as they reveal. Hence, it is also useful to consider a more provincial or at least subnational perspective. A province-by-province review cannot be done here, but it is useful to focus to some extent on Ontario, because it has followed a rather different approach with its municipalities and also with its 1990s reforms, and because the province is so large that its numbers can skew the national averages.

Subnational data indicate that Ontario is different. It has a relatively large municipal sector – 25.5 percent of consolidated provincial local expenditure, compared with 14.1 percent in the other provinces. Furthermore, unlike elsewhere, this sector has actually grown since 1997 (from 22 percent); see figure 4.

As in the other provinces, Ontario municipalities have become more reliant on their own revenues. However, the burden of own-source revenue as a percentage of PDI increased in only five other provinces, but the increases in them were swamped by the 1.6 percentage point increase (to 6.62 percent of PDI) in Ontario. The average burden of own-source revenue elsewhere actually

Figure 4: Program Expenditure Trends: Ontario and Other Provinces

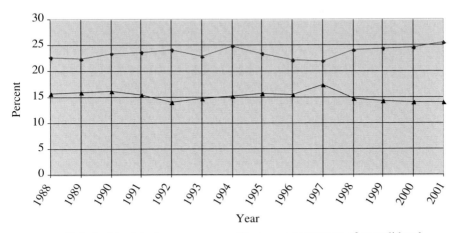

—◆— Ontario: Municipal program expenditures as a percentage of consolidated provincial and local program expenditures

—▲— Canada less Ontario: Municipal program expenditures as a percentage of consolidated provincial and local program expenditures

Sources: Statistics Canada, ibid.

declined marginally to 5.34 percent of PDI. The municipal real property tax burden (as a share of PDI) has increased in all provinces to meet rising own-revenue requirements, but this is especially so in Ontario, where it rose from 2.14 to 3.52 percent between 1988 and 2001, compared with an average increase from 2.25 to 2.57 percent in the other provinces.[14] Figure 5 shows the time paths of the own-source and real property tax burdens in Ontario and in Canada less Ontario. The sharp and significant changes in Ontario are obvious.

An interesting difference also appears in Quebec. Provincial data indicate that Quebec was the only province not to reduce transfers to its municipalities. Between 1988 and 2001, total transfers to Quebec municipalities increased from 8.0 to 14.0 percent of municipal expenditures. However, this growth was not entirely smooth. The latest data show that for the two years 1999 and 2000, transfers were at least 20 percent below their previous level but then

Figure 5: Municipal Own-Source Revenue and Real Property Taxes as a Percentage of Personal Disposable Income, Ontario and Canada less Ontario, 1988–2001

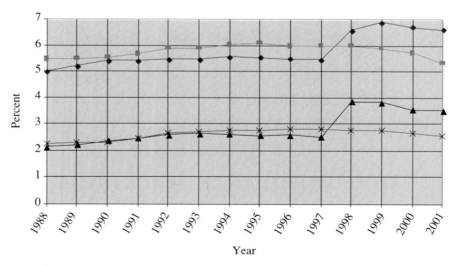

Sources: Statistics Canada, ibid.

recovered quickly to levels now at about 13 percent of expenditures. Also unique, as part of Quebec's fiscal restraint effort, the province required an annual contribution of $356 million by its municipalities for three years (1998–2000) to a Local Activities Special Financing Fund as part of their contribution to the province's fiscal restraint effort (Quesnel 2000, 119).[15] The $356 million annual contribution was equivalent to about 30 percent of the transfers then in place.[16]

Changes in social service financing in Nova Scotia also deserve comment. During the last half of the 1990s, social service outlays fell from one-quarter of municipal expenditures in 1995 to 4.5 percent in 2001 as the province assumed greater responsibility for social services. Because provincial transfers funded about three-quarters of municipal social service outlays, transfers to the municipalities declined as well, and the drop in transfers for social services accounted for 74 percent of the reduction in the total grants to municipalities over that period. Thus, the substantial fall in grants as a percentage of municipal expenditures (from 24.8 to 5.9 percent between 1988 and 2001) results partly from a provincial-municipal reallocation of responsibilities. A better comparison is that had the 2001 social service arrangements been in place in 1995, transfers would have represented about 15 percent of municipal expenditures. A decline in the contribution of transfers from 15 to 5.9 percent is still substantial but is more modest than the simple numbers suggest.

The pressure to maintain services in the face of declining grants during an economic slump posed problems for municipalities across the country throughout much of the 1990s. The result was fiscal pressure, especially from the revenue side. In general, though, the municipal governments seem to be coping relatively well. Although they rely more on own-source revenues and on real property taxes in particular, program expenditures are being maintained. However, the burden put on Ontario municipal governments and their taxpayers appears extraordinary, to the extent that the results suggest that the municipal fiscal squeeze may primarily be an Ontario problem.

Intergovernmental Transfers

Municipal governments receive transfers from both the federal and the provincial governments. The federal transfers are small. Even at their peak in the mid-1990s, they never exceeded 1.35 percent of expenditures ($19 per capita). In 2001 they amounted to 0.42 percent ($6.50 per capita). Federal transfers are specific purpose, small, and, at least recently, variable. Respecting provincial jurisdiction over municipalities, the federal transfers have been arranged through federal-provincial or federal-provincial-municipal agreements, which have often left the municipalities feeling that they are, if not outsiders, at least underrepresented. About one-half of the transfers have been directed to transportation and housing. Until the mid-1990s, federal money accounted for one-sixth of municipal spending on housing, but by 2001 it had fallen to only 2.3 percent. Beyond housing, only for resource conservation/industrial development and for "other" did federal transfers account for more than 1 percent of municipal outlays in the area. Currently, the federal contribution is very minor in all areas of municipal expenditure. Still, it may be significant to certain small subprograms not recognized at this level of aggregation.

The provincial transfers are much larger – about 16 percent of municipal expenditures overall (down from a peak of more than 24 percent). The magnitude and allocation of provincial grants vary considerably among the provinces. In 2001 provincial grants amounted to only about 5 percent of expenditures in British Columbia and Nova Scotia but amounted to about 20 percent in Ontario and Newfoundland. The per capita dollar amounts range from $40 in Prince Edward Island to $389 in Ontario. While the provinces do make unconditional transfers, the conditional (or specific purpose) grants dominate in all provinces except New Brunswick, and nationally they account for 13.9 of the 16.2 percent of municipal expenditures met through provincial transfers.

There is also considerable variation in the distribution of provincial grants. Ontario devotes almost 80 percent of its grants to social services. Outside Ontario, municipalities have very small social service responsibilities or none at all. Transfers for transportation, typically a major grant category, range from 4.9 percent of conditional transfers in Nova Scotia to 75 percent in Alberta. Large variations can also be found among the provinces in transfers to aid other categories of spending – for example, health, environment, and debt changes.

The contribution of transfers to municipal spending in the various areas is also of interest. In general, provincial transfers tend to be relatively large in comparison to expenditures in those areas for which municipalities normally have limited responsibilities (social services, health, housing, and conservation); but, with the exception of transportation and recreation, they are of less importance for those purposes that are major municipal expenditure areas. Even for transportation, specific purpose transfers exceed 12 percent of category expenditures in only four provinces.

THE MUNICIPAL SITUATION FROM A FISCAL FEDERALISM PERSPECTIVE

Thus far, this paper has outlined what exists. Very little has been said about why it is this way, what the positive and negative features are, or how improvements might be made. To be normative, standards or criteria are needed. Work by economists and political scientists on fiscal federalism provides a model useful for understanding and assessing intergovernmental fiscal relations. Although the main features can only be highlighted here, they are detailed elsewhere.[17] This assessment of the municipal situation is based on the fiscal federalism model.

The assignment problem is at the heart of fiscal federalism. The assignment problem is how to assign among governments (a) expenditure and service responsibilities and (b) revenue raising and tax powers. The major roles of government are often seen to be stabilization, distribution, and allocation (Musgrave 1959). For reasons of small size and interjurisdictional spillovers, neither stabilization nor (re)distribution is deemed an appropriate function for municipal government. However, allocation (using resources to provide services efficiently) is well suited to municipalities. Once there, the problem is to find the mix of responsibilities and funding that will realize that goal. Desirable characteristics for effective local government typically are said to include autonomy, responsiveness, accountability, and strong benefit-cost linkages for local services.[18]

EXPENDITURE RESPONSIBILITIES

Decentralization, or subsidiarity, is central to fiscal federalism. The principle is that responsibility for services should be assigned to the lowest level of government capable of providing the service effectively. When preferences or conditions vary geographically, devolution enhances efficiency plus responsiveness, autonomy, and accountability in a democratic environment. Substantial interjurisdictional spillovers, economies of scale, or decision-making costs may offset the advantages of decentralization and require alternative or modified solutions.

The services typically provided by Canadian municipalities are those well suited to local government: protection (fire, police), transportation, environment (water, sewerage, solid waste), recreation and culture, general services, conservation/development, and regional planning. These services – which together account for more than 75 percent of municipal spending nationally – essentially provide local benefits (that is, there are limited spillovers) for which tastes vary and for which local management and a local scale of operations are efficient. Such services are suited to the duties of a government limited to user charges and property taxes. An important and interesting feature of local government in Canada over the past twenty years has been the expanding provincialization of school finance, effectively make schooling entirely a provincial responsibility (despite the local school boards).

Social expenditures by municipalities – those for health, social services, education, and housing – are minor in most provinces. In eight provinces, they amount to 4 percent or less of total outlays. While municipal support for schooling makes Nova Scotia stand out, the striking anomaly is Ontario, where social spending represents one-third of municipal expenditures. Local governments are not well suited to financing redistributive services. This is why social services in particular, and social spending generally, have been progressively reduced (most recently in Nova Scotia) or virtually eliminated (in

eight provinces) as a municipal responsibility. Ontario makes concessions towards social spending via transfers, but those directed specifically at social
spending offset just over half of its costs. Thus, Ontario municipalities are
still left with an unusually large share of social costs relative to the other
provinces and to recommended practice. Ontario's reforms of the 1990s ag-
gravated the situation, because although it was initially claimed that they were
intended to be revenue neutral, "the numbers did not work out" as someone
said. Ontario is the most obvious case of service responsibility downloading.
Elsewhere, though arguably less so in Quebec, downloading has taken the
form of shifting added revenue-raising (funding) responsibility onto municipal governments.

REVENUE RESPONSIBILITIES

Once there is a multitiered structure of government, tax assignment becomes
an issue. Taxes on immobile tax bases – notably, property – and fees and
charges on service beneficiaries are well suited to municipal government.
Because efficient resource allocation is seen to be the major municipal objective, a close link between local public benefits and local public levies is strongly
recommended; that is, the benefit principle should prevail. As Bird (1993,
111) has noted, "the essential economic role of local government is to provide
local residents with those public services for which they are willing to pay."
In addition, the levies to be imposed on local citizens in order to finance local
services should be determined by their local government. Benefit-related finance and local determination of local levies are fundamental criteria.
Furthermore, it is desirable that revenue sources are adequate, predictable,
fair, visible, not exportable, and easily administered.

The revenue structure of Canadian municipalities conforms rather well to
the model outlined. Own-source revenues account for 83 percent of revenues
and they are almost entirely locally determined.[19] One-half of total revenues
come from property and related taxes, and one-quarter come from user charges.
Lot levies and special assessments (about 4 percent of own-source revenues)
fit the benefit criteria well. More debatable is the business tax (about 3 percent of own-source revenues). Business taxes (because they are additional to
the regular property taxes) and high property taxes on nonresidential property
raise questions about tax shifting and exporting (Kitchen 2003a; Kitchen and Slack
1993). Further reliance on user charges is often advocated, especially for environmental and recreational services (e.g., Dewees 2002). Yet larger service charges
have not figured predominately in the municipal response to the decade's fiscal
stresses. Instead, greater real property taxes have carried the load.

Municipalities have not had revenue sources that correspond well to their
major expenditure area – transportation. In particular, there is no mechanism
with which municipalities can allocate costs directly to vehicles and their users,

since fuel taxes and licence fees are the realm of the provincial and federal governments. Tolls have been limited to a few specific projects and to public transit.

The adequacy and appropriateness of the property tax can be questioned when municipalities are being asked or expected to meet significant social expenditures (without compensating transfers). Ontario is the obvious concern. There, social expenditures are now 33.2 percent of municipal budgets – at least half again as much as they were in 1988. In other provinces, social expenditures by municipalities have risen only marginally, if at all. A notable concern in the case of Ontario is not only that social expenditures have actually increased markedly but also that the responsibility for social spending has increased at the municipal level in the face of provincial and federal cutbacks.

The assumption of full financial responsibility for schooling by more provinces (for example, Alberta, British Columbia, and Ontario) has been a feature of recent local-provincial finance. The paralleling feature is their failure to fund schooling from traditional provincial revenue sources, instead choosing to convert the local school property tax to a provincial property tax. The school property tax, which does not relate well to school benefits or ability to pay, made sense when a local contribution to schooling was required and the only sufficient local tax base was property. Elimination of provincial property taxes for schooling (at least on residential property) might enhance the municipalities' ability to fund spending from traditional revenue sources.

INTERGOVERNMENTAL TRANSFERS

Objective and independent assignments of expenditure and revenue-raising responsibilities do not ensure either an efficient or an equitable fiscal system. One potential problem is a mismatch of fiscal capacity and expenditure responsibilities, resulting in a fiscal gap that calls for some reshuffling of responsibilities or revenue sources, or for unconditional gap-reducing intergovernmental transfers. Even if there is no fiscal gap at the municipal level overall, there still may be "rich" and "poor" municipalities and legitimate demands for (unconditional) equalization grants. Interjurisdictional spillovers of benefits and/or taxes call for grants to correct distortions and to improve fairness. Such grants are specific to the spillover activity. Specific purpose (or conditional) grants are a means by which different tiers of government can share responsibility for services that do not fit neatly into any single level. Schooling has been such a responsibility. Such transfers are also one way for one level of government to (essentially) contract with another level to perform specific services. There are also political reasons for intergovernmental grants. Raw political power may be a motivation, but a more positive view is that some grants are a means of motivating cooperation and contributions while stretching the grantor's budget. Hence, grants may exist for various reasons.

Because grant programs often appear to be aimed at meeting more than a single objective, assessment is complicated.

Unconditional grants to municipalities are provided only by the provincial governments and, typically, in relatively modest amounts. For Canada as a whole, unconditional assistance averages 2.4 percent of municipal revenues, with the largest relative contributions coming in Manitoba (7.9 percent) and New Brunswick (12.4 percent). These funds normally come from provincial general revenues, but in Manitoba they come from a well-established revenue-sharing program. These grants are distributed by formulae on some type of equalizing basis. Often, the available funds are not sufficient to meet the equalization requirements implied by the distribution mechanisms. Typically, some funds are allocated to every municipality; hence, the unconditional transfers may be motivated partly by fiscal gap-closing objectives. Given the modest size of these grants, the provinces must see the municipal fiscal gap problem as minor.

Conditional transfers in most provinces are for transportation, environmental services (water and sewerage), and recreation and culture. The externality element in transportation is obvious (external users) and also in the case of public transport and environmental considerations; but for the others, it is more obtuse.[20] Funding is predominantly for capital projects (or for debt service costs). Uneven subsidies for capital versus operating expenditures raises questions about potential misallocations between capital and operating costs.

A striking feature of conditional transfers is the variation in their relative contribution to municipal spending for a particular purpose. For example, transfers for transportation meet 2.9 percent of expenditures in Ontario but 42 percent in Alberta. However, spillovers are usually not easily determined and priorities can vary. It is interesting that the transfers for policing, a service probably involving significant externalities for most (if not all) municipalities, make only very small contributions to costs, yet for recreation, which is likely to provide local benefits, transfers cover a far higher share of its costs.

Ontario's loading of significant social expenditures on municipalities is exceptional. This unusual arrangement could be quite workable as a responsibility-sharing arrangement given the appropriate transfer programs; that is, with generous conditional social transfers and effective equalization. Ontario's social transfers still leave the municipalities to meet half these costs, which amount to about 16 percent of their total expenditures – a level that far exceeds the municipal social expenditure outlay in any other province.

Federal transfers to municipalities are small (0.4 of municipal expenditures in 2001), and they are directed mostly to social housing and transportation. With recent reductions, the federal contribution to expenditures in any of the main areas has become very minor, the largest in 2001 being to housing, where federal transfers provided 2.33 percent (down from 16 percent in 1995).[21] Federal transfers may contribute in important ways to various subprograms, but the overall contribution has been small and declining.

The analyst would expect federal transfers to be in areas involving national externalities or in areas of federal jurisdiction that benefit from municipal input and cooperation. Efforts to alleviate poverty – such as social housing, immigrant settlement, and off-reserve Aboriginal uplift – seem logical. Typically, as seems reasonable, these programs operate under federal-provincial-local agreements. However, it is debatable whether the allocation of responsibilities and cost sharing under these agreements, as well as the burdens that the underlying problems now impose, are appropriately distributed. Although housing has been identified as a component of the federal urban strategy, the levels planned will not notably enhance the federal role. The fiscal priority of the recent and announced federal strategy has, interestingly, been infrastructure.[22] Apart from the fact that federal visibility from input into municipal projects affords broad local public benefit (as opposed to small social projects benefiting narrow groups of disadvantaged people), the national interest in and benefit from many of these investments is difficult to imagine.

OPTIONS AND PROSPECTS FOR THE FUTURE OF MUNICIPALITIES' INTERGOVERNMENTAL FISCAL RELATIONS

The prevailing message from the municipal sector is that Canadian municipalities are bearing a greater and possibly unsustainable fiscal burden which, unless corrected, will have a negative impact on the development of municipalities, especially Canadian cities, and in turn on the social and economic future of the country. That the share of municipal expenditures met from own-source revenues has grown is without doubt (overall, about 83 percent in 2001, compared with 77 percent in 1988). Although the required adjustment has been relatively rapid and definitely difficult, the fact that municipalities generally are unable to sustain the larger burden is less obvious, especially when the bulk of the readjustment has been concentrated in one province, Ontario. The data examined here suggest that many of the claims of municipal crisis and incapacity may be overstated. For the most part, municipalities appear to have coped relatively well through rather difficult times. But this relatively positive assessment does not imply inaction is an acceptable response. There is still substantial scope for improving the fiscal environment of municipalities of all types. In this section, consideration is given initially to the prospects for easing the existing municipal fiscal burden through expanded transfers. This avenue is likely to be the most popular alternative with municipalities and, though with less enthusiasm, also with the provincial and federal governments. Because the transfer option may be inadequate or (at least in the minds of some) second best, options for making the municipal fiscal burden more manageable through expansion of own-source revenues are also considered.

INTERGOVERNMENTAL TRANSFERS

Although recent developments may suggest otherwise, it is difficult to hold much hope for substantial fiscal relief emerging from the federal government. In part, this view emerges simply because the federal transfers have traditionally been so small; even at their mid-1990s peak, they amounted to only 1.35 percent of municipal expenditures. However, there has been some expansion in federal infrastructure programs for municipalities. More notable has been the emergence of Prime Minister Paul Martin as the champion of a "New Deal" for municipalities, a cause he initiated during his campaign for leadership of the Liberal Party and one that is mostly associated with a sharing of federal fuel tax revenues (Martin 2003). Towards this initiative, the federal budget of 2004 provided municipalities full (versus the partial 57 percent) relief from the federal goods and services tax (GST). This measure was estimated to provide municipalities with $580 million in sales tax relief in its first year. The 2005 federal budget announced the New Deal for Cities and Communities program, which is to provide $5 billion in funds for municipalities over the next five years, starting with $600 million in 2005–6. The 2005 budget and the New Deal proposal are now mired in the uncertainties of minority government. Assuming that the program materializes, $600 million translates into about $18.75 per capita today, or about 1.2 percent of 2001 municipal expenditures. Immediate potential funding from the New Deal, plus the added savings from the GST, is equivalent to about 2.4 percent of 2001 municipal expenditures. Clearly, this is a healthy increase from recent levels of federal government transfers. However, even if the New Deal reaches the $2 billion annually projected after five years, these funds could be expected to amount to only about 3 percent of municipal expenditures. Whether more would become available is hard to say. The federal government faces many demands, and the municipalities are a provincial responsibility. However, federal transfers amounting to 3 percent of expenditures represent almost 40 percent of what the provinces collectively trimmed from their transfers to the municipalities. Hence, in a sense, the enhanced federal funding is as much a benefit to the provinces as to the municipalities. Perhaps, along with the fact that the New Deal funds flow through agreements with the provinces, this is why the provinces are strangely silent on this significant federal initiative into the municipal area.

The provinces are and will continue to be the source of the bulk of transfers to the municipalities. It is the provinces, too, that imposed the most burdensome cuts in these transfers. The cuts were imposed when most provincial economies were listless and the provinces were struggling with deficits and restoring fiscal balance. Both of those situations have improved considerably, so perhaps, with provincial budgets in better condition, the provinces will be more amenable towards restoring municipal transfers. While not indicating a negative trend, the latest (2003) data show no notable evidence of a recovery in transfers to municipalities (relative to their revenues and expenditures). Bearing in mind that health care and other demands place continuing pressures on provincial treasurers, perhaps the changes are yet to come. Some of the recent provincial budgets offer encouragement. For example, the Ontario government has initiated a sharing of the provincial gas tax with its municipalities to support public transit. And Alberta – an exceptional case, faced as it is with the infrastructure demands of strong growth but enjoying the benefits of the accompanying growth in resource revenues – is embarking on a program transferring $600 million (currently the equivalent of $180 per capita) annually to its municipalities for five years.

A careful analysis of the logic for and practice of transfers might sway provincial governments towards being somewhat more generous. A close look at the assignment and financing of social programs in Ontario should head the list. The entire package in all the provinces would likely benefit from review.

The re-examination of transfers might result in a more coherent system, but it might not result in a great deal more funding. To illustrate, Edmonton City Council received a report outlining inequities in the city's fiscal relationship with the province (Edmonton 2002). The report identified $88 million in costs which the city bore on behalf of the province and for which it should receive consideration. While a considerable sum, this represented only 6.3 percent of the city's total budget for the coming year. Many may have expected a larger share. In addition, the Alberta government may have some reasonable rebuttals and an independent analyst may propose something else again. Regardless, the gains from improved (rather than simply enlarged) transfer systems might not be large.

Indirect transfers are another possibility. In 2003, Ontario introduced Ontario Opportunity Bonds to fund municipal infrastructure lending, the interest on which was not subject to provincial income tax. This tax concession lowered the interest rate charged on municipal debt (a tax expenditure), providing an indirect subsidy to borrowing municipalities.[23] While on the surface appealing, such bonds distort incentives to investors, induce municipalities to rely more on debt to finance capital, encourage the substitution of capital investment for operating costs, and favour high-income investors most. Both the TD Bank (2002) and the C.D. Howe Institute (Mintz 2003) considered the Opportunity Bonds flawed. The federal government, and many would say wisely, did not provide a parallel tax concession.[24] Ontario's newly elected McGuinty government soon dispensed with the tax exempt status of infrastructure bonds and reformed the province's infrastructure lending authority.

Enhanced intergovernmental transfers do not appear to offer great opportunities for reducing the present fiscal pressures on municipalities. However, unexpected and substantial improvements in the fiscal situation of the federal government and especially the provincial governments could change that (as occurred in Alberta, for example). If so, it could start municipal government on another cycle of transfer volatility. Senior governments are fickle friends when it comes to providing grants. Some transfers are necessary for efficiency and equity reasons, so a well-designed and appropriately funded grant system is desirable. Even then, changing circumstances and political perspectives can be expected to ensure that some volatility will persist. While the expansions are normally regarded positively, the contractions are unpleasant. Municipalities may have more success in resolving their fiscal problems if they advance and secure improvements in their own-source revenues.

OWN-SOURCE REVENUES

Four topics are addressed here. While there are many possible alternative mechanisms for augmenting municipal revenues and many of those have been suggested in various contexts, most have very limited revenue-generating capacity (even collectively) and many have other drawbacks. Attention is focused here on options that offer significant revenue potential or potential improvements, or have gained some attention in the Canadian context.

The Property Tax

Growth in the property tax burden has been striking and may have heightened resistance to further increases. About 40 percent of property taxes are not municipal taxes; except in Manitoba and Saskatchewan, they are provincial taxes primarily supporting schooling. Provincializing the school property tax afforded a convenient transition, but as there are better alternatives, the provincial property tax (at least on residential property) should be phased out. Doing so would be a revenue-neutral change for the provinces – a reshuffling of (not an increase in) provincial taxes. Doing so would also rationalize the tax structure better. Especially when school property taxes are paid to the province, there is, at best, a weak connection between tax and benefits. As a benefit-related tax, the property tax is much better suited to municipal government. Even if the provinces were to abandon general property taxes, it is unlikely that this would create a tax room windfall for municipalities. Municipal taxpayers would still look for the quid pro quo and would carefully scrutinize the pros and cons of any proposed property tax increase.

Vehicle-Related Taxes

The absence of vehicle-related revenues for municipalities is striking, given the importance of their transportation expenditures. This anomaly detracts from the benefit-cost linkage considered important for municipal finance. It is reasonable that municipalities have access to vehicle fuel tax revenue. Hence, some have suggested that municipalities be permitted to levy their own vehicle gas taxes. While superficially attractive, the logic for individual municipal gas taxes is weaker. Vehicles are mobile, and drivers in many municipalities could easily make the choice of avoiding or minimizing this tax. Multijurisdictional communities afford the greatest opportunity to avoid local fuel taxes, and undoubtedly some municipalities would find gas stations a more attractive alternative to fuel taxes. Even for large municipalities (or where regional associations of municipalities agreed to cooperate) where the travel costs necessary to avoid a fuel tax would be larger, border problems would persist. To illustrate, near the City of Lloydminster on the Alberta-Saskatchewan border, the higher Saskatchewan fuel tax is graduated with distance from the border. In addition, in the regional context, while border problems diminish, the accountability problem is exacerbated. In the multijurisdiction environment with fuel tax levies collectively determined, who is held accountable for increased fuel taxes? Finally, even without the border problem, gas tax bases will vary greatly. Consider the major pit stops along the main intercity highways. Of the few places where local fuel taxes are in place in Canada (for example, the Greater Vancouver Regional District), they are provincially determined. Because of the potential social costs of tax avoidance efforts, the distortions to business location, and the uneven base, vehicle fuel taxes become a candidate for revenue sharing. The fuel taxes which the federal and provincial governments already collect could be shared, or an additional (dedicated municipal tax) could be collected for sharing. While administratively convenient and avoiding the noted distortions, revenue sharing poses problems of determining the appropriate amount of revenue to be raised, its distribution, potential arbitrary changes by the "sharing" government, and a weak tax-benefit linkage to local expenditures. Clearly, there are tradeoffs to be considered.

For a locally determined tax, a municipal vehicle registration charge is an attractive option. Owners of vehicles live in a particular municipality and, to a large extent, use their vehicles there. Since vehicle registration is linked to residence, the tax could not easily be avoided (especially if significant fines accompanied improper registration). Commercial vehicles used primarily outside the "home" community could be levied a representative supplementary provincial registration fee, to be shared among municipalities. Piggy-backing local fees onto the provincial registration system would minimize administration and compliance costs. A local vehicle registration fee relates user benefits to transportation costs only in a simple way, but since there is less potential for tax avoidance and tax exporting, it seems superior to local fuel taxes. Such a fee would be ineffective in easing congestion and would not account for use outside the municipality (excepting the aforementioned suggestion for certain commercial vehicles). However, provincial licence fees and fuel taxes, plus federal fuel taxes, go far towards taking account of certain externalities.

Roadway congestion charges are virtually nonexistent in Canada, so a local vehicle registration fee would be neutral on that front. However, the case for and appeal of congestion charges is increasing, and it deserves further attention, though it can be considered only briefly here.

Tolls geared to traffic volume are suited for controlling congestion in urban areas, and technology is making their use more and more feasible. Note, for example, the developments in throughway tolling in California, the well-established toll system in Singapore, and the charge recently introduced in central London, England. In fact, the British are considering developing a nationwide road-use toll system. Toll revenue should be shared among the governments responsible for providing and maintaining the roads (much as one would think should occur with the existing fuel taxes and registration fees).

General Sales Taxes

The municipal sales tax is another option for an expanded local tax base. Municipalities could be permitted to levy a general sales tax within their jurisdiction, to be collected by piggy-backing it onto a provincial sales tax or the federal GST. Local general sales taxes are relatively common in the United States but are not often found elsewhere beyond southern Europe. Municipal sales taxes can raise considerable revenue, and partly for this reason they have attracted some proponents in Canada (e.g., Kitchen 2000b, 2003a; TD Bank 2002). They account for about 10 percent of local tax revenue in the United States. There are, however, numerous criticisms of local sales taxes. Because consumers are mobile, local sales taxes affect where they buy and where businesses locate. Hence, as with municipal fuel taxes, economic activity can be subject to fiscal distortions. Also, the sales tax base is not uniformly distributed so access to sales taxes may disadvantage some (for example, rural jurisdictions) but be attractive to others, in part because of the potential for tax exporting. Because these social costs are rather obscure, municipal sales taxes may appear more attractive than is warranted. Hence, sales taxes may be better suited as a source of funds for revenue-sharing programs. Again, revenue sharing has its own set of problems; there are some significant tradeoffs involved with the local sales tax, the pros and cons are not always obvious, and they differ with the particular circumstances.

Personal Income Taxes

Municipal personal income taxes are another option. Although frequently overlooked,[25] they are not all that unusual.[26] They are the mainstay of municipal government in the Scandinavian countries, but municipal governments there have extensive responsibilities, especially in the social services area. In the

United States, which more closely parallels the Canadian situation, about 3,700 local governments levy local personal income taxes (compared with 6,500 using the sales tax), and those taxes generate 5.9 percent of local tax revenue (compared with 10 percent for local sales taxes). Municipal income taxes are especially popular with cities in the United States.[27] Canadian municipalities only lost their income tax powers with the 1941 federal-provincial tax rental agreement. Before then, local income taxes in Canada sometimes exceeded the provincial income tax collections.

A municipal personal income tax is typically levied at a low flat rate on the personal income of residents. A 1 percent rate is not unusual. Corporate income is not taxed, largely because of tax-exporting problems. However, to capture personal income comprehensively in Canada, the income of professional and small corporations may need to be included. The treatment of commuters varies and is debatable. A municipal income tax offers various advantages. It can easily be piggy-backed on provincial personal income taxes to minimize administrative and compliance costs. Because the tax (and the benefits it would help to finance) is based on residence, it is, like the property tax (but unlike municipal sales taxes), a relatively non-distorting revenue source. The personal income tax relates better to ability-to-pay than the property tax, so in combination with the property tax it might facilitate a better matching of benefits and costs at the municipal level (especially of social programs). Unlike sales taxes, neither rural nor urban municipalities are disadvantaged by access to this revenue source. Also, like the property and sales taxes, it is a visible tax that promotes accountability. On the negative side, a municipal income tax would (like a municipal fuel or sales tax) add a third tax authority to a shared tax base. Also, it might have some marginal adverse incentive effects on income earners. Again, there are tradeoffs to consider. A 1 percent tax could generate about 8 percent of municipal revenues, or the equivalent of 20 percent of the revenues from the real property tax. If the federal government were to offer to collect a low municipal personal income tax, this option would be open for discussion.[28]

SUMMARY AND CONCLUSIONS

THE FISCAL PICTURE

Municipal governments in Canada supply and finance services benefiting their own local residents. More than 83 percent of the costs of municipal services now come from own-source (locally raised) revenues, property and property related taxes, and user charges. This assignment of responsibilities and revenue sources conforms quite well with the recommendations of fiscal federalism analysis. For the most part, functions are decentralized appropriately and there is a

strong benefit-cost linkage at the municipal level. Intergovernmental transfers account (on average in 2001) for 17 percent of municipal funding.
Provincial transfers, representing 16.6 of the 17 percent, dominate. Transfers
to municipalities are predominately (85 percent) for specific purposes rather
than being unconditional grants.

Over the past decade, municipal government has been pressured by a fiscal
squeeze precipitated by a sharp reduction in transfers (except to Quebec),
from about 25 to 16.6 percent of municipal expenditures.[29] Reduced interest
rates (and, in turn, lower debt service charges) softened the blow, but reduced
grants erased for municipalities the fiscal dividend that they would otherwise
have realized from falling interest rates.

The downloading of responsibilities has been a widespread complaint and
concern of the municipal sector. Although widely spoken of, evidence of notable downloading on the expenditure side is much more muted. Between 1988
and 2001, there was hardly any change in municipal total expenditure as a
percentage of GDP, of municipal program expenditure as a percentage of GDP,
and of municipal program expenditure as a percentage of consolidated provincial and local program expenditure. However, municipal real dollar per
capita expenditures increased 15 percent (from $1,262 to $1,453) over that
period. This evidence does not necessarily demonstrate the absence of expenditure downloading, but it does demonstrate that, to the extent that it
occurred and to the extent that municipal government has responded, it has
not resulted in the growth of municipal government relative to the economy
or relative to the subnational (notably, provincial) government sector.

Developments on the revenue side are more substantial. Reduced grants
meant an increased reliance on own-source revenues. While user charges have
become somewhat more important, the increase in real property taxes has been
dramatic. Between 1988 and 2001, real property taxes increased from 32.2 to
41.9 percent of municipal revenues – a 30 percent increase. The burden of municipal property taxes moved in parallel, increasing as a percentage of personal
disposable income (PDI) by almost 34 percent (from 2.21 to 2.96 percent).

Municipal property taxes are only part of the story. Provinces (and school
boards in some provinces) also levy property taxes. Together, the aggregate
property tax reached 5.6 and 5.7 percent of PDI during much of the 1990s.
Canadians have not experienced this level of property taxation since the 1960s,
when those levels contributed to school finance reforms. One might legitimately ponder whether the recent concern about municipal finance might stem
from the escalating and high property tax burdens of the 1990s and whether
pressure for reforms to relieve the property tax burden will escalate or be
stayed by the gains of the recent economic recovery.

A subnational perspective offers further insights. Ontario stands out. A significant downloading of responsibilities to the municipalities occurred there.
Municipal government increased in relative size only in Ontario. Also, while

the municipal real property tax burden rose elsewhere, Ontario shifted to a new, higher plateau after 1998, which resulted in an increase from 2.14 to 3.52 percent of PDI between 1988 and 2001, while the average of the other provinces rose from 2.25 to 2.57 percent. The consolidated provincial and local property tax had a parallel shift. Ontario municipalities have experienced a substantial fiscal squeeze from both the expenditure side and the revenue side. In the other provinces, the squeeze was a revenue squeeze and was more modest.[30] Overall, while there has been a municipal fiscal squeeze across the country, the squeeze is the biggest in Ontario, and it appears to be primarily an Ontario problem.

FUTURE DIRECTIONS

Conventional Transfers

Reduced transfers have been the source of many of the municipalities' recent fiscal difficulties. Is there much likelihood of relief from this same source now that the federal government and most provincial governments have their fiscal houses in better shape? Perhaps, but there are many obstacles. The federal government has been a minor player in the municipal grant programs (contributing only 0.4 percent of municipal revenues in 2001). Even with the shift of municipalities in the federal priorities under the Martin government (with the full GST rebate and the New Deal for Cities and Communities), the effective additional relief afforded municipalities in the short term will amount to about 2 percent of municipal expenditures. While still relatively small, the new federal contributions are not trivial and are welcomed by municipalities. The provinces have been unusually quiet about this initiative of the federal government in an area of provincial jurisdiction, probably because they see federal assistance to municipalities as easing the expectations and burden on themselves – that is, it is a form of indirect assistance to the provinces. Despite these initiatives, the federal government should not neglect transfer programs involving municipalities in areas of federal responsibility (immigrant settlement and Aboriginal improvement) and those largely redistributive programs (such as affordable housing) where there is a relative advantage to national funding.

Changes in the much larger provincial transfers could be expected to have a more significant impact. A careful review of them might result in improved design and possibly expanded funding. Even so, the amounts might not be that large, and grant funding seems less dependent on grant rationale than on the availability of funds. To be realized, a change in priorities is required. To date, there has been little evidence of a major turnaround in provincial transfers to municipalities developing in most provinces.

Should federal transfers to municipalities increase and play a more important role? This is not a simple question to answer. Provincial transfers, it could be argued, will better reflect regional needs, interests, and priorities. However, if they are not emerging because of differences in the fiscal pressures on the federal and provincial governments or because of different priorities, greater federal transfers might be an acceptable alternative (although it could be argued that it might be more appropriate for the federal government to address provincial fiscal capacity and let decisions regarding municipalities be made there). At projected levels, added federal transfers will not undermine the reliance on local revenues and the local benefit-cost linkages relative to what they were a decade or more ago. Also, if modest and well designed, they are unlikely to distort local priorities or encourage inefficiencies – at least, not any more than provincial grants do. On the other hand, an expanded federal grant system adds complexity to intergovernmental relations. Perhaps worthy of note is that federal-municipal fiscal relations vary widely among federations, and the minimal interaction found in Canada is unusual.

Sustainability of the Status Quo and Some Direct Implications

If the prospects for a reinstatement of the conventional transfers must be viewed cautiously, can municipalities function effectively under the current situation with the heavier reliance on the property tax? Improved economic and fiscal conditions have raised PDI and diminished the relative burden of the property tax. Whether this easing will suffice is yet to be determined. The prospects here look more positive outside Ontario. Ontario, however, should rethink its municipal social expenditure assignment (or its funding). There are good reasons why social expenditures by municipalities are almost zero elsewhere.

An option for reducing the property tax burden in many provinces is to reduce provincial property taxes.[31] With access to superior alternatives at the provincial level for financing schools, a provincial property tax (at least on residences) could be eliminated without any increase in the overall provincial tax burden. Elimination of provincial property taxes would leave the property tax for municipal government. The municipalities, however, would still need to convince their taxpayers that additional municipal levies were warranted.

Some Less Conventional Options

A large share of municipal expenditure is related to vehicle transportation, but municipal government lacks the mechanisms to charge or tax vehicles or their use. Some have suggested that municipalities be granted the authority to levy municipal fuel taxes. Others propose municipal sales taxes as a solution to the broader fiscal problem. Consumer mobility (creating border problems and economic distortions), especially in multijurisdictional environments, and uneven tax bases could make these unattractive options. Fuel and sales taxes are better suited for revenue sharing, but that puts control of the revenue (and its distribution) in the hands of the sharing government. Municipal governments might be reluctant to endorse this option, given their recent experience with transfers, and the sharing governments might want municipal governments to take (greater) responsibility for the taxes from which they benefit.

There are other taxes that may be better suited to municipal government. Individual municipalities should levy a municipal vehicle registration fee (rather than fuel taxes), and congestion tolls deserve consideration, especially in large cities. A municipal personal income tax surcharge is another option. Like the vehicle registration fee, it could be collected through the existing collection systems. Both these taxes are residence based, and because residence is less mobile than consumption, they are less subject to distortion than taxes based on sales.

There is relatively little evidence to suggest that the provinces are inclined towards these less conventional options. In 2003 the City of Winnipeg advanced a carefully crafted New Deal Initiative that, among a variety of measures, included innovative proposals for a municipal general sales tax of 1 percent and a municipal fuel tax of $0.05 per litre.[32] The province, however, was unwilling to give the city new taxing powers. In Alberta, in 2002, the minister of municipal affairs created a high-level Provincial/Municipal Council on Roles, Responsibilities and Resources. This council was exposed to a wide range of alternatives across the three areas, and some innovative recommendations were advanced, including some for expanded municipal tax bases.[33] However, the council kept a very low profile, never issued public reports, and seemed to come to a close in 2004 with no resolution. The Canada West Foundation (Gibbins et al. 2004) issued a report that appeared to be aimed at outlining the council's unfinished agenda. Flush with energy revenues and facing an election, the province opted for reverting to a very large expansion of conditional transfers to support infrastructure development. Other provinces lack the fiscal flexibility of Alberta. Still, Ontario, in the fall of 2004, started sharing one cent per litre of the fuel tax (to reach two cents in 2006) with its municipalities. Hence, there seems to be little enthusiasm by the provinces for expanding municipal taxing capacity; instead, where possible, the provinces prefer to revert to conventional transfers.

FURTHER OBSERVATIONS

This discussion is limited in several respects. For one, the fiscal problems of municipalities may well differ among different types of municipalities. It has not been possible to address those differences here (largely for lack of suitable data by municipal type). It is, however, important to recognize that differences do exist and that possible solutions may not be universally applicable. There is also a problem that capital and operating budgets have not been separated (again a data problem). Municipalities are responsible for the bulk of total government infrastructure investment, and it is often argued that they suffer an infrastructure deficit. Hence, municipal capital warrants further attention.

Finally, there are many dimensions to municipal intergovernmental fiscal issues. Money matters, but it is not the only consideration, though it often overlaps with others. Fortunately, other aspects are considered elsewhere in this volume.

NOTES

The author thanks Harry Kitchen and the Public Institutions Division of Statistics Canada for providing data. He also thanks Junaid Jahangir for research assistance. Additional tables further documenting the data reported in the paper are available from the author or at the conference section of the Institute of Intergovernmental Relations website, where an extended version of this paper appears. Enid Slack and two anonymous referees are thanked for their comments. Various people are thanked for insightful comments and valuable references.

1 For a good overview of developments, see Kitchen 2003 and Garcea and LeSage 2005. The latter cover the extension of "natural person powers" to municipalities. Distinct from these developments, but not to be overlooked, are the changes in school finance (i.e., the provincialization of school finance) and the school district amalgamations that have occurred in parallel (e.g., Alberta, British Columbia, and Ontario).

2 For example see Berdahl 2002, who draws from many of these studies. More recent CWF publications relating to municipal finance have tended to focus on infrastructure.

3 Note the activities of the Federation of Canadian Municipalities. Recent assessments are provided by, for example, Kitchen 2000a, TD Bank 2002, and Vander Ploeg 2001, 2002a and b.

4 Before 1988, data were available only for local government; that is, for the combination of (the comparably sized) general purpose local authorities (municipalities) and local school authorities (school boards). The data suggest that, since 1965, the relative magnitude of local government has been quite stable.

5 The latest numbers from Statistics Canada Financial Management System (for 2002 and 2003) suggest that, although municipal social assistance expenditures continued to decline, there has been no further reduction in overall municipal social service spending in Nova Scotia since 2001.

6 For details, see, for example, Kitchen 2003b.

7 Transfers in Prince Edward Island also are relatively small (7.2 percent of total revenue), but municipal expenditures there are low.

8 The most recent data on municipal revenues and expenditures have revised the 2001 numbers, and that revision affects the 2001 values reported here. Note that the updated data show transfers to municipalities as accounting for 15.4 percent of municipal expenditures and revenues in 2001 (not the 16.6 and 17 percent reported here). The important implication of this is that the reduction in transfers to the municipalities is actually greater than indicated in the text of the paper. The volume of calculations using the earlier data prevent recalculation of all the numbers, so other changes are not noted (nor is the above change made in the text). More than marginal changes are not expected for most figures.

9 Due to the slow growth in GDP during the economic funk of the early and mid-1990s, the ratio in intermediate years rose because of the adverse effect on the denominator of the ratio. This affected several of the series examined. Fortunately, the initial and final years of the study period are both periods of relative economic prosperity and so are comparable.

10 Program expenditures are expenditures less debt-servicing costs; that is, expenditures directly on services (programs) for the community.

11 Nominal dollars are adjusted using the GDP price index. There is no price index for municipal government expenditure, but the GDP index seems more appropriate than the consumer price index, and it also approximates the index for (total) government current expenditures.

12 Because local taxes are paid from disposable income, it is reasonable to look at the municipal tax burden relative to disposable income, although that figure is affected by income taxes. For those interested, own-source revenues increased from 4.15 to 4.47 percent of personal income (a somewhat smaller 7.7 percent increase).

13 Also, the move to development charges has helped alleviate the problems of infrastructure financing.

14 The total (provincial and local) property tax burden (relative to personal disposable income) also increased between 1988 and 2001. In Ontario it rose from 4.70 to 6.05 percent, and the average increase in the other provinces was from 3.71 to 4.46 percent. Ontario has a particularly high provincial property tax, matched only by the school taxes in Saskatchewan.

15 Also see section 3, "Measures Regarding the Local Sector," of Quebec's 2000–2001 Budget.

16 Note, too, that as part of the municipal reform process in the two provinces, both Ontario and Quebec amalgamated many municipalities – a move rationalized in part by arguments for potential cost savings. These amalgamations were unpopular at the local level. The new Liberal government in Quebec allowed demerger referendums in 2004. Of the 213 merged municipalities in Quebec, 89 called for a referendum and the demerger vote carried in 31. While some municipalities have sought de-amalgamation in Ontario, the provincial government has not yet approved any.

17 Most undergraduate public economics texts have a chapter on fiscal federalism (e.g., Rosen, et al. 2002); the original work of Oates 1972 is valuable. References

directed more to local government include Bird 1993 and McMillan, forthcoming, a and b.

18 A variation on these points is (i) decentralized decision making, (ii) local autonomy, (iii) effective provision, (iv) interjurisdictional and interpersonal equity, and (v) adequate resources.

19 The leading exceptions are federal and provincial government payments in lieu of property taxes, which are included under own-source property and related taxes. These payments, however, are intended to approximately parallel taxes on similar private property.

20 Subsidies for environmental outlays are about half as large relative to the relevant municipal expenditures as those for transportation. Part of the reason for this may be that there is greater public acceptance of the idea that the polluter should pay the cost of avoiding (reducing) pollution (i.e., to meet environmental standards) than that road users should pay for local roads or for (and thus reduce) the congestion costs that they impose on others. Resistance to congestion pricing is diminishing, as is evidenced by the congestion tolls introduced recently in London, England, for example.

21 Of interest is the fact that, despite the fluctuations in federal funding, consolidated federal, provincial, and local expenditures for housing held quite stable at close to 1 percent of consolidated expenditures throughout the 1988–2001 period.

22 See, for example, OECD 2002 and Liberal Party of Canada, Prime Minister's Caucus Task Force 2002.

23 See Kitchen 2003a and McMillan 2003 for some discussion.

24 If the tax concession game is to be played, a more neutral concession would be to provide a refundable personal income tax credit for property taxes paid that are not now tax deductible; that is, essentially for owner-occupied residences. For further discussion, see McMillan 2003.

25 Note Vander Ploeg 2002a and b. Also, the TD Bank 2002 report cavalierly dismissed municipal income taxes with a reference to the inappropriate municipal taxation of corporate income.

26 See Kitchen 2003a and McMillan, forthcoming, a and b, for discussions of local income taxes.

27 Payroll taxes are a common form of taxing income at the local level in the United States and are encompassed in the reference to U.S. local income taxes. Local income taxes as suggested here do not include payroll taxes, because they typically are aimed in part at nonresidents and are incomplete in their coverage of their own residents. A local income tax piggy-backed on the federal-provincial personal income taxes requires explicit consideration of the tax-exporting issue and avoids the latter problem.

28 See Kitchen and Slack 2003 for discussion of alternative municipal taxes. Of particular interest is that they provide estimates of the revenues and tax rates associated with local income and of sales and fuel taxes for numerous Canadian cities. For a

discussion of the merits of alternative municipal taxes and of the experience in the United States, see Oates and Schwab 2004 and Sjoquist et al. 2004.

29 Recall that the latest data indicate that transfers in 2001 account for 15.4 percent of expenditures (not 16.6 percent), so the reduction in transfers was actually somewhat larger than stated; that is, from 25 to 15.4 percent.

30 Recall, too, that the bulk of the transfer reduction in Nova Scotia resulted from the province assuming responsibility for social assistance outlays (uploading, if you like) and thus reducing its transfers to the municipalities for that purpose.

31 Alternatively, where schooling is still largely funded by local school taxes, increased provincial school funding would enable a reduction in local school property taxes.

32 Information on Winnipeg's proposal can be found at www.winnipeg.ca/NewDeal.

33 For example, see Patterson et al. 2003.

REFERENCES

Berdahl, Loleen. 2002. *Structuring Federal Urban Engagement: A Principled Approach.* Calgary: Canada West Foundation, November

Bird, Richard M. 1993. "Threading the Fiscal Labyrinth: Some Issues in Fiscal Decentralization." *National Tax Journal* 46 (June): 207–27

Boothe, Paul, ed. 2003. *Paying for Cities: The Search for Sustainable Municipal Revenues.* Edmonton: Institute for Public Economics, University of Alberta

Canadian Tax Foundation. 2002. "Municipal Finance and Governance Reform Symposium." *Canadian Tax Journal* 50 (1, 2 and 3)

Dewees, Donald N. 2002. "Pricing Municipal Services: The Economics of User Charges." *Canadian Tax Journal* 50 (2): 586–99

Edmonton. 2002. *Identifying and Addressing Inequities in the City of Edmonton's Relationship with the Provincial Government.* Edmonton: Corporate Services Department, December

Garcea, Joseph, and Edward C. LeSage Jr., eds. 2005. *Municipal Reform in Canada: Reconfiguration, Re-Empowerment, and Rebalancing.* Toronto: Oxford University Press

Gibbins, Roger, Loleen Berdahl, and Casey Vander Ploeg. 2004. *Foundations for Prosperity: Creating a Sustainable Municipal-Provincial Partnership to Meet the Infrastructure Challenge of Alberta's Second Century.* Calgary: Canada West Foundation, September

Hobson, Paul A.R., and France St-Hilaire, eds. 1997. *Urban Governance and Finance: A Question of Who Does What.* Montreal: Institute for Research on Public Policy

Kitchen, Harry M. 2000a. "Provinces and Municipalities, Universities, Schools and Hospitals: Recent Trends and Funding Issues." In *Canada: The State of the Federation 1999/2000. Towards a New Mission Statement for Canadian Federalism*, ed.

Harvey Lazar, 295–336. Kingston: Institute of Intergovernmental Relations, Queen's
University; Montreal: McGill-Queen's University Press

– 2000b. "Municipal Finance in a New Fiscal Environment." *Commentary*. Toronto:
C.D. Howe Foundation, no. 147, November

– 2003a. "Financing Cities and Fiscal Sustainability." In *Paying for Cities*, ed. Paul
Boothe, 19–36. Edmonton: Institute for Public Economics, University of Alberta

– 2003b. *Municipal Revenue and Expenditure Issues in Canada*. Toronto: Canadian
Tax Foundation, Tax Paper no. 107

Kitchen, Harry M., and Melville L. McMillan. 1985. "Local Government and Canadian Federalism." In *Intergovernmental Relations*, ed. Richard Simeon (research
coordinator), 63:215–61. Research studies of the Royal Commission on the Economic Union and Development Prospects for Canada. Toronto: University of Toronto
Press

Kitchen, Harry M., and Enid Slack. 1993. *Business Property Taxation*. Government
and Competitiveness Project Discussion Paper no. 93-24. Kingston: School of Policy
Studies, Queen's University

– 2003. "New Finance Options for Municipal Governments." *Canadian Tax Journal*
51 (6): 2215–75

Liberal Party of Canada. Prime Minister's Caucus Task Force on Urban Issues. 2002.
Canada's Urban Strategy: A Blueprint for Action. Chair, Judy Sgro. Final Report.
[Ottawa: The Task Force] (accessed at www.judysgro.com)

McMillan, Melville L. 2003. "Rapporteur: What Have We Learned?" In *Paying for
Cities*, ed. Paul Boothe, 105–21. Edmonton: Institute for Public Economics, University of Alberta

– forthcoming a. "Designing Local Governments for Performance." In *Handbook on
Public Sector Performance Reviews*. Vol. 5, *Fiscal Federalism: Principles and Prac-
tices*, ed. Robin Boadway and Anwar Shah, chap. 11. To be published by Oxford
University Press for the World Bank

– forthcoming b. "Local Perspective on Fiscal Federalism." In *Handbook of Public
Sector Performance Reviews*. Vol. 6, *Macrofederalism and Local Finances*, ed. Anwar
Shah, chap. 7. To be published by Oxford University Press for the World Bank

Martin, Paul. 2003. "Towards a New Deal for Cities." Paper presented at the Creative
Cities Conference, Winnipeg, 29 May (accessed at www.paulmartintimes.ca)

Mintz, Jack M. 2003. "Ontario's Bond Bust." *Financial Post*, 15 May

Musgrave, Richard A. 1959. *The Theory of Public Finance*, New York: McGraw-Hill

Oates, Wallace E. 1972. *Fiscal Federalism*. New York: Harcourt Brace Jovanovich

Oates, Wallace E., and Robert M. Schwab. 2004. "What Should Local Governments
Tax: Income or Property?" In *City Taxes, City Spending: Essays in Honor of Dick
Netzer*, ed. Amy Ellen Schwartz, 7–29. Northhampton, Mass.: Edward Elgar

OECD. 2002. *OECD Territorial Reviews: Canada*. Paris: Organization for Economic
Co-operation and Development

Patterson, Ernie, Jack Hayden, Bill Smith, and Dave Bronconner. 2004. Proposal to
the Minister's Council on Roles, Responsibilities and Resources. Edmonton: Alberta

Urban Municipalities Association, September. www.munlink.net/policy/Reports/ 121903MuniCouncilProposal.pdf

Quesnel, Louise. 2000. "Municipal Reorganization in Quebec." *Canadian Journal of Regional Science* 23 (1): 115–34

Rosen, H.S., B. Dahlby, R.S. Smith, and P. Boothe. 2002. *Public Finance in Canada,* 2nd edn. Toronto: McGraw-Hill Ryerson

Seidle, F. Leslie. 2002. *The Federal Role in Canada's Cities: Overview of Issues and Proposed Actions.* Ottawa: Canadian Policy Research Networks, Discussion Paper F/27, November

Sjoquist, Davil L., Sally Wallace, and Barbara Edwards. 2004. "What a Tangled Web: Local Property, Income, and Sales Taxes." In *City Taxes, City Spending: Essays in Honor of Dick Netzer,* ed. Amy Ellen Schwartz, 42–70. Northhampton, Mass.: Edward Elgar

Slack, Enid. 2002. "Funding Our Cities." Paper presented at the Metro West II Conference. Canada West Foundation, held in Winnipeg in October

TD Bank Financial Group. 2002. *A Choice Between Investing in Canada's Cities or Disinvesting in Canada's Future.* TD Economics Special Report. Toronto, April

– 2004. *Minding the Gap: Finding the Money to Upgrade Canada's Aging Public Infrastructure.* TD Economics Special Report. Toronto, May

Vander Ploeg, Casey. 2001. *Dollars and Sense: Big City Finances in the West, 1990– 2000.* Calgary: Canada West Foundation

– 2002a. *Big City Revenue Sources: A Canada-U.S. Comparison of Municipal Tax Tools and Revenue Levers.* Calgary: Canada West Foundation

– 2002b. *Framing a Fiscal Fix-Up: Options for Strengthening the Finances of Western Canada's Big Cities.* Calgary: Canada West Foundation

Young, Robert. 2002. "The Politics of Paying for Cities." In *Paying for Cities,* ed. Paul Boothe, 83–97. Edmonton: Institute for Public Economics, University of Alberta

4

Citistates and the State of Cities: Political-Economy and Fiscal-Federalism Dimensions

Thomas J. Courchene

Les villes, plus particulièrement les villes-régions internationales, sont devenues les plaques tournantes de l'ère de l'information. Bien que ces villes-régions aient actuellement une fiscalité fragile et n'aient pas de référence constitutionnelle en matière juridique, leur ascension est telle qu'elles deviendront entièrement et formellement intégrées au sein de la structure et du processus fédéral politique et institutionnel. Par conséquent, les objectifs de ce chapitre sont, en premier lieu, d'expliquer l'ascendance des villes dans ce nouvel ordre global, et en deuxième lieu, de se concentrer sur différentes solutions qui permettront aux villes de développer leurs compétences, leur autonomie fiscale et l'élargissement et l'intensification de leurs rapports avec les autres paliers de gouvernement. En développant ces thèmes, ce chapitre s'inspire de l'expérience internationale similaire qui se rapporte aux états tant fédérés qu'unitaires, en se donnant la possibilité d'imiter le système allemand où certains länder sont des villes-états (Berlin, Brême et Hambourg), comme le titre « villes-états » de ce document le sous-entend.

The world, economically and in management terms, has become a network of prosperous regions, prosperous city-regions.

Kenichi Ohmae, 2000

It is certain that the future of democracy as the capacity of people to act on their own future, at the juncture of social identities and personal subjectivities, will be at the local level.

Michel Autès, 1997, citing A. Touraine, 1994

INTRODUCTION

These quotations speak directly and dramatically to the economic, political and democratic ascendancy of cities in the knowledge-based economy (KBE), and especially to the ascendancy of what have come to be referred to as citistates or global city-regions (GCRs). In line with this vision, the role of the ensuing analysis is essentially twofold. The first is to elaborate on why and how GCRs have become the new and dynamic motors of the information era. This is a global development, not unique to Canada. The second role of the paper is, however, quintessentially Canadian: Given that our GCRs are fiscally weak in a comparative context and jurisdictionally constitutionless in the Canadian context, how might they evolve so that they can indeed fulfill their promise as the empowering engines of our local, national, and global economies?

Toward these ends, the analysis begins with "Global City-Regions in Ascendancy," which focuses on a range of new roles and rationales that are catapulting cities onto the policy and jurisdictional centre-stage. Included under this rubric will be brief discussions of why cities are now the key players in both the old geography (the space of places) and the new (the space of flows). This will be followed by a discussion of GCRs as magnets for attracting what Richard Florida calls the "creative class," together with an assessment of how Canadian GCRs are doing in this regard. Rounding out this discussion is a focus on the differing needs of all cities, on the one hand, and those of the GCRs, on the other.

Under the heading "The Fiscal and Jurisdictional Challenges Facing Canada's GCRs," the analysis then addresses the revenue and expenditure patterns of Canadian cities in comparative domestic and international contexts. This is followed by a review of the recent evolution of federal-provincial political and fiscal relations and the manner in which this is impinging on the prospects for Canada's GCRs. The section concludes with a brief note on the relationship between fiscal autonomy and democracy/accountability.

The final substantive section, "Alternative Policy Futures for the GCRs," addresses the various avenues by which Canada and Canadians might capitalize on the KBE potential of our global city-regions. This begins by focusing on the variety of possibilities for enhancing the revenue autonomy of cities, both by increasing reliance on the full range of existing (but often unused) revenue sources and by tapping new sources, including tax-sharing options from senior government levels. Next, attention is directed to the ways in which the federal-GCR interface is already evolving, with a discussion of the prospects for further creative evolution. This is followed by a similar assessment of the likely evolution of the provincial-GCR interface. The analysis ends by redirecting attention back to the GCRs themselves, including some speculation relating to the option of their achieving citistate or city-province status along the lines of the German city-Länder of Berlin, Bremen, and Hamburg.

The paper ends with a brief conclusion that highlights the prospects for Canada's GCRs to achieve the lofty societal heights articulated in the opening quotations.

While this paper is intended, in principle, to have general application across Canada and across all GCRs, most examples will be drawn from Ontario. Readers will have to judge for themselves how much this impinges on its intended generality.

GLOBAL CITY-REGIONS IN ASCENDANCY

GCRs AS THE DOMINANT EXPORT PLATFORMS IN THE SPACE OF PLACES

Were one to parse the new societal order into its globalization component and its KBE component, in terms of the former the most straightforward rationale for the enhanced role of GCRs is that they are in the forefront of regional and global economic integration. All Canadian regions (and at last count, all but one of Canada's provinces) are more integrated with the United States in terms of aggregate trade flows than they are with the rest of Canada. This led Colin Telmer and me to proclaim that Ontario (and perhaps by now several other provinces as well) had donned the mantle of what we labelled a North American economic region-state (Courchene and Telmer 1998). Yet it is patently evident that the evolution of Ontario's region-state status is, for all intents and purposes, about the evolution of Toronto and the Greater Toronto Area (GTA) in the direction of becoming a global city-region (Courchene 2000). More generally, Vancouver, Edmonton/Calgary, Winnipeg, Toronto, Montreal, and Halifax, among others, are the driving force behind their respective regions' and provinces' integration in NAFTA economic space. Hence, cities and, in particular, global city-regions have achieved pride of place in conventional economic geography – or what Manuel Castells (2001) refers to as the "space of places."

GCRs AS NATIONAL NODES IN THE GLOBAL SPACE OF FLOWS

More recently, however, cities have also come to be viewed as the paramount jurisdictional players in terms of the KBE component of the new societal order – or what Castells calls "the space of flows." One facet of this is that in the KBE, knowledge and human capital are progressively at the cutting edge of competitiveness. Another facet is that the network, powered by the Internet, has become the dominant space-of-flows organizational form (Castells 2001, 1). In tandem, these hallmarks of the information era come to the fore in global cities, since it is in these cities that one finds the requisite dense concentrations of human capital, research and development, high-value-added services, et cetera, that allow GCRs to become the key coordinating and integrating networks in their regional economies while also performing as dynamic national nodes in the international networks that drive growth, trade, and innovation in the global economy. While this resulting space-of-flows or networked geography is a new form of space, it is not placeless. Indeed, as Lever (1997, 44) notes, underpinning the importance of these global cities is that they assume the (network) role of a command, control, and management centre for their domestic and international economies. Phrased somewhat differently, the GCRs breathe life into the emerging regional-international interface that is replacing the traditional nation-nation interface as the dominant integration linkage. Perhaps the role of GCRs – embracing as it does both the space of places and the space of flows – is best described as the "space of networked places" (Castells 2001, 235).

Thus, in this framework, GCRs assume two economic roles – as dynamic export platforms and as learning and innovation platforms – which in tandem attract industry clusters, which in turn attract talent (human capital) in search of rewarding and remunerative work. Yet this people-to-jobs or people-to-industry causation is now being complemented – and in some ways even supplanted – by the opposite industry-to-people causation, arising from the human-capital and quality-of-life aspects of city competitiveness, to which this analysis now turns.

THE "CREATIVE CLASS," COMPETITIVE ADVANTAGE, AND GCRs

Appropriately, the third perspective by which to envision the rise of GCRs puts the focus on the GCRs themselves. In his international bestseller *The Rise of the Creative Class* (2002; 2004), Richard Florida builds on the human-capital/knowledge paradigm by introducing human creativity, or the "creative class," as a GCR's ultimate economic resource (Florida 2004, xiii). Specifically, Florida views these GCRs as the key economic and social organizing units of our era, and he believes that the cities that come out on top will be those that fare best in terms of his "3 Ts": technology (as measured by innovation and high-tech industry concentration), talent (as measured by the number of people in creative occupations), and tolerance (as measured by the amenities and opportunities available for every possible lifestyle). Cities that score well, especially with respect to the tolerance component, will become places where the creative class will cluster. For their part, companies will then cluster in those same places to draw upon the concentrations of the various creative classes and their ability to power innovation and economic growth. Florida labels this the "creative capital theory" of regional economic growth and development.

Even though creative capital theory is likely to be oversold initially, as is the case with many new ideas, it is nonetheless a most welcome addition to the literature on the competitiveness of cities because, as noted, it is centred on the management and organizational attributes of cities. While it will still be an advantage to have a world-class university in your midst, or to be sitting on a major resource deposit, or to have access to the full range of high-value-added business services, the new reality is that initial endowments are no longer as determining, let alone as predetermining, and that by positioning themselves high in the quality-of-life features GCRs can come out on top in the competitiveness sweepstakes. In Florida's words:

> It's often been said that in this age of high technology, "geography is dead" and place doesn't matter any more. Nothing could be further from the truth: Witness how high-tech firms themselves concentrate in specific places like the San Francisco Bay Area or Austin or Seattle. Place has become the central organizing unit of our time, taking on many of the functions that used to be played by firms and other organizations. Corporations have historically played a key economic role in matching people to jobs, particularly given the long-term employment system of the post World War II era. But corporations today are far less committed to their employees and people change jobs frequently, making the employment contract more contingent. In this environment, it is geographic place rather than the corporation that provides the organizational matrix for matching people and jobs. Access to talented and creative people is to modern business what access to coal and iron ore was to steelmaking. It determines where companies will choose to locate and grow, and this in turn changes the ways cities must compete. As [former] Hewlett Packard CEO Carly Fiorina once told this nation's governors: "Keep your tax incentives and highway interchanges; *we will go where the highly skilled people are.*" (Florida 2004, 6, emphasis added)

In *A State of Minds: Toward a Human Capital Future for Canadians* (2001), I asserted that the knowledge/information revolution would do for human capital what the Industrial Revolution did for physical and financial capital. Florida expands this analogy to go beyond human capital to embrace "human creativity." His core message is that "human creativity is the ultimate source of economic growth. Every single person is creative in some way. And to fully tap and harness that creativity we must be tolerant, diverse, and inclusive" (2004, vi). This is part and parcel of the emerging reality that citizens, individually and collectively, are not only the principal beneficiaries of the KBE but are also the driving force underpinning the burgeoning of the KBE itself. Florida's insight is that successful GCRs, as well as providing an inviting environment where the creative class can cluster, will also supply an organizational spatial and network matrix for matching talent and jobs.

CANADA'S GCRs AND FLORIDA'S "3 Ts"

Given the multicultural nature of Canadian society, it should come as no surprise that Canadian GCRs, especially major immigration-receiving cities such as Toronto, Vancouver, and Montreal, rank very high in terms of Florida's tolerance index. This is because the index is a combined measure of the high-profile gay index, the bohemian index (the percentage of artistically creative citizens), the melting pot or mosaic index (the percentage of foreign-born population), and the racial integration index (a measure of the geographical diversity of racial groups).

Table 1, based on data from Gertler et al. (2002), shows how Canada's largest cities rank on selected elements of Florida's index, where the comparison is among the forty-three North American city-regions with a population in excess of one million. Toronto ranks fourth in terms of the bohemian index and first in terms of the mosaic index, thanks in part to its large immigrant population. Where Toronto does not perform all that well is in terms of Florida's other two Ts – the talent index (percentage of population with a university degree) and the technology index (high-tech concentration). As Gertler et al. (2002) note (again among forty-three North American city-regions), Toronto ranks twenty-fourth and fifteenth for talent and technology, respectively. Rankings for other Canadian GCRs with populations over one million are qualitatively similar, although Ottawa receives particularly high marks for talent.

Table 1: Rank of Canadian Cities for Various Elements of the "3 T index" among 43 North American Cities

	Talent	*Mosaic*	*Bohemian*	*Technology*
Toronto	24	1	4	15
Montreal	43	7	10	13
Vancouver	31	2	3	29
Ottawa	10	9	14	23

Source: adapted from Gertler et al. (2002)

Confirmation that Canada's cities should be the focus of policies to address lagging prosperity – and that our cities need in particular to improve their position in terms of the indexes for talent and technology – comes from related research that Roger Martin and James Milway (2003) carried out for the Institute for Competitiveness and Innovation and summarized in the *National Post.* Martin and Milray note that the entire gap between per capita GDP in Ontario and that of the average U.S. state is an *urban gap.* Rural Ontario more than holds its own with the rural United States, but this is not the case for Canadian cities versus U.S. cities. Closing this gap, according to Martin and Milway, requires redressing four factors: attitudes (for example, lower university enrolment in Ontario); investments (private investment to enhance productivity and public investment in education and human capital); incentives/motivation (higher tax rates in Canada); and fiscal and governance structures.

While GCRs can and must play key roles in creating a learning and innovative environment, addressing the talent and technology shortfall, whether defined by Gertler et al. or by Martin and Milway, requires a societal commitment to what might be termed "policy infrastructure," and this clearly transcends the boundaries and powers of the GCRs. Arguably, the most important component of this policy infrastructure relates to the creation of human capital. In *A State of Minds*, I went as far as to propose a formal "human capital mission statement" for Canada and Canadians as the cornerstone of twenty first-century public policy (Courchene 2001, 154): "Design a sustainable, socially inclusive and internationally competitive infrastructure that ensures equal opportunity for all Canadians to develop, to enhance and to employ in Canada their skills and human capital, thereby enabling them to become full citizens in the information-era Canadian and global societies." Were Canada to embrace such a mission statement, our GCRs and Canadian society generally would clearly climb in the rankings of Florida's talent and technology indexes. In any event, the message here is that the jurisdictional responsibility for undertaking societal policies of this type – increasing the human capital of all Canadians – must reside well beyond the city level, even if cities end up as the jurisdiction that most benefits from such a policy. In this regard, we should all welcome Ottawa's recognition in the 2004 federal budget that we trail the Americans in terms of the percentage of university graduates, and we should also welcome the creative policies the budget adopted to close this gap.

Along similar lines, the "employ in Canada" component of the above mission statement is related to another policy requisite for cities' success, namely that Canada must ensure that our tax rates on mobile factors – physical, financial, and human capital – are competitive with rates existing internationally, and particularly with those prevailing in the United States. If ensuring that these tax rates are competitive leaves the federal or provincial governments with a revenue shortfall, the way to restore any such shortfall is via an export/import neutral consumption tax, for example, the GST. Canadian GCRs will not achieve their potential if, because of unlevel playing fields on the tax front, they become only temporary stopping points for our talent and human capital en route to sunnier economic climes elsewhere.

GCRs VERSUS OTHER URBAN CENTRES

Obviously, many of the forces privileging GCRs are also privileging other cities. For example, the falling cost of information allows for the delivery of more services to be assigned, in accordance with the principle of subsidiarity, to the jurisdiction that is "closer to the people," as it were. Whereas the term "decentralization" in the Canadian federation has typically meant passing powers from Ottawa to the provinces, the implications of the subsidiarity principle in the KBE would suggest that selected powers can and should be devolved from both Ottawa and the provinces to GCRs and, for many services, to cities generally. Likewise, the need to increase the fiscal autonomy of GCRs in order to improve efficiency, accountability, and citizen participation would also apply to the entire municipal sector.

However, as already noted, the raison d'être of this paper is that the GCRs are different, not only because of their size per se but because of the critical roles they play in the KBE. Some of these roles have already been outlined – export platforms, dense nodes of human capital, and centres of concentration for business services, research and development, and information technology – all of which combine to drive KBE innovation and competitiveness. Moreover, GCRs typically have infrastructure, transit, and logistics challenges of a magnitude not shared by smaller urban areas. And as the principal immigrant and refugee receiving areas, GCRs are saddled with very substantial settlement costs (language and skills training, income support, housing, etc.). Finally, but hardly exhaustively, GCRs are large enough to employ a critical mass of civil servants so that for many of the functions they have the analysis and design capacity to compete in terms of policy formation with federal and provincial bureaucrats.

Simon Fraser's Richard Harris has aptly captured the essence of all of this when he asserts (2003, 50) that the collective future of Canadians depends on how our global cities will perform relative to U.S. global cities. Indeed, over the last decade Canada's six biggest urban areas have enjoyed a 30 percent increase in total employment, double the percentage advances for smaller metropolitan areas and for Canada's towns and rural areas (Little 2004). Moreover, international research shows that a doubling of city population leads to a 4–5 percent increase in productivity as measured by output per capita (Strange 2003).

Having thus made the case for special treatment for Canada's GCRs in order that they may achieve their information-era potential, the remainder of this analysis identifies the two Achilles' heels of Canada's GCRs. The first is their lack of fiscal autonomy and the associated view that they are ideal places from which to redistribute revenue, whereas the emerging KBE reality is that GCRs ought to be able to retain a much larger share of the revenue generated from within their boundaries. The second, and related, challenge facing GCRs is that they are constitutionless – they are creatures of their respective provinces. The next section will identify and document, often in comparative context, these fiscal and federal challenges. The section following that will address the range of alternative policies, instruments, and processes that would allow the GCRs to become more fiscally and federally integrated into our KBE future.

THE FISCAL AND FEDERAL CHALLENGES FACING CANADA'S GCRs

THE FISCAL CHALLENGE

The fiscal reality facing the GCRs is that they rely almost exclusively on property taxation and provincial transfers for their revenues, which means that they typically do not have access to a tax base that automatically grows apace with incomes and population (such as a share of income taxes, of general sales taxation, or even of specific excises such as gasoline taxes). In turn, and almost by definition, this lack of revenue-raising capacity serves to constrain the GCRs' expenditure autonomy. As the TD Bank (2002a, press release) noted, "Canada's cities have much to offer including a highly diverse workforce, geographical proximity to the large US market and a competitive cost base. Yet ... in many cities infrastructure is deteriorating rapidly. Social housing, water systems, sewers, roads and public transit systems all require massive re-investment, but cash-strapped cities are in no position to deliver." What follows is a brief review of the fiscal position of Canadian cities in a domestic and an international context, beginning with expenditures.

Expenditures

Table 1 of Melville McMillan's paper (this volume) reveals that for the calendar year 2001 there were very substantial variations in per capita municipal expenditures across provinces – from a low of $378 for Prince Edward Island's municipalities to nearly $2,000 for those in Ontario, for an all-Canada average of $1,545. The principal reason for these wide disparities is that cities shoulder different responsibilities across provinces. For example, as McMillan's table 1 indicates, Ontario cities spend 25 percent of their budgets on social services – a proportion that is over five times more than second-place Nova Scotia (and more than ten times more in terms of per capita spending). On the other hand, Nova Scotia municipalities spend nearly 15 percent of their budgets on education, whereas in all other provinces the municipalities spend negligible amounts, since responsibility for education has been taken over by the provinces.

While it is likely the case that cross-province differences in municipal spending are as large as cross-country differences, some international comparisons are nonetheless in order. In an earlier paper, McMillan (1997) compares data for selected cities in the mid-1990s. He notes that Melbourne spends only US$723 per capita (in large measure because police and schooling are the responsibility of the Australian states), whereas Pittsburgh (which shoulders much of education spending) spends US$2,894, and Toronto spends US$1,839. In terms of cities in federal systems, Frankfurt tops McMillan's list at US$4,979. The German federation may be rather unusual among developed federations because the Basic Law (the German constitution) states that communities must be guaranteed the right to regulate all the affairs of the local community within the limits set by law; and to accommodate this on the revenue side, in addition to receiving revenues from real estate and business taxation, the Basic Law provides for the communes to receive a share of personal income tax and corporation tax (articles 106(6) and 107(1), respectively). For example, personal income taxes are shared equally between the federal government and the Länder governments, with each government level then transferring 7.5 percentage points of the personal income tax to the communes or municipalities. This type of constitutionally mandated tax sharing and regulatory responsibility for municipalities also exists in other federations – in Mexico, for example. However, it is in stark contrast to the Canadian reality where, as already noted, Canadian cities are not mentioned in the *Constitution Act, 1867* (except of course to place "Municipal Institutions in the Province" under the exclusive jurisdiction of the provinces (section 92(8)).

Intriguingly, cities in unitary states frequently tend to have *greater* expenditure and revenue-raising autonomy than Canadian cities do. This is less puzzling than it might at first appear, because any commitment to the principle of subsidiarity in unitary states necessarily means greater powers for cities, since this is the only subnational government level in unitary states. In the Canadian context, the frequent calls for more decentralization nearly always mean transferring powers from Ottawa to the provinces. However, as noted earlier, for many policy areas decentralization to the city/municipal level is, thanks to the information revolution, increasingly possible as well as being consistent with the subsidiarity principle. Partial evidence in the direction of confirming the proposition that unitary states pass more authority down to cities is that Stockholm's per capita spending is US$10,644 (McMillan 1997), more than double Frankfurt's and close to six times Toronto's per capita spending.

Revenues

Mcmillan's table 2 (this volume) reveals that property taxes account for between 48.3 percent (Ontario) and 73.1 percent (Nova Scotia) of overall municipal funding, with an all-Canada average of 52.2 percent of overall revenues (and 63 percent of own-source revenues). Note that since Ontario's cities are the highest per capita spenders, this should imply (all other things being equal) that property taxes account for a smaller proportion of revenues for Ontario cities. Sales of goods and services (including fees and charges) are the other major component of own-source revenues, averaging 28 percent (and 23 percent of overall revenues). Transfers from other levels of government account for 17 percent of overall revenues. For the most part, these are in the form of conditional transfers (14.6 percentage points of the 17), which may not relate to the internal priorities of cities. The remaining 2.4 percentage points take the form of unconditional grants. Note that the overwhelming proportion of these transfers are provincial-municipal transfers; direct federal-municipal transfers in 2001 were less than 3 percent of total transfers and only 0.4 percent of overall municipal revenues.

By way of international comparisons, Frankfurt obtains much of its revenue from a 15 percent share of federal and Länder income taxes, whereas 35 percent of Stockholm's significant revenues come from a sharing of Sweden's personal income tax (McMillan 1997). It is true that cities in some provinces also have access to shared taxes. For instance, Manitoba municipalities receive a share of provincial personal and corporate income taxes; Alberta cities receive a capital grant for roads and transit based on fuel consumption in each city; and Vancouver, Victoria, and Montreal have access to a share of gasoline taxes). Nonetheless, the resulting tax sharing does not loom large in terms of the overall fiscal needs of cities. However, these examples are important in that they provide excellent models of appropriate tax sharing, which needs to be broadened, enriched, and, of course, replicated elsewhere.

As a bridge between this section on the fiscal gap and the following one on the jurisdictional gap, it is appropriate to note that Canada's cities frequently suffer from "unfunded mandates," or fiscal downloading from both levels of government. For example, Ottawa's decisions with respect to immigrants and refugees will duly commit Toronto to a range of settlement services, which Ottawa only partially funds (especially in light of what Ottawa transfers to Quebec for such services). Likewise, Queen's Park has devolved responsibility for social housing onto Ontario's cities, but not with sufficient funding, at least from Toronto's perspective. In the years immediately following the huge cuts in the Canada Health and Social Transfer (CHST) in the 1995 federal budget, the provinces could legitimately make the case that they were merely transferring to the cities part of what Ottawa had downloaded onto them. While this is small comfort to the cities, their current situation is even less encouraging, because the provinces have become trapped in what I have elsewhere referred to as "hourglass federalism" (Courchene 2004). This will be part and parcel of the following discussion of the GCRs' fiscal and political role in the federation.

THE JURISDICTIONAL CHALLENGE

Ottawa, Nation Building, and Cities

In the prime of the resource-based economy and paradigm, much of nation building tended to be bound up with resources and megaprojects – oil, hydro, pipelines, railways, mining, potash, the Seaway, and the like. In the KBE, nation building has much more to do with human capital and therefore with citizens. Moreover, what now sells electorally are such issues as health, quality of life, democratic participation, and, of course, developing skills and human capital to be successful in the KBE. Whereas megaprojects were likely to be resource-based and rural, nation building in the KBE is predominantly citizen-based and, perforce, largely urban.

As already highlighted, knowledge and human capital are at the cutting edge of competitiveness in the information era. And where competitiveness is at stake, Ottawa *will* become involved, regardless of what the written constitutional word may say. For present purposes, it is sufficient to note that cities and especially the GCRs are the principal repositories of human capital and therefore of KBE competitiveness, which in turn implies that Ottawa will necessarily become strategically as well as politically involved in city matters.

Hourglass Federalism

Ottawa has, of course, grasped the enormous significance of this marked shift in the determinants of nation building, competitiveness, and political salability. However, cities fall under provincial jurisdiction, as do many of the policies relating to citizens and to competitiveness in the KBE. Not surprisingly, the result has been and will continue to be a jurisdictional tug-of-war between Ottawa and the provinces in terms of addressing KBE-related city issues. For the federal government, the challenge is how to make inroads into these areas of provincial jurisdiction. "Hourglass federalism" is the label that in my view rather aptly describes the way in which Ottawa has unwittingly gone about doing this.

As part of the adjustment to the dictates of the KBE, Ottawa transferred aspects of old-paradigm nation building (forestry, mining, energy, etc.) to the provinces, presumably in part to make room on the federal policy plate for new-paradigm policies and programs. The key initiative, however, was the set of deep cuts in the CHST transfers to the provinces contained in Paul Martin's 1995 federal budget as part of a series of measures to eliminate the deficit. To be sure, these cuts were part of Canada's remarkable fiscal turnaround and its emergence, in the words of the *Economist*, as the "fiscal virtuoso" of the G7. However, there were some rather dire consequences for the provinces associated with these CHST cuts. Specifically, as Ottawa shifted away from direct transfers to the provinces (by abolishing the Canada Assistance Plan and reducing the CHST), it began to replace them with direct transfers to citizens (such as millennium scholarships, Canada Research Chairs, and the Canada Child Tax Benefit) and with direct transfers to cities (such as homelessness grants, the GST exemption, and the proposed federal gas tax sharing).

As the federal deficit downloading to the provinces began increasingly to constrain the provinces' fiscal position, an even more problematic fiscal dynamic came into play. Because of the electoral salience of medicare, the provinces have been unable to reduce expenditures on health care. Indeed, all provinces have increased health-care expenditures. But this meant that they were forced to starve virtually every other provincial policy area in order to feed medicare's voracious appetite. Not surprisingly, Canadians and cities alike began to be very receptive to new federal initiatives in these policy-starved areas.[1]

Thus, as Ottawa bypasses the provinces to deal directly with Canadians and with cities in areas typically viewed as falling under provincial jurisdiction, the provinces find themselves as the squeezed middle of the division-of-powers hourglass – hence, hourglass federalism. Intriguingly, with health-care spending heading towards 50 percent of program spending, the provinces will continue to find themselves trapped in this squeezed middle unless they can either download aspects of medicare to citizens or upload aspects to Ottawa. The Ontario Liberal government did the former when it delisted several previously insured items (eye examinations, physiotherapy, and chiropractic services) and introduced a dedicated and income-tested health-care levy. At the July 2004 meeting of the Council of the Federation at Niagara-on-the Lake, the premiers proposed a two-tiered strategy to combat the challenges posed by hourglass federalism: (1) upload pharmacare to Ottawa, and (2) request dramatic increases in health and equalization funding. At the fall 2004 first ministers' meetings, Ottawa took a pass on the first option but agreed to provide nearly $75 billion new transfer money to the amounts already committed over the next ten years. While this may go a long way to alleviate much of the medicare cost overhang, it is not clear that it will be enough for the provinces to redress their spending deficits elsewhere in their budgets, including municipal funding. In any event, the message here is that the politics and economics of hourglass federalism have served to worsen the fiscal position of Canada's cities and to pave the way for the federal government to embark on a series of initiatives designed to foster a closer relationship with the cities.

For their part, the cities have obviously welcomed the federal initiatives and overtures. Indeed, via the Federation of Canadian Municipalities and other associations such as the C5 (Toronto, Montreal, Vancouver, Winnipeg, and Calgary), cities have actively lobbied for these federal initiatives. Fundamentally, it is arguably preferable from the cities' point of view to have two patrons rather than just one. And on the more substantive side, Canada's GCRs look with a combination of competitive concern and envy at their sister GCRs in the United States which have direct access to Washington for infrastructure funding. This is a levelling-the-playing-field argument, important in its own right, but it takes on added importance in the current context where the provinces are squeezed by hourglass federalism. As we shall see below, Ottawa has clearly heard and heeded the cities' call.

By way of a final challenge facing Canada's cities, attention is now directed briefly to issues relating to democracy and accountability.

DEMOCRACY AND ACCOUNTABILITY

The growing influence of the GCRs has generated an increasing interest in big city politics, as evidenced by the star status of former Winnipeg mayor Glen Murray, Vancouver's Larry Campbell, and the excitement associated with the election of Toronto mayor David Miller. Indeed, Canada's GCR mayors will in all likelihood become better known internationally than their respective provincial premiers. Certainly, the mayors of New York City and Chicago have typically been better known than the governors of New York and Illinois. (Admittedly, the governor of California is a notable exception!)

Nevertheless, while cities may in theory be ideal places for democracy and accountability to flourish, the Canadian reality is, with some notable exceptions, very different. Understandably, citizens will not become too excited about democracy and accountability at the city level as long as cities are largely administrative units. Indeed, as long as cities are kept under a tight fiscal leash by their respective provinces, the collective citizen mind-set will tilt towards the administrative/rent-seeking mode rather than the policy-intensive and, therefore, participation/accountability-enhancing mode.

ALTERNATIVE POLICY FUTURES FOR THE GCRs

The first substantive section of this paper focused on the variety of ways in which globalization and the knowledge/information era have been privileging cities, especially GCRs. It may well be that the assertion that "this is the century of the city state" (Gillmor 2004, 42) is going a bit far, but it nonetheless captures the spirit of recent thinking both here and abroad. The next section of this paper was a reality check of sorts, highlighting some of the fiscal and federal roadblocks that stand in the path of cities trying to reach this potential. It follows, therefore, that much of the task in the remainder of this paper involves articulating a series of proposals and recommendations that will overcome or otherwise circumvent these roadblocks in order to enable our cities to prosper. These proposals include rethinking and reworking both the provincial-GCR interface and the federal-GCR interface, as well as considering a range of creative, albeit sometimes controversial, options that may be open to GCRs if other avenues remain blocked. This analysis begins with the revenue challenge facing municipalities generally.

DIVERSIFYING REVENUE SOURCES

Increasing Reliance on Existing Sources

While addressing options for providing cities with new revenue sources remains uppermost in policy circles as well as in the media, attention needs to be focused initially on cities' existing but frequently unused or overlooked revenue sources. Canadian cities would do well to cast their eyes internationally to recognize their untapped revenue opportunities. Thankfully, Winnipeg and its former mayor Glen Murray have been leading the way in recognizing them. A recent *Saturday Night* feature entitled "The City Statesman" elaborates as follows on Murray's views and proposals:

> Under the Canadian Constitution, cities aren't designated as a separate order of government; they operate under provincial jurisdiction. In effect, they are glorified utilities. Their means of raising revenue are limited, with property taxes being the main source. Winnipeg relies on property taxes for over 50 per cent of its revenue. But property taxes in Winnipeg are already high, and they are a flat tax: they don't rise as economic activity increases. For cities to prosper, Murray argues, they need a piece of the growth revenues, including sales tax, GST, income tax and corporate tax.
>
> He [Murray] proposes a complete overhaul of an antiquated tax system, which would reflect a closer relationship between taxation and behaviour. Thus, a fuel tax would punish SUVs and trucks and have a marginal effect on fuel-efficient vehicles. According to Murray, 80 per cent of police calls are alcohol-related, and so a liquor tax would go toward the police budget. A fee for garbage pickup would have the greatest impact on those who fail to recycle. (Gillmor 2004, 40)

Leaving the sharing of sales and income taxes to the following section, it can be seen that each of Murray's specific tax or user-fee proposals would (as well as raising revenue) fall into one or more of the following categories: accountable, pro-environment, transparent, efficient. Thus, it is surprising that Canadian cities have not followed their sister cities internationally in being more actively engaged in these user-fee and optimal-pricing approaches. Part of the problem here may be that Canada does not have a tradition of "pricing" the outputs of the public sector generally – for example, the lack of peak-load pricing for electricity and lack of incentive pricing for conserving water. (Perhaps the real, but unstated, fear here is that the imposition of user fees in these municipal service areas would open the door to thinking about applying them elsewhere in the provincial domain, in particular in the health-care area.)

Well before Glen Murray aired his proposals, Berridge (1999) provided a framework capable of incorporating and even expanding on these Winnipeg proposals:

> [Toronto and the GTA] have to decide what activities the city-region should not finance off the tax base, scrutinizing all the operating municipal services businesses – electricity, water and waste water, garbage, transit – and creating new organizations largely able to meet their own needs. Toronto is one of the few world cities that still operates these services as mainline businesses. The ability to use the very substantial asset values and cash flows of these municipal businesses is perhaps the only financial option to provide the city-region with what is unlikely to be obtainable from other sources: its own pool of re-investment capital. Such an urban infrastructure fund would have remarkable leverage potential, both from public-sector pension funds and from other private-sector institutions.

Hence, it is important to underscore the fact that there is much that cities can do to increase their revenue (and, by extension, their expenditure) autonomy by drawing on the revenue opportunities within their own jurisdiction. Creative experimentation along the lines of the Winnipeg mayor's proposals would be most welcome.

Despite the potential for raising revenue within current jurisdictional constraints, this avenue will fall short of meeting cities' expenditure requirements. As a result, current attention is focused primarily on ways in which the senior levels of government can share their revenues with, or devolve new revenue bases to, the cities.

Finding New Revenue Sources

The increasing awareness of the strategic economic importance of GCRs and the serious challenges they face is exemplified by three (thus far) ambitious policy reports on the future of Canada's cities published by the TD Bank. The titles of these reports are of interest in their own right: *A Choice Between Investing in Canada's Cities or Disinvesting in Canada's Future* (22 April 2002); *The Greater Toronto Area (GTA): Canada's Primary Economic Locomotive in Need of Repairs* (22 May 2002); and *The Calgary-Edmonton Corridor: Take Action Now to Ensure Tiger's Roar Doesn't Fade* (22 April 2003). This series is a clarion call for a new way of thinking about Canadian cities so that they will become more robust and vibrant and will also become an integral part of the TD Bank's overarching vision for Canada, namely that Canada surpass the United States' standard of living within fifteen years.

As part of this new way of thinking about Canadian cities, the TD Bank argues for a national approach to this challenge, one that provides cities with the administrative and financial power to move forward without increasing the overall regulatory or tax burden for Canadians. Toward this end, the TD report's recommendations stress that "Canadian municipalities should be granted additional taxation powers to ensure that they have access to independent sources of revenues – sources that enhance accountability, transparency, efficiency and equity. The best option is a new excise or sales tax collected on behalf of cities by the provincial or federal governments. Provinces should also allow municipalities the flexibility to levy property taxes, user fees and development charges" (2002a).

While Frankfurt and Stockholm have, as noted earlier, access to a significant share of their countries' income taxes, most of the attention in Canada has focused on cities gaining a share of sales or excise taxes – the federal GST, provincial and/or federal excises on gasoline, and provincial sales taxes (PSTs). But given that both the provinces and Ottawa now have access to the personal income tax (PIT) base, sharing the PIT should also be included in the set of choices. This option is especially relevant if the aim is to privilege the GCRs, because sharing the PIT on a derivation basis will provide the GCRs with a larger per capita value than typically would be the case for smaller cities.

The TD report went on to note that while federal and provincial grants can be used to address cities' accumulated funding shortfalls, such grants are the wrong vehicles for financing cities' ongoing financial needs; the preferable way to finance ongoing needs is by sharing the revenues of a growing tax base. A discussion of the pros and cons of tax sharing versus intergovernmental grants, as well as the variety of ways that tax bases can be shared, can be found in the appendix to this paper.

Summary

The core message here is that Canada's cities need enhanced fiscal autonomy. While much of the ongoing public debate has focused on cities gaining access to new revenue sources via tax sharing, it is important to reiterate that there also exist significant but unutilized revenue opportunities that are fully within the cities' own jurisdiction. In any event, the underlying rationale for enhanced revenue autonomy is to allow cities greater expenditure autonomy. At one level, this will serve to activate the principle of subsidiarity at the city level. At another, the traditional emphasis on competitive federalism and the importance of provincial experimentation in terms of the financing, design, and delivery of public goods and services will in effect be "decentralized" to cities. In this regard, it is instructive to recall that the seminal "Tiebout model" of competitive federalism was in effect a "competing-local-governments" model.

Moreover, enhancing the link between revenues and expenditures is a way to improve accountability, as well as allowing cities more flexibility in responding to their citizens' policy wishes. This has the potential not only for increasing the static and dynamic efficiency of Canada's cities but, also for drawing citizens into greater civic involvement, since much more will now be at stake in city governance.

These dynamic efficiencies arising from enhanced fiscal autonomy and competition among cities are appropriate for all cities, small and large. However, since Canada's employment growth, competitiveness, and living standards depend on how our GCRs fare in relation to their international counterparts, privileging the GCRs in terms of enhanced fiscal powers as well as more formal integration into the operations of Canadian federalism must rank high on the policy agenda at both the federal and the provincial level. For example, while Canada has traditionally viewed the GCRs as appropriate places to redistribute from, it is critical for the success of Canadian GCRs in a NAFTA environment that they be able to retain a larger share of the revenues generated within their boundaries. This may be a tough sell politically, though one of the noteworthy features of the 2004 federal election was that it brought cities and city issues (along with medicare, of course) to the policy centrestage.

In addition to this political economy challenge, the institutional and jurisdictional hurdle is likely to be every bit as daunting – namely, how to integrate Canada's GCRs more fully and more formally into the operations of Canadian federalism. We begin the assessment of the prospects for creative approaches to Canada's GCRs by addressing the options for the federal-GCR relationship.

RETHINKING THE FEDERAL-GCR INTERFACE

Recent Federal Initiatives

In the 2004 federal budget, Finance Minister Ralph Goodale outlined a series of rather remarkable fiscal initiatives directed towards cities:

- rebates for GST and HST taxes paid on the provision of municipal services and community infrastructure, estimated to be worth $7 billion over ten years;
- accelerated funding of the $1 billion Municipal Rural Infrastructure Fund, with spending to be now undertaken over the next five years instead of the next 10;
- a commitment to work with the provinces to share a portion of gas tax revenues with cities or to introduce other fiscal mechanisms that achieve the same goals.

Of even more significance in the 2004 budget were the various jurisdictional measures:

- appointment of a parliamentary secretary (elevated to Minister of State for Infrastructure and Communities after the 2004 election) to lead federal efforts to obtain a new deal for communities;
- creation of the External Advisory Committee on Cities and Communities (chaired by former Vancouver mayor and former B.C. premier Mike Harcourt);
- participation of municipal representatives in federal budget consultations;
- a promise to give municipalities a stronger voice in shaping federal programs and policies that affect them.

Most appropriately, Goodale hailed these initiatives a "historic commitment to forge a New Deal for Canada's communities" (Goodale 2004, 165).

In the federal budget of 23 February 2005, Goodale detailed the manner in which Ottawa would share a portion of its federal gasoline tax with Canada's communities. Like most other spending items in the 2005 budget, this tax sharing was backloaded – rising from $600 million in fiscal 2005–6 (the equivalent of 1.5 cents per litre of gas tax revenues) to $2 billion in 2009–10 (or 5 cents per litre), for the promised $5 billion over five years. Since the 2005 budget continues with the New Deal label for these programs for cities and communities, one would assume that the 5 cents per litre in 2009–10 will be carried forward to future years as well, but there appears to be no direct commitment to this effect in the 2005 budget.

While the GCRs lobbied for the federal gas tax sharing to go preferentially to large cities, this was not to be the case. The first two principles underpinning the New Deal made this abundantly clear: "Provide municipalities, both large and small, with a long term, reliable and predictable source of funding"; and "Ensure equity between regions and between large and small communities" (Goodale 2005, 199). Not surprisingly, "to ensure that gas tax revenue allocation results in stable, predictable and equitable funding, the Government will allocate funds to the provinces, territories and First Nations on a per capita basis, with a minimum amount of funding assured for the smallest jurisdictions equal to 0.75 percent of total funding or $37.5 million over five years" (ibid., 204). These monies will be allocated in line with the following objectives and priorities:

> Eligible investments will include capital expenditures for environmentally sustainable municipal infrastructure. As the needs of large urban centres are different from those of smaller communities, eligible projects will depend on the size of the community and the region. In each large urban centre, investments will be targeted to one or two of the following priorities: public transit, water and

wastewater, community energy systems, and treatment of solid waste. In smaller municipalities, eligible funding will be considered more broadly to provide flexibility to meet priorities. In all municipalities, some funds may also be used for capacity-building initiatives to support sustainability planning. (ibid., 204)

It is fair to suggest that Ottawa's New Deal for communities is not the constructive step forward for federal-GCR relations that Canada's larger cities had hoped for. Ottawa's penchant for redistribution and equalization was too strong to allow the privileging of Canada's GCRs. This is surprising, since there was a recognition of the role of GCRs in advancing a culture of innovation and enhancing our competitiveness and living standards. Paul Martin had himself championed the role of GCRs in the new global order well before he succeeded Jean Chrétien as prime minister.

A bolder federal vision for GCRs could have taken as its basis a proposal penned by the late Tom Plunkett and aptly entitled "A Nation of Cities Awaits Paul Martin's 'New Deal': Federal Funds for 'Creatures of the Provinces'":

Does the mere fact that a province utilizes its powers to establish cities and other forms of local government mean that the province is required to monitor or participate in every relationship that its cities may have with the federal government? Most provinces are not that much interested in their largest cities. Their primary municipal interest seems to be in the small towns and rural areas. Can a province not simply agree to permit its largest cities to work out revenue sharing or other arrangements with the federal government? Some examination of these questions might lead to the possibility of a realistic and productive federal/city relationship. (2004, 23)

In terms of what would presumably have qualified as a "realistic and productive relationship" from the GCRs' perspective would, as noted earlier, be sharing a portion of the personal income tax on a derivation basis (as in Germany or Sweden) on the revenue side; or, on the expenditure side, participating in an infrastructure fund dedicated to addressing mass transit and logistics challenges.

Yet Ottawa failed to step up to the plate. Rather, the recent fiscal initiatives have actually discriminated against the GCRs relative to smaller cities and rural communities. A more apt headline for recent federal initiatives might be "A Nation of Villages Awaits Paul Martin's New Deal for Equalization and Regional Development." For example, the ratcheting up of equalization payments, with 3.5 percent indexing over the next ten years, resulted in new money for equalization totalling $33.4 billion – surprisingly close to the additional $41.3 billion allocated to health. And in the 2005 federal budget, Ottawa allocated a further $800 million to regional development as well as providing enhanced access to EI benefits, complete with their regional preferences relating both to accessing benefits and to the duration of payments. Indeed, as discussed later, Ottawa's New Deal as it relates to the gas tax is, in effect, yet another equalization program, this time effectively transferring funds from GCRs to municipalities. The reality remains that Ottawa continues to view GCRs as an ideal place from which to redistribute.

Other Federal Linkages

These budget initiatives will serve to refocus the GCRs' attention on their respective provinces, but as we shall see in the next section, our GCRs will nonetheless continue with their lobbying activities in the corridors of federal power. High on the GCRs' agenda should be the creation of a dedicated infrastructure fund along the lines already existing in the United States, and cast politically to be the counterpart of the regional development programs. To be sure, the Canada Strategic Infrastructure Fund goes some way towards this objective and could serve as a model for addressing the GCRs needs in terms of areas such as mass transit; but the most obvious avenue for the GCRs to pursue would be to seek full cost-recovery for expenditures undertaken in connection with their implementation of federal policy initiatives, particularly those relating to immigrant and refugee settlement costs. While Ottawa does have a program in place that contributes to these services, the allocation of funds bears little relationship to where immigrants and refugees locate. For reasons of both equity and efficiency, Ottawa should bear the full cost of these payments and should transfer them through the provinces to the GCRs on an equal-per-newcomer basis. Relatedly, Canada needs better policies and programs to recognize the newcomers' training and credentials in order to respond "to the growing recognition of the enormous waste of immigrants' human capital in Canada" (Alboim, Finnie, and Meng 2005, 20). Not only would such a policy have to be directed primarily to GCRs, but enabling immigrants to obtain the credentials needed to apply their knowledge or ply their trades would serve to improve Canadian GCRs' scores in terms of Florida's "3 Ts" and, as a result, our competitiveness in NAFTA economic space. If Ottawa wants to foster a closer relationship with Canada's major cities, removing this funding inequity and inefficiency is an excellent place to start.

Summary

The political and economic implications of the KBE are such that some version of the New Deal was bound to find the light of legislative day. Moreover, it is likely to be viewed as a successful initiative on many fronts. Cities welcome the invitation for consultation with Ottawa on policies related to Canada's communities. Given that the proceeds of the sharing of the federal gas tax will help develop environmentally sustainable municipal infrastructure, this measure will find support in the environmental community as well. Ottawa benefits because the gas tax transfer enhances the visibility of the federal government; and in the process, some progress has been made towards increasing the revenue autonomy of cities. Plaudits all around, or so it would appear.

However, as already noted, Ottawa's New Deal for communities is not the creative federal-GCR relationship that Canada's largest cities had in mind. The best light that the GCRs can put on this is that federal politics are such that Ottawa probably had to begin its relationship with cities by treating all cities in a similar manner. The reasoning would presumably be that only when the federal-city relationship develops further could the GCRs expect to receive special treatment. Yet pinning too much in the way of effort and aspirations on an improving federal-GCR relationship may be a questionable gambit for at least two reasons. The first is that while the Plunkett assertion that some provinces "are not much interested in [their] cities" may be traditional wisdom, the mere fact that the GCRs are actively lobbying Ottawa will hardly be lost on the provinces. Apart from the fact that the provinces may now be more receptive, the second reason is that the constitutional reality is such that the GCRs are eventually going to have to deal with or through their respective provinces. This being the case, we now turn our attention to the provincial-GCR relationship.

RETHINKING THE PROVINCIAL-GCR INTERFACE

At one level, the provinces are obviously fully on the side of their GCRs. Consider, for example, Ontario's 1999 "economic mission statement." As part of the province's commitment to "build on the potential of Ontario's city-regions," the mission statement asserts:

> Around the world, cities are the focal points for creativity, innovation, production and the supporting infrastructure. Ontario's seven largest urban areas account for 70% of all jobs in the province and will continue to be central in all economic development strategies ...
>
> Priority attention [must be directed] to the economic challenges and opportunities facing the Greater Toronto Area and surrounding Golden Horseshoe – Canada's only global scale city-region. (Ontario Jobs and Investment Board 1999, 64)

Presumably one can find similar rhetoric about Montreal, Vancouver, Calgary/ Edmonton, Winnipeg, and others from their respective provincial governments.

At another level, however, the provinces have heretofore largely failed their GCRs, and cities generally. Whereas Ottawa has to go "through" the provinces to deal with the GCRs, the provinces have always been free to deal with them directly and as they see fit. For example, it has always been open for the provinces to privilege their GCRs by allocating a share of sales taxation or personal income taxation to cities on a derivation basis. Yet the reality is that the very opposite has occurred. As the earlier evidence indicates, Canadian cities are among the most fiscally constrained cities in the world. Indeed, it was this reality that encouraged cities to take their concerns to Ottawa in the first place.

The further reality is that the provinces have been backed into a fiscal and political corner by both Ottawa and their own cities. With respect to Ottawa, the provinces have been caught in the fiscal vise of "hourglass federalism," as elaborated earlier. And in this fiscally constrained environment, the GCRs and cities backed their respective provinces into a political corner by openly lobbying for a stronger fiscal and political relationship with Ottawa.

The upshot is that the provinces have begun to mount a counterattack. On the political front, they responded to Ottawa's plan for direct consultations with municipalities by proposing that cities participate, where appropriate, in the meetings of the Council of the Federation, and that the premiers would then carry the cities' concerns to the first ministers' table. While it is surely unlikely that the GCRs would view this as adequate compensation for refusing Ottawa's offer, it nonetheless opens the door to a broader range of interactions with the Council and, perhaps more importantly, with their respective provinces.

On the fiscal front, the move by Manitoba to transfer some of its own gasoline tax to its cities (in the pre-2004 budget period when Ottawa decided to postpone its proposed gas tax transfer) arguably was an important signal to all provinces. Ontario's response to the eventual transfer to cities of 5 cents per litre of the federal gas tax was to transfer 2 cents per litre of its own gas tax to cities. The allocation of this tax across the province's cities and municipalities is as follows: 30 percent on the basis of population and 70 percent on the basis of public transit ridership. Thus, while Ontario will likely allow the federal tax sharing to be determined in accordance with Ottawa's guidelines, its own gas tax allocation will proportionally favour the larger cities.

But provinces should go further with tax sharing in order to address the GCRs' pressing need for own-source revenues that will grow with the economy. The obvious options here are provincial sales taxes and income taxes. Likewise, the appropriate initial approach to sharing either of these revenues is via revenue sharing rather than tax-base sharing, with the share of revenues allocated on a derivation basis (see the appendix). While this would be a significant shift in terms of the fiscal evolution of cities, it would not be all that dramatic in dollar terms, since the sharing could, in the initial years, replace a given portion of provincial-municipal cash transfers. An alternative approach, one that may be preferable initially, would be for the province to index existing provincial-municipal transfers to the rate of growth of, say, provincial personal income taxes, an approach that held sway in Ontario during the 1970s (Sewell

2005b). This caveat aside, some province will surely at some time be enticed (or forced) into sharing its growth taxes with its cities and municipalities, perhaps with an accompanying municipal equalization program if per capita differences become too large. The game will then be afoot.

For this to occur, let alone be sustained, there need to be structures and processes to facilitate such privileged status for the larger cities. That this may not come easily is clear from the ongoing Ontario experience. Recently, the Ontario government signed a memorandum of understanding with the Association of Municipalities of Ontario (AMO) to consult with it on any legislation, regulations, and negotiations with Ottawa that affect municipalities. Toronto mayor David Miller objected to this because Toronto, as the sixth largest government in Canada, should be consulted directly and not via the AMO which, Miller points out, is not even a government (Campbell 2004). Indeed, Toronto has threatened to withdraw from the AMO, and the AMO in response is threatening to move its upcoming conference out of Toronto. From the perspective of the foregoing analysis, two observations are in order. First, it was only a matter of time before the GCRs-municipalities confrontation would develop. Second, the provinces will find it difficult not to provide formal or informal recognition of the special nature of GCRs. John Sewell (2005a) notes that the City of Toronto has recommended that Ontario adopt a consultation model similar to that in Alberta, where the provincial government consults with Calgary and Edmonton and with municipal associations, recognizing that these two cities are different from the other municipalities. Toronto suggests that Ontario conduct separate consultations with Toronto and perhaps some other large cities, in addition to its consultations with the AMO. While this would represent the beginning of a provincial-GCR interface in Ontario, it would not be the final word, because the GCRs ultimately want more legislative powers.

THE GCRs AND THE FISCAL IMBALANCE ISSUE

Readers will recognize that the demand for more powers on the part of GCRs has a very familiar federal ring. And so it should, for many of the traditional federal-provincial issues are now going to be replayed at the provincial-municipal level. From the vantage point of the GCRs, there is also a fiscal imbalance in the GCR-provincial relationship which they want rectified by, say, receiving a tax-point transfer from the provinces. They do not want to settle for additional equal per capita intergovernmental transfers from their respective provinces, since that would exacerbate their fiscal problems relative to both the provincial government and other municipalities. This is because the per capita value of sales and income tax revenues is higher in the GCRs than in other municipalities. To "send" this money to the province and then receive it back in equal per capita grants clearly disadvantages the GCRs.

Much more preferable would be the transfer of an equivalent value of sales or income tax room to the GCRs.

This is precisely the argument that Ontario's Dalton McGuinty is making to the federal government. Ontario, McGuinty notes, is contributing $23 billion more to the federal coffers than it receives in federal spending and transfers. Part of the McGuinty argument is that Ontario contributes more than its population share of federal revenues, so when Ottawa turns round and transfers these back in terms of equal per capita revenues in areas of provincial jurisdiction, this is tantamount to yet another equalization program. Hence, the frequent call for Ottawa to transfer additional income tax points to the provinces, which would then be equalized through the formal equalization program. The provinces would surely be willing to allow this income tax transfer to "pass through" to selected spending areas, in the same way as they likely will allow the gas tax to pass through. In any event, the point here is that our long-standing federalism debates will progressively be replayed at the provincial-GCR/city level.

Arguably, in at least one dimension Toronto may find it easier to make its case with Queen's Park than Queen's Park has been able to do with the federal government. Specifically, the operative assumption in the federation and embodied in the equalization program is that a given level of per capita revenues provides an equivalent level of public goods and services across all provinces. In other words, there is no recognition in the equalization formula that one should take the cost of providing services (i.e., capitalization) into account when assessing fiscal adequacy. As a relevant aside, in some recent exploratory work, I showed that taking into account the costs of providing public goods and services would leave Ontario with the lowest effective fiscal capacity of all provinces (Courchene 2005). It appears, however, that in terms of Toronto (or GCRs generally) there is a growing recognition that they require greater revenues than the smaller cities, both because of the range of their responsibilities and because we all benefit if they can be competitive with their U.S. counterparts. Given that the GCRs themselves also recognize this, the stage is set for some much bolder thinking by our global city-regions.

GCRs AS CITISTATES

The thrust of the foregoing analysis is that Canada's GCRs desire and require much more revenue and expenditure autonomy. Phrased differently, they want a more formal role in the operations of Canadian federalism. Moreover, not only are they acquiring the coordination and management capacity to undertake a broader range of functions and responsibilities than their smaller sister cities, but they are also approaching the critical mass of civil servants needed for them to become competing policy centres vis-à-vis their respective provincial governments with respect to the design and implementation of GCR policies. Finally, given that Ottawa looks after medicare as well as income support for children and the elderly, Canadian GCRs have much more room than their American counterparts to manoeuvre on the allocative or efficiency front without compromising the social fabric. So why not attempt to follow in the footsteps of the German city Länder (Berlin, Bremen, and Hamburg) and seek to become Canadian city-provinces with full constitutional powers? Toronto has not quite gone this far, at least not yet. But it has adopted a blueprint for a bold future within the federation – the Greater Toronto Charter:

The Greater Toronto Charter

Article One   The Greater Toronto Region form an order of government that is a full partner of the Federal and Provincial Governments of Canada.

Article Two   The Greater Toronto Region, and its municipalities, be empowered to govern and exercise responsibility over a broad range of issues, including:

child and family services; cultural institutions; economic development and marketing; education; environmental protection; health care; housing; immigrant and refugee settlement; land-use planning; law enforcement and emergency services; recreation; revenue generation, taxation and assessment; transportation; sewage treatment; social assistance; waste and natural resource management; and water supply and quality management, with the exception of those matters as are mutually agreed upon with other levels of government that are best assigned to another level.

Article Three   The Greater Toronto Region have the fiscal authority to raise revenues and allocate expenditures with respect to those responsibilities outlined in Article Two.

Article Four   The Greater Toronto Region be governed by accessible, democratic governments, created by their citizens and accountable to them for the exercise of the governments' full duties and responsibilities.

Article Five   The Greater Toronto Region continue to fulfill its obligation to share its wealth, innovation and other assets with the rest of Canada, through appropriate mechanisms developed in concert with other levels of government.

Guided by two fundamental principles of democracy – subsidiarity and fiscal accountability – the citizen-initiated and citizen-drafted Greater Toronto

Charter has been endorsed by business leaders, community activists, former politicians, journalists, and academics and was enthusiastically received by the Committee of Greater Toronto Mayors and Regional Chairs. While city charters are not particularly novel in Canada – Vancouver, Winnipeg, Montreal, Saint John, and Newfoundland's two major cities all have them – the timing and breadth of the Toronto charter are significant; its timing coincides with the resurgence of cities and particularly the GCRs, and clearly the starting point of the charter is to view Toronto (or the GTA) as an order of government that is a full partner of the federal and provincial governments. Much of the rest of the charter follows rather axiomatically from the operations of federalism. Specifically, under the provisions of the charter, the GTA would aspire to:

- acquire, along the lines of the principle of subsidiarity, both exclusive and shared or concurrent powers/responsibilities;
- achieve fiscal autonomy with respect to both revenues and expenditures;
- be democratically accountable to its citizens;
- work with other governments to integrate the GTA, politically and economically, into the workings of the Canadian federation.

Even without providing further details, it is clear that this charter is, in principle, much closer to the concept of a city-province than it is to Toronto's status quo.

While there are some important advantages of the informal charter model over a formal (that is, constitutionalized) citistate model (for example, the appropriate boundaries of a Toronto city-province would probably need to be defined once and for all), the citistate model nonetheless represents an important reference point for many of the issues addressed in this paper. For example, under a citistate model, the GCRs would automatically retain more of the revenues generated within their boundaries. As already noted, since our GCRs will be competing head-to-head with American GCRs more than with Canada's smaller communities, it is essential that they have revenue and expenditure autonomy adequate to this task. This is especially so because the higher level of business activity in GCRs tends to be capitalized into higher wages, rents, and the like, so the GCRs need more revenues per capita than smaller municipalities in order to provide the same amount of public goods and services. Moreover, the fact that citistates are a viable model in the German federation provides additional leverage to Canada's GCRs in pressing their case with both Ottawa and the provinces.

However, there is a major concern associated with both the citistate and the charter model, even beyond that relating to political feasibility. It is that despite the merits of the model, there is precious little that the GCRs have done to earn this degree of power and autonomy. The most obvious issue here is that most of Canada's GCRs have shown little interest in accessing the untapped revenue sources that lie within their jurisdiction. By wanting to run before they learn to walk, the GCRs are in effect calling their own bluff in terms of their aspirations to become charter cities, let alone citistates or city-provinces. Nonetheless, the very presence of the charter, as well as the existence of the German city Länder, may serve to propel GCRs' actions more in line with their aspirations.

CONCLUSION

The tandem of globalization and the information revolution have catapulted global city-regions into the policy limelight. Because of their role as the dynamic export and innovation platforms of the new economy, their future is Canada's future. Hence, we need to find ways – politically, institutionally, and perhaps eventually constitutionally – to accommodate our GCRs' needs in the KBE. As Bradford points out, this may not be easy: "The concern here is that Canada's national policy machinery and intergovernmental system remains ill-adapted to changing policy realities and spatial flows. While governments at all levels are active in cities, there is little evidence of a coherent agenda, systematic coordination, or even appreciation of the importance of place quality to good outcomes" (2004, 40). Among other things, Bradford sees this challenge as involving "new thinking ... that respects provincial constitutional responsibility for municipal governments while fully recognizing that metropolitan policy issues, from the environment and housing to employment and immigration, transcend the jurisdictional compartments" (ibid., 41). More optimistically, Bradford goes on to note that "using a mix of principles, programs, and networks, the EU in the 1990s developed multi-level governance to implement more place-sensitive policies and programs" (ibid., 43). The lesson that we ought to draw from this is that if the European Union can accomplish this multijurisdictional relationship within a multinational and even supranational context, it should be all the more easy to accomplish in a national context. Ottawa's most important role will be to provide the leadership so that the issue of what needs to be done is sorted out before attention turns to turf warfare or who does what.

The good news here is that Canadians have traditionally excelled at the art of federalism. We were able to centralize our fiscal system during wartime and then decentralize it again. We were able to create decentralized yet national programs in health, education, and welfare. We were able to accommodate Quebec's interests in terms of several national programs, including personal income taxes and the Canada/Quebec Pension Plan. Through changes in the magnitude of and incentives within the transfer system, we were effectively able to alter the division of powers between Ottawa and the provinces. And we did all this without any change in the *Constitution Act,*

1867. Rather, we did it through creative instruments and processes – the federal spending power, opting out, altering the nature of federal-provincial transfers, cost sharing, delegation of powers, and the like. Jean Chrétien's Team Canada missions and the provinces' Council of the Federation are more recent examples of these creative instruments and processes at the national and provincial levels, respectively.

In short, if there is a societal will, there is a federal way. Since our collective future economic and social well-being depends on the success of our GCRs, Canada and Canadians will find a way to ensure that our global city-regions become more fully and more formally integrated into the operations of Canadian fiscal and political federalism.

APPENDIX: ANALYTICAL PERSPECTIVES ON TAX SHARING

SHARING TAX REVENUES

There are at least three features of tax sharing that need elaboration. The first has to do with whether the cities are *sharing the revenues* from a given tax base or whether they are *sharing the tax base* itself and therefore have the freedom to alter the tax rate. For example, under the former, the cities would presumably receive a fixed share of the revenues collected by the relevant senior government (for example, a given percentage, or a given number of the eight percentage points of Ontario's PST, or in the case of sharing the federal gas tax, a given number of cents per litre). Under tax-base sharing, however, Ontario would, for example, reduce its provincial sales tax rate from 8 to 6 percent and then allow cities to take up the tax room by setting their own rate, say between zero and 4 percent. This latter version would give the cities tax-rate flexibility and therefore would allow them to determine their own revenues at the margin.

The second issue relates to the *allocation* of the shared revenues. For example, the proceeds of revenue sharing for the cities could be allocated according to the "derivation principle" (in accordance with where revenues are derived from in the first place) or in some other manner (for example, equal per capita). For such taxes as the multilevel GST, for which it can be difficult to ascertain geographically where the revenues actually come from, allocation would probably have to be done on a basis other than the derivation principle. It is far easier to allocate shares of a gasoline tax or a PST on a derivation basis (by quantity of gas sold in a given location or by the location-related PST-eligible final sales, respectively), though they could also be allocated on an equal per capita basis. Typically, when taxes are allocated on the derivation principle, richer (and generally larger) cities receive greater per capita revenues, so pressures might develop to supplement this by some sort of equalization program.

The third issue relates to the nature of shared revenues – should they be conditional (earmarked) or unconditional? For example, the revenues from the proposed gasoline tax are intended to be earmarked for transportation infrastructure, making them more like a "benefit" tax or a user fee. If revenues from GST or PST sharing are made conditional, this will presumably have less to do with efficiency than with attempting to ensure that cities carry out the preferences of the donor government. Obviously, fiscal autonomy is enhanced when revenues are transferred to cities without any conditions in terms of how and where they are spent.

Not surprisingly, there is a relationship among these three issues. For example, allowing provinces to set their own tax rates (on a federally or provincially determined tax base) leads rather naturally to the allocation of the resulting revenues on a derivation basis, as well as favouring unconditionality in terms of how these revenues are to be spent.

INTERGOVERNMENTAL TRANSFERS AND REVENUE SHARING

The second role of this appendix is to compare revenue sharing with traditional transfers. Motivating this analysis is the TD Bank's assertion (quoted in the text) that federal and provincial grants should be used to address cities' accumulated funding shortfalls – but they are the wrong vehicle for financing cities' ongoing financial needs. Presumably, one of the reasons for this claim is that intergovernmental grants or transfers are open to arbitrary change (for example, the CHST cuts) or are subject to arbitrary "conditioning." Moreover, they are unlike tax-base sharing, which allows cities to increase or decrease their revenues at the margin.

However, it is possible to make too fine a distinction between revenue sharing and intergovernmental grants. Consider the following two examples. The first draws from actual experience in Australia, namely, the operations of the Commonwealth Grants Commission (CGC). Recently, the Commonwealth government and the Australian states agreed that: (a) a new 10 percent value-added tax called the GST will be introduced and collected by the Commonwealth government; (b) the 10 percent tax rate cannot be changed without agreement of the Commonwealth and all of the states; (c) the *entire proceeds* of the GST are to be transferred to the states; (d) these revenues will be "equalized" for both revenue means and expenditure needs via the operations of the Commonwealth Grants Commission; (e) the resulting grants are unconditional; and (f) the GST replaces a series of pre-existing state taxes that cannot be reintroduced. In terms of the three issues alluded to above, one would (presumably) refer to this as tax sharing (but at a 100 percent rate), with the proceeds being allocated under the equalizing provisions of the CGC and where the resulting revenues are unconditional. As a relevant aside, the Australian states are particularly delighted with one feature of this system –

not only is the GST a broad-based tax but it is growing faster than GDP, so aggregate state revenues are rising as a percent of GDP. One of the themes of this paper is that Canada's cities too need access to a growing tax base.

Now compare this to another example. Suppose the federal government were to initiate annual grants to the cities of, say, $4 billion, escalated annually by the rate of growth of federal GST revenues. Assume that these grants would be unconditional and allocated to cities on an equal per capita basis. Since $4 billion annually is roughly equal to one percentage point of the GST (and over time would remain at roughly one percentage point given the nature of the indexing), this is not all that different from the above Australian revenue-sharing example. In other words, there would appear to be enough flexibility in terms of the design of intergovernmental transfers to replicate most features of sharing the revenues of a tax base. This is especially the case if creative ways are found to ensure that these transfer arrangements could not be altered arbitrarily by the donor government.

NOTES

This paper "appropriates" the title of a book by Neil Peirce (1993). My thinking on city issues had its origins in a series of discussions with then-president of the C.D. Howe Institute, Tom Kierans, who encouraged me to extend my work on federalism to incorporate cities and especially what are referred to below as global city-regions. In the present context it is a pleasure to acknowledge the comments and encouragement from Robert Young. Thanks are also due to France St-Hilaire and Jeremy Leonard of IRPP for many valuable organizational and substantive suggestions on earlier drafts. I also wish to acknowledge the support from the SSHRC Major Collaborative Research Initiative (Multilevel Governance).

1 In a recent *Globe and Mail* column, Jeffrey Simpson (2005) noted that government spending in British Columbia over the last four years and the next four is forecast to increase by $2.7 billion. Health-care expenditures over the same eight years are also forecast to increase by $2.7 billion. This is hourglass federalism at its finest!

REFERENCES

Alboim, Naomi, Ross Finnie, and Ronald Meng. 2005. "The Discounting of Immigrants' Skills in Canada: Evidence and Policy Recommendations." *IRPP Choices,* February
Autès, Michel. 1997. "Public Action, Local Democracy, and the Challenge of Economic Globalization." In *Cities, Enterprises, and Society on the Eve of the Twenty-First Century,* ed. Frank Moulaert and Allen J. Scott, 229–43. London and Washington: Pinter

Berridge, Joseph. 1999. "There Is No Need to Sit and Wait for a Handout." *Globe and Mail,* 7 June

Bradford, Neil. 2004. "Place Matters and Multi-Level Governance: Perspectives on a New Urban Policy Paradigm." *Policy Options/Options politique,* February, 39–44

Campbell, Murray. 2004. "Is a New Deal for Cities Doomed by Political Spat in Ontario?" *Globe and Mail,* 26 August

Castells, Manuel. 2001. *The Internet Galaxy.* New York: Oxford University Press

Courchene, Thomas J. 2000. "Responding to the NAFTA Challenge: Ontario as a North American Region State and Toronto as a Global City Region." In *Global City-Regions: Trends, Theory, Policy,* ed. A. Scott, 158–92. New York: Oxford University Press

– 2001. *A State of Minds: Toward a Human Capital Future for Canadians.* Montreal: Institute for Research on Public Policy

– 2004. "Hourglass Federalism." *Policy Options/Options politiques,* April, 12–17

– 2005. "Vertical and Horizontal Fiscal Imbalance: An Ontario Perspective." Presentation before the Standing Committee on Finance, House of Commons, 4 May (Available from IRPP)

Courchene, Thomas J., and Colin Telmer. 1998. *From Heartland to North American Region State: The Fiscal, Social, and Federal Evolution of Ontario.* Toronto: Centre for Public Management, Rotman School of Business, University of Toronto

Florida, Richard. 2002; 2004 (paperback). *The Rise of the Creative Class.* New York: Basic Books

Gertler, Meric, Richard Florida, Gary Gates, and Tara Vinodrai. 2002. "Competing for Creativity: Placing Ontario's Cities in the North American Context." Toronto: A Report Prepared for the Ontario Ministry of Enterprise, Opportunity, and Innovation and the Institute for Competitiveness and Prosperity

Gillmor, Don. 2004. "The City Statesman." *Saturday Night,* April, 38–44

Goodale, Ralph. 2004. *New Agenda for Achievement: The Budget Plan 2004.* Ottawa: Department of Finance

– 2005. *Budget 2005: Delivering on Commitments.* Ottawa: Department of Finance

Harris, Richard G. 2003. "Old Growth and New Economy Cycles: Rethinking Canadian Economic Paradigms." In *The Art of the State: Governance in a World without Frontiers,* ed. Thomas J. Courchene and Donald J. Savoie, 31–68. Montreal: Institute for Research on Public Policy

Lever, William F. 1997. "Economic Globalization and Urban Dynamics." In *Cities, Enterprises, and Society on the Eve of the Twenty-First Century,* ed. Frank Moulaert and Allen J. Scott, 33–53. London and Washington: Pinter

Little Bruce. 2004. "Canada's Big Cities Are Racking Up Big Job Growth Too." *Globe and Mail,* 26 July

McMillan, Melville L. 1997. "Taxation and Expenditure Patterns in Major City-Regions: An International Perspective and Lessons for Canada." In *Urban Governance and Finance: A Question of Who Does What,* ed. Paul Hobson and France St-Hilaire, 1–58. Montreal: Institute for Research on Public Policy

Martin, Roger, and James Milway. 2003. "Ontario's Urban Gap." *National Post*, 4 July

Ohmae, Kenichi. 2000. "How Regions Can Prosper from Globalizaiton." In *Global City-Regions: Trends, Theory, Policy,* ed. A. Scott. New York: Oxford University Press

Ontario Jobs and Investment Board. 1999. *A Road Map to Prosperity: An Economic Plan for Jobs in the Twenty-First Century.* www.ontario-canada.com/jobgrow

Peirce, Neil. 1993. *Citistates: How Urban America Can Prosper in a Competitive World.* Santa Ana, Calif.: Seven Locks Press

Plunkett, T.J. 2004. "A Nation of Cities Awaits Paul Martin's 'New Deal': Federal Funds for 'Creature of the Provinces'." *Policy Options/Options politiques,* February, 19–25

Sewell, John. 2005a. *Local Government Bulletin No. 53.* January. www.localgovernment.ca

– 2005b. *Local Government Bulletin No. 54.* February. www.localgovernment.ca

Simpson, Jeffrey. 2005. "Watch for the BC Pattern Across Canada." *Globe and Mail,* 16 February, A17

Strange, William C. 2003. "Agglomeration Economics and the Future of Cities." PEAP Policy Study no. 200301. Toronto: Policy and Economic Analysis Program, Department of Economics, University of Toronto

TD Bank Financial Group. 2002a. *A Choice Between Investing in Canada's Cities or Disinvesting in Canada's Future.* TD Economics Special Report. Toronto, April

– 2002b. *The Greater Toronto Area (GTA): Canada's Primary Locomotive in Need of Repairs.* TD Economics Special Report. Toronto, May

– 2003. *The Calgary-Edmonton Corridor: Take Action Now to Ensure Tiger's Roar Doesn't Fade.* TD Economics Special Report. Toronto, April

Touraine, A. 1994. *Ou'est-ce que la démocratie?* Paris: Fayard

III

Restructuring

5

Why Municipal Amalgamations?
Halifax, Toronto, Montreal

Andrew Sancton

Entre 1995 et 2001, trois provinces de l'est du Canada, soit la Nouvelle-Écosse, l'Ontario et le Québec, ont légiféré pour la fusion des municipalités au sein de leurs grandes métropoles. Il y a trois raisons qui peuvent expliquer l'adoption de politiques similaires dans ces provinces : (1) les gouvernements provinciaux faisaient face, directement ou indirectement, à la pression du mouvement de mondialisation (2) les gouvernements provinciaux répondaient aux demandes de forces politiques internes, qui pouvaient être ou ne pas être similaires dans chaque province, mais qui étaient clairement indépendantes du mouvement de mondialisation; ou (3) les gouvernements provinciaux agissaient de façon autonome, avec peu d'égard aux pressions politiques internes. Le point majeur soulevé par ce chapitre est que la troisième explication semble celle qui concorde le mieux aux faits. Ce point est développé en donnant plus de précisions d'abord sur chacune des deux autres explications, et en examinant ensuite plus en profondeur les raisons politiques des fusions municipales à Halifax, Toronto et Montréal.

Between 1995 and 2001 legislation was passed in three eastern Canadian provinces – Nova Scotia, Ontario, and Quebec – to implement major municipal mergers within the largest of their respective metropolitan areas. There have been three types of explanation for the adoption of these similar policies: (1) provincial governments were responding, directly or indirectly, to pressures caused by globalization; (2) provincial governments were responding to demands of internal political forces, which may or may not have been similar in each province but were clearly independent of globalization; or (3) provincial governments were acting "autonomously," with little regard to internal political pressures. The main argument of this paper is that it is the third type of explanation that best fits the facts. This argument will be advanced first by exploring each of the other two types of explanation and then by examining, in more detail, the political causes of municipal amalgamation in Halifax, Toronto, and Montreal.

DID GLOBALIZATION CAUSE AMALGAMATION?

Globalization involves the increasing interconnectedness among different regions of the world, involving trade, rapid communication (especially through the internet), and the formation of social and economic networks – some very powerful – that transcend national boundaries.[1] Different analysts emphasize different characteristics of globalization, and as a result the whole concept is deeply contested. It has been considered at one time or another as a possible cause of almost any significant development in various societies around the world. Municipal amalgamations are no exception. By definition, however, globalization is widespread. If it has a direct impact on the structure of governmental institutions, we should expect to see similar changes everywhere. But, contrary to what many in Canada have assumed, the recent round of municipal amalgamations in eastern Canada has not been part of any worldwide trend (Sancton 2000). Since 1990, municipal amalgamations in the Western world outside Canada have occurred only in New Zealand, parts of Australia, a very few local authorities in England, post-apartheid South Africa, and, most recently, Denmark. If globalization causes municipal amalgamations, surely there should be many more cases than these. In particular, we would expect to find them in the United States.

If anything, pressure in the United States has been for municipal secession, not municipal amalgamation. In the early 1990s, there was a movement on Staten Island to have it secede from New York City, but the plan was blocked in the state assembly (Benjamin and Nathan 2001, 80). On the eve of the centennial of the New York consolidation in 1898, the Brooklyn borough president saw no reason to celebrate. He wrote, "If consolidation had not taken place ... continued independence for Brooklyn, Long Island City or Queen's and New York would have fostered intense competition among the municipalities, resulting in dynamic economic growth and an even stronger metropolitan region than we have today" (ibid.).

It has been in Los Angeles, however, where the issue of municipal secession has been most prominent. In the end, as a result of local referenda, the City of Los Angeles continued with its same boundaries, but only after secession had been impartially evaluated by a government agency and only after all the plans for its implementation had been made. The case of Los Angeles is therefore highly significant for anyone claiming that there is a direct link between globalization and municipal amalgamation.

Although there were various other proposals for breaking up Los Angeles (including the establishment of a new City of Hollywood), the main one involved the establishment of a new city in the San Fernando Valley. The valley had been incorporated into the City of Los Angeles in 1915. By 2002 its population was over 1.3 million, while that of all of Los Angeles was 3.7 million. For almost ninety years, the valley had been part of the city. At various times during this period, secessionist movements had appeared, but none was stronger than the one that developed during the 1990s. Under the state rules that were legislated in 1985, any proposed municipal breakup of a city within Los Angeles County required the approval of the Local Agency Formation Commission for Los Angeles County (LAFCO). Before it could allow a local referendum, a detailed study needed to be made of all of the implications, the theory being that voters needed to know what was at stake and that implementation plans needed to be worked out before the breakup was approved, rather than after.

On 24 April 2002 the executive officer's report on the *Special Reorganization of the San Fernando Valley* was released. It is a landmark document for the study of municipal secession because it lays out exactly how a secession would be implemented, including a detailed financial plan for the new city to compensate the City of Los Angeles for its fiscal losses as the result of the secession. On the subject of the implications for future municipal costs resulting from the establishment of the new city, the report stated:

The academic studies on this topic have found that economies of scale are relevant only among the smallest of cities.

For larger metropolitan cities the literature suggests that *dis*economies [emphasis in original] of scale exist in policing as well as refuse collection, general government and fire services. This means that the per capita costs of providing of local government *rise* as city population, crime or other measures of government output increase ...

The evidence does indicate that in the area of street maintenance and possibly, sanitation, there are likely economies of scale. The Executive Officer encourages the parties [i.e., the two potential cities] to consider a long-term contractual relationship in such areas with clear efficiencies from a large-scale operation. (Local Agency Formation Commission for Los Angeles County 2002, 24 and 26)

When LAFCO approved the implementation plan derived from this study, the stage was set for the referendum that took place on 5 November 2002.[2] Within the boundaries of the proposed City of San Fernando Valley that had been established by LAFCO, the proposal was narrowly approved: 51 percent to 49 percent. The relatively high vote against secession has been attributed to all kinds of factors: high spending by opponents of secession; fears of increased electricity costs in an independent city; and a poor campaign strategy by the secessionists. In any event, the proposal also had to be approved by voters in the entire city, and here it lost by 67 percent to 33 percent.

The results of the referendum in Los Angeles will no doubt be analysed by students of urban politics in Los Angeles for many years to come. Meanwhile, the secession movement provides plenty of opportunity for theorizing about what was really going on (Hogen-Esch 2001; Haselhoff 2002). The most creative of such attempts has been by Roger Keil, who has explicitly compared developments in Toronto and Los Angeles and linked both cases to globalization. The heart of his argument is: "Both current developments, the amalgamation of government in Toronto and the push towards secession in Los Angeles, are reactions to new urban realities created by globalization. Ideologically, there are many similarities between the secessionists' desire for smaller government, fairer taxation and better services on the one hand, and the Ontario Tories' neoliberal agenda of more accountable, streamlined government on the other" (Keil 2000, 776).

Creative as such theorizing may be, it relies primarily on linking globalization to the obvious ideological similarities between San Fernando Valley secessionists and Mike Harris's Conservatives. But it does not help much in understanding the practical politics of the two cities. Globalization, according to Keil's line of argument, can explain everything, even plans for institutional change that are the opposite of each other. If globalization explains the rise of the secessionist movement, does it also explain the fact that the secessionist movement has, temporarily at least, been defeated? Does it explain why there was a binding referendum in Los Angeles and not in Toronto? And what about the impact of globalization on the vast majority of North American metropolitan areas (including Vancouver), where dozens or hundreds of municipalities continue to exist and where there have been no significant movements for either secession or consolidation? Finally, how do we explain the consolidation of New York City in 1898? Was it caused by globalization? (Answer: Possibly.) How do we explain the creation of Unicity in Winnipeg in 1971? Or the many European municipal amalgamations of the 1960s and 1970s?

Globalization is indeed having a profound effect on the physical, societal, and economic characteristics of our metropolitan areas. These changes have been well documented by scholars from a wide variety of disciplines in the social sciences (Scott 2001). Many of these changes in turn lead to pressures for new governmental arrangements of one sort or another. There is absolutely nothing new, however, in the claim that municipal structures need to be changed to meet changes in the pattern of urbanization, changes caused by streetcars, automobiles, new methods of (fordist) industrial production, or globalization. Such claims have been made for at least a century and a half. Just because the occasional politician claims that globalization requires amalgamation – or secession – does not mean that academic analysts should accept such a claim as being empirically true (Boudreau 2003, 180–3).

Some credence to the claim that globalization requires amalgamation has recently come from Thomas J. Courchene. As part of his argument about Ontario becoming a North American region-state, he applauds the Harris government for implementing market-value assessment for Ontario's property-tax system. He claims that, for the new system to be workable,

> there needs to be some restructuring of boundaries to internalize the externality arising from the fact that there is a divergence in terms of where citizens earn their incomes and where they consume services. Hence the rationale for amalgamation, not only for the megacity of Toronto but for other Ontario cities as well. And as an added bonus from the province's vantage point, the creation of the megacity merged the high-business-tax preferences of the former city of Toronto with the more competitive-oriented policies of the other five former municipalities. Arguably the new megacity is now more attuned to a global city-region mentality and more attuned to the larger vision of Ontario as a North American region-state. (Courchene 2001, 180)

Arguments about internalizing externalities and equalizing taxation levels have nothing to do with globalization. Such arguments have been made in the literature on metropolitan government for at least a century. Given that Courchene is trying to situate Ontario in its North American (rather than Canadian context), it is mystifying that he thinks municipal amalgamation is at all relevant to anything with which he is concerned. Why is the new mega-city any more attuned to its global or North American reality than the former municipalities were? The American reality is that municipal amalgamations have not taken place for a century. The global reality is that they have had nothing to do with the public-sector reforms that have swept all industrialized countries since the time of Margaret Thatcher and Ronald Reagan.[3]

WAS THERE POLITICAL PRESSURE FOR AMALGAMATION?

Pluralist, corporatist, and Marxist views of the state all assume that forces in civil society ultimately determine state actions; they reject the notion that the state itself is an autonomous actor (Nordlinger 1981, 44). Marxist views are consistent with the notion that economic forces associated with globalization have caused central governments to restructure municipalities in particular ways. Pluralist and corporatist approaches suggest that particular groups – business corporations, labour unions, or organizations representing people with particular policy interests (the environment, for example) – are the causes of policy changes. A pluralist approach to the politics of municipal restructuring would, at some stage, look for all the groups favouring such a policy. It is an interesting question whether municipalities themselves can be classified as groups or interests within the pluralist universe. Some may wish to classify them as being part of the state itself; others (especially in the Anglo-American tradition) may emphasize their distinct legal existence apart from the central state (Frug 1999, 26–53).

It is extremely difficult to argue that there were strong societal forces urging Canadian provincial governments in the 1990s to implement sweeping municipal amalgamations in major metropolitan areas. In Halifax, the Royal Commission on Education, Public Services, and Provincial-Municipal Relations called for a single municipality as early as 1974. In 1992 the provincially appointed Task Force on Local Government arrived at a similar conclusion. In neither of these cases was there great public interest in the issue. None of the municipalities – not even the City of Halifax – was urging that the amalgamation be implemented. It is true that the Halifax Board of Trade supported the amalgamation plan after it was announced, but there is no evidence from the relevant government reports that it actively promoted such a policy beforehand (Sancton 1994, 51).

In Toronto in the early 1990s, the Golden Task Force on the Greater Toronto Area (GTA) received 211 written submissions, including a number from various kinds of business associations (Ontario 1996, 244–9). Only two individuals and three municipalities argued for any form of municipal consolidation within the GTA, and no one argued for the amalgamation of all the municipalities within the territory of the Municipality of Metropolitan Toronto (Sancton 1996, 281–2). It is true, of course, that influential forces need not write reports for government task forces. In the case of supporters of municipal amalgamation in Toronto, Graham Todd has suggested exactly how such powerful forces are comprised:

> The current coalition of large downtown firms (banks and consumer retail outlets), media outlets (like the Toronto Star), politicos (such as Paul Godfrey the former appointed chair of Metro and publisher of the Toronto Sun), and politically connected law firms (like McCarthy Tetreault which reportedly helped draft the legislation and which was represented on the province's "transition team" for the new city) is organized around the Toronto Board of Trade. In one form or another these interests have pushed for amalgamation since the early 1970s. At present the main concern of this group – whose membership might better fit the definition of an urban regime – has been how to translate the amalgamation victory into further tax reductions (commercial office space has already received a windfall from property reassessment). (Todd 1998, 206–7)

Unfortunately, Todd presents no evidence to support this claim; it is not accompanied by footnotes or references. Looking for evidence, we discover that, of the entities mentioned above, only the Board of Trade of Metropolitan Toronto made a submission to the GTA task force. It was concerned primarily with levels of commercial and industrial property taxation and made no reference to amalgamations. The closest reference was this: "Governance design changes in the GTA are not essential to the resolution of commercial/industrial tax problems in Metro."[4] It was only after the government announced that it would be implementing amalgamation that the board came out in favour. The chronology was similar for the editorial positions of the *Toronto Sun* and *Toronto Star*, although in past debates about municipal structures in Metro, the *Star* had officially supported amalgamation.

It may well be true that Paul Godfrey pushed privately for amalgamation before to the governments's announcement, but he does not personally comprise a regime. In fact, whatever involvement he may have had was likely more closely linked to his activities as a backroom activist in the Ontario Progressive Conservative Party than as a representative of a business or media elite. If Todd or anyone else wants to argue that business interests played a profound role in the creation of Toronto's mega-city, they should produce some evidence. Then, given that there have been no similar amalgamations in the United States for more than a hundred years, they will need to explain why business interests in American cities either take a different position or are less powerful.

In the Montreal amalgamation, it seems that there is little or no evidence that business groups favoured such a policy before its adoption by the Quebec government. For example, the Chambre de commerce du Montréal métropolitain, which eventually supported the provincial government's policy on amalgamation in 2000, stated the following in its brief to the Bédard Commission on 2 October 1998:

> Municipalities must be encouraged to reorganize, even to amalgamate. Although the chamber does not take a dogmatic position about a specific size, we are convinced that Quebec unduly wastes public funds in having here almost twice as many municipalities as Ontario, with almost 1,500 for a population of seven million compared to 700 for a population of ten million in Ontario.
>
> Municipalities must be encouraged to amalgamate by a program of financial incentives that will bring value to citizens through a reduction in taxes (author's translation).[5]

Among other things, this passage indicates how important it was for the chamber of commerce that Quebec follow Ontario's example in amalgamating municipalities. Nevertheless, there was no specific reference in the brief to the need to create only one municipality within Montreal Island – roughly the territory covered by the Communauté urbaine de Montréal (CUM). Indeed, the chamber clearly implies that the CUM should continue to exist: "The chamber believes that the CUM is an important level of decision-making and of fiscal redistribution and that its mandate should be enlarged to manage on a truly metropolitan basis common services relating to transport, land-use planning, and perhaps waste management and the environment, even though it appears difficult to reach consensus on jurisdiction" (author's translation). This does not look like pressure from the business sector to amalgamate all the municipalities within the CUM. Unlike the cases of Halifax and Toronto, the central city of Montreal promoted amalgamation long before the provincial government did. But there is no evidence that any particular interest groups ever adopted the city's position.

AUTONOMOUS POLICYMAKING BY THREE PROVINCIAL GOVERNMENTS

The main argument of this paper is that recent municipal amalgamations in Canada can only be explained by a state-centred account of policymaking. Provincial leaders sponsored amalgamations because they thought this was the right policy in the circumstances, even though there was little or no societal demand for such a policy and even though there were many other possible courses of action. This is not to say that the actions of one provincial government did not have an impact on others; it is especially evident that the actions of the Quebec government (and its interlocutors, as we have seen above) were significantly affected by what had happened in Ontario. The rest of this paper is largely concerned with describing and analysing the particular circumstances under which each province acted.

Amalgamation in Halifax had first been called for by the Graham Commission in 1974. The Task Force on Local Government – comprising six provincial public servants, three senior staff members from three different municipalities, the executive director of the Union of Nova Scotia Municipalities, and an accountant with a major accounting firm (Nova Scotia 1992, 51) – resurrected the idea in 1992. There is no evidence in the task force's report of any consultation outside provincial and municipal circles. Premier Donald Cameron, a Progressive Conservative, announced in late 1992 that amalgamations would proceed in Cape Breton and Halifax. But in May 1993 he was replaced by John Savage, a Liberal and former mayor of Dartmouth, who had proclaimed during the election campaign that amalgamation in Halifax was "a crazy idea."[6] In mid-1994 Savage's government sponsored legislation to create the single-tier Cape Breton Regional Municipality, primarily to prevent the impending bankruptcy of some of the existing cities and towns in industrial Cape Breton (Sancton, James, and Ramsay 2000, 25–39). The process went relatively smoothly and probably contributed to Savage's decision later in the year to impose a similar structure in Halifax, but for different reasons.

Everyone who has addressed Savage's decision accepts that it was his alone, taken at a time when he was convinced that dramatic action needed to be taken to reduce public spending and promote economic development. Debate continues on what exactly he was trying to accomplish (Stewart 2000), but no one has argued that he was in any way pressured to implement amalgamation. The Halifax Board of Trade had supported Cameron's initiative and also supported Savage's, but it always appeared to be following rather than leading.

The best explanation for Savage's action is that he was convinced that Nova Scotians had to understand that major sacrifices were needed to extract the province from its fiscal and economic problems. Things could not go on as before. What better way to demonstrate this than for Savage, recently mayor of Dartmouth, to sponsor legislation merging his former municipality with its arch-rival, Halifax, especially when one of the municipal critics of his Cape Breton merger legislation had claimed, "Fish will fly when this happens in metro Halifax" (quoted in Stewart 2000, 206). Savage no doubt genuinely believed that money would be saved, that economic development would be easier, and that his policy of "service exchange" would be facilitated by sharing the central city's tax base with the outlying areas (Vojnovic 1999). But amalgamation was either of dubious value in achieving such objectives, or the objectives could be accomplished in other ways. Amalgamation for Halifax was implemented primarily for its symbolic value. It was something dramatic that Savage could do without affecting most people in any direct way. Amalgamation was implemented not because there were societal pressures to do so but because there were no significant societal pressures on either side. It was the perfect opportunity for autonomous state action.

The Toronto case was quite different. It turned out that there were significant societal pressures against amalgamation in Toronto, though these were obviously grossly under-estimated by Mike Harris's government when it made its initial decision. John Duffy, a "Liberal strategist," has been quoted as saying that the decision to amalgamate Toronto was, for the Harris government, "the Mistake that Ate the Agenda" (Ibbitson 1997, 240). There are three contending state-centred explanations of why the Harris government acted as it did. The first appears on the surface to be linked with the globalization hypothesis. It was advanced by John Ibbitson in his book *Promised Land*. Ibbitson claims that when Harris went abroad to "sell Ontario," he found that no one knew anything about Ontario, but people did know about Toronto. In order for Toronto to compete with the major cities of the world, however, it needed to be "bigger, stronger, bolder ... And so the plan to amalgamate the cities of Metropolitan Toronto was born" (Ibbitson 1997, 242).

As a globalization explanation for amalgamation, this approach fails completely. There is simply no connection between the municipal organization of a metropolitan area and its rank in the hierarchy of global cities. For example, would anyone have considered that Los Angeles had lost a significant portion of its global role if the San Fernando Valley had seceded? As a relatively parochial and uninformed provincial politician, Premier Harris possibly believed that municipal size mattered for global competition. But this does not mean that he was right – or that the more sophisticated globalization hypothesis advanced by scholars such as Keil and Courchene is right.

Ibbitson's claim actually takes state-centred explanations of policymaking to new heights. The strongest version of this approach is that states sometimes adopt policies for which there is little or no societal support (Nordlinger 1981, 28–9). Ibbitson is actually claiming that the Government of Ontario (a North American region-state, as Courchene insists) adopted a policy for which there was little or no societal support, for which there turned out to be much active opposition, and which was based on the completely faulty premise that Toronto (as a global city, not as a municipality) could be made "bigger, stronger, and bolder" by enlarging its boundaries to take in neighbouring municipalities which, in any analysis by business consultants (let alone academics) of Toronto as a global city, would have been included as part of Toronto anyway.[7]

Perhaps the Ibbitson explanation is only partly true; perhaps it helps us understand Harris's frame of mind as he approached this issue, even if it was not itself the determining factor. In any event, there are two other more plausible – and not mutually exclusive – state-centred explanations of the Toronto amalgamation. The first is the better known. It is that the amalgamation was a deliberate effort by the Harris government to eliminate the power of the dominant left-wing majority on Toronto City Council by swamping the amalgamated city council with more conservative representatives of the suburbanites. The fact that Mel Lastman of North York defeated Barbara Hall of Toronto in the first mayoral election in the amalgamated city is the most dramatic evidence available of how the strategy was allegedly meant to work.

Did the downtown big-business community dream up this strategy and suggest it to top Harris operatives? We shall probably never know. What we do know is that their prime concern was with excessively high taxes on commercial property within the old City of Toronto. Since the mega-city was created, this problem is in the process of being fixed, partly by market-value assessment and partly by caps on commercial tax increases. The point, however, is that both these policies were implemented by the provincial government through different pieces of legislation that were entirely separate and apart from the amalgamation itself. Neither policy was in any way dependent on the amalgamation being in place. In any event, former mayor Mel Lastman became (publicly at least) a strident critic of the provincially imposed cap on commercial property tax increases. If he had been operating as the tool of downtown business interests, he disguised it well. Unlike many American central-city mayors who rely on local bankers for access to capital funding, Canadian mayors (especially in prosperous cities such as Toronto, in which there are provincially imposed limits on campaign contributions) have few reasons to take instructions from local business elites. On the other hand, they do have electoral reason to listen to homeowners whose taxes are going up largely because of commercial tax freezes.

As noted previously with respect to the Golden Task Force, business groups in Toronto had little interest in promoting amalgamation until after it became government policy. In fact, it is much more plausible to suggest that business supported the government's policy on amalgamation as a trade-off for getting tax relief by other means than it is to suggest that business supported amalgamation as an end in itself. Provincial governments in Canada (and the national government in the United Kingdom, as concerns England) have unlimited legal authority with respect to municipalities. Since the mid-1960s, any informal political conventions about the sanctity of established local governments have been almost completely eroded, a development that has not occurred in the United States. There appeared to be no constraints on what a determined Harris government could do to its municipal political enemies in the old City of Toronto.[8] In the absence of such constraints, the Harris government acted. It was precisely because the amalgamation policy was such an obvious attack on the established and articulate middle-class political interests within the old city that the reaction was so quick and effective (Horak 1998). But the Harris government realized that it would lose too much by backing down, and it pushed the measure through at considerable short-term political cost.

The other state-centred explanation relates more to the "state" (of Ontario) as a whole than to the political interests of its leaders. Both the Golden Task Force and Harris himself, when in opposition, were leaning towards eliminating the Metro level of government, not the lower-tier municipalities. Metro was to be replaced by some new form of authority for the entire Greater Toronto Area. This plan did have political costs for Harris, because it brought the "905" voters – his core support group – much closer to Toronto political issues than they ever wanted to be. But there were also severe practical, governmental difficulties that even the Golden Task Force did not fully work out. These difficulties related especially to the fate of some services (notably, the police) that could not be uploaded to the new GTA authority or to the province or be downloaded to the area municipalities. Furthermore, even leaving aside the preferences of "905" voters, there were real practical difficulties in determining how a GTA authority would actually work. Harris could dispense with these problems – and meet his electoral promise of abolishing Metro – by creating the mega-city. The fact that no one was actually advocating such a policy was irrelevant.

The Montreal amalgamation is in many ways more complicated, in part because the mayor of Montreal, Pierre Bourque, was a fervent advocate of it. He obviously played a significant role in affecting the final decision of Lucien Bouchard's provincial government, and in this sense the decision is arguably less state-centred, though advocates of such a position presumably have to claim that a mayor of a major city is not part of the state apparatus. One point is clear: Bourque himself was not responding to any societal forces (business or otherwise) that were urging Island-wide amalgamation – they did not exist. In many ways, Bourque's success in having his unlikely policy adopted can be seen as the most remarkable accomplishment ever of a Canadian mayor.

Before beginning the Montreal analysis, we must take account of a few contextual factors. First, like Toronto but unlike Halifax, there has never been (before 2001, at least) any official report sponsored by the Province of Quebec advocating the amalgamation of all the municipalities covered by the original metropolitan government (the CUM), despite the fact that dozens of such reports have examined municipal issues in the Montreal area. Second, unlike Toronto and Halifax, the merger in Montreal was implemented by a provincial law (Bill 170) that simultaneously merged municipalities elsewhere (Quebec City, Gatineau, and Longueuil). Third, unlike Toronto and Halifax, the merger in Montreal was directly linked to sensitive issues relating to constitutionally recognized linguistic minorities.[9]

In 1999, Mayor Pierre Bourque of Montreal was already working hard to accomplish his objective of amalgamating all the municipalities on Montreal Island into a new City of Montreal. The suburbs – francophone and anglophone alike – were resisting. The political dynamics were almost identical to what they had been when Mayor Drapeau of Montreal launched a similar campaign in the 1960s (Sancton 1985, 93–5). The main difference was that, at the level of the Quebec government and in the anglophone municipalities, there was a heightened sense of the linguistic implications. For the Quebec government, the concern was that an amalgamated City of Montreal would have only a razor-thin francophone majority and could conceivably be captured politically by declared non-sovereignists – even by partitionists, who could threaten to have Montreal separate from a newly independent Quebec.[10] For the anglophone suburbs, the concern was that under the provisions of Quebec's *Charter of the French Language*, their territories would lose their bilingual status if they were absorbed by a city whose majority was French-speaking. In the mid-1960s, sovereignty, partition, and language laws were not serious political issues. In the late 1990s they were.

But these were issues that could not be raised by mainstream politicians, francophone or anglophone, provincial or local. This is why they do not appear in any official reports, including the Bédard report on municipal fiscal issues (Quebec 1999), a report that favoured a drastic reduction of municipalities on Montreal Island, but not total amalgamation. The unspoken linguistic problem with any such proposal is that it involved, at a minimum, the merger of some francophone-majority municipalities on the West Island into a new and populous anglophone-majority municipality. In practical political terms, this simply was not possible.

The point, of course, is that total amalgamation seemed equally impossible. This was confirmed in June 1999 when both Premier Lucien Bouchard and Louise Harel, the minister of municipal affairs, explicitly rejected the plan espoused by Mayor Bourque. Premier Bouchard was quoted as saying, "One island, One city is not in the picture for us. But we know that we cannot leave the situation as it is" (author's translation). [11] A modest reorganization, such as one that would bring the municipalities of Westmount and Outremont into the City of Montreal, might have made sense to those who wanted to bolster the social and economic strength of the central city, but it would have been seen by many as an arbitrary and stopgap measure that could only be achieved at a huge political cost.

By September 1999, the option of complete amalgamation was back on the table. As with Premier Harris in Ontario when he had promised to do something about municipal structures in the Toronto area, the option of amalgamation re-emerged for Premier Bouchard after his own outer suburban MNAs rejected the option of a strong directly elected authority for the entire Montreal region. In April 2000, at the same time as it released its White Paper on municipal reform (Quebec 2000a), the government appointed chairs of advisory committees for municipal structures in Montreal, Quebec City, and the Outauoais area. For Montreal, the chair was Louis Bernard.

Bernard's report was made public on 11 October 2000. Although it called for the creation of a single City of Montreal covering the entire island, it also noted that it was important "to preserve the link between citizens and their immediate political environment, to reinforce the feeling of attachment to a way of life, and to encourage the development of social and cultural diversity" (author's translation). He also made reference to the need to "preserve the cultural and historical roots of diverse communities." Nevertheless, the report made no explicit reference to language (Quebec 2000b, 6–7). There was no evidence that Bernard consulted anyone other than municipal officials.

The report created a crucial political challenge for Montreal's larger suburban municipalities, especially the anglophone ones, because it went much further to accommodate suburban demands than anyone had predicted. Bernard proposed the creation of twenty-seven boroughs, each with a council that would have the authority to manage a significant range of local services and to levy a tax on property within the territory of the borough to pay for these services. Boroughs that were formerly autonomous suburbs could even maintain responsibility for negotiating collective agreements with their unions, a provision that enraged the existing unions within the City of Montreal Never in Canadian municipal history had a serious proposal for an amalgamation been accompanied by such a high degree of political and financial decentralization. Indeed, the most compelling criticism of the Bernard plan was that it effectively involved the creation of a three-tier system of local government for Montreal Island: the newly created Montreal Metropolitan Community covering the entire metropolitan area; the new City of Montreal covering the island; and the twenty-seven boroughs.

On 15 November 2000 the government announced the content of Bill 170. Boroughs were not given any authority to levy taxes or to enter into collective agreements. It appears that Premier Bouchard had decided he could not take on both union and suburban opposition at the same time (Milner and Joncas 2002). With some suburban municipalities objecting to the Bernard report just as strenuously as the unions in the City of Montreal, it is not surprising that Bouchard opted to gain at least some significant political support by satisfying the unions and limiting the autonomy of the boroughs. Nevertheless, even without any authority over taxation and collective agreements, the boroughs were given more legal authority over local services than similar bodies that were established after amalgamation in other Canadian cities, including Halifax and Toronto.

The language issue emerged in a much more public way at this same time. The government announced that boroughs formerly within anglophone municipalities would retain their bilingual status under the *Charter of the French Language*. This policy required in the West Island that the francophone municipalities be grouped together to form a single borough, even though their territories were not contiguous. Furthermore, the section of Bill 170 concerning Montreal opened with the declaration, "Montreal is a French-speaking city." Taken together, these provisions indicate how carefully the government had balanced the various linguistic imperatives it faced, both from within the Parti Québécois and from the anglophone minority.

The government's careful handling of the language issue shows that its imperatives were in fact more important than the amalgamation itself. In many respects the very existence of the boroughs is merely a mechanism to work around the language issues which the amalgamation created. But why did the Bouchard government choose the amalgamation option in the first place? One answer, as we have seen, is that the alternative of creating a new, stronger metropolitan authority was not acceptable to its own core supporters in the outer suburbs. Just as Harris amalgamated Toronto in order to be seen to be doing something to address an apparent crisis of governance in the province's largest city, so did Bouchard amalgamate Montreal. Bouchard had the added justification that he was merely following Ontario's example.

Unlike Harris in Ontario, Bouchard and his colleagues pointed to the benefits of equalizing taxes and services across the new city. These were powerful arguments for the more social democratic elements of the Parti Québécois. But if they were so intrinsically important, it is difficult to understand why they were rejected for so long by the government after Mayor Bourque first started advancing them. In any event, even if we assume that this was the government's real motivation, it is clearly a state-centred explanation. No one except Bourque was calling for an amalgamation of the entire CUM, not even the various groups, such as unions, that traditionally supported the Parti Québécois and would normally be expected to favour political action leading to increased equality. But there is one additional fact that must be kept clearly in mind: by the time Premier Bouchard had formally committed himself to amalgamation, he had already announced that he was leaving. There is perhaps no easier time for state-centred policymaking than in a parliamentary system after a popular first minister has announced his or her impending retirement.

While the Bouchard government was pushing Bill 170 through the National Assembly, a strong anti-merger movement appeared in affected areas of the province, especially on the western part of Montreal Island (Aubin 2004). Opposition leader Jean Charest promised that, if elected, he would establish a democratic mechanism for residents of merged municipalities to decide if they wanted their area to demerge. To the surprise of many, after the 2003 provincial election, Premier Charest kept his promise and introduced complex legislation (Bill 9) that provided for local decisions on demergers. On 20 June 2004, residents of fifteen former municipalities on Montreal Island voted in sufficient numbers to demerge (Whelan and Joncas 2005). Although many observers have pointed to the complexity and confusion surrounding the new arrangements that will come into force on 1 January 2006, there is little or no evidence that societal interest groups in Montreal are particularly concerned about the demerger process one way or another.

State-centred policy forcing municipal mergers in Quebec provoked societal opposition, which prompted an opposition party, later the government party, to provide for demergers, which in turn took place without much involvement by actors outside conventional municipal politics. If there had been strong societal interests favouring the mergers in the first place, surely we would have heard more from them during the demerger process.

CONCLUSION

This paper is not concerned with the political rationale for amalgamations; it is concerned with academic explanations. Just because we cannot know exactly how and why politicians behave in particular situations (Young 2003) does not give us the luxury of starting with some "broad force" such as globalization and deducing how it must have affected a particular policy decision. We must at least allow for the possibility that even the broadest and most powerful of such forces might, in certain situations, be of no relevance at all to a particular decision. This is precisely the point being made here about municipal amalgamations in Canada: there is very little about the broader politics of these amalgamations that was not present in amalgamation controversies in the United States during the nineteenth century. What is obviously different is the presence of the linguistic issue in Montreal and the relative importance of the three provincial premiers on the one hand and the relative unimportance of American state governors on the other.

In the American system, state governors could do nothing without cajoling a majority in each of two houses in the state legislature to support an amalgamation initiative. Incentives for such support were very small, especially when it was generally accepted that even if an amalgamation proposal were accepted by the state legislature, it would still have to be approved in some form of local referendum. In short, American state politicians advocating municipal amalgamations understood that they had to mobilize a great deal of societal support or else it would not happen. There is plenty of evidence of pluralist, or society-centred, policymaking in any of the nineteenth-century American cases. Exactly the same claim can be made about the politics of the recent San Fernando Valley secession attempt – and for the same reasons.

There are no sweeping conclusions to be drawn from this attempt to understand why municipal amalgamation policies have been pursued in Nova Scotia, Ontario, and Quebec over the last ten years. These policies were brought in with little or no thought by provincial premiers, who acted as they did in response to the particular political circumstances in which they found themselves. They made little or no effort to mobilize consent for these policies, beyond a small group of cabinet ministers, who in turn helped control obedient caucuses. The adoption of these policies demonstrates how easy it is – in some circumstances, at least – for those who control the apparatus of the provincial state to have their way. Such a demonstration raises two questions: Is it a good idea for provincial premiers to be able to do what they want without having to mobilize political support? Or is the municipal sector in some way unique or unusual, such that similar state policymaking autonomy would not be possible in other sectors?

NOTES

1 There is, of course, a huge literature on globalization. This definition derives from one of the more recent contributions; that of Newman and Thornley 2005, 13–15.
2 For details, see www.latimes.com/news/local/la-secede-sg.gallery.
3 The best-known popular account of these reforms is Osborne and Gaebler 1992. The book is full of municipal examples, but none of them involve municipal amalgamations.
4 Letter from the Board of Trade of Metropolitan Toronto to Anne Golden dated 18 May 1995, reproduced in the CD-ROM accompanying Ontario 1996.
5 In response to my request in June 2003, a copy of the brief was graciously provided to me by Francis Letendre, a research assistant for the Chambre de commerce.

6 As quoted in Kevin Cox, "Halifax-area Leaders Fuming over Plan for Supercity," *Globe and Mail*, 28 October 1994.

7 Savitch and Kantor (2002) treat the territory of the Municipality of Metropolitan Toronto as metropolitan Toronto's "centre city," even for the period prior to amalgamation.

8 This was confirmed in legal terms by the results of the court challenge. See Milroy 2002.

9 For Guy Bertrand's legal argument on this point, see www.guybertrand.com/pdf/memoire2.pdf. The argument was rejected by the courts. For other approaches that emphasize the importance of the language issue, see Boudreau 2003 and Serré 2003.

10 Lysiane Gagnon, "Why the Suburbs Resist Merging with Montreal," *Globe and Mail,* 12 June 1999. For details on the partitionist movement, see Stevenson 1999, 225–9.

11 As quoted in Kathleen Lévesque, "25 élus dirigeront la suprarégion de Montréal," *Le Devoir*, 15 June 1999.

REFERENCES

Aubin, H. 2004. *Who's Afraid of Demergers? The Straight Goods on Quebec Megacities.* Montreal: Véhicule Press

Benjamin, G., and R.P. Nathan. 2001. *Regionalism and Realism: A Study of Governments in the New York Metropolitan Area.* Washington, D.C.: Brookings Institution Press

Boudreau, J.A. 2003. "The Politics of Territorialization: Regionalism, Localism, and Other Isms ...The Case of Montreal." *Journal of Urban Affairs* 25 (2): 179–99

Courchene, T.J. 2001. "Ontario as a North American Region-State, Toronto as a Global City-Region: Responding to the NAFTA Challenge." In *Global City-Regions*, ed. A.J. Smith, 158–90. Oxford: Oxford University Press

Frug, G. 1999. *City Making: Building Communities without Building Walls,* Princeton N.J.: Princeton University Press

Haselhoff, K. DeF. 2002. "Motivations for the San Fernando Valley Secession Movement." *Journal of Urban Affairs* 24 (4): 425–43

Hogen-Esch, T. 2001."Urban Secession and the Politics of Growth: The Case of Los Angeles." *Urban Affairs Review* 6 (6):783–809

Horak, M. 1998. "The Power of Local Identity: C4LD and the Anti-Amalgamation Mobilization in Toronto." Research Paper 195. Toronto: Centre for Urban and Community Studies, University of Toronto

Ibbitson, J. 1997. *Promised Land: Inside the Mike Harris Revolution.* Toronto: Prentice-Hall

Keil, R. 2000. "Governance Restructuring in Los Angeles and Toronto: Amalgamation or Secession." *International Journal of Urban and Regional Research* 24 (4): 758–81

Local Agency Formation Commission for Los Angeles County (LAFCO). 2002. *Special Reorganization of the San Fernando Valley*: *Executive Officer's Report*, 24 April

Milner, H., and Joncas, P. 2002. "Montreal: Getting through the Megamerger." *Inroads* 11: 49–63

Milroy, B.M. 2002. "Toronto's Legal Challenge to Amalgamation." In *Urban Affairs: Back on the Agenda,* ed. Caroline Andrew, Katherine A. Graham, and Susan D. Phillips. Montreal & Kingston: McGill-Queen's University Press

Newman, P., and Thornley A. 2005. *Planning World Cities: Globalization and Urban Politics*. Basingstoke, England: Palgrave Macmillan

Nordlinger, E.A. 1981. *On the Autonomy of the Democratic State*. Cambridge, Mass.: Harvard University Press

Nova Scotia. Task Force on Local Government. 1992. *Report to the Government of Nova Scotia*. Halifax, April

Ontario. Task Force on the Future of the Greater Toronto Area. 1996. *Greater Toronto: Report of the GTA Task Force*. Toronto: Queen's Printer

Osborne, D., and Gaebler, T. 1992. *Reinventing Government: How the Enrepreneurial Spirit Is Transforming the Public Sector*. Reading, Mass.: Addison-Wesley

Quebec. La Commission nationale sur les finances et la fiscalité locales. 1999. *Pacte 2000*. Quebec: Publications du Québec

– Municipal Affairs and Greater Montreal. 2000a. *Municipal Reorganization: Changing the Ways to Better Serve the Public*. Quebec: Gouvernement du Québec

– 2000b. *Regroupements municipaux dans la région métropolitaine de Montréal: recommendations du mandataire*. www.mamm.gouv.qc.ca/accueil/livre_blanc_2000/documents/montreal/rap_mand_ber.pdf

Sancton, A. 1985. *Governing the Island of Montreal: Language Differences and Metropolitan Politics*. Berkeley: University of California Press

– 1994. *Governing Canada's City Regions*. Montreal: Institute for Research on Public Policy

– 1996. "Reducing Costs by Consolidating Municipalities: New Brunswick, Nova Scotia, and Ontario." *Canadian Public Administration* 39 (3): 267-89

– 2000. *Merger Mania: The Assault on Local Government*. Montreal & Kingston: McGill-Queen's University Press

Sancton, A., James, R., and Ramsay, R. 2000. *Amalgamation vs. Inter-Municipal Cooperation*: *Financing Local and Infrastructure Services*. Toronto: ICURR Press

Savitch, H.V., and Kantor, P. 2002. *Cities in the International Marketplace: The Political Economy of Urban Development in North America and Western Europe*. Princeton: Princeton University Press

Scott, A.J., ed. 2001. *Global City-Regions: Trends, Theory, Policy*. Oxford: Oxford University Press

Serré, P. 2003. "La reconfiguration de l'echiquier politique au Québec: l'impact de fusions municipales de 2001." *Policy Options* 24 (4): 51–6

Stevenson, G. 1999. *Community Besieged: The Anglophone Minority and the Politics of Quebec*. Montreal & Kingston: McGill-Queen's University Press

Stewart, I. 2000. "The Dangers of Municipal Reform in Nova Scotia." In *The Savage Years: The Perils of Reinventing Government in Nova Scotia*, ed. Peter Clancy et al. Halifax: Formac

Todd, G. 1998. "Megacity: Globalization and Governance in Toronto." *Studies in Political Economy* 56 (Summer): 193–216

Vojnovic, I. 1999. "The Fiscal Distribution of the Provincial-Municipal Service Exchange in Nova Scotia." *Canadian Public Administration* 42 (4): 512–541

Whelan, R., and Joncas, P. 2005. "Montreal Demergers: An Update." *Inroads* 16 (Winter-Spring): 94–9

Young, R.A. 2003. "The Politics of Paying for Cities." In *Paying for Cities: The Search for Sustainable Revenues*, ed. Paul Boothe. Edmonton: Institute of Public Economics, University of Alberta

6

Revisiting Municipal Reforms in Quebec and the New Responsibilities of Local Actors in a Globalizing World

Pierre Hamel and Jean Rousseau

Ce chapitre permet d'examiner les incidences des récentes réformes municipales au Québec. Bien que cette restructuration des politiques locales et municipales soit reliée au dernier courant de réformes, la conjoncture économique et politique est différente. Dans le contexte actuel, la décentralisation, la mondialisation et la redéfinition des responsabilités politiques des municipalités font dorénavant partie du programme politique. Le gouvernement du Québec légitime ses nouveaux projets de réforme en se référant à une structure de « gouvernance ». Cette structure serait celle qui relèverait le plus adéquatement les nouveaux défis urbains et métropolitains. Le Québec n'a toutefois pas mis en œuvre cette approche. Il a plutôt adopté l'approche technocratique, qui se préoccupait davantage des structures institutionnelles et est la continuité des courants de réformes municipales qui ont suivi la Révolution tranquille. Cette stratégie s'est avérée inadéquate et désuète, plus particulièrement pour ce qui est de la région de Montréal, parce qu'elle n'a pas tenu compte de l'apprentissage inhérent à tout projet de réforme majeur. Le gouvernement du Québec aurait dû être au courant de l'importance stratégique de mobiliser un système pour soutenir ses projets. Cette ligne de conduite aurait pu instaurer une gouvernance plus coopérative ce qui aurait été plus approprié dans la conjoncture actuelle.

Over the last fifteen years, Canada's city-regions, like other city-regions in the world, have been facing several changes that can be associated with globalization. This brought to the fore a series of questions about the role of territory or space, the availability of resources for municipalities to cope with new responsibilities, the capacity of local power to adapt to external pressures, and the forms of cooperation that municipalities should establish on a metropolitan scale with economic actors, other local institutions, and upper tiers of government. These issues have been explored at length in the recent literature on urban governance and new forms of regionalism (Frisken and Norris 2001; Swanstrom 2001).

Surprisingly, in Quebec such questions have not been at the top of the research agenda for social scientists. This does not mean that local political actors and the Quebec government were inactive in this field. It has in fact been the other way round. Until now, politicians, technocratic civil servants, and a small network of experts have led the debate about the restructuring of local and municipal politics.

Our intent here is not so much to explain why social scientists have paid so little attention to the restructuring of local power in Quebec. Rather, we want to highlight some of the shortcomings of the recent municipal and metropolitan reform that took place at the turn of the new millennium by referring to contextual changes. However, although these changes help us understand why the institutional and governance framework has to be adapted to the new urban reality, this does not explain the political choices that were made by the Quebec government in its aim to modernize the municipal and metropolitan systems. That requires paying attention to the normative and political dimensions of those governmental choices – that is, looking at values, political opportunities, and institutional constraints. This represents the particular angle that shapes our discussion of these reforms.

In this paper, we shall discuss some of the limits deriving from the political choices that were made by the Quebec government with regard to municipal reforms. In doing so, we shall bring out an ambiguity inherent in the government strategy, which was particularly evident with the approach adopted by the Quebec government for the metropolitan region of Montreal. While trying to implement a new model of reforms based on what we call a governance framework, the government continued to use a technocratic model, involving a top-down perspective, which has been framing the various reform projects since the 1960s. The governance framework is based on the mobilization of municipalities and local actors with interests in metropolitan development, and the establishment of forms of decision making in which the government appears to be one important actor but is no longer the only one. This framework has come to be seen as the most relevant for dealing with challenges imposed by globalization,[1] especially for increasing the competitiveness of the city-regions. In this perspective, the emphasis is on the development of flexible and variable strategies of development that can cope with economic restructuring and the creation of new sectors of world-led economic activities. A key issue with governance is the process itself by which actors are mobilized and participate in decision making; the setting up of an institutional structure with a clearly delimited sphere of intervention is no longer the main issue. But even though the challenges imposed by globalization have been raised in some reports and studies – and by the government itself from the 1980s onwards – the Quebec government chose nonetheless to reproduce its technocratic model.

The emergence of governance reveals a deeper transformation of Quebec politics that is still going on. It is linked to an attempt to redefine the role of the government within a new political context that is characterized by a decrease of the state's legitimacy and a questioning of its level of institutional capability. This new political context indicates a significant transformation of the framework structuring the public realm with regard to state intervention and citizen participation. We shall argue in this paper that the Quebec government did not take into account this new political setting when launching the recent wave of municipal reforms. Given its contested legitimacy and its limited resources, the Quebec government should have planned this process of reform better, especially by adequately explaining the rationale of the project and by creating a large regional consensus among the various local actors that would have helped legitimate the project. The learning dimension of municipal and metropolitan reforms was largely ignored. Although, in some respects, the Quebec government came to invoke the governance approach for justifying its decision, its intervention turned out to be a move against such an approach, for the government finally chose to put into practice an outdated model of reform that paid attention primarily to institutional structures.

Our paper is divided into three parts. First, we will recall the historical context of Quebec municipal reforms since the Quiet Revolution. In many ways, the recent wave of municipal reforms is a continuation of the previous ones. Second, we will present an overview of the recent wave of municipal reforms. We will look more closely at the political and institutional changes that have been implemented in Montreal and will highlight the predominance of the technocratic approach. Finally, we will analyse these reforms, discussing some of their limitations. We will refer to the recent debates in the literature concerning urban restructuring and governance in the context of globalization. Some issues explaining the limitations of the recent municipal and metropolitan reforms will also be discussed.

THE HISTORICAL CONTEXT OF QUEBEC MUNICIPAL REFORMS (1960 TO MID-1990s)

The Quiet Revolution put the issue of reforming municipal structures at the front of the governmental agenda. The election of the Liberal Party in 1960 under the leadership of Jean Lesage marked the end of the long Duplessis era which, according to the leaders of the Quiet Revolution, had been a period of great backwardness – *une grande noirceur*. This election was recognized as the beginning of a new period in Quebec history. In this context, the modernization of municipal politics was seen as a prerequisite that would clearly reflect this historical step. From the 1960s to the 1990s, several parliamentary commissions, study groups, reports, projects, and bills sought to transform and rejuvenate municipal institutions in conformity with the diagnostic that had been posed during the first years of the Quiet Revolution. However, none of them brought efficient and definitive answers. Thus, despite the intention to transform the municipal system, the project of thoroughly reforming the political values and structures of municipalities has remained on the political agenda.

IN THE AFTERMATH OF THE QUIET REVOLUTION

The 1960 electoral defeat of the Union Nationale government marked the end of the "Duplessism" that had permeated Quebec politics during the previous two decades. During those years, the predominant political discourse on Quebec society had been centred on the protection of its rural, Catholic, French-speaking, and conservative dimensions (Meynaud and Léveillée 1973; Bissonnette 1982; Bourque and Duchastel 1996). Premier Maurice Duplessis's ideology had been based on the promotion of rural values. This representation of Quebec society had helped give rural municipalities a symbolic and political importance. At the same time, it served to mask the increasing gap between the Quebec polity and the socio-economic reality of Quebec society (Simard 1979; Dickinson and Young 1995). In contrast to the Duplessis discourse, Quebec society was already urbanized and industrialized at the turn of the twentieth century. The political weight given to rural municipalities and county councils by the Duplessis government was misleading.[2]

The election of Jean Lesage opened the door to a major restructuring of the Quebec political system in a very short time. First, the predominant political discourse came to emphasize the urban and industrial character of Quebec society and stressed Quebec's backwardness compared with other countries and other provinces, especially Ontario. From the beginning, the liberal government insisted that Quebec society needed to be modernized and that the best way to achieve this was through a reform of public institutions.

Second, the discourse on Quebec's need to catch up with its neighbours revealed a significant change in social relations. Three different groups that had become allied through their opposition to the Duplessis regime carried it out: the labour unions, the French-speaking petite bourgeoisie, and a group of Liberal intellectuals. They called into question the role of the old elites (clergy, rural leaders) and the representations of Quebec society associated with them. The election of the Liberal Party provided them with the opportunity to be empowered.

The third type of change introduced by the Quiet Revolution was the broadening of the field of state intervention. The Quebec government became recognized as the key actor that would enable the province to catch up with other modern societies. This brought a major restructuring of the field of state intervention ranging from the complete replacement of the clergy in the education, social services, and health sectors to the establishment of new state agencies for promoting Quebec's economic development. This restructuring was based on a technocratic approach in which the Quebec government was presented as the key player in leading the reforms. With its strong legitimacy and significant resources, the government succeeded in implementing these reforms and mobilizing large sectors of the population. The province's public sector built up an expertise that has helped reinforce its central role in Quebec politics. The changes opened the door to the establishment of a new framework delimiting the boundaries of the Quebec public realm and specifying its forms of intervention and participation. This technocratic model of public action became predominant in the debate about regional development and municipal reforms.

THE INTERVENTIONS AT THE MUNICIPAL LEVEL

The municipal system was not left out of this process of restructuring. The need to reform municipal structures was a major issue, since municipalities were perceived as outdated and inefficient (Meynaud and Léveillée 1973; Bissonnette 1982; Hamel 2001). The political and legal association between the municipality and the parish was called into question in connection with the requirements of an urban and industrial society. Moreover, the close links that had existed between the rural elite and the Duplessis government caused the municipalities to be suspect; they were easily seen as being opposed to the new and modern rationality advocated by the Liberal government.

This perception was reinforced by the increasing discussion about the specific problems faced by municipalities, notably the fiscal difficulties, especially in the case of rural municipalities. While having to face new demands for financing schooling and health services, the rural municipalities were confronted with a demographic decline and then with a diminution of their sources of revenue. Their lack of resources was also noticeable with respect to the funds required to support the establishment of industrial firms. In this context, the municipalities were increasingly dependent on governmental transfers and grants (Hamel and Jalbert 1991, 176–80).

Pierre Laporte, minister of municipal affairs under the Lesage government, became a strong advocate of municipal reforms (Meynaud and Léveillée 1973; Bissonnette 1982). In 1963–64 he established three commissions of inquiry: the Bélanger Commission on municipal fiscal issues, the La Haye Commission in charge of examining the urban question, and the Blier and Sylvestre Commission on the intermunicipal problems in the Montreal region. As minister, Laporte undertook a provincial tour, during which he discussed with municipal representatives the project of municipal amalgamation. He insisted that municipalities had to be merged in order to reduce their number, and he emphasized the importance of intermunicipal cooperation. Amalgamation, he argued, would overcome rural isolationism and the fragmentation of Quebec territory into small units that could no longer cope with the requirements of a modern society. It would allow better and more diversified services to be provided to citizens. It would help municipalities attract businesses more easily and adopt rules on urban planning. And it would re-establish a better equilibrium between rural and urban municipalities while allowing for an improved and more rational management of Quebec territory.

THE BEGINNING OF A LONG PROCESS OF REFORMS

Over the three following decades, various bills, reports from study groups, parliamentary commissions, and proposals from organizations representing municipalities were released and debated. Of course, these discussions did not follow a direct trajectory. From the 1960s to the mid-1970s, the discussions about municipal reforms were framed by the tenets of the discourse on regional development diffused by the leaders of the Quiet Revolution (Bissonnette 1982; Divay and Léveillée 1981). They were part of the whole project of imposing a centralized management of Quebec territory in response to the imperatives of a modern, urban, and industrial society. All this followed the top-down approach, in which the municipal representatives were seen as potential obstacles whose attributes needed to be transformed. Following the economic difficulties faced by the Quebec government in the 1970s, the discussions began to be less ambitious and were no longer thought of as a great leap. The idea of planning at all political levels was gradually dropped and was replaced by a pragmatic management of the existing municipal actors and structures.

During the 1960s and 1970s some significant reforms had been introduced. In 1965 the Liberal government adopted Bill 13 on the voluntary merger of municipalities. However, the adoption of this bill did not result in a great movement towards amalgamation. Since the municipal representatives were recognized as the initiators and did not have any incentives or constraints, the amalgamation of municipalities occurred very slowly. Then, in 1966, Pierre Laporte tried to replace the existing county councils with modern regional organizations that would simultaneously represent urban and rural municipalities; but this proposal was set aside with the electoral defeat of the Liberal Party, and three years passed before these reforms were introduced.[3]

One important reform was the creation in 1969 of three supramunicipal communities: the Communauté urbaine de Montréal (CUM), the Communauté urbaine de Québec (CUQ), and the Communauté urbaine de l'Outaouais (CUO). These new structures were supposed to provide more efficient and, in some cases, new services to the population, reinforcing the autonomy of municipalities (Meynaud and Léveillée 1973).

The reform momentum was modified somewhat with the election of the Liberal Party under the leadership of Robert Bourassa in 1970.[4] Despite the persistence of a technocratic bias, new elements were introduced. The economic role of Montreal in relation to developmental issues for the whole province was increasingly discussed. The government referred to the notion of "profitable federalism," opening the door to a greater collaboration with the federal government.[5]

A more decisive shift in government strategy occurred when the Parti Québécois government adopted Bill 125 in 1979. The intention was to implement a comprehensive framework for the planning and management of Quebec territory, and also to redefine territorial management through the creation of regional county municipalities (RCMs). Even though these institutional structures implied a centralized control over the activities of municipalities, René Lévesque's government justified this reform by discoursing on the decentralization of responsibilities and the democratization of regional politics. Nonetheless, some of the objectives discussed during the Quiet Revolution finally came to be achieved. The creation of ninety-four RCMs covering Quebec territory (excluding the territory covered by the three supramunicipal communities created in 1969) led to the demise of the county councils and established a new institutional structure for managing the municipal system.

THE TRANSFORMATION OF THE SOCIO-POLITICAL CONTEXT OF
MUNICIPAL REFORMS

The preliminary discussions around Bill 125 revealed a change in governmental approach.[6] They showed the government's intention to integrate local and regional decision makers further into the process of reform. This came to be seen as a prerequisite to a successful implementation of government intervention. In the meantime, significant changes had occurred in regional and local politics. Resistance at the local and regional levels helped to democratize these political spaces, which could no longer simply be seen as the persistence of rural conservatism. Other representations of these spaces, highlighting their cultural and social dimensions, became discussed in the debates. Of course, the political and institutional changes introduced by the Quebec government, such as the RCMs and the bills regarding territorial development and the protection of agricultural lands, transformed the local and regional institutions and structures.

However, the change in the government's position did not mean that local and regional representatives became the main instigators in the development of policies on regional development and urban affairs. Although some changes were noticeable in the government's discourse, the implementation of the reform turned out to be a continuation of the predominant model of public intervention associated with the Quiet Revolution. The setting up of RCMs was instigated by the Quebec government. The RCMs' weak management capacity and the lack of sustained effort to increase their legitimacy reflected the government's desire to avoid greatly altering the power relations between the central government and the regional and local levels. Since then, the centralizing and top-down approach has remained predominant within the Department of Municipal Affairs.

THE RECENT WAVE OF MUNICIPAL REFORMS IN QUEBEC (MID-1990s)

A NEW CONTEXT FOR MUNICIPAL POLITICS

From the mid-1990s on, the Quebec government again began to discuss launching a process of municipal reform. However, since the adoption of Bill 125 in 1979, the political situation has changed significantly. The current political and economic context is different from that of the Quiet Revolution (except for the constitutional disputes about jurisdictions between the Quebec government and the federal government). The government no longer presents itself as the driving force orienting society towards the achievement of collective goals. The discourse on planning has been replaced by one emphasizing the establishment of partnerships with the private sector and the need to provide efficient, cheap, and competitive services to citizens, who are regarded as well-informed clients. The socio-economic summits organized by Lucien Bouchard's government in 1996 – which were attended by representatives of the business sector, labour unions, youth organizations, and the women's movement, among others – reflected a representation of the state as the creator of synergy and as a facilitator. This perspective also shapes the policy adopted by the Quebec government on regional development, in which the government is primarily defined as a supporter of regional initiatives (Quebec 1997).

In this context, the discourse on decentralization took on further importance. While allowing the state to revise its mission, the discourse on the decentralization of services opened the door to a restructuring of services along the lines of efficiency and proximity. This was the case with the 1992 reform of the health sector, which involved transferring some health services to new regional health boards (Michaud 2000). It should be mentioned that the discourse on decentralization has been shaped by neoliberal tenets on privatization and deregulation. More recently, the discussion on decentralization has included new elements – the establishment of new models of governance that include the government, the private sector, and "civil society" (community groups and non-profit-making organizations). This discourse on governance refers to the limited resources of the state, which needs to find new forms of financing. It emphasizes the need to set up decentralized decision-making processes and to mobilize various actors to implement policies and reforms.

The other important element of this new context is globalization, which has come to be discussed as the new political horizon, both for the Quebec government and for the municipalities. These discussions refer mainly to the economic aspects of globalization. Indeed, globalization is most often synonymous with a global market imposing constraints on national and local actors, thereby revealing the predominance of a neoliberal and corporatist discourse (Boyer and Drache 1996). The strengthening of the global competitiveness of national economies has been presented as the most appropriate avenue for facing the challenges raised by globalization. The signing of the Free Trade Agreement and the North American Free Trade Agreement, both of which were supported by the main political parties in Quebec, has helped to justify this economic reading of globalization.

One of the consequences of these discussions on the role of the state and globalization has been a new perspective on the role of local actors, especially metropolitan regions. This has involved repositioning them, so that instead of being seen as a subordinate and dependent tier of national government, they are seen as strategic actors that should develop new spheres of intervention that will allow them to compete in the global marketplace. This presupposes the adoption of a more flexible regulatory framework and the elaboration of strategies that would allow them to deal with national governments and external economic forces, such as multinational corporations. This brought up the question of Montreal, which requires a different perspective. Its economic vitality and its ability to establish economic and political relations in the international arena, notably for developing its own niche, became important political issues for the Quebec government.

Since the 1990s, the discussions about changing the governance of the municipal system in order to overcome what the government called the status quo began to be more and more intense. Paving the way for the municipal reform were various factors: the debates about the adoption of a policy on rurality, indicating the necessity of rethinking urban planning and the occupancy of rural territory; the 1996 Politique de consolidation des communautés locales, which aimed to facilitate municipal amalgamation; the adoption in 1997 of Bill 92 on the Commission for the Development of the Metropolis (CDM), which pointed out the need to address the problems of Montreal as a city-region;[7] and the debates on fiscal equity and the management capacity of municipal institutions.

It is important to mention that the creation of the CDM was an important shift in the government's discourse. The debates on the setting up of this commission revealed the increasing influence of a governance approach. Indeed, in 1996, when the provincial government announced its intention to promote the Montreal metropolitan region, it stressed the importance of setting up adequate processes of consultation and participation. The involvement and cooperation of local actors were presented as a key element. This orientation framed to a large extent the unsuccessful attempt made by the provincial government to implement the CDM. It was to have been presided over by the minister of municipal affairs and the metropolis, and elected officials were supposed to rub shoulders with representatives of socio-economic groups and para-public institutions. However, the emphasis on processes was overtaken two years later by an approach focusing on institutional structures.

The failure of this strategy resulted from the difficulty of bringing together the interests of people living in the central city with those in the outer suburbs on the North and South Shores. The suburbanites held that they did not need the central city in order to survive and, more importantly, they did not want to pay for the central city's mismanagement of public services. The challenge of the metropolitan reform in 1996 was to convince the citizens from the outer suburbs that it was not fair to let only the citizens from the central city pay for regional functions that benefited the whole metropolitan community. However, this challenge turned out too problematic to be undertaken.

THE WHITE PAPER ON THE RESTRUCTURING OF MUNICIPAL GOVERNANCE

The publication in 2000 of the White Paper by the minister of municipal affairs and the metropolis marked the beginning of the implementation of a new wave of municipal reforms. It reveals the influence of the traditional perspective, in which the creation or transformation of institutional structures was a major concern. In this way, this new wave of reforms was a continuation of the previous ones that had been based on a technocratic approach.

The portrait of the municipal situation in the White Paper appeared very complex.[8] The justification for the reform was linked to the resolution of many issues. First of all, as in the 1960s, the problem of municipal fragmentation as a result of having too many municipalities was pointed out. In addition, it was noted that the small size of the municipalities imposed severe limits on their capacity to address issues that go beyond their territorial limits and to assume new responsibilities. The large number of municipalities (more than thirteen hundred) raised important problems: the lack of a global vision on municipal politics; unproductive and unequal competition among them; a multiplication of structures, causing additional costs; and fiscal disparities between municipalities. The existing forms of intermunicipal collaboration, it turns out, were too limited with regard to these problems. The existing system of government grants had not created incentives to adopt these forms of cooperation or to implement amalgamations.

In addition, urban agglomerations were confronted with the problem of urban sprawl and with the lack of strong socio-economic dynamism that would increase their competitiveness at the national and global levels. A section of the White Paper was dedicated to the specific situation of the three urban communities (Montreal, Quebec City, and Hull-Gatineau). Despite their achievement in many ways, their structures should be redefined to increase their competitiveness and their management capacity while achieving economies of scale. In the governmental perspective, increasing the management capacity of the supramunicipal tier should do this. The White Paper also discussed the implementation of the government policy on rurality. The objective would be to reinforce the decision-making capacity of the rural communities, which might imply amalgamating municipalities or strengthening the role of the RCMs.

The implementation of the municipal reform proposed in the White Paper rested on two complementary strategies.[9] The first was the forced merger of local municipalities, which the government went on to apply in the urban agglomerations of Montreal, Quebec City, and Hull-Gatineau. The second strategy was the creation of metropolitan tiers of governance, with the object of making urban agglomerations more competitive.

THE IMPLEMENTATION OF THE REFORM: THE EXAMPLE OF MONTREAL

In the Quebec government's discourse on the rationale for reform in the metropolitan region, the government referred to the arguments raised in the White Paper. In order to justify the new reform, the minister of municipal affairs and the metropolis referred to the need to build a more competitive city-region. To achieve this objective, the main tool appeared to be the reduction of municipal fragmentation through the amalgamation of municipalities. Two other dimensions also were present in the government discourse. One was planning and coordinating municipal activity on a regional scale. The other was reducing the gap, in terms of fiscal efforts, between municipalities. Fiscal disparities were a major concern in financing the infrastructure and services needed to develop the city-region, because the central city fiscal situation was a matter of serious concern.

The Quebec government used the former technocratic approach to implement this reform and imposed it by passing a law, despite the protestations and the opposition of many local mayors; the government did not attempt to build up a consensus on a metropolitan scale. This turnaround – the idea of imposing its view instead of convincing the population – was not explained by the provincial government, apart from its mentioning that there had to be a limit to the obstructionism of the local mayors.

With Montreal, the government followed a two-step strategy. The first step was the amalgamation of the municipalities on Montreal Island – the same strategy it employed with other urban agglomerations, such as Longueuil and Quebec City. Under Bill 170, it created a mega-city of 1.8 million inhabitants that came into existence on 1 January 2002. The government also established an updated territorial-management structure through the creation of twenty-seven boroughs. These boroughs respected the former borders of the main urban neighbourhoods of Montreal and also those of the former suburbs. The new boroughs are responsible for delivering such services as urban planning, fire prevention, waste removal, social and economic development, culture and recreational activities, borough parks, local roadwork, and enforcing the ban on converting buildings into condominiums. In fact, the boroughs have only two exclusive competencies – fire prevention and infringements regarding the conversion of buildings. As for their other responsibilities, these are shared with the administration of the City of Montreal. The boroughs have no power of taxation. Their budget comes from the city council's grants. Consequently, the boroughs are administrative and consultative structures rather than deci-sion-making centres. In other words, the municipal reform tends to reinforce the institutional basis of the City of Montreal while broadening its spheres of competency. Its new functions are supposed to allow Montreal to answer the challenges it faces in the contemporary context.

The second step of the municipal reform was the creation under Bill 134, of the Montreal Metropolitan Community (MMC), which covers the territory of the census metropolitan region defined by Statistics Canada and includes more than 3.4 million inhabitants. By creating the MMC, the government wanted to establish a strategic authority with specific competencies: area plan-ning, protection of the environment, economic development, international promotion, and management of metropolitan activities.[10] The MMC is com-posed of representatives chosen from the elected officials of the sixty-four municipalities within the five administrative regions that constitute the met-ropolitan region. The government gave the MMC the mandate of developing a metropolitan plan for area planning and development. The goal of this plan is to set up "a strategic vision of economic, social, and environmental develop-ment aiming at facilitating a coherent exercise of the Community's powers" (Quebec 2000, art. 127, par 1; our translation). The MMC's mandate also includes the supervision of agencies with a metropolitan vocation (the Met-ropolitan Transport Agency, the Agricultural Consultative Agency, and Montreal International) and the supervision of special commissions. In May 2001 five commissions were established in the following areas: transport, land-use planning, economic planning and metropolitan facilities, environment, and social housing.

Despite its metropolitan vocation in planning and management, the MMC does not constitute a regional government as such. Until now, it has had few powers and resources to convince the municipalities and economic actors to develop and share a common vision of metropolitan interests. Its capacity to design a real development strategy for the metropolitan region seems rather limited. In that context, it can hardly be assumed that a common vision and a substantial intervention strategy would arise from the MMC's activities. It does not have the political or administrative powers that would allow it to establish some form of governance on a regional scale, in spite of the government discourse.

THE RECENT MUNICIPAL REFORMS IN THE CONTEXT OF LOCAL AND GLOBAL RESTRUCTURING: SOME THEORETICAL REMARKS

The imposed metropolitan solution in 2002, based on the merging of munici-palities on Montreal Island and the South Shore, coupled with a supramunicipal tier of coordination and planning on a regional scale – the Montreal Metro-politan Community – revealed the prevalence of the old technocratic model. By acting in a directive manner on Montreal Island and the South Shore while at the same time counting on the cooperation of the municipalities and other regional actors to achieve metropolitan governance, the Quebec government was sending contradicting messages to the local actors and municipalities.

Whereas the preceding sections examined the main municipal reforms since the Quiet Revolution, this section will analyse recent reforms. The strategy adopted by the government appears to be deficient, whether we look at the objectives of the reform or the manner of its implementation. The difficulties faced by the government can be explained from two complementary angles. At first, it based its reform on an inadequate understanding of the new reality of the city-regions. Recent socio-economic changes have given rise to a new framework for political action that calls into question the technocratic model. In addition, the Quebec government made some huge mistakes in planning its process. One of them was the lack of attention given to the learning compo-nent of the reform. In discussing this dimension, we shall attempt to provide some explanations of why the reforms failed, taking into account the contem-porary urban context.

SOME REFLECTIONS ABOUT THE NEW METROPOLITAN CHALLENGES

In 2001, 80 percent of Canada's population was living in urban centres, an increase of 5.2 percent compared with 1996 (Liberal Party 2002, 1). Since 1941, the urban population has grown steadily. This increase is concentrated mainly in four extensive urban regions, including Montreal. After the Second World War, like other metropolitan regions in the Western world, Montreal underwent economic processes of restructuring that were closely linked to changes in urban forms. These transformations took place on a metropolitan scale and involved a new experience of mobility and centrality for residents (Ascher 1998). At the outset, the political and administrative consequences of these changes were difficult to grasp. Since the 1960s, they have been put back on the policy agenda (Andrew, Graham, and Philips 2002).

Over the last thirty years, metropolitan regions have experienced a series of transformations that have fundamentally affected city life, city forms, and the overall urban structures (Soja 2000; Bassand 2001; Dear 2002). The increasing segmentation of the labour market, coupled with the prevalence of the service-sector economy, has brought about a restructuring of the urban economy (Corade and Lacour 1995). One important consequence of this restructuring has been the relocation of social and economic activities, resulting in a redefinition of the hierarchy within and among cities. The new urban hierarchy has often been explained by referring to economic globalization (Kratke 1992). The impact of economic globalization on cities is noticeable in the new waves of immigration, among other things. It is also visible in several social and cultural changes that can be analysed in terms of the opportunities or constraints experiences by the inhabitants (Bauman 1998).

Such a perspective is in tune with the move to bring cities or other places back into our analyses of economic globalization. Several reasons are given by Saskia Sassen to explain the importance of including cities in our understanding of global processes, beginning with the fact that it "allows us to see the multiplicity of economies and work cultures in which the global information is embedded" (Sassen 1999, 141). The impact of globalization on localities varies depending on the leeway available to them as a result of market conditions and public resources. Thus, cities "behave strategically" in diverse ways, according to their capacity to mobilize local resources or to count on government support (Savitch and Kantor 2003).

The issue of regulating the new urban reality can be connected to a growing tension arising from the breakup of its main components and on the need to provide coherence for public action (Le Galès 1998). This tension raises several questions. Under what conditions can the central city or the city-region become a collective actor (Bourdin 2000) able to deal with superior tiers of government and external economic forces? Consequently, what are the dominant interests of the central city compared with those of the city-region? To start with, can the central city and the city-region share the same collective project, with all its economic, social, cultural, environmental, and urban components, as Dreier, Mollenkopf, and Swanstrom (2001) suggest?

These questions are particularly important in the new metropolitan context. The need to revise the old planning institutions and the local political system in order to take into account the expansion of the metropolis's territorial boundaries goes hand in hand with a repositioning of local actors. Here it is interesting to notice, following Christian Lefèvre (1998), how recent metropolitan governance reforms in most Western countries have been conducted with the cooperation of local actors, unlike the top-down approach of previous attempts. This strategy is linked to the "disappearance of central government as the holder of supreme legitimacy and capable, by itself, of imposing, or at least shaping, a particular idea of public action" (Lefèvre 1998, 18). In this regard, the institution is not created in advance or in a "ready to use" form. Its appearance is the result of a constitutive process. From then on, "metropolitan governance does not consider the institution to be pre-established – on the contrary. The objective to be achieved is not fixed in advanced, but becomes the product of the system of actors as the process unfolds" (Lefèvre 1998, 18). In other words, the top-down approach has been replaced by a collaborative approach with local actors.

HOW TO EXPLAIN THE RESISTANCES TO THE REFORM? THE IMPORTANCE OF
THE LEARNING PROCESS

Two questions should be raised regarding the strategies which the Quebec government chose to adopt. First, why did the Quebec government see in amalgamation a solution to Montreal's problems, describing them in relation to a series of economic, spatial, social, and environmental processes, whereas their causes and consequences seem often to have been intertwined and can be connected to the weak economic performance of the city-region compared with the urban regions of other North American metropolises? Second, if it seems so important to organize planning on the scale of a city-region to make Montreal more competitive in this globalizing world, why did the government decide to build such a weak example of coordination and planning as the MMC?

For the time being, we do not have satisfactory answers to give. Nonetheless, it is necessary to recognize that, to a large extent, the diagnosis upon which the government based its reform may be considered adequate. What is problematic remains on the normative side – namely, how the forced amalgamation was privileged over other courses of action, such as a consensus-building solution on a metropolitan scale, in order to elaborate a pragmatic approach in reference to governance. We know that such an approach was attempted in the mid-1990s, but it was inadequate.

When it comes to municipal and metropolitan regionalism, one of the main issues remains the fragmented nature of local government. How is it possible to make planning work and to combine diversified, if not opposite, interests through steering institutions such as metropolitan coalitions or a metropolitan tier of government? Is it sufficient for a metropolitan entity or a specialized unit of planning to implement regulation and coordination for the whole region? Conversely, do we need a metropolitan government to limit suburban sprawl, to redistribute resources among the municipalities of the whole region (especially to the central city), and to take care of infrastructure, equipment, and services of regional or metropolitan range?

In the literature on metropolitan regionalism, two different paths have been explored in reference to these questions. In brief, some researchers suggest that a coercive structure is required, while other researchers think that cooperative forms of governance are preferable. For example, Mitchell-Weaver,

Miller and Deal have argued that "top-down directives, though out of favour, are necessary for managing metropolitan development and ensuring fiscal equalization" (2000, 868), but other authors think that piecemeal or ad hoc cooperation is preferable, because of the context of uncertainty within which local and metropolitan actors are evolving: "It is a question of a community which must be built by using existing resources, an arduous task, and one which does not seem sufficiently established for the question of the legitimacy of the metropolitan institutions to be considered definitively settled (Lefèvre 1998, 23)." In this respect, governance solutions appear to be a kind of institutional "bricolage" that has to be contrasted with sustainable political institutionalization.

What was at stake in this reform can be considered from a planning angle. In his conception of planning in the French context after the Second World War, Lucien Nizard (1973) brought to our attention the main functions that planning practices have to achieve in order to attain their objectives. One of these functions is particularly important in relation to the last municipal and metropolitan reform in Quebec – the function of learning, which is often coupled with the function of decision. As Nizard states, planning is defined in systemic terms as an attempt to regulate in a systematic way a part or the entirety of a social system, on which planning can act by reflecting its content.

Even though the learning function appears secondary in comparison to the decision function, its role remains difficult to bypass. More importantly, the learning function must be well managed. It is responsible for convincing those who will be affected (both by the planning process and by the new frame of action that is being implemented) that these are legitimate interventions that will improve the situation for everybody in the long term. So if the learning function is not well managed by the planners, the planning process and the subsequent process of implementation of the reform can fail.

With the recent municipal and metropolitan reform in Montreal, one can ask whether it was not the learning function, above all, that was not properly understood by the provincial planners in charge of the reform? We are referring here not only to those who were opposed to the forced mergers but more generally to all the local actors at one level or another who were concerned about the reform. The recent demerger movement reflects only one aspect of this. Other aspects are related to the sense of belonging to the metropolitan region, which was not of any concern to the planners during the implementation of the reform, although one of its main aspects was defined in terms of metropolitan governance. In other words, how can one create a metropolitan identity? What is the responsibility of planners in this regard? Is it necessary to create or build a metropolitan citizenship? Can a metropolis act as a collective actor? What are the conditions or the prerequisite for this?

At present, if Montreal is a metropolitan region in statistical terms, it is far from being one in social and political terms. Maybe we should look at the recent municipal reform as the beginning of a planning process instead of seeing it as the result of a completed one.

CONCLUSION

In April 2003 the provincial election in Quebec brought back on the policy agenda the issue of municipal and metropolitan reform. This can be explained principally by the electioneering motives of the Liberals, who promised before the electoral campaign – and stuck to the position during the campaign – to provide the municipalities with the opportunity to recover their previous autonomy.

After their election, the Liberals did not wait long to take action on these matters. Two decisions were taken. The first was to amend Montreal's city charter in order to increase the powers of the borough councils that had been created with the mega-city of Montreal. The second was to organize a referendum to give residents of the municipalities where the merger process – organized by the previous government – had taken place to be consulted, and to offer them the possibility of recovering a part of the powers lost by their municipalities through the creation of the mega-city. On Montreal Island, twenty-two former suburban municipalities decided to hold a referendum in June 2004. Fifteen of the twenty-two succeeded in getting back, in part, the position of their local municipality, as it had been before the forced mergers. There is no doubt that this move introduced renewed uncertainty on the local scene.

It is too early to assess the impact of the demerger process on the management of the City of Montreal. However, it is true that the Liberal government added a supplementary difficulty to the ones that the City of Montreal and the old suburban municipalities were already facing as they adjusted to the reforms introduced in 2000 and 2001. In other words, the reform on Montreal Island was not yet fully completed when the municipalities were confronted with a new political and administrative reality. At the same time, it is important to minimize the impact of the demerging process. Although fifteen municipalities had opted for demerger, they are small municipalities. Before the demergers, the population of the City of Montreal was of 1.8 million. Since the demergers, its population is now around 1.6 million.

Many analysts have seen the recent wave of reforms on the local and urban scene as producing a messy situation. It reveals that local issues are sensitive ones. The sense of belonging to local communities remains strong. It is true, however, as the defenders of the reform argue, that other values, such as equity and administrative performance, should counterbalance localism.

In the urban and economic environment affected by globalizing forces, social inequalities are increasing as much as conflicts of interest (Faure 2003).

Political urban leaders are experiencing a new role in connection with the growing importance of local milieu on the political scene.

Before the Quebec government directly intervened, we did not necessarily have the impression that the municipalities and the city-region were new political actors, especially during the debate over amalgamation and the creation of the MMC. The minister of municipal affairs and the metropolis considered municipalities an inferior tier of governance. This was clearly reflected in the top-down approach that was chosen by the Quebec government to implement the reform. In addition, some of the main issues that municipalities and city-regions are dealing with – for instance, environmental problems, social poverty, the social and economic integration of immigrants – were not thoroughly discussed during these events, even though they were mentioned in the White Paper. Institution building on a metropolitan scale, which is increasingly important to resolve the problems mentioned above, was not seriously discussed either.

When looking back to the beginning of the 1960s and considering what has been achieved since then in terms of urban and municipal restructuring, one should keep in mind that the Quebec government was obsessed with the technocratic discourse and rationality. In this respect, local actors should be very cautious about any initiatives taken by the government regarding reform of the municipal system. In other words, it seems that the responsibility of making social and political choices adapted to the needs of their own milieu depends on local actors above all. Consequently, it is the responsibility of local actors to bring back on the agenda not only the issue of power sharing among municipalities and with the provincial government, but also urban problems and the challenges related to the building of city-regions. It is more than ever on a metropolitan scale that these urban problems are increasingly experienced nowadays. This has to be reiterated strongly one more time.

NOTES

1   We are aware that globalization has become a buzzword over the last decades. While being the object an imposing literature, globalization constitutes also a controversial political issue. One important issue that has been discussed in the literature on globalization is that of local matters, especially the redrawing of local politics. We can mention in this regard the concept of "glocalization proposed by Robertson (1992), which draws attention to the rearticulation between the global and the local. One important field of research on the transformation of the local revolves around the notion of global cities. The latter would constitute new actors that call into question the centrality of national states, notably by developing new spheres of intervention that were previously assumed by states, such as technological development and immigration. On the other hand, some authors focus

on the emergence of regions that would become global actors. Without necessarily supporting their premises, our analysis can be seen as a dialogue with these perspectives.

2 In 1960 the number of rural municipalities or, in legal terms, the municipalities of counties, was estimated to be around 1,300, representing 20 percent of the Quebec population. A council represented each municipality within the county, which also constituted at that time an electoral circumscription. It was composed of all the mayors and one prefect. In 1944 the Union of the County Councils was established. This association was a close and strong ally of the Duplessis government.

3 The release in 1968 of the report from the La Haye Commission on urbanism also contributed to reactivate the discussions about the need for municipal reform. While reinforcing the need to plan the urban development, the report also insisted on the idea of recognizing some centres for stimulating and at the same time orientating regional development. The report recommended the adoption of regional, interlocal, and local plans (Bissonnette 1982).

4 It should be mentioned that, some weeks before the election, the Union Nationale government had released the Remur program. Following from the creation of the three regional urban communities, this plan proposed the creation of twenty additional regional municipalities in the peripheral regions (four urban and sixteen regional communities) within the limits of the existing administrative regions. The emphasis was placed on the necessity of creating viable communities with some administrative autonomy.

5 This recognition of the participation of the federal government in regional development followed the signing of a Quebec-Canada accord in 1968 with the newly created federal Department of Regional Economic Expansion. This agreement recognized the involvement of the federal government with regard to regional development, calling into question the Lesage government's claim for exclusive competency in this matter. This new orientation by the Bourassa government was influenced by the Higgins-Raynauld-Martin report on the future orientation in matters of regional economic development. Among other things, the report emphasized the economic importance of Montreal as a pole of development (Bernier 1992).

6 The change in the government's attitude did not only result from the economic difficulties it faced. The government was also confronted with the constraints imposed by Canadian and U.S. economic relations. The Quebec government's space to manoeuvre appeared to be much more limited. This governmental orientation was also linked to ideological changes in Quebec politics. With the election of the Bourassa government, the ideology of planning was called into question and was gradually replaced by an ad hoc strategy.

7 Bill 92 was to a large extent a result of the report of the Groupe de travail sur Montréal et sa région (GTMR) set up in 1992. The mandate given to this group was to evaluate the situation and propose solutions to the economic, social, and administrative problems of the Montreal region. The report emphasized the need to improve the management capacity of local actors. These discussions about the

situation of Montreal pointed out the necessity of reforming the municipal organization and the administrative procedures (Hamel 2001, 108–9).

8 Indeed, in the introduction of the White Paper, the minister mentioned that local institutions have to address common issues that are at the heart of the social, cultural, and economic development of Quebec society: territorial planning; protection of the environment; economic development in the context of a globalising economy; fiscal equity; and social justice (Quebec 2000, ix).

9 The government identified three specific objectives of the reform: (1) the adoption of a collective vision on the future of the communities; (2) taking into account the government's objectives with respect to planning and sustainable development, involving, among other things, prevention of urban sprawl and respect for agricultural activities; (3) increasing the efficiency of the municipal sector, which would allow for a decrease of the fiscal burden and at the same a more equitable fiscal repartition (Quebec 2000, 55–7).

10 The MMC has exclusive competencies only with respect to metropolitan-level facilities, infrastructure, services and activities, and the international promotion of the region. Regarding its other competencies, it has to share its powers with the City of Montreal and the city's boroughs.

REFERENCES

Andrew, C., K.A. Graham, and S.D. Philips, eds. 2002. *Urban Affairs: Back on the Policy Agenda*. Montreal & Kingston: McGill-Queen's University Press

Ascher, F. 1998. *La République contre la ville*. Paris: Éditions de L'Aube

Bassand, M. 2001. "Métropole et métropolisation." In *Enjeux de la sociologie urbaine*, ed. M. Bassand, V. Kaufmann, and D. Joye, 3–16. Lausanne: Presses polytechniques et universitaires romandes

Bauman, Z. 1998. *Globalization: The Human Consequences*. London: Polity Press and Blackwell

Bernier, G. 1992. "Les politiques fédérales de développement régionale au Québec." In *Bilan québécois du fédéralisme canadien*, ed. F. Rocher, 268–302. Montreal: VLB éditeur

Bissonnette, R. 1982. "La régionalisation municipale au Québec (1960–1980): visées technocratiques et résistances locales." MA thesis, École des études supérieures, Université d'Ottawa

Bourdin, A. 2000. "Pourquoi on s'en encombore ou: la ville de la gouvernance," *Espaces et sociétés* 101–2: 75–89

Bourque, G., and J. Duchastel. 1996. *L'identité fragmentée: nation et citoyenneté dans les débats constitutionnels canadiens, 1941–1992*. Montreal: Fides

Boyer, R., and D. Drache, eds. 1996. *States against Markets: The Limits of Globalization*. London: Routledge

Corade, N., and C. Lacour. 1995. *La métropolisation: les commandements.* Cahiers de recherché de l'IERSO. Bordeaux IV: Université Montesquieu

Dear, M., ed. 2002. *From Chicago to L.A.: Making Sense of Urban Theory.* Thousand Oaks and London: Sage

Dion, L. 1975. *Nationalisme et politique au Québec.* Montreal: Hurtubise HMH

Dickinson, J., and B. Young. 1995. *Brève histoire socio-économique du Québec.* 2nd edn. trans. Hélène Filion. Sillery: Septentrion

Divay, G., and J. Léveillée. 1981. *La réforme municipale et l'État québécois (1960–1979).* No. 27, Montreal: INRS-Urbanisation

Dreier, P., J. Mollenkopf, and T. Swanstrom. 2001. *Place Matters: Metropolitics for the Twenty-First Century.* Lawrence: University Press of Kansas

Faure, A. 2003. "Une île, une ville, un laboratoire politique?" *Possibles* 27 (1–2): 15–27

Frisken, F., and D.F. Norris. 2001. "Regionalism Reconsidered." *Journal of Urban Affairs* 23 (5): 467–78

Hamel, P. 2001. "Enjeux métropolitains: Les nouveaux défis," *Revue internationale d'études canadiennes* 24: 105–27

Hamel, P., and L. Jalbert. 1991. " Local Power in Canada: Stakes and Challenges in the Restructuring of the State." In *State Restructuring and Local Power: A Comparative Perspective*, ed. C. Pickvance and E. Preteceille, 170–96. London and New York: Pinter

Higgins, B., F. Martin, and A. Reynauld. 1970. *Les orientations du développement économique régional dans la Province du Québec.* Ottawa: Ministère de l'expansion économique régionale

Kratke, S. 1992. "Villes en mutation. Hiérarchies urbaines et structures spatiales dans le processus de restructuration spatiale: le cas de l'Allemagne de l'Ouest." *Espaces et sociétés* 67: 39–68

Lefèvre, C. 1998. "Metropolitan Government and Governance in Western Countries: A Critical Review." *International Journal of Urban and Regional Research* 22 (1): 9–25

Le Galès, P. 1998. "Les politiques locales et la recomposition de l'action publique." In *Politiques locales et transformations de l'action publique en Europe*, ed. R. Balme, A. Faure, and A. Malibeau, 101–14. Grenoble: CERAT

Liberal Party of Canada. Prime Minister's Caucus Task Force on Urban Issues. 2002. *La stratégie urbaine du Canada: une vision pour le XXIe siècle.* Chair, Judy Sgro. Interim Report. [Ottawa: The Task Force]

Meynaud, J., and J. Léveillée. 1973. *La régionalisation municipale au Québec.* Montreal: Éditions nouvelle-frontière

Michaud, J. 2000. "The Restructuring of the Health Care System in Québec: Its Impact on the Women's Health System." *Studies in Political Economy* 61: 31–48

Mitchell-Weaver, C., D. Miller, and R. Deal Jr. 2000. "Multilevel Governance and Metropolitan Regionalism in the USA." *Urban Studies* 37 (5–6): 851–76

Nizard, L. 1973. "Administration et société: planification et régulations bureaucratiques." *Revue française de science politique*, April, 199–229

Quebec. Ministère des Affaires municipales et de la Métropole. 2000. *La réorganisation municipale*. Quebec: Gouvernement du Québec

– Secrétariat au développement des régions. 1997. *Politique de soutien au développement local et régional*. Quebec: Gouvernement du Québec

Robertson, R. 1992. *Globalization: Social Theory and Global Culture*. London: Sage

Sassen, S. 1999. "Cracked Casings: Notes toward an Analytics for Studying Transnational Processes." In *Sociology for the Twenty-First Century: Continuities and Cutting Edges*, ed. J.L. Abu-Lughod, 134–45. Chicago: University of Chicago Press

Savitch, H.V., and P. Kantor. 2003. *Cities in the International Marketplace*. Princeton: Princeton University Press

Simard, J.J. 1979. *La longue marche des technocrates*. Montreal: Éditions coopératives Albert Saint-Martin

Soja, E.W. 2000. *Postmetropolis: Critical Studies of Cities and Regions*. London: Blackwell

Swanstrom, T. 2001. "What We Argue about When We Argue about Regionalism." *Journal of Urban Affairs* 23 (5): 479–96

7

Intergovernmental Relations and Polyscalar Social Mobilization: The Cases of Montreal and Toronto

Julie-Anne Boudreau

Les années 1990 ont vu l'ascension de mouvements d'autonomie locale qui résistaient aux fusions municipales ou qui les réclamaient. La recrudescence des réformes territoriales durant cette décennie a permis aux mouvements sociaux de déployer des stratégies de mobilisation territoriale. En opposition aux stratégies sectorielles, qui se concentrent sur des secteurs politiques précis (le logement, la santé, etc.), les stratégies territoriales instrumentalisent les espaces à plusieurs échelons dans le but d'influencer la gouvernance. En observant les modèles des défenseurs des droits des anglophones de Montréal et des réformistes de Toronto, ce document explore l'évolution des stratégies de mobilisation, à partir du lobbying sectoriel au partitionnisme, la résistance aux fusions et la sécessionisme. Les litiges engendrés par les amalgamations à Montréal et Toronto sont considérés dans un contexte plus large, qui est respectivement celui des droits linguistiques et celui du réformisme municipal. La conclusion entraîne la réflexion suivante : est-ce que la tendance vers des stratégies de mobilisation territoriale et d'action polyscalaires au Canada et ailleurs est un indicatif d'une réorientation non seulement des compétences de réglementation, mais aussi du processus politique complet, comprenant la légitimité, l'autorité et l'allégeance.

Beginning in the mid-1990s, municipal amalgamations were implemented by provincial legislation in Montreal, Toronto, and many other Canadian cities. Interesting work has been written in trying to understand the motivation behind these institutional and territorial reforms (see Sancton in this volume for a critical synthesis). This paper seeks to analyse the mobilizing strategies developed by local autonomy movements that reacted against these municipal reforms.

Resistance to municipal consolidation is certainly not a new phenomenon. At the turn of the twentieth century, residents reacted to the wave of annexations that swept North America. Similarly, suburbanites on Montreal Island were adamantly opposed to Mayor Drapeau's dream of "One Island, One City" in the 1960s. With the new wave of city-regionalism that began in the 1990s, we are witnessing the resurgence of local autonomy movements throughout North America after two decades of relative quietness. These movements take the form of resistance to mergers, or calls for a reorganization of intergovernmental relations, or for local secession. They have now increased in number and have seemingly been more successful in capturing the political agenda than previous attempts were.[1] While resistance to consolidation in Montreal and Toronto did not ultimately prevent mergers, local autonomy movements have had a significant impact on the political process, particularly in influencing agenda setting. In thinking about Canadian intergovernmental relations, it is thus important to understand how and why these local autonomy movements contribute to a continued redefinition of political autonomy.

In both Montreal and Toronto, opponents to mergers and coalitions advocating a general reform of intergovernmental relations in Canada have developed a series of mobilizing strategies on different scales, forming alliances with various levels of government and pitting them against one another. While rarely discussed directly in intergovernmental relations studies, this polyscalar approach exploited by civil-society actors has had an important impact on the kinds of institutional and territorial reorganization undertaken by state actors, particularly in a context where the decision-making process has been opened to a variety of non-state actors.

In the past decade, states have undergone important territorial and institutional restructurings that have emphasized the importance of the city-regional and supranational levels more than the national level (Marks 1996; Brenner 1997; Clarke and Gaile 1998; Keating 1998; Keil 1998; Le Galès and Harding 1998). Brenner argues that a new scalar division of regulatory capacities is being implemented as state functions are pushed upward towards the supranational level, downward towards regional and local levels, and outward towards private or semi-private agencies. This has led to an increase in policy responsibilities at these governmental levels, the proliferation of city-regional and supranational institutions, and a number of bilateral and multilateral initiatives coming directly from these levels of government without passing through the national government.

The hypothesis put forward by Brenner is that the rise of neoliberal policies in the 1980s has created what Soja would call a "restructuring-generated crisis" (Soja 2000). In this context, a complex set of actors, including policymakers and elected representatives, are (sometimes explicitly but very often unintentionally) redefining authority and policy at different territorial scales. This is what Brenner calls a process of "rescaling." Indeed, the end result of this chaotic, unplanned process may be some rather important over-all changes in the scales at which governance and policymaking now work.

These changing intergovernmental relations are particularly striking in the European Union. A number of research projects have demonstrated the prolif-eration of new institutions and political mobilization at the European level on the one hand and at the subnational level on the other.[2] While this develop-ment is becoming very important in Europe, similar trends are also observable in North America. The two most obvious are the devolution of responsibilities to the subnational level and the increasingly proactive role of city-regional institutions in local and regional economic development, as demonstrated by Clarke and Gaile for the United States (Clarke and Gaile 1998). At the supranational level, NAFTA institutions do not have the same political weight on national sovereignty as European institutions do. Nevertheless, Keating, for example, has shown how Canadian provinces and U.S. states have devel-oped bilateral cooperative agreements without passing through their respective federal governments. For instance, in the 1980s alone, Ontario and U.S. states signed 25 agreements, and Quebec negotiated 101 agreements with U.S. states between 1980 and 1993 (Keating 1996). With the ratification of NAFTA in 1994, these trends were reinforced.

The question that arises from this empirical literature is, to what degree is there not only proliferation of institutions at the supranational and subnational levels but also a rescaling of the exercise of power. There is no definite answer, for rescaling processes involve diverse actors interacting in complex ways. Yet, it is worth exploring whether demands for political autonomy at various territorial levels may be signs of a substantive rescaling of political power.

This hypothesis rests on the conception of territory as a malleable rather than static element. The literature on the restructuring of territory is particu-larly enlightening in pointing to the fact that the spatial and institutional organization of the polity is determined by a political process, by what Jones calls a process of "spatial selectivity," whereby specific functions are secured spatially and provide differential privileges to actors in their access to state power (Jones 1997; Keating 1998). Because control over territory is, as Sack reminds us, a "means to power," this territorial and institutional restructuring has pro-found implications on who makes decisions and where decisions are made, what kinds of policies are implemented and through what channels, and what access citizens have to institutions at various scales (Sack 1986; Mann 1997).

One of the hypotheses explored in this research is that there has been a strategic territorialization of citizen mobilization in the past decade and that this has explicitly politicized state reform processes. It is suggested that the intensification of intergovernmental reform processes has created a situation of territorial flux, which has opened opportunities for citizens to develop their own territorial mobilization strategies, thus challenging the state's monopoly over decisions on the territorial organization of the polity. Claims for local autonomy could be conceptualized as one manifestation of this strategic territorialization of civil-society movements. Another characteristic of this territorial flux is that civil-society actors adopt polyscalar mobilization strategies – that is, they act at multiple scales of governance simultaneously.

While local autonomy movements in Montreal and Toronto were shaped by their respective local and provincial contexts, and thus differ in important ways, analysing them in relation to one another sheds light on important processes occurring in different city-regions. Moreover, these relations are based on empirically observable networking practices between activists. This is not to downplay the specific "political opportunity structures" favouring the resurgence of local autonomy movements in each city-region (Tarrow 1998). But it is useful to recognize this general trend towards a rescaling of sociopolitical mobilization, which in turn interacts with reforms in intergovernmental relations.

This field of research on the changing scales of political practices, while familiar to students of intergovernmental relations and federalism, is also rapidly evolving in many other disciplines (geography, sociology, political science, urban planning). As mentioned by Sancton in this volume, more research on the policymaking and decision-making process that leads state functions to be pushed to supranational and subnational levels would help clarify how reforms of intergovernmental relations actually happen. Most crucially for this paper, this field would gain enormously by looking at rescaling as more than state-centred and seeing it as a transformation of political autonomy and of the scales of political struggles more generally.

The analytical lens proposed here to understand local autonomy movements requires going beyond the literature on metropolitan fragmentation versus consolidation that has developed since the beginning of the twentieth century (for excellent overviews, see Keating 1995; Stephens and Wikstrom 2000; Brenner 2002). By comparing two separate cases in great detail and situating them in the broader context of an increase in the number of similar claims, I suggest that the strengthening of local autonomy movements in the 1990s is due to a much more complex set of factors, both structural and contextual, than that suggested by the metropolitan consolidation vs fragmentation literature. These coalitions are related to a general redefinition of supranational and federal-provincial-municipal relations in Canada and elsewhere.

Hence, two interrelated research questions are at the root of this paper:

1 Do local autonomy movements in many North American city-regions today represent an overall trend that tends to redefine relations between different scales of government?
2 Do claims for political autonomy at the local level, expressed in the form of secessionist movements or resistance to mergers, represent a more general phenomenon of the rescaling of political authority in the contemporary world?

Below is a brief historical overview of the two broad coalitions studied: Montreal's anglophone rights activists and Toronto's reformists. The paper then turns to specific examples of territorial and jurisdictional strategies of mobilization.

JURISDICTIONAL AND TERRITORIAL STRATEGIES OF MOBILIZATION IN MONTREAL AND TORONTO

Toronto is wealthy, hard-working, and creative – the entrepreneurial engine of the country. Our resources are essential to the rest of Ontario and indeed the nation – reportedly $3 billion in taxes goes out of the city annually. A fair share from this city to help equalize opportunities and support our common life as Canadians is a reasonable demand from federal and provincial governments. But all around us in the city we see ugly unmet needs – homelessness, lack of affordable housing, the highest child poverty rate in the country. These unmet needs underline the fact that the present structures and division of powers are unsustainable. We cannot go on lacking the means and the powers to tackle our grave problems. (Creighton 2000)

When reading the Quebec Government's Bill 170 [merger bill], I began feeling physically ill. Nervous flutters, a sinking feeling in the pit of my stomach ... symptoms I recognized from the weeks prior to the 1995 Quebec referendum. The feeling I had when I felt that I might lose my country was one that I will never forget. Now I feel that the PQ Government wants to take away my town, my home, my community and my way of life. (Housefather, 2000)

In these two statements, activists in Toronto and Montreal express how they envision political autonomy as nested in intergovernmental relations, and how they sense the need to mobilize using these various levels of governments strategically. The point here is not to argue that this polyscalar outlook on sociopolitical mobilization is a new phenomenon. Strategically, forming alliances with various levels of government has long been common practice. The objective of this paper is to highlight these often unnoticed polyscalar strategies and to examine their influence on reforms of intergovernmental relations in a context in which such reorganizations occur (in various forms) in many different countries. If we accept the premises of the work on rescaling discussed above, it is important to open up the argument to a non-state-centred analysis and thus to explore rescaling processes from the standpoint of civil society as well. The interaction between intergovernmental reforms and polyscalar sociopolitical mobilization strategies point towards what could perhaps be termed a rescaling of political struggles.

The starting point is that these general (yet locally specific) processes of state jurisdictional reorganization have created a situation of territorial flux that has provided opportunities for civil-society actors to develop their own competing territorial and jurisdictional strategies. In the case of Montreal and Toronto, claims for local autonomy are not the ultimate aim; but rather they can be understood as instruments developed to affirm cultural differences in the case of Anglo-Montrealers, and to sustain a specific vision of urban life, in the case of reformist Torontonians. In other words, these local autonomy movements are not simply ad hoc reactions to municipal mergers; the reason they were able to mobilize effectively was that they were part of a broader struggle specific to each city. Although the immediate threat of municipal amalgamation was taken as a rallying point, one has to place this mobilization in the wider context of the struggle for cultural affirmation in Montreal and for a reformist view of urban life in Toronto. Significant here is that, from the perspective of these wider sociopolitical struggles, resistance to the mergers does not represent two independent new movements; rather, it represents a mobilizing strategy embedded in larger struggles. In this sense, resistance to mergers can be interpreted as a territorial and jurisdictional strategy for the anglophone rights and the reformist movements.[3]

An analysis of the mobilizing strategies developed by these coalitions in Toronto and Montreal reveals a trend towards an increase of jurisdictional and territorial strategies compared with sectoral strategies.[4] Sectoral strategies of political claims channel efforts into specific policy sectors (housing, language, health, education, etc.). Jurisdictional and territorial strategies of political claims are attempts by civil society to use one level of government against another or to create a new level of government altogether by asking for a remapping of political and administrative boundaries.

In what follows, examples of mobilizing strategies in the anglophone rights coalition in Montreal and reformist coalition in Toronto are discussed with the goal of examining civil society's use of jurisdictional and territorial strategies and their relation to intergovernmental reorganization. But first it is useful to present a brief historical overview of these two coalitions and their role in each city's amalgamation debate.

ANGLO-MONTREALERS' STRUGGLES:
FROM BILL 22 TO PARTITIONISM AND RESISTANCE TO MERGERS

Throughout the nineteenth century and much of the twentieth, Anglo-Montrealers were engaged in organizing economic development in the city and in the whole St Lawrence basin. Their influence thus radiated beyond the city throughout Canada. In creating municipalities with a majority of middle and upper-class anglophone residents concentrated on the West Island, they did not think in terms of local autonomy. This residential pattern was the result of elite separation based on language more than a claim for local autonomy. By the 1970s, a significant shift of power affected Anglo-Montrealers. First with Bill 22, declaring French the only official language of the Province of Quebec (1974), and then with Bill 101 (1977), which regulated access to anglophone schools, workplace language use, and public signs, the anglophones began to see themselves as a minority within Quebec. From a situation in which they did not need to claim political autonomy because of their economic and cultural influence, they found themselves wanting to mark their territory and to gain power over it. This situation was further exacerbated by the gains Toronto was making over Montreal as Canada's economic engine, as well as by the departure of many Anglo-Montrealers to other provinces. Since the Quiet Revolution of the 1960s, Quebec had gained more power over social policy (transferred from both the churches and the federal government), and Anglo-Montrealers had become more isolated from their compatriots in the rest of Canada. They had become active in securing services in English, asserting their rights as a minority, fighting discrimination against them, and protecting a good quality of life in their local environment.

When they first began to act as an organized political force, the anglophones turned to the Quebec Liberal Party (PLQ) as their natural allies against French nationalism. But when the PLQ was unable to prevent the adoption of many linguistic policies, its hold on Anglo-Montreal loyalties was seriously challenged. Seeking other ways of securing their rights, many turned to Alliance Quebec, a lobby organization created in 1981 and funded by the federal government to protect minorities. Tired of Alliance Quebec's conciliatory lobbying strategies, the Equality Party was created in 1989. It gained four seats in the provincial legislative assembly, but the momentum faded away. Anglophone rights activists then retrenched to their local communities, developing strategies of conflict avoidance. The rule of the thumb was "to avoid language politics" and focus instead on local volunteerism and community activities.

With the 1995 referendum, partitionism came forcefully on the agenda, starting a chain of jurisdictional and territorial mobilizing strategies. The goal of securing services in English, fighting language discrimination and protecting a good quality of life remained. But the strategies to achieve them evolved. Many anglophone leaders have reduced their involvement in professional lobbying, party politics, and even community development, and have chosen to emphasize territorial autonomy. They perceive the territory as a tool with which to exert political pressure on the Quebec government for more political power. Municipalities are used to pass motions on partition or demerger in the name of local autonomy but are clearly aiming at cultural affirmation. This is well illustrated in the argument for the legal challenge to the merger bill developed by partitionist lawyer Guy Bertrand: "The existence of a non-sovereign local government in Baie d'Urfé has served and must serve again as a rampart against an important reduction of the Anglophone minority rights, if not against its pure and simple assimilation to the francophone majority of Quebec" (Guy Bertrand et Associés 2001, 48).

The anglophone rights movement was certainly not the only one active in resisting mergers and pushing for demergers, but it was one of the most vocal elements of this local autonomy coalition on Montreal Island. Similarly, cultural affirmation was not the only issue at stake in the struggle against mergers. More traditional fears easily identifiable in the consolidation-versus-fragmentation debate, such as the will to protect suburban lifestyles, a fear of decreasing service levels, or a fear of higher taxes, were also involved. Nevertheless, the question this paper asks is, Why did the anglophone rights movement get involved in this struggle against mergers? A response is that it was a logical continuation of the trend towards territorial and jurisdictional mobilizing strategies that began in the 1990s.

TORONTO'S REFORMISTS: FROM THE SPADINA EXPRESSWAY
TO C4LD AND LOCAL SELF-GOVERNMENT

Aided by a remapping of the City of Toronto's ward boundaries in 1968, a loose alliance of reformists won the 1972 municipal elections. Reformists came from more conservative and more radical backgrounds and introduced a new planning ideology in the central city, exacerbating tensions with pro-development suburbs. They rejected the "growth at any cost" philosophy that was prevailing at the time. Reformists fought inner-city expressways such as the Spadina Expressway, car dependence, private apartment redevelopment, urban renewal and housing segregation. They also resented the increasing pressure of office space in central neighbourhoods; between 1962 and 1973 office space had more than doubled.[5] Reformists rejected low-density suburbs and favoured medium-density and mixed-use planning. They did not like high-rise buildings, advocating instead the conversion of houses into apartments, and they promoted outlying office centres (such as those in North York) in order to protect central neighbourhoods.

While these reformists never formed a municipal party, they voted together on certain common issues. Their main concern was to encourage recognition that planning is a political exercise and that citizens ought to have a say (Lorimer 1970; Sewell 1972; Harris 1987; Caulfield 1988b; Sewell 1993; Caulfield 1994; Allen 1997). They created citizen advisory boards and decentralized some city employees moving them to site offices. With a higher proportion of renters in the City of Toronto than in the rest of the region, they were able to focus attention on issues other than property values. Yet young urban professionals and newly gentrified homeowners were still very concerned about property values. For one stream of reformists, it was not development per se that was a problem but its pace and style; as well, they were concerned about the preservation of lively (middle-class) neighbourhoods in the city core. As Caulfield notes, "It is not accidental that the principal early hotbeds of middle-class reform were gentrifying neighbourhoods"

(Caulfield 1988a). Other reformists were more concerned about the distributive consequences of housing development, the lack of affordable housing, the profits made, and the control exercised by development mega corporations.

This reformist planning ideology came to be integrated in City of Toronto practices and formed the basis of an urban progressive middle-class regime. As Caulfield noted in 1988, "Concerns of middle-class reform, have, today, been sufficiently absorbed into municipal orthodoxy that there is no imminent danger of another uprising of restless bourgeois" (1988a, 482). When amalgamation was imposed on Metro Toronto, the reformists felt threatened.[6] They coalesced in a movement called Citizens for Local Democracy (C4LD), which was led by the former reformist mayor, John Sewell (1978–80). In the first five months of the struggle to defeat Bill 103, which was imposing amalgamation on Toronto, many other groups gravitated around the coalition. C4LD saw its role as a catalyst to attract energy and to mobilize support for maintaining a reformist regime in Toronto.[7] Its meetings attracted more than a thousand people in peak times. With local autonomy threatened, reformists had to turn to jurisdictional and territorial strategies of mobilization.

C4LD was not successful in preventing amalgamation, but its territorial and jurisdiction mobilizing strategies continued. In the first years of the new city, C4LD acted as a watchdog of the new council and became involved in a number of other issues. Even though the immediate purpose of the coalition (resisting amalgamation) was no longer relevant and the appellation C4LD gradually faded, the reformist movement – as a loosely defined network – remained active. Secession was probably the first important issue that many C4LDers embarked on. They did so in coalition with some municipal bureaucrats and politicians, a number of philanthropic business leaders and academics, and the Federation of Canadian Municipalities, the Association of Municipalities of Ontario, the Toronto Board of Trade, and the Toronto Environmental Alliance (Keil and Young 2001).

A variety of secessionist activities emerged at much the same time in different circles. Perhaps the most colourful was a declaration by mayor Mel Lastman, at a meeting in Florida in the fall of 1999, that Toronto should be its own province. He later pulled back from his statement, but it had already unleashed waves of ironic (and also serious) comments back in Toronto (Gwyn 1999; Sewell 1999; Benzie 2000d, 2000b, 2000c, 2000a, 2000e; Comeau 2000; Gollom 2000; Sewell 2000b; Welsh 2000). Most observers knew that, constitutionally, the creation of a new city-province would be virtually impossible. But Jane Jacobs had already toyed with the idea, especially during a conference held in her honour in October 1997, and also in her deputation to the committee hearing on Bill 103 (Hume 1997c, 1997a, 1997b, 1997d; Jacobs 1997). The proposals varied from the creation of a Province of Southern Ontario to the creation of a new designation for city-states which could include Montreal and Vancouver.

Some C4LDers formed the Committee for the Province of Toronto a "community group committed to achieving Provincial Status for Toronto under Canada's Constitution" (Vallance 2000). The committee supported a notice of motion to City Council, presented by Councillor Michael Walker on 9 December 1999 and officially deposited in February 2000. Building on the widespread opposition to amalgamation in 1997 and the widespread discontent with downloading policies, the motion demanded that the City of Toronto (1) "hold a public referendum as part of the 2000 municipal election to determine public support for proceeding with separation from the Province" and (2) "develop an extensive communications package outlining the argument (financial, social) for and against separation and a plan to provoke full participation and debate on the part of the citizens prior to the referendum" (Walker 1999). This movement, which included members of City Council and other citizens, eventually faded, and mobilization focused on securing a charter for the city.

These various citizen activities show continuity with the 1970s reform movement, both in the people involved and in the political ideas. But there is an important difference: the evolution of mobilization strategies. Reformists had been in power in the former City of Toronto for three decades, but the threats posed by amalgamation forced these activists and municipal politicians to craft territorialized strategies in order to maintain a progressive political regime in place.

EXAMPLES OF POLYSCALAR MOBILIZATION IN MONTREAL AND TORONTO

In both city-regions, other coalitions have also been territorializing their mobilization strategies as a result of amalgamation. A good example can be found by looking at how grassroots organizations have been mobilizing at the borough level in what were the neighbourhoods of the former City of Montreal. With amalgamation, the City of Montreal was subdivided into boroughs to complement the boroughs created out of former local municipalities. This new territorial structure provided grassroots organizations with a framework for mobilization.[8] Space constraints do not permit expansion here on all of the examples of territorialization. However, in this last section, three examples of jurisdictional and territorial strategies deployed by the anglophone and reformist coalitions are discussed in order to illustrate further the interaction between intergovernmental reorganization policies and polyscalar sociopolitical mobilization.

Strategic territorialization occurs on various scales, from the neighbourhood to the borough to the municipality to the metropolitan level. The focus here is on Toronto reformists' strategies at the metropolitan scale (secession, charter) and on Anglo-Montrealers' focus on the local municipal scale (partition, demerger).[9] Regardless of the scalar focus of these examples, civil society's territorial strategies of mobilization usually necessitate incorporating negotiation between levels of governments.

PUTTING URBAN AFFAIRS BACK ON THE FEDERAL AGENDA

Although municipal affairs are under provincial jurisdiction, the coalitions in Toronto and Montreal, in their struggle against amalgamation, attempted to influence federal electoral outcomes in order to pressure their respective provincial governments. This is a typical jurisdictional mobilizing strategy. The 2000 federal election resulted in a significant loss of votes for the Bloc Québécois (BQ) when the federal Liberal Party publicly exhorted Quebecers to vote Liberal in order to make a statement against the provincial Parti Québécois (PQ). The election supervisor later warned the Liberals to be careful, as anti-merger expenses in Montreal might be tallied as campaign expenses for the federal party. When C4LD in Toronto attempted to put "local democracy" on the agenda during the federal election of 1997, federal parties refused to get involved. The cultural stakes were obviously different. But this renewed openness towards municipal affairs at the federal level is related to the strategies of mobilization on multiple scales developed in the 1990s by local autonomy movements across Canada, and particularly in Montreal and Toronto.[10]

This urban pressure at the federal level is slowly making its way as a legitimate federal issue, resulting in a rescaling of the level at which political autonomy is claimed by civil-society actors. For Anglo-Montrealers, it makes sense to support these municipal-federal alliances, for they decrease the autonomy of the francophone-controlled Quebec government. These jurisdictional strategies can be traced back at least to the constitutional negotiations leading to the 1987 Meech Lake Accord.[11] At the time, the Federation of Canadian Municipalities (FCM) was pushing to have municipalities recognized as a third order to government. Aboriginal people were also calling for self-government. If these measures had been enshrined in the accord, they would have rescaled autonomy profoundly in Canada, taking away some provincial powers. However, the two proposals were not fully integrated in the amendments unanimously approved by all provincial premiers back in June 1987, and the concessions made in the 1992 Charlottetown Accord were ultimately rejected by Canadian citizens. But these ideas made their way, and many civil-society actors, including reformists and Anglo-Montrealers, were mobilizing in order to change the locus of political autonomy in Canada. The 2002 election of the reformist Toronto councillor and former FCM president, Jack Layton as the New Democratic Party's leader is a sign of the advances made by this polyscalar mobilization.[12]

PARTITIONISM AND DE-MERGERS:
MUNICIPAL RESOLUTIONS AND FEDERAL AND PROVINCIAL POLICIES

Although neither a recognition of municipalities as a third order of government nor Aboriginal self-government was fully incorporated in the Meech Lake Accord, the recognition of Quebec as a distinct society was. Anglophone leaders in Quebec then developed their own competing territorial strategy. As Scowen wrote, "A territorial approach brings important psychological benefits. It will allow the English to see themselves as exercising some real influence in at least a part of the province. It permits and encourages all kinds of local initiatives, a strengthening of local institutions, and political action ... A territorial approach to the English community in Quebec does not involve a denial of individual rights. It is the logical extension of these rights into practical collective action. It does not mean that English Quebec is creating a ghetto for itself, any more than Quebec is a ghetto within Canada or North America" (Scowen 1991, 111).

It was in this climate, in 1995, that the PQ launched a referendum campaign on Quebec sovereignty. Reacting to the referendum's very close results, many anglophones rallied for partition. The Equality Party and Alliance Quebec, as well as most anglophone municipalities on Montreal Island worked with this territorial strategy in two ways. First, a number of partitionist motions were adopted by local municipal councils stating their will to remain part of Canada if Quebec unilaterally declared its independence. Second, a campaign was launched with the federal government and through the court system, led by Guy Bertrand, to obtain a decision on the constitutionality of secession. The Supreme Court decision (1998) states that the Province's territory would be up for negotiation if Quebec went with secession. Based on this court decision, the federal government adopted the *Clarity Act,* which details the conditions under which Canada would negotiate if a clear majority of Quebecers voted for sovereignty in a future referendum. Should partition be implemented, it would have important territorial consequences, not the least being a complex redrawing of Quebec's territory according to small units of the voters' choice, most probably the ridings.

When the Quebec government imposed mergers on Montreal Island in 2000, much of this activity on partition, which relied on local municipal boundaries, was threatened. Moreover, even anglophones who did not support partition were affected, for their traditional mobilization strategies were threatened by the loss of local institutions. This has resulted in a significant move towards territorial and jurisdictional strategies in an effort to preserve these local institutions and boundaries, which were seen as secure spaces for community well-being in the face of increasing urban and linguistic tensions.

Another example of this strategy is demerger resolutions passed by municipal councils. Westmount's former mayor Peter Trent and the citizen antimerger group DemocraCité developed the idea of pressuring the Quebec Liberal Party to promise to adopt a demerger policy if it was elected in the April 2003 election. Several municipal councils in the Montreal area had adopted demerger resolutions immediately after the merger legislation was approved. This gave a clear signal to Jean Charest and the Liberals. The procedure for demerging was similar to the California municipal secession policy adopted in 1997 in response to pressure by San Fernando Valley secessionists: a referendum is to be held on demerging if 10 percent of the population signs a petition against amalgamation.[13] Since January 2006, 15 municipalities were demerged on the Island of Montreal, amounting to 237,949 residents.

THE CHARTER MOVEMENT: CROSS-CANADIAN ALLIANCES

While demerging has not been on the agenda in Ontario, the secession of newly amalgamated Toronto from the rest of the province was briefly discussed by various citizens and by Councillor Walker. These earlier formulations eventually evolved into a Canadian charter movement similar to the U.S. home rule movement at the turn of the twentieth century.

As Keil and Young note, in the Canadian institutional framework, three avenues are possible for providing more autonomy to municipalities: (1) amending the federal constitution to recognize municipalities as a third order of government; (2) amending provincial municipal acts; and (3) a provincially approved city charter, which would grant municipal autonomy in specific areas under a provincial-municipal contract (Keil and Young 2001). After initially flirting with the first two options, several Toronto actors opted to lobby the provincial government for a city charter (Chief Administrative Officer 1999, 2000a, 2000b, 2000c, 2000d; Grewal 2000; Rowe 2000; *Toronto Star*, 2000; Welsh and Moloney 2000).[14]

Toronto City Council took over the charter idea, motivated partly by a budget crisis in 2001–2, when the council faced a shortfall that led to service cuts, higher transit fees, and an increase in property taxes. The civic-spirited business leader Alan Broadbent initiated meetings and drafted a charter in association with a number of academics, ex-mayors, and various civic leaders (Broadbent 2000; Rowe 2000). The Toronto Environmental Alliance also drafted a charter focusing on regional governance (Keil and Young 2001). This was accompanied by pressure for a change in the provincial *Municipal Act*, which could provide the city with enhanced revenue sources, regulating abilities, and protections from unilateral provincial changes of municipal boundaries.

These various jurisdictional and territorial strategies in Toronto and across Canada are monitored by a network of reformist activists led by John Sewell (see their website, www.localgovernment.ca). As the website's *Local Self-Government Bulletin No. 3* indicates, "the Toronto debate goes beyond asking for autonomy and respect, and raises the question of the kinds of power which should be exercised by a big city" (Sewell 2000a). The website offers a good source of information illustrating the cross-Canada alliances developing on the issue of local autonomy.

Activists in Montreal and Toronto have insisted on the importance of local territorial boundaries while developing a number of jurisdictional strategies playing one level of government against another (particularly during the 1997 and 2000 federal elections). These strategies have multiplied the scales at which claims to autonomy are made in a country in which such claims were long dominated by the provincial level of government.

CONCLUSION

This paper has taken a civil-society-centred approach to Canadian intergovernmental relations, examining how polyscalar mobilization strategies exploited by certain social actors can influence the kinds of institutional and territorial reorganization undertaken by state actors. Do local autonomy movements in many North American city-regions today represent an overall trend that tends to redefine relations between different levels of government? Do claims for political autonomy at the local level, expressed in the form of secessionist movements or resistance to mergers, represent a more general phenomenon of the rescaling of political authority in the contemporary world? Despite the fact that most of the examples discussed here were only partly successful on the proximate issue of local autonomy, the cases of Toronto and Montreal point towards a positive answer to these two research questions, given that new opportunities have been opened for territorial strategies of mobilization to be developed.

By situating the struggles against amalgamation in Montreal and Toronto in the context of larger sociopolitical struggles – namely, the anglophone rights coalition and the reformist coalition – it was possible to see the campaigns against mergers as jurisdictional and territorial strategies of mobilization. The starting point was that in the general process of intergovernmental reforms, a situation of territorial flux provided opportunities for social actors to develop their own competing territorial and jurisdictional strategies. Claims for local autonomy were thus not the ultimate aim of these coalitions but were an instrument developed to affirm cultural differences, in the case of Anglo-Montrealers, and to sustain a specific vision of urban life, in the case of Torontonians.

Various examples of jurisdictional and territorial strategies were discussed, including pressure to put urban affairs back on the federal agenda, partitionism and demerger, and the emergence of a Canadian charter movement. The object was to highlight these polyscalar strategies and to examine their influence on state restructuring in order to explore rescaling processes from the standpoint of civil society. The interaction between intergovernmental reforms and the strategic multiplication of the scales at which claims to autonomy are made begin to illustrate that we may be witnessing a rescaling, not only of institutions but of the exercise of power. The impact of this territorialization of civil-society activities on political debates and social justice is difficult to assess at this point. But certainly the scale at which social actors focus their political claims will affect redistributive policies – a central yet not always openly articulated element of the struggle in both Toronto and Montreal.

NOTES

1   In the United States alone, local secessionism rose in the 1990s with active move-ments in more than fifteen cities, the most prominent being in the populous (1.4 million) San Fernando Valley of the City of Los Angeles. To provide a point of comparison, the aggregate population of all territories detached from all munici-palities in the United States as a whole between 1970 and 1985 was only 119,000 (Briffault 1992, 777). In Canada, local autonomy movements tend to take a wider range of modalities (from resistance to mergers to a Canadian charter movement), but U.S.-style local secessionism also exists. For instance, the California proce-dure for secession has directly influenced the Quebec Liberal Party's procedure for demergers (interview with Roch Cholette, 4 June 2001). Secession was also briefly on the agenda of Toronto activists in the aftermath of amalgamation.

2   For excellent empirical analyses of these phenomena in Europe, please refer to three edited books: Balme 1996; Le Galès and Lequesne 1997; Balme et al. 2002. In the latter book, Balme, Chabanet, and Wright have asked contributors to reflect not only on the proliferation of institutions at the supranational and subnational levels but also on the Europeanization of social and political mobilization, that is, on the appearance of the EU as a target of political mobilization, on the prolifera-tion of EU interest groups and the effect of the construction of Europe on national interest groups, and on the access to European institutions for subnational authorities.

3   Anglophone rights and reformist movements are conceived in this paper as politi-cal formations that are more loosely organized than political parties or interest groups but not necessarily socially transformative like social movements. The terms "coalitions" and "civil-society actors" are used to designate this type of sociopo-litical mobilization. It is also important to note that these coalitions are visible mainly through their leaders and their most militant activists; they do not neces-sarily embody the views of all the citizens they claim to represent.

4   The analysis of mobilizing strategies appearing in this article consisted in the com-pilation of a list of actions and issues undertaken by the anglophone rights and reformist activists in the 1990s (obviously this list cannot be exhaustive). Infor-mation on strategies came from documents produced by their main organizations,

from interviews, from media coverage, from direct observation, and from secondary studies. The list was then categorized according to the variables (1) sectoral and (2) territorial and jurisdictional, in order to determine the dominant type of strategy at a specific period (Boudreau 2003a, 2003b).

5 Between 1970 and 1980 there was an increase of 78 percent, and there was a further 71 percent increase between 1980 and 1993 (Lemon 1996, 274; Filion 2000, 173).

6 The term "reformist" is used here to designate local councillors adhering to reformist ideals, as well as activists.

7 The argument against amalgamation was not specifically cast as a will to preserve this regime. This would have alienated potential suburban allies in the struggle to prevent mergers. Rather, the argument was framed on the more neutral ground of "local democracy" (for a detailed analysis, see Boudreau 2003a).

8 I am indebted to Jean-Pierre Collin for this observation.

9 The reader may have noticed that the Montreal Citizen Movement (MCM) remains absent from the present analysis. The MCM could be seen as the equivalent of the Toronto reformist coalition. At first glance, it may seem surprising that these two reformist coalitions took opposite positions on amalgamation. A careful comparative analysis of their positions might be an extremely interesting exercise to undertake in another paper. Suffice it to say here that part of the explanation may be that the language component of the struggle in Montreal had an important influence beyond the typical reformist claims. Moreover, Montreal's and Toronto's levels of decentralization and democratic traditions before amalgamation were very different. Finally, the Harris government's neoconservative motives for amalgamation contrasted with the PQ's stated objectives.

10 Business elites were also very active in pushing for federal involvement in cities. This was done through traditional lobbying practices but also through alliances with other civil-society actors, such as local autonomy movements. This is the case, for instance, of the Toronto City Summit Alliance (Boudreau and Keil 2004; Keil and Boudreau 2005).

11 The Federation of Canadian Municipalities already had lobbied the federal government for a greater role for Canadian cities; it had done so in 1982 when the constitution was patriated to Canada.

12 Toronto Mayor David Miller continues to invite federal government representatives to come to municipal committee meetings on relevant issues (particularly transportation and immigration) in an effort to build stronger ties between the two levels of government, bypassing the provincial level (interview with David Miller, 8 April 2002).

13 Roch Cholette (who was urban affairs critic when the PLQ was in opposition in Quebec) has studied the California secession procedure very closely, and the demerger proposal put forward by Quebec's Liberal premier Jean Charest is considerably less stringent than California legislation (AB62). In California, for an area to secede from a municipality, a petition of 25 percent of registered voters

in the secessionist area has to be submitted to a state agency, which then under-takes a "feasibility study" that has to prove secession would be revenue-neutral. Then secession is put on the ballot and has to be approved by a double majority: in the secessionist area, and in the city at large.

14 Jane Jacobs also initiated, in May 2001, a meeting of the mayors of the country's five biggest cities to discuss strategies for gaining more autonomy (Coyle 2001; James 2001).

REFERENCES

Allen, Max. 1997. *Ideas That Matter: The Worlds of Jane Jacobs*. Owen Sound, Ont.: Ginger Press

Balme, Richard. 1996. *Les politiques du néo-régionalisme*. Paris: Economica

Balme, Richard, et al. 2002. *L'action collective en Europe/Collective Action in Europe*. Paris: Presses de Sciences Po

Benzie, Robert. 2000a. "City to Debate Referendum on Secession." *National Post*, 10 May. www.nationalpost.com

– 2000b. "Harris' Stinging Letter Propels Vote on City-State." *National Post*, 12 May. www.nationalpost.com

– 2000c. "Lastman Insists He'll Fight for Toronto City-State." *National Post*, 5 May. www.nationalpost.com

– 2000d. "Referendum on Separation Here? Council to Decide." *National Post*, 12 April. www.nationalpost.com

– 2000e. "Toronto Still Plans to Seek More Control over Affairs." *National Post*, 16 May. www.nationapost.com

Boudreau, Julie-Anne. 2003a. "Local Autonomy Movements in North American City-Regions: Territorial Strategies and the 'Local Democracy' Argument." Doctoral thesis, Department of Urban Planning, University of California at Los Angeles

– 2003b. "The Politics of Territorialization: Regionalism, Localism, and Other isms ... The Case of Montreal." *Journal of Urban Affairs* 25 (2): 179–99

Boudreau, Julie-Anne, and Roger Keil. 2004. "In Search of a New Political Space? City-Regional Institution-Building and Social Activism in Toronto." Paper presented at the Annual Meeting of the Association of American Geographers, 15–19 March, Philadelphia

Brenner, Neil. 1997. "State Territorial Restructuring and the Production of Spatial Scale: Urban and Regional Planning in the FRG, 1960–1990." *Political Geography* 16 (4): 273–306

– 2002. "Decoding the Newest 'Metropolitan Regionalism' in the USA: A Critical Overview." *Cities* 19 (1): 3–21

Briffault, Richard. 1992. "Voting Rights, Home Rule, and Metropolitan Governance: The Secession of Staten Island as a Case Study in the Dilemmas of Local Self-Determination." *Columbia Law Review* 92 (4): 775–850

Broadbent, Alan. 2000. *Towards a Greater Toronto Charter*. Toronto: Avana Capital Corporation

Caulfield, Jon. 1988a. "Canadian Urban 'Reform' and Local Conditions: An Alternative to Harris's 'Reinterpretation'" *International Journal of Urban and Regional Research* 12: 477–84

– 1988b. "'Reform' as a Chaotic Concept: The Case of Toronto." *Urban History Review/Revue d'histoire urbaine* 17 (2): 107–11

– 1994. *City Form and Everyday Life: Toronto's Gentrification and Critical Social Practice*. Toronto: University of Toronto Press

Chief Administrative Officer. 1999. *Legislative Proposals for Local Government*. www.localgovernment.ca (accessed 22 August 2002)

– 2000a. *Charter Status for the City of Toronto*. Toronto: City of Toronto

– 2000b. *Provincial Local Services Realignment: Making it Work*. Toronto: City of Toronto

– 2000c. *Towards a New Relationship with Ontario and Canada*. Toronto: City of Toronto

– 2000d. *Towards a New Relationship with Ontario and Canada: Staff Report*. Toronto: City of Toronto

Clarke, Susan E., and Gary L. Gaile. 1998. *The Work of Cities*. Minneapolis: University of Minnesota Press

Comeau, Pauline. 2000. "The City-State: More Than a State of Mind." *Forum: Canada's National Municipal Affairs Magazine*. Winter, 20–5

Coyle, Jim. 2001."Role for Cities in Confederation Needs to Be Fixed." *Toronto Star*, 24 May. www.thestar.com

Creighton, Phyllis. 2000. *Councillor Michael Walker's Motion on Toronto as a Future Province*. Toronto

Filion, Pierre. 2000. "Balancing Concentration and Dispersion? Public Policy and Urban Structure in Toronto." *Environment and Planning, C: Government and Policy* 18: 163–89

Gollom, Mark. 2000."City Councillors Sidestep Secession Debate Again." *National Post*, 14 April. www.nationalpost.com

Grewal, San. 2000. "'Province 416' Proposed: Budget Spurs Call for Autonomous Toronto." *Toronto Star*, 4 May. www.thestar.com

Guy Bertrand et Associés. 2001. *Argumentaire de Me Guy Bertrand et Me Gratien Boily*. Superior Court of Quebec

Gwyn, Richard. 1999. "Lastman Catches Attention on City-State." *Toronto Star*, 26 November. www.thestar.com

Harris, Richard. 1987. "A Social Movement in Urban Politics: A Reinterpretation of Urban Reform in Canada." *International Journal of Urban and Regional Research* 11: 363–79

Housefather, Anthony. 2000. *Municipal Reorganization Is a Disaster*. www.notomergers.com (accessed 23 November 2000)

Hume, Christopher. 1997a. "The City That Jane Helped Build." *Toronto Star*, 12 October

- 1997b. "A Gentle but Frighteningly Incisive Vision." *Toronto Star,* 12 October
- 1997c. "Jacobs Sees Humanity Amid Urban Concrete." *Toronto Star,* 18 September
- 1997d. "We Forget How Lucky We Are" *Toronto Star,* 12 October

Jacobs, Jane. 1997. "Deputation Given to the Standing Committee in General Government Conducting Hearings on the City of Toronto Act – Bill 103." Toronto: Citizens for Local Democracy

James, Royson. 2001. "Canada Risks the Death of Big 5 Cities, Jacobs Warns." *Toronto Star,* 25 May. www.thestar.com

Jones, M.R. 1997. "Spatial Selectivity of the State? The Regulationist Enigma and Local Struggles over Economic Governance." *Environment and Planning, A* 29: 831–64

Keating, Michael. 1995. "Size, Efficiency, and Democracy: Consolidation, Fragmentation, and Public Choice." In *Theories of Urban Politics*, ed. D. Judge, G. Stoker, and H. Wolman. Thousand Oaks, UK: Sage

- 1996. "Les provinces canadiennes dans la concurrence inter-régionale nord-américaine." In *Les politiques du néo-régionalisme*, ed. R. Balme. Paris: Economica
- 1998. *The New Regionalism in Western Europe: Territorial Restructuring and Political Change*. Cheltenham, UK: Edward Elgar

Keil, Roger. 1998. "Globalization Makes States: Perspectives of Local Governance in the Age of the World City." *Review of International Political Economy* 5 (4): 616–46

Keil, Roger, and Julie-Anne Boudreau. 2005. "Is There Regionalism after Municipal Amalgamation in Toronto?" *City* 9: 1

Keil, Roger, and Douglas Young. 2001. "A Charter for the People? The Debate on Municipal Autonomy in Toronto." Paper presented at the RC 21 Meeting of the International Sociological Association," 15–17 June, Amsterdam

Le Galès, Patrick, and Alan Harding. 1998. "Cities and States in Europe." *West European Politics* 21 (3): 120–45

Le Galès, Patrick, and Christian Lequesne. 1997. *Les paradoxes des régions en Europe*. Paris: La Découverte

Lemon, James T. 1996. "Toronto, 1975: The Alternative Future." In *Liberal Dreams and Nature's Limits: Great Cities of North America since 1600*, ed. J.T. Lemon. Toronto: Oxford University Press

Lorimer, James. 1970. *The Real World of City Politics*. Toronto: James Lewis and Samuel

Mann, Michael. 1997. "The Autonomous Power of the State." In *Political Geography: A Reader*, ed. J. Agnew. London: Arnold

Marks, Gary. 1996. "An Actor-Centred Approach to Multi-Level Governance." *Regional and Federal Studies* 6 (2): 20–38

Rowe, Mary W. 2000. *Toronto Considering Self-Government*. Owen Sound, Ont.: Ginger Press

Sack, Robert David. 1986. *Human Territoriality: Its Theory and History*. Cambridge: Cambridge University Press

Scowen, Reed. 1991. *A Different Vision: The English in Quebec in the 1990s*. Don Mills, Ont.: Maxwell Macmillan Canada

Sewell, John. 1972. *Up Against City Hall*. Toronto: James Lewis and Samuel

– 1993. *The Shape of the City: Toronto Struggles with Modern Planning*. Toronto: University of Toronto Press

– 1999. " Welcome to the Year of the Slingshot." *Eye*, 30 December. www.eye.net

– 2000a. *Local Self-Government Bulletin No. 3*. January 2000. www.localgovernment.ca (accessed 29 August 2002)

– 2000b. "No Whipping Boy: Toronto Searches for the Power to Govern itself." *Eye*, 22 June. www.eye.net

Soja, Eward W. 2000. *Postmetropolis: Critical Studies of Cities and Regions*. Oxford: Blackwell

Stephens, G. Ross, and Nelson Wikstrom. 2000. *Metropolitan Government and Governance: Theoretical Perspectives, Empirical Analysis, and the Future*. New York: Oxford University Press

Tarrow, Sidney. 1998. *Power in Movement: Social Movements and Contentious Politics*. Cambridge: Cambridge University Press

Toronto Star. 2000. "Toronto Needs Its Own Charter." 22 June. www.thestar.com

Vallance, David. 2000. "Toronto, the Province, Is a Marvelous Idea." *Annex Gleaner*, n.p.

Walker, Michael. 1999. "Secession of the City of Toronto from the Province of Ontario." Motion presented to Toronto City Council, 9 December

Welsh, Moira. 2000. "Toronto Charter Plan Boosts Independence." *The Toronto Star*, 14 June

Welsh, Moira, and Paul Moloney. 2000. "Committee Passes Toronto Charter." *Toronto Star*, 23 June

8

Recent Changes in Provincial-Municipal Relations in Ontario: A New Era or a Missed Opportunity?

David Siegel

Il semble que l'on soit à un moment décisif de l'histoire pour ce qui est des interactions provinciales-municipales en Ontario, et même, des administrations municipales dans l'ensemble de la province. La réforme des gouvernements locaux s'est faite à bâtons rompus au cours des années et les récentes réformes dont il est question dans ce document, sont les plus déterminantes du système municipal de l'Ontario depuis la création du système actuel par le Baldwin Act en 1849. Cependant, on doit considérer l'importance de la persistance comportementale lorsqu'on analyse l'impact de ces changements. Les municipalités se sont longtemps vues comme la progéniture de la province. Et, depuis tout aussi longtemps, la province a joué un rôle empreint de paternalisme envers ses municipalités. Ce chapitre évaluera la situation actuelle et examinera si elle constitue le début d'une ère nouvelle ou une occasion ratée.

Municipal reform in Ontario has moved in fits and starts over the years. The pattern has been repeated over several cycles. There are periods when municipalities are simply ignored; then suddenly there is a relatively short period of intense interest in municipal reform, during which the actual changes fall short of the early intentions; then the next period of quietude sets in. It is fitting to review municipal reform in Ontario at this point because we seem to have just completed one of these cycles and are entering a new period of quietude. However, the real impact of some of these changes is still unfolding. The result could be a major change in the provincial-municipal relationship or a missed opportunity and a reversion to the old way of doing things.

The beginning of responsible municipal government in Ontario is usually dated from the Baldwin Act of 1849. For over a hundred years after the establishment of responsible government, the municipal system experienced steady growth and incremental change but no major shocks. The creation of Metropolitan Toronto in 1954 was the first major structural change in the system (Rose 1972; Colton 1980; Frisken 1993). This was sufficiently revolutionary to generate international interest; but after this flurry, the somnolence returned for more than ten years, until the Smith Committee (the Ontario Committee on Taxation) in 1967 recommended that all southern Ontario be restructured in the form of regional governments like that of Metro Toronto (Ontario, Committee on Taxation 1967). This led to the creation of ten regional governments (mostly in the Golden Horseshoe around Toronto, plus Ottawa and Sudbury) in the years 1969–74, after which there was another stretch of somnolence (O'Brien 1993; Sancton 1991). The period 1996–99, following the election of the Harris government in 1995, saw the most comprehensive reform of municipal government since 1849. This brief but very important spurt of activity and its aftermath will be the topic of this paper.

The paper will assess whether this flurry of activity will result in any real lasting change in the system. The first section of the paper provides a description of the changes that have been made. The second section analyses these changes to determine what their real impact is likely to be.

THE COMMON SENSE REVOLUTION

In 1995 Mike Harris and his Conservatives swept the previous NDP government out of power with promises of major changes in the political landscape. The Conservatives' success was attributed in part to the Common Sense Revolution. This was outlined in a short pamphlet that stated in a very clear and succinct way what the Conservatives would do when they came to power. Their campaign strategy, which they started pursuing several years before the election, was to develop this clear and fairly simple document and hammer on it throughout the election campaign to make sure that everyone knew where they stood.

While the Common Sense Revolution document made many of the Conservatives' policy goals very clear, it said little about municipal government, so it was not clear what the Conservatives' goal for local government reform was or even if they had a goal (Sancton 2000). Some have suggested that the government's real goal was to reform the primary and secondary education systems and that municipal reform was almost an unintended consequence (Ibbitson 1997; Graham and Phillips 1998). While this may be an accurate analysis of the genesis of reform, it was clear that reform was ultimately pursued with such vigour that it could not really be considered an unintended consequence. At some point, the impetus for municipal reform took on a life of its own.

This paper will discuss the municipal reforms under a number of headings, beginning with financial, since there is some evidence that this was the prime motivator and starting point for the more extensive changes.

FINANCIAL REFORM

Before the Common Sense Revolution, boards of education had received about half their funds from the property tax and the other half from provincial transfer payments.[1] Ontario's chosen method of obtaining more leverage over boards of education was to shift this balance so that almost all education funding would be provided by the province. Then control would follow funding. Of course, the province did not have the funds simply to increase the level of transfers, and even if it had been able to do so, it would have created a windfall if it had allowed the school boards to retain the property tax.

The province's original plan was to provide a significant increase in transfer payments to boards of education but to require them to relinquish their hold on the property tax. Municipalities could then occupy the property tax room vacated by boards of education so that ratepayers would barely be aware that the destination of their property taxes had shifted. Since the municipal property tax take would increase, the province could then reduce its transfer payments to municipalities and use that money to increase transfer payments to boards of education. This was very similar to shifts that had already occurred in Alberta and Quebec (Lapointe 1980). It was a grand circular movement that could have worked very well if the numbers had fitted together better. In practice, the numbers did not work, and school boards are still in the property tax business to a reduced but still fairly significant extent. However, the main point is that this shift did occur to a certain extent.

The most significant outcome of the financial reforms is that municipalities are much more reliant on revenue from their own sources, such as the property tax and user charges, and are considerably less reliant on provincial transfers payments. Table 1 illustrates the extent of this shift. The reduction in provincial transfer payments was greeted with howls of indignation by municipalities, though the increased availability of the property tax was accepted with considerably more equanimity. As will be discussed below, this shift from spending someone else's money to spending revenue from their own sources will have an impact on the municipalities' level of autonomy.

The shift to a greater reliance on the property tax was affected by a major change in the property assessment system. The property tax assessments used in some municipalities in Ontario were fifty years out of date, while assessments in other municipalities were virtually up to date. This created many problems of equity between individual taxpayers, classes of taxpayers, and municipalities.

The province brought in a system of current value assessment that was a very positive change because it would have solved the equity problems

Table 1: Shift in Municipal Revenue

	1996		2003	
	$ millions	% of total revenue	$ millions	% of total revenue
Real property tax	7,171.7	42.2	11,794.1	49.0
User charges	3,349.7	19.7	5,696.2	23.6
Other own-source revenue	1,050.7	6.2	1,596.8	6.6
Total own-source revenue	11,572.1	68.1	19,087.1	79.2
Conditional grants	4,542.9	26.7	4,320.8	17.9
Unconditional grants	881.6	5.2	679.4	2.8
Total grants	5,424.5	31.9	5,000.2	20.8
TOTAL	16,996.5	100.0	24,087.3	100.0

Source: Statistics Canada, Cansim II, table 3850004

mentioned above and created a more transparent taxation system (Slack 2002). However, serious problems arose when changes in individual tax liability arose from the movement from the previous inequitable system. For political reasons, the province capped the increase in taxes payable by commercial and industrial taxpayers. This meant that almost the full burden of any tax increase would fall on residential taxpayers, since they were the only group without a cap. The effect of this has been to limit the ability of municipalities to increase taxes because any increase would be focused almost entirely on one group.

FUNCTIONAL REFORM

At the same time that municipal reform was taking place, the province was working on the commitment made in the Common Sense Revolution to re-duce government expenditure, reduce the debt and deficit, and ultimately reduce taxes. Thus, it was clear that whatever was done by way of municipal reform could not increase provincial expenditure and ideally would reduce it. This contrasted sharply with the 1970s reform period when the province was willing to throw money at the new system of regional government to ease the transition. As table 1 indicates, the shift in the property tax discussed in the previous section meant that municipalities enjoyed a fairly significant increase in revenue. This provided the province with the opportunity to shift certain expenditures to municipalities – which leads to another part of the story.

The complex web of provincial-municipal relationships had developed in a fairly haphazard way over many years. Everyone involved in the system recognized that the web of approval requirements, funding arrangements, and mutual persuasion was so complex that it had become dysfunctional. Previous governments had attempted to simplify the system without success. When the Conservatives came to power they appointed the well-respected former mayor of Toronto, David Crombie, to head the "Who Does What" task force. This was actually a group of committees charged with trying to simplify this complexity by going back to first principles to determine which level of government should be responsible for which services and what type of interaction should take place between the levels of government. The idea was to take a fresh look at each service and allocate it to the appropriate level of government, eliminating unnecessary interactions and approval requirements between the two levels. In cases where shared responsibility was necessary, the idea was to structure the interaction in a more functional manner (Meyboom and Richardson 1997).

The task force made its recommendations based on a set of rational principles which flowed from the idea that a service should be allocated to the level of government that was best equipped to handle it. However, when the province began to implement the recommendations, it was clear that the ugly face of expediency impinged on the elegance of the task force's recommendations. In the end, the decisions made about the allocation of responsibilities were heavily influenced by the financial considerations mentioned above; that is, provincial expenditures had to be restrained.

The most significant variation between recommendation and action was in the field of social assistance. The "Who Does What" task force recommended that social assistance be moved to the provincial level, a move that would have brought Ontario into line with the other nine provinces. Instead, the province restructured the system in ways that imposed greater responsibility for social assistance on the municipal level and moved social housing – which had previously been a provincial responsibility – to the local level. Thus, its actions were exactly the opposite of what the Crombie task force had recommended.

At the beginning of this process, the term "revenue-neutral" was used quite a bit. At various stages in the process, scorecards were prepared which purported to show the dollars associated with various transfers. This produced considerable debate, because the amounts to be assigned to various transfers were contentious. And even if the total impact on the municipal system could be determined, the nature of the changes was such that they had very different effects on different municipalities. For example, the requirement that every municipality would now pay for the cost of policing had no impact on the large and medium-sized municipalities, which were already paying this cost, but had a devastating effect on smaller municipalities, which would be paying this for the first time. Over time, the term "revenue-neutral" seems to have dropped out of use. Municipalities talked a lot about "downloading," whereas the provincial phrase was "local services realignment."

Table 2 summarizes some of the changes in the responsibility for functions and some related changes. It avoids the rigid scorecard approach, but it does show whether a particular change was a benefit (+) or a cost (−) to the municipalities. There are many more minuses than pluses in the table, but that can be misleading. For example, the one plus associated with Education Property Tax reform brought in much more money than some of the cost factors.

STRUCTURAL REFORM

Structural reform is tied to the other elements of reform because the Common Sense Revolution promised that the municipal system would be rationalized and the overlap in the layers of government reduced. Structural reform is also tied to financial reform because structural reform was seen as a way of saving money and thus offsetting the reduction in provincial transfer payments to municipalities.

In practice, structural reform meant the amalgamation of municipalities and the restructuring of two-tier counties and regional governments into single-tier governments. The highest profile amalgamation was the 1998 creation of one City of Toronto from Metropolitan Toronto and its six area municipalities. This was followed in 2001 by the creation of large single-tier municipalities in what were the regional municipalities of Hamilton-Wentworth, Ottawa-Carleton, and Sudbury. Throughout this time there were many smaller amalgamations occurring within county systems, including the creation of some large single-tier municipalities, such as Chatham-Kent and Prince Edward County. The extent of the amalgamations can best be appreciated by the fact that in 1995 there were 850 municipalities in Ontario, and by 2001 this number had been approximately halved.

In some cases, these amalgamations were accomplished by provincial edict, particularly in the case of Toronto, Hamilton, Ottawa, and Sudbury. In other cases, there was a strategy of persuasion, with some level of coercion waiting in the wings. The legislation that applied to all of southern Ontario except the regional governments provided mechanisms that allowed municipalities to amalgamate voluntarily, but the legislation also allowed the minister of municipal affairs to appoint a commissioner if requested to do so by any municipality. The commissioner had binding authority to order any type of structural change. A strong message about the use of commissioners was sent when the first commissioner ordered a complete amalgamation of the twenty-three municipalities in the Kent County–City of Chatham area in spite of the fact that none of the local actors wanted such an extensive change. This decision sent many other municipalities scurrying to effect smaller amalgamations before something so extensive was imposed on them. A typical arrangement

Table 2: Changes in the Provincial-Municipal Relationship

Before Common Sense Revolution	*After Common Sense Revolution*	*Change[1]*
EDUCATION PROPERTY TAX		+

Province had been funding a declining portion of total education cost.[1]
    The major portion of education funding came from local school boards through the property tax. Education portion of the property tax had been increasing more rapidly than the municipal portion.
	Province funds approximately 50% of cost of education.
	    School boards reduced their residential property tax levy, which resulted in rates being reduced by about 50%; municipalities were able to increase their tax rates accordingly. Province has specified uniform school tax rate for commercial and industrial properties.	

FARM TAX REBATE		−
Farmer paid 100% of property tax to municipality and received 75% rebate from province.	Farmer now pays 25% of residential tax rate to municipality; no provincial involvement. Municipal bears this cost instead of province.	
PROPERTY ASSESSMENT		−
Responsibility of province.	Responsibility of municipalities. Performed by autonomous entity funded collectively by municipalities.	
SOCIAL ASSISTANCE		−
Province funded some programs 80/20, others 50/50; administration costs shared 50/50.	All programs shared 80/20; administration still shared 50/50.	
SOCIAL HOUSING		−
Province funded most of the deficit through a variety of means.	Province agreed to spend $215 million in capital upgrades, after which municipalities will be responsible for future deficits.	
MUNICIPAL TRANSIT		−
Province provided some grants for both capital and operating.	Existing commitments for capital grants honoured, then no further grants for either capital or operating.	

... continued

Table 2 continued

Before Common Sense Revolution	*After Common Sense Revolution*	*Change[1]*
	GO-TRANSIT	–
	(commuter rail in the Greater Toronto Area)	
Province met deficit.	Operation assumed by the Greater Toronto Services Board and its successors. No provincial funding.	
	ROADS	–
Province maintained some roads within municipalities. Province provided conditional grant.	Many roads switched to municipalities. One-time maintenance funding provided. Grants eliminated.	
	FERRIES AND AIRPORTS	–
Province provided most funding.	Most ferries and airports turned over to municipalities, except those in sparsely populated areas.	
	POLICING	–
OPP provided service free to small municipalities.	All municipalities responsible for the cost of policing. This could be handled through contracts with OPP or establishing a local police service.	
	LIBRARIES	–
Province provided grant.	Grant reduced.	
	PUBLIC HEALTH	–
Most programs were funded by 80–100% grants from the province.	Province continues to fund 50% of mandatory programs.	
	AMBULANCE SERVICE	–
Provided by province.	Municipalities responsible for land ambulance, province funds 50% of approved expenditure; province provides air ambulance.	
	GROSS RECEIPTS TAX	–
Collected by municipalities.	Must be turned over to province.	

Table 2 continued

Before Common Sense Revolution	After Common Sense Revolution	Change[1]
	PROVINCIAL OFFENCES REVENUE	+
Collected by province.	Net proceeds (after adjudication and prosecution costs) directed to municipalities.	
	WATER AND SEWER	0
Province provided service to smaller municipalities on a user-pay basis.	Municipalities are responsible for service, but this was self-funding in most municipalities before anyway.	
	COMMUNITY REINVESTMENT FUND AND TRANSITIONAL ASSISTANCE	+
	Unconditional grant provided. Total amount has varied over time because this is the balancing figure which is intended to make the entire package revenue neutral. Will be discontinued at some point, to be replaced by special circumstances funding on application from municipalities each year.	

[1]Municipal benefit +
Municipal cost –
No change 0

Source: Hollick and Siegel 2001

occurred in Elgin County, where fifteen municipalities were restructured into seven and some realignment of services between the county and the lower tiers was achieved. Outside Toronto and a few other places, the changes were frankly more incremental than earth-shattering.

In many cases, there was a great deal of acrimonious debate about the amalgamation. On the one side, the province promised that larger units of government would generate significant efficiencies that would result in lower taxes. On the other side, many local citizens feared a deterioration in services and a loss of local community spirit. As frequently happens in such cases, neither extreme view seems to have come to fruition. None of the amalgamated municipalities have reported major efficiencies and tax reductions, but there are no major examples of serious deterioration in the quality of service.

There have been concerns in Toronto about problems associated with the amalgamation, but John Barber, the local affairs columnist for the *Globe and Mail*, has argued that many of the sins laid at the door of amalgamation are simply examples of old-fashioned bad management, which can occur in organizations of any size (Barber 2001). A colleague and I have done extensive residents' surveys in three amalgamated municipalities, and they indicate that local residents have not seen a deterioration in the quality of service or sense of community since the amalgamation (Kushner and Siegel 2005).

The outcome of most of these amalgamations gives one cause to wonder whether all the focus sometimes placed on organizational structure is worthwhile. Maybe structure does not matter very much. Structures mean a lot to people who work in them and to academics who study them, but to the average citizen they are not nearly as important as having the garbage picked up on time.

LEGISLATIVE REFORM

A final reform was the first major revision in the municipal legislation in Ontario since the Baldwin Act of 1849. The new Act, which was passed in 2001 and took effect on 1 January 2003, was consciously modelled on the Alberta legislation passed in 1994. The Baldwin Act was a very detailed piece of legislation that had been interpreted in line with the classic Dillon's Rule – a municipality could take no action unless it was given express authority to do so under some piece of provincial legislation.

The purpose of the new Act was to give municipalities greater autonomy by providing them with a broader "permissive policy framework," rather than the narrower "restrictive regulatory framework" (Garcea 2004, 18). This was done by identifying ten spheres of jurisdiction in which municipal councils have considerable latitude to operate. The spheres are:

1 highways, including parking and traffic on highways
2 transportation systems, other than highways
3 waste management
4 public utilities
5 culture, parks, recreation, and heritage
6 drainage and flood control, except storm sewers
7 structures, including fences and signs
8 parking, except on highways
9 animals
10 economic development services (Ontario, *Municipal Act, 2001*).

The Act also gives municipalities "natural person powers," meaning that they are allowed to carry out duties within these general spheres of jurisdiction without needing the kind of detailed delegation found in the previous Municipal Act. Specifically, this should provide municipalities with greater flexibility in the areas of entering into contracts, suing and being sued, hiring and dismissing employees, delegating administrative responsibilities to council committees and staff, entering into innovative service delivery arrangements such as public-private partnerships, and purchasing and disposing of property (Garcea 2004).

In addition to natural person powers, municipalities are granted some governmental powers, such as "the authority to tax, to regulate or prohibit certain activities, to require individuals to do certain things, to expropriate property and to establish a system of licences, permits, approvals and registrations" (Ontario, Ministry of Municipal Affairs 2001, 7). Many of these powers already existed in a number of different pieces of legislation, but the new Municipal Act brings them together in one place.

There are certain limits on these new powers. Municipalities cannot pass bylaws that conflict with federal or provincial legislation; they must respect certain procedural requirements in making decisions; and there are some limitations on their financial activities.

CONSEQUENCES

The cumulative effect of all these changes could provide municipalities with more autonomy. The previous sentence is worded in a cautionary manner because much depends on how municipalities react to the opportunities presented to them and how the province responds to these municipal initiatives. The remainder of this paper will consider some of the opportunities that municipalities have, and will provide a preliminary assessment of how they have used these opportunities so far.

MORE POWERFUL MAYORS

Politicians gain a great deal of their authority from the size of the area and the number of people they represent. Currently, the City of Toronto has twenty-two members of parliament, twenty-two members of the provincial legislature, and one mayor. It is not difficult to figure out who will speak with the greatest authority about the needs of the people of Toronto. This will also have an impact when mayors speak collectively. Three of the largest cities in Ontario are now of the amalgamated, single-tier type. The mayors of Hamilton, Ottawa, and Toronto represent more than 30 percent of the total population of the province.

Of course, political power has a significant personal component as well. There will be mayors who are unable or unwilling to wield the amount of power they have available to them, and it will be some time before this pattern develops to its full extent, but there can be little doubt that these mega-cities have the potential to produce mega-mayors.

SIZE MATTERS

Not only are the amalgamated cities quantitatively larger, but there are qualitative differences that occur as municipalities become larger. Courchene has argued that Toronto is in the process of attaining the status of a global city-region with all the accoutrements of power that this brings (Courchene 2001). Larger and more economically powerful municipalities are able to hire more staff and more highly qualified staff. The larger municipalities have more money, and because of their size they can attract politicians and staff who want the challenge of managing in a larger place. For an aspiring politician, being mayor of a large city looks more attractive than being an MP or MPP. On the staff side, larger municipalities can hire people with more specialized expertise in such areas as policy analysis and intergovernmental affairs. This kind of appointment is sometimes seen in municipalities in other provinces and in the United States, but is not common in Ontario. It could allow municipalities to develop a level of expertise that might rival that of the province.

This has not happened very much so far in Ontario. The traditional view held by many councillors and staff is that local government is about delivering services and minimizing taxes. They consider that policy analysis is something done by other governments; local governments do not waste time considering broader policy issues – a fact that is all too often true. And since intergovernmental relations are handled by the head of council, there is thought to be no need for specialists. This is an area where local governments could improve their position, but they have been slow to move.

SINGLE-TIERS SPEAK WITH ONE VOICE

Two-tier governments were supposed to be desirable because they would provide for economies of scale in the upper tiers and citizen participation in the lower tiers. This has not worked as well as anticipated because there are relatively few economies of scale to be captured, and the goal of citizen participation has been weakened because of the confusion caused by two tiers of government. In practice, two-tier local governments have become vehicles that allow politicians in one tier to spend a great deal of their time and taxpayers' money fighting politicians at the other level (who are spending a great deal of time and taxpayers' money to defend themselves). Blame shifting has become a major activity in two-tier governments.

Mayors of larger municipalities speak with considerable authority, and the mayor of a large, single-tier municipality can speak with greater authority than the chair of an upper-tier county or region. The downside of this is that the kinds of territorial disputes that used to occur between municipalities now occur within council. This is obviously a problem, and the greater the geographic area of the municipality and the larger the council, the greater is this problem. However, there are established mechanisms for resolving these disputes within council, and they do not involve the same level of visible acrimony as intermunicipal disputes.

MORE UNTIED MONEY

Table 1 above indicated that municipal revenue has increased significantly in the last few years. The shift from a heavy reliance on tied money, in the form of conditional transfers, to greater availability of own-source revenue, in the form of property taxes and users charges, is as significant as the amount of the increase.

Municipal politicians would be quick to point out that these were not exactly windfalls in that the increase in revenues has been accompanied by the downloading of major responsibilities for service provision. Municipal politicians would also point to the political cost and practical constraints on increasing property taxes and user charges. However, the increase in the amount of untied money does give municipalities more levers in making policy. Downloaded responsibilities cannot be ignored, but the lack of conditional transfers, which forced municipalities to spend in certain areas, means that municipalities now have autonomy to decide how much attention (and funding) to focus on these downloaded responsibilities. Municipalities will soon figure out what provincial governments learned some time ago in their dealings with the federal government – that in the absence of conditional grants, it is very difficult to enforce standards and require other governments to engage in particular activities. Municipalities will be able to make policy decisions to move funds around if they choose to do so.

MORE LEGISLATIVE AUTHORITY

The establishment of spheres of jurisdiction and the provision of natural person powers can amount to a notable increase in the powers that municipalities have available to them. These changes constitute a change from the rigid principle of Dillon's Rule to greater flexibility and autonomy in decision making. However, Garcea has argued that the real impact of these changes will be determined by how the municipal governments use them, how the provincial government responds to what municipalities do, and how courts interpret the legislation (Garcea 2004).

A few months after the legislation has come into force, the rhetoric at municipal council meetings has not changed very much. Many councillors would still rather complain about the intrusiveness of provincial rules than actually make policy themselves. New-found power can be both intoxicating and frightening. Municipal councillors are so comfortable with possessing limited powers and being able to blame the province or the other level of municipal government for problems or missed opportunities that these patterns of behaviour will be slow to change. Smith and Stewart, in their paper in this volume, have provided examples of cases where Vancouver politicians have acted proactively to push the envelope of municipal autonomy in the face of reluctant provincial officials. It would be difficult to find comparable examples in Ontario.

From the provincial perspective, it may be difficult to loosen the reins of municipal government that have been in place for so long. Although the new legislation gives municipalities more autonomy, there are enough restraints in the legislation and in other powers held by the province that it would be easy for the province to revert to its paternalistic role. The constraints preventing this occurring are based more on goodwill than on legislative enactment. For example, the province has recently raised the idea of requiring municipalities to hold a referendum before they increase property taxes. If this idea is followed through, it will have a significant impact on the development of municipal autonomy that I have suggested above. Another effect of this suggestion and the way it was announced is that it has had a devastating impact on the level of trust that was developing between the two levels of governments. As mentioned above, there are levers in the legislation that allow the province to return to a very restrictive position. At first, municipalities believed that the province would not be quick to use these. However, this recent musing about referendums has shaken that confidence.

CONCLUSION

Local government reform in Ontario has come by fits and starts over the years. However, the recent reforms discussed in this paper are the most significant set of reforms made in Ontario's municipal system since the current system was created by the Baldwin Act in 1849. There were financial reforms that have reduced the municipalities' reliance on provincial transfers and given them greater access to own-source revenue. There were functional reforms that have given municipalities much more scope for service provision. There were structural reforms that have reduced the number of municipalities by half, often by replacing two-tier municipalities with very large single-tier municipalities. There were also major legislative reforms that have given municipalities more autonomy from provincial control.

The importance of behaviour persistence needs to be considered in assessing the real impact of these changes. For a long time, municipalities have viewed themselves as creatures of the province; and for an equally long time, the province has taken a paternalistic view of municipalities. These roles will not change quickly, even with all sorts of structural changes.

Municipalities have been conditioned to see themselves as service-delivery vehicles, trying to squeeze as much money as possible from the province so that they can keep property taxes low. Municipal councillors see their role almost entirely in terms of minimizing property taxes and delivering the mandated services. Ten years ago, Frances Frisken wrote: "[M]ost Canadian municipalities tend to use their powers primarily to protect themselves from the impacts of change, not to accommodate or manage it." (Frisken 1994, 30) Changing this perspective to a more proactive, policy-oriented role will be very difficult. Since councillors generally see their entire role in financial terms, the additional powers available to them in the new *Municipal Act* have not attracted a great deal of attention.

There are important caveats on the provincial side as well. While there are mechanisms in place to allow more municipal autonomy, there are also mechanisms that could allow that autonomy to be withdrawn. There is a great deal of goodwill in the Ministry of Municipal Affairs and Housing right now because the architects of the new legislation are still there. However, provincial people move around. Will the next group inherit the same spirit of cooperation? Or will they overreact to the first problems that develop in a municipality? Much of this goodwill could be squandered by one quick announcement of a referendum requirement for property tax increases.

A further complication is that the Ministry of Municipal Affairs and Housing is only one ministry in the provincial government. Many other ministries also deal with municipalities, and it seems doubtful that all of them have heard the autonomy message; some are still imposing the kind of detailed control on municipal activity that the Ministry of Municipal Affairs and Housing would like to leave behind.

We seem to be at a significant juncture in the history of provincial-municipal relations – even of municipal government generally – in Ontario. There have been major structural changes in the last few years that pave the way for what could be the greatest change in municipal government since the creation of municipalities in 1849. However, it would be easy to slide back to the old ways of doing things. The next few years will determine what happens.

NOTES

The author would like to thank Lionel Feldman, Enid Slack, and Shaun Young for their helpful comments on an earlier version of this paper. The analysis and conclusions are the responsibility of the author.

1 Actually, the two largest boards (Ottawa and Toronto) did not receive any provincial funding.

REFERENCES

Barber, John. 2001. "The Nasty Job of Mucking Out Megacity Stables." *Globe and Mail,* 1 December

Colton, Timothy J. 1980. *Big Daddy: Frederick G. Gardiner and the Building of Metropolitan Toronto.* Toronto: University of Toronto Press

Courchene, Thomas J. 2001. "Ontario as a North American Region-State, Toronto as a Global City-Region: Responding to the NAFTA Challenge." In *Global City-Regions: Trends, Theory, Policy,* ed. Allen J. Scott, 158–92. Oxford: Oxford University Press

Frisken, Frances. 1993. "Planning and Servicing the Greater Toronto Area: The Interplay of Provincial and Municipal Interests." In *Metropolitan Governance: American Canadian Intergovernmental Perspectives,* ed. Donald N. Rothblatt and Andrew Sancton, 153–204. Berkeley: Institute of Governmental Studies Press, University of California; Kingston: Institute of Intergovernmental Affairs, Queen's University

– 1994. "Metropolitan Change and the Challenge to Public Policy." In *The Changing Canadian Metropolis: A Public Policy Perspective,* ed. Frisken, 1–35. Berkeley: Institute of Governmental Studies Press, University of California

Garcea, Joseph. 2004. "Modern Municipal Statutory Frameworks in Canada." *Revue gouvernance* 1 (1): 18–31

Graham, Katherine A., and Susan D. Phillips. 1998. 'Who Does What' in Ontario: The Process of Provincial-Municipal Disentanglement." *Canadian Public Administration* 41 (2): 175–209

Hollick, Thomas R., and David Siegel. 2001. *Evolution, Revolution, Amalgamation: Restructuring in Three Ontario Municipalities.* London, Ont.: Department of Political Science, University of Western Ontario

Ibbitson, John. 1997. *Promised Land: Inside the Mike Harris Revolution.* Scarborough, Ont.: Prentice-Hall Canada

Kushner, Joseph, and David Siegel. 2000. "Restructuring Poll." *Chatham Daily News,* 3 November

– 2005. "Citizen Satisfaction with Municipal Amalgamations." *Canadian Public Administration* 48 (1): 73–95

Lapointe, Jean-Louis. 1980. "La réforme de la fiscalité municipale au Québec." *Canadian Public Administration.*23 (2): 269–80

Meyboom, Peter, and Dana Richardson. 1997. "Changing Who-Does-What in Ontario: Ontario's Approach towards Municipal Empowerment – Process, Results, and Lessons Learned." Paper presented at conference of the International Institute of Administrative Sciences, Quebec City, 14–17 July.

O'Brien, Allan. 1993. *Municipal Consolidation in Canada and Its Alternatives.* Toronto: Intergovernmental Committee on Urban and Regional Research

Ontario. Committee on Taxation. 1967. *Report.* Toronto: Queen's Printer

– Ministry of Municipal Affairs and Housing. 2001. *New Directions: A New Municipal Act for Ontario.* Toronto: Queen's Printer for Ontario

– *Municipal Act, 2001.* SO. 2001, c. 25, s. 11.

Rose, Albert. 1972. *Governing Metropolitan Toronto: A Social and Political Analysis.* Berkeley: Institute of Governmental Studies, University of California

Sancton, Andrew. 1991. *Local Government Reorganization in Canada since 1975.* Toronto: Intergovernmental Committee on Urban and Regional Research

– 2000. "Amalgamations, Service Realignment, and Property Taxes: Did the Harris Government Have a Plan for Ontario's Municipalities?" *Canadian Journal of Regional Science* 23 (1):135–56

Siegel, David. 2001. "Measuring Citizen Satisfaction in an Amalgamated Municipality: The Case of Chatham-Kent, Ontario," Paper presented to the Annual Conference of the Urban Affairs Association, Detroit, Michigan, 26 April

Slack, Enid. 2002. "Property Tax Reform in Ontario: What Have We Learned?" *Canadian Tax Journal* 50 (2): 575–85

IV

Policy

9

Ethnocultural Diversity, Democracy, and Intergovernmental Relations in Canadian Cities

Christian Poirier

Bien que la dimension multiculturelle de plusieurs villes canadiennes ne fasse aucun doute, le rôle joué par les municipalités en matière de politique dans ce domaine et les relations intergouvernementales qui font partie de ce processus demeurent néanmoins obscures. Comparant Montréal et Ottawa, ce chapitre analyse le développement historique de la question de l'immigration au niveau des politiques publiques municipales, la nature de la relation entre les autorités municipales et les gouvernements fédéral et provinciaux, et le degré d'autonomie locale en place. S'intéressant à la fois à l'aspect discursif et à l'aspect pratique, ce chapitre soutient que ces deux villes peuvent jouer un rôle important à différents niveaux. Les associations multiculturelles reconnaissent d'ailleurs de plus en plus qu'elles ont un rôle politique important à jouer. Elles ne sont toutefois pas entièrement perçues comme de vrais partenaires politiques par les autres niveaux de gouvernement.

INTRODUCTION

In the management of ethnic diversity, federalism and intergovernmental issues are extremely important. Immigration, according to the *Constitution Act, 1867*, is an area of shared jurisdiction (article 95). Many provinces, including Quebec, play an active role in this field and, through a series of agreements with the federal government, select the candidates and are responsible for their integration. However, since immigrants settle mainly in urban areas, municipal governments have been increasingly involved, especially those large cities that have received the majority of recent immigrants (Montreal, Ottawa, Toronto, and Vancouver). The numbers are stunning: approximately 220,000 immigrants and refugees enter Canada each year, and 85 percent of them settle in urban centres (Canada 2001). In 1996, 85 percent of all immigrants and 93 percent of those who had arrived in the country between 1991 and 1996 were living in a census metropolitan area, compared with 57 percent for people born in Canada (Canada 1996).

While there is no doubt about the multicultural dimension of many cities, the political and policy roles played by municipalities in this area – as well as the intergovernmental relations involved in the process – are more obscure. There is a growing Canadian literature on municipal public policy in this field (Abu-Laban 1997; Abu-Laban and Derwing 1997; Edgington and Hutton 2002; Germain and Dansereau 2003; Germain and Rose 2000; Milroy and Wallace 2002; Paré, Frohn, and Laurin 2002; Siemiatycki et al. 2001; Wallace and Frisken 2000). However, there has not been much comparative work, since most of the studies relate to one specific city (exceptions would be Edgington et al. 2001; Quesnel and Tate 1995).

This paper compares the policies dealing with the management of ethnocultural diversity in Montreal and Ottawa, two ethnically diverse cities. From 1997 to 2001, 78.3 percent of the immigrants that came to Quebec settled in Montreal (Quebec 2002); overall, 13 percent of new immigrants to Canada chose Montreal. In 2002 Montreal, with a total population of 1.8 million (the second largest in Canada), had an immigrant population of 26 percent; of the overall population, 35 percent had origins other than Canadian, Québécois, French, British, or Aboriginal, and 19 percent belonged to a visible minority. In Ottawa, in 2002, immigrants made up 21 percent of the population. Nearly 30 percent of the population had origins other than Canadian, Québécois, French, British, or Aboriginal, while 15 percent belonged to a visible minority. The total population of Ottawa was 791,300, making Ottawa-Gatineau the fourth largest metropolitan area in Canada.

Four elements will be examined in order to analyse the nature and dynamics of the intergovernmental factor regarding immigration and settlement. First, it is important to consider how migration issues became matters of local public policy. Specifically, we will consider how Canadian cities became involved in this field. Second, we need to assess how local policies are linked to policies developed or promoted at the provincial and federal levels. It is here that we will address the management of ethnic diversity, both its practical aspects (policies, programs, and administrative and political mechanisms) and discursive ones (the models for the management of ethnocultural heterogeneity that lie behind government actions). Each city has certain policy tools that it can use to influence the patterns of integration of ethnocultural groups. On the practical side, many activities can be created (for example, festivals) and many mechanisms can be put in place (for example, creating an advisory council on multicultural issues, or implementing an equal employment opportunity program for the municipal public service). The discursive aspect is linked to the three broad models used in Western countries to integrate immigrants: civic universalism, multiculturalism, and interculturalism.

Third, we will consider whether there are formal partnerships or agreements and consultations between the levels of governments. Both Montreal and Ottawa constantly position themselves in the complex set of interrelations – involving conflict as well as cooperation – that exist between them and the governments of Quebec, Ontario, and Canada. In Montreal, the relationship with the Quebec government has always been one of ambivalence, exhibiting both distance and connection. Various Montreal mayors, often feeling "abandoned" or misunderstood, have argued for a greater understanding of the importance of the social, cultural, and economic role of Montreal for the Province of Quebec as a whole. Indeed, the Quebec government did react favourably, at least to some extent, and the Ministry of Municipal Affairs became, during the second half of the 1990s, the Ministry of Municipal Affairs and the Metropolis. Also, a city contract signed in January 2003 between Montreal and the Quebec government gave the city some political autonomy. However, the imposition of the municipal amalgamations, even though this major restructuring was shared (or even suggested) by many of Montreal's political elite, created considerable discontent at the municipal level.

Although relationships between Montreal and the federal government are somewhat more distant, the recent proposals formulated by the Canadian government have generally been well received by the Montreal political authorities, for they indicate a more active federal role in urban issues (for example, the infrastructure program; the agreement with the provinces on low-cost rental housing; the national Homelessness Initiative; the Prime Minister's Caucus Task Force on Urban Issues; and the agreement regarding the gas tax).

Intergovernmental relations are very different in Ottawa. Since it is the national capital, it is the federal government that is very close and the province more distant. Relations with the federal government are, however, ambivalent. Specifically, the city has had some difficulty in developing an autonomous local identity. The strong role played by the National Capital Commission has certainly complicated the role for the city. As part of its mandate, this federal agency aims at building the image of the capital in order to strengthen the Canadian identity and its symbols. This leaves little room for Ottawa to create its own references, linked (or not) to ethnocultural diversity. However, as in Montreal, the recent federal statements about an interest in urban affairs have met with general approval.

Relations between Ottawa and the Ontario government are more distant. They were clearly antagonistic when the Conservatives were in power, since the latter saw Ottawa as a bastion of the opposition. This was partly on account of the mayor's previous role as a Liberal MPP but also because of the city's near defiance of the province on the implementation of the Ontario Works program. The downloading of such activities as social services, housing, and public transportation has certainly fuelled a feeling of frustration on the part of the municipal council. For instance, a conflict emerged when the province blocked the municipal decision to restructure the ward boundaries, an action that was seen as having been motivated by partisan goals – those of protecting rural councillors more sympathetic to the neoliberal views of the provincial Conservatives. Obviously, relations are much more harmonious now that there is a Liberal government in Ontario.

Finally, we will consider more generally the role of the city as a political actor and a producer of identity, and we will analyse the extent of local autonomy on this issue. We think that what can be learned from Montreal and Ottawa could very well be extended to other cities. We will attempt to show that the management of diversity reveals a great deal about the state of local governance in Canada, the development of local identities, and the evolution of intergovernmental relations at the present time.

In sum, we will try to demonstrate in this paper that both cities, even if they are not involved with the same intensity in diversity matters, do play an important role in this field and are relatively autonomous from the upper levels of government. Unfortunately, the latter do not often recognize them as real and legitimate political actors.

ETHNOCULTURAL DIVERSITY AS AN ISSUE FOR LOCAL PUBLIC POLICY

The policy on immigration has evolved substantially in Canada (Berthet and Poirier 2000). Immigration was first seen as a matter related to the workforce, and public policy was situated in terms of international relations and economic development. Without entirely losing this focus, immigration came to be seen, in the period after the 1960s and 1970s, as part of social and cultural policies. In addition to attracting immigrants that will contribute to Canada's economic growth, public policy must increasingly look at issues linked to ethnic cohabitation. It is only fairly recently that municipalities have entered the field of managing ethnocultural relations. Their initiatives were not the result of formal agreements about decentralization. It was more like opening a policy window, in the sense of John Kingdon's (1995) treatise – that local authorities take up an issue because they perceive that there are advantages to be gained and because other levels of government are not really involved.

Municipalities that have developed initiatives relating to the integration of immigrants all have a considerable number of ethnocultural associations, either consisting of people from the same ethnocultural group or bringing together a variety of people around issues such as anti-racism, human rights, and anti-discrimination. Many local governments (for example, Vancouver) have supported the work of these associations in order to facilitate service delivery that is more culturally sensitive and thus may prevent conflicts from arising. A number of local elected officials have been particularly sensitive to the demands of these groups and have included the issue of cultural diversity in the construction of local identities as well as in the political legitimization of the municipal level of government. So it would seem that community-based groups, rather than incentives from other levels of government, have been extremely important in pushing Canadian cities to take more account of ethnocultural diversity.

The federal policy regarding multiculturalism has also had a significant impact on the mobilization of ethnocultural communities. Since the 1980s especially, the Secretary of State for Multiculturalism (now part of Canadian Heritage) has worked to build the capacity of the immigrant community to take collective responsibility for dealing with the causes of inequality and for developing mobilization strategies – including judicial recourse – so that its members can exercise their rights at all levels of government.

Provincial policies, too, have had an indirect impact. This is largely a result of the crisis of the welfare state and the downloading of many services linked to social issues (which have an impact on immigration issues) from federal to provincial governments and from provincial to municipal governments (Germain and Harel 1985). As well, many responsibilities have been privatized to civil society organizations. Recently, the Quebec Liberal government cut quite extensively the budget of the department responsible for immigration and the funds allocated to the programs aimed at facilitating the integration of immigrants. In that context, Montreal has no choice but to try to find some solutions.

In addition, some municipalities took initiatives in areas (such as culture, social services, and the environment) that had not been their traditional spheres of activity, and in this way they illustrated a desire to be more autonomous. In this context, the strength of municipal governments is their capacity to bring the full range of social actors to the table to act together. Public action at the local level therefore involves many organizations (civil, private, and public), and it is the convenor and networking capacity of local governments that determines their policy capacity.

Another factor that Kingdon stresses in explaining policy initiative is the importance of having solutions for identified problems. In this respect, the actions of the Federation of Canadian Municipalities (FCM), the official spokesperson for Canadian municipalities at the federal level, can be seen as facilitating municipal action for the management of diversity. In 1986 the FCM adopted its first policy statement on interracial relations (FCM 1986). In order to facilitate municipal activity, this interest group published a series of pamphlets, starting in 1987. The first of these underlined the need for municipal action because, despite existing laws and policies (such as the federal policy on multiculturalism, the *Canadian Charter or Rights and Freedoms*, and provincial laws), discrimination on the basis of race and unequal access to institutions remained significant problems (FCM 1987).

The FCM put forward a program that has been taken up by a number of municipalities interested in the management of diversity. It includes the creation of festivals and multicultural celebrations; consultation with ethnocultural groups in order to adapt municipal services; and the adoption of programs and policies by municipal councils to promote increased participation of ethnocultural minorities in the social, economic, cultural, and political life of the community. The FCM's basic argument was that good interracial relations could translate into greater economic development and an enhanced quality of urban life. Cities should be leaders in this area, argued the national organization, because they are the first point of contact for citizens and ethnocultural communities and are major facilitators of community action. For the FCM, the improvement of interracial relations is clearly a municipal responsibility (FCM 1987, 1988, 1990, 1991, 1992).

The FCM stated in 2002 , "A major part of the impact of immigration is felt at the local level, and it is the local initiatives and programs that assure the success of our national immigration policies" (FCM 2002, 2). This led the federation to call for official recognition of the increased municipal responsibility in the area of immigration: "The municipal governments should be at the table with the federal and provincial governments when decisions are being made about immigration and refugee policies and programs" (ibid.). The FCM's discourse has gone from one of encouraging municipalities to become involved in this policy area (in the 1980s and 1990s) to insisting on intergovernmental recognition of the municipal role (in the 2000s).

Finally, the municipal responsibility for police and transit was an important element in the movement towards municipal activity in managing diversity. For instance, in Montreal, the actions taken by the Communauté urbaine de Montréal (CUM) were clearly motivated by the attempt to reduce tensions stemming from crisis situations between the police, the public transit commission, and some ethnocultural communities. Indeed, in many municipalities (including Ottawa), the first actions relating to the management of diversity were often linked to the police, in many cases arising from specific incidents.

In sum, Canadian cities involved in ethnocultural issues have been doing so because of a proactive attitude by city councils, pressure from ethnic interest groups, incentives from the Federation of Canadian Municipalities, and the relative absence in (or retreat from) this field by the upper levels of government.

MANAGING DIVERSITY: POLICIES AND DISCOURSES

While immigration policies (the number of people allowed to enter the country each year, the types of immigrants wanted, the acquisition of citizenship, etc.) are mainly influenced and determined by the federal government and some provinces, we must underline that large Canadian cities are increasingly involved in the business of attracting immigrants. In a globalized world, cities are in competition with one another, and they try to attract skilled immigrants (for example, in the multimedia and pharmaceutical sectors in Montreal and the computer and software sectors in Ottawa). Also, settlement policies are mainly left in the hands of provinces and, more and more, in the hands of municipalities, with the other levels of government providing financial help to specific programs or to multicultural and ethnic associations.

Montreal has been involved in settlement issues since the 1980s. In 1985 the CUM created the Advisory Committee on Intercultural and Interracial Relations, and in 1990 it issued a declaration on intercultural and interracial relations. The public transportation agency (Société de transport de la Communauté urbaine de Montréal) provided intercultural training to its drivers and established a program of employment equity in 1987. The CUM police did likewise. The City of Montreal created its own Advisory Committee on Interracial and Intercultural Relations in 1990 (in 1995 the name was changed to the Advisory Committee on Intercultural Relations), with a mandate to advise and make recommendations to City Council.

The new amalgamated (in 2002) City of Montreal intends to make the management of diversity and the elimination of barriers one of its priorities. In 2003 the city created the Intercultural Council (replacing the former Advisory Committee on Intercultural Relations). This council has the responsibility of advising City Council and the executive committee – either on its own initiative or by request from the city – on services and policies designed to facilitate the integration and participation of members of ethnocultural communities in the political, economic, social, and cultural life of the city (Montreal 2001, 1). In addition, the Intercultural Council hears delegations, solicits opinions, and undertakes research studies. The City of Montreal also established the Office of Intercultural Relations, charged with implementing recommendations and ensuring follow-up; the office is also responsible for the relations between the city and its ethnocultural communities.

The main activities undertaken by the City of Montreal are the following: establishment of a program of employment equity for municipal employees; financial and technical support for ethnocultural associations; information and translation services; activities to raise awareness (workshops, intercultural days, debates, publicity campaigns, information in local newspapers, displays in libraries, visits to schools, work with the media); financing festivals and multicultural celebrations; consulting ethnocultural communities about ways of adapting municipal services; integrating multiculturalism into leisure and sports activities; adopting a declaration on intercultural and interracial relations, and a declaration against discrimination and racism.

Montreal's civic groups have also incorporated a concern for this issue, presenting candidates from ethnocultural communities. Selected elected representatives were given responsibility for intercultural relations, particularly at the level of the executive committee. Both the public transportation agency and the police service established a program of employment equity many years ago. More recently, the Montreal Summit, held in June 2002 to define the main policy orientations of the new amalgamated city, discussed the issue of diversity (Montreal 2002).

The former City of Ottawa first set up an advisory committee on visible minorities in 1982 (Andrew and Rajiva 1996). In the early 1990s the city also had an administrative structure that dealt with human rights and employment equity, and in the late 1990s the Diversity and Community Access Project Team was created to tackle the issue of diversity (Ottawa 2000). The new City of Ottawa (which was amalgamated in 2001, one year earlier than Montreal) set up an enlarged network of advisory committees, including one on equity and diversity. The Equity and Diversity Advisory Committee (EDAC), which met for the first time in August 2001, covers a number of dimensions of diversity. Its terms of reference include working towards the elimination of discrimination within the City of Ottawa, advocating on behalf of racially and ethnically diverse groups, developing a strong lobbying network with other organizations, and promoting a better understanding of different cultures (Ottawa 2002c).

However, the functioning of EDAC has not been without problems (Poirier and Andrew 2003). Indeed, all of the advisory committees of the new city have questioned their roles and their relations with city staff and elected officials. The major problem seems to be access to the political agenda. As one of the members of EDAC said, "How can we advise if we don't know what the issues are?"[1]

Ottawa is also extensively involved in the diversification of its workforce and has put in place various activities oriented towards dialogue between religions (as a result of 9/11). The Ottawa Police and OC Transpo are also very active on issues of diversity. However, Ottawa City Council is almost exclusively "white," unlike Montreal City Council, and the Ottawa 20/20 official plan (which will broadly guide City Council for twenty years) gives rather limited visibility to the issues of diversity (Ottawa 2002a).

It is now time to consider the ways in which Montreal and Ottawa describe their policy objectives and activities. In doing so, it will be possible to understand the fundamental approach that each takes in relation to the management of diversity. Broadly speaking, we can identify three models: civic universalism, multiculturalism, and interculturalism.[2]

In the model of civic universalism, the public sphere is seen as an area where all citizens should be on an equal footing in relation to the rules and values of collective life. Differences (in moral choice, religious belief, behaviour, and taste) are not denied but are confined to the private space. By contrast, multiculturalism is a political project which states that the common good and the search for social justice must take into account the cultural conceptions of minorities living in the same territory. Differences are valorized in the political and public spheres, while collective rights or different privileges can be accorded to specific minorities.

The intercultural model emerged as a result of the criticisms that were levelled at both models. The central question it poses is the following: How can we remain different while sharing certain common reference points? Whereas universalist models were criticized for ignoring differences and for proposing the homogenization of ideas and lifestyles in the name of an abstract citizenship, multiculturalism was criticized for producing communities and groups isolated from one another. Interculturalism is a sort of multiculturalism but with the construction of common reference points (for instance, the necessity to learn French in Quebec); the immigrant as well as the host society should both adapt to each other.

Montreal's model is traditionally inspired by interculturalism. During the Montreal Summit, the description of the city's policy emphasized intercultural relations and links between the ethnocultural communities and the city as a whole. The interculturalist model is also present in the publicity campaign "Nous sommes tous Montréalais" ("We are all Montrealers"), created during the years of Pierre Bourque's administration. The image shows a variety of people representing different ethnocultural communities, with the idea that all of these groups share a common Montreal identity. The links between them are what forms their commonality; Montreal is the strong common reference point, and it provides the links between different groups.

At the same time (and more recently), Montreal's discourse also contains universalist references. The documents prepared for the Montreal Summit dealing with diversity refer to citizenship and universal rights. All sectors of the population must be able to exercise their citizenship fully. The policies for managing diversity are only one part of a broader policy aimed at creating a universal citizenship. In this sense, the conception of a person as being a member of a specific culture cohabits with the reference to citizens having the same rights and duties as other citizens. Multiculturalism references are also present, although less strongly.

The Government of Quebec surely had a strong influence on Montreal on the level of discourse. Traditionally, Quebec has articulated a very clear intercultural stance, most notably in 1990–91 with the establishment of a "moral contract" between Quebecers and immigrants (Quebec 1990). This contract recognizes diversity while emphasizing the importance of a common public culture (including French).

The intercultural reference moved towards a universalist approach during the latter part of the 1990s. In 1996 the Quebec government stopped using the term "cultural communities," which had been introduced in the 1970s, and the Ministry of Cultural Communities and Immigration became the Ministry for Relations with Citizens and Immigration, while Intercultural Week became

Quebec Citizenship Week. The Quebec government readopted Intercultural Week in 2003. According to the Ministry for Relations with Citizens and Immigration, the government policy is to promote an understanding of the rights and responsibilities of all citizens without discrimination (Quebec 2001, 20). The discourse is of civic participation and good civic relations, rather than intercultural relations. This evolution from interculturalism to universalism has clearly influenced the Montreal discourse. Also, the multi-ethnic orientation of associations is encouraged rather than the promotion of single ethnocultural groups, as is the case with the federal government's policy.

The influence of the Canadian government, with its policy of multiculturalism, is rather limited in Montreal, except for the financing of multicultural associations. Heritage Canada and the Canadian Human Rights Commission are occasionally mentioned as playing a role in local activities, but generally speaking, the federal government is relatively discreet in the management of diversity in Montreal. The federal government also moved, especially after the referendum on Quebec sovereignty in 1995, towards a universalist approach aiming at strengthening and unifying the Canadian nation and Canadian identity. This kind of discourse was not really well received in Montreal.

The City of Ottawa's discursive universe plays on two registers: one universalist (which is dominant) and one multicultural. Every policy and discourse put forward by the city stresses the equality of all citizens. At the same time, other policy orientations are influenced more by a multicultural approach (Ottawa 2002b, 10). Some papers from EDAC argue for financial and other support to specific ethnocultural groups and for the creation of a Multicultural Day. The Ottawa Police refers to a "cultural mosaic" – clearly a multicultural approach, with the idea of communities coexisting side by side. Ottawa's draft official plan (Ottawa 2002a) also builds on the idea of a city of distinct communities, each with its own identity and pride of place.

There are also a few intercultural references. One paper refers to the importance of links between the various ethnocultural communities: "The City must provide active support for diversity through strategies which build inclusion, create shared points of contact, and build a shared commitment to the City as a place in common – in other words, a home" (Ottawa 2002a, 11). EDAC also talks of encouraging formal and informal contacts between community groups in order to promote a better understanding of different cultures. But despite these references, the dominant approaches in Ottawa are those of universalism and multiculturalism.

The Ontario legislation on employment equity during the 1990s was a major influence on the activities of the former City of Ottawa. Given that Mike Harris's Conservative government had abolished the legislation on employment equity and gave little priority to the recognition of diversity, it is not surprising that there was little influence from the provincial level at that time.

However, the previous New Democratic government had used a multicultural approach, and certainly this did correspond to the municipal approach. It is too soon to assess the influence of the Liberal government of Dalton Mcguinty. There may also be some influence from the federal government in terms of its multicultural approach and its universal approach focusing on the Canadian identity, which had been very well received in the City of Ottawa.

This section has demonstrated that both cities, in varying degrees, are involved in ethnocultural issues. Both have shown leadership in this field and are relatively autonomous from the provincial and federal governments, though they are sometimes influenced by the senior levels of government, most notably in terms of discourses. We have also seen that both cities use – often at the same time – a combination of different models. In fact, they constantly switch from one to another, according to the circumstances. However, the consequence of this "reframing" of ethnic issues is that variations can be observed between the discourses and the policies put in place. For instance, if Montreal officially puts forward an intercultural discourse, variations between districts can be evident, with some districts allowing specific swimming hours for Muslim women (a multicultural approach) while others do not (a universal one). But these variations clearly demonstrate, even in times of financial restraint, that cities possess a degree of autonomy in this field. Cooperation with other levels of government is also possible. This is what we shall consider in the following section.

FORMALIZED INTERGOVERNMENTAL RELATIONS?

In the case of Montreal, there are a number of joint activities that relate to ethnocultural diversity. There are agreements between the Quebec Ministry of Relations with Citizens and Immigration and the City of Montreal relating to the integration of new immigrants and the learning of French. There is also an intergovernmental agreement supporting interculturalism in the area of cultural activities. In addition, Montreal participates in coordinating activities organized by the Quebec government, most notably those bringing together agencies working with refugees and immigrants and those dealing with visible minority youth. The new city contract signed in January 2003 between the Quebec government and the City of Montreal recognizes that Montreal plays – and must play in the future – an important role in such areas as the management of ethnic diversity, housing, transit, community development, and tourism.

In Ottawa, there are no formal agreements between the city and the Government of Ontario. Through the Newcomer Settlement Program, Ontario's Ministry of Citizenship and Immigration supports community-based delivery of settlement services. Funding is provided to community agencies that are working directly with newcomers and providing project support to the settlement sector. The main impact of the provincial government on the City of Ottawa is perhaps the equal opportunity program of the 1990s, which promoted the elimination of barriers in the private as well as the public sector. It provided the municipality with access to information, resources, and role models that could help with the implementation of its own equal opportunity initiatives. In 2004, Citizenship and Immigration Canada and the Ontario Ministry of Citizenship and Immigration announced that they had signed a letter of intent that paves the way for municipalities to have a voice in immigration issues in negotiations towards a future Canada-Ontario immigration agreement.

The federal government is far less visible in both cities. Formal agreements (such as the Canada-Quebec Accord regarding immigration) are with the provinces, not the cities. They have, however, an important indirect impact on the cities. The Canada-Quebec Accord is the most comprehensive of the agreements signed between the federal government and the provinces. It gives Quebec selection powers and control of the settlement services, while Canada keeps responsibility for the definition of immigrant categories, the levels of immigration, and the refugee as well as family categories. There are also agreements with British Columbia, Alberta, Saskatchewan, Manitoba, New Brunswick, Nova Scotia, Newfoundland, Prince Edward Island, and Yukon. The agreements with British Columbia and Manitoba give them responsibility and funds for settlement services and the power to attract business immigrants. The other agreements generally imply that the provinces will select immigrants to meet specific labour-market needs. Since immigrants settle mainly in large cities, these federal-provincial agreements undoubtedly have an impact on them. As we noted above, the governments of Canada and Ontario are currently negotiating such an agreement.

The Department of Citizenship and Immigration has some settlement and language programs, but there are no formal agreements between it and the city. The same applies to the multiculturalism programs of Canadian Heritage and the Secretary of State for Multiculturalism. The targets of all these programs are community-based groups or private organizations, not cities. There are, however, partnerships between Montreal, Ottawa, and the Department of Human Resources Development to operate Partners for Jobs, an employment program that helps immigrants find work. In addition, the Prime Minister's Caucus Task Force on Urban Issues has called for more active involvement by the federal government in the management of ethnic diversity at the local level; it reported that current programs are too often driven by a short-term perspective and that municipalities often must fill the gaps with their own support programs (Liberal Party 2002, 23).

The task force also proposes the enactment of formal trilevel relations in the field of immigration and settlement. It recommends a cohesive approach in this field, involving coordination between all orders of government as well as non-governmental organizations. It also proposes to review, with the provincial and municipal levels, the formula for funding settlement, integration programs, and services, and to convene a biannual conference on immigration with all orders of government (Liberal Party 2002, 24).

It is also noteworthy that in 1996 the federal government created the Canadian Metropolis project and linked it to the international Metropolis, a forum for research on public policy relating to migration, cultural diversity, and the integration of immigrants in cities. Metropolis is thus supported by a consortium of federal departments and agencies (including Citizenship and Immigration Canada, the Social Sciences and Humanities Research Council, Health Canada, Canadian Heritage, Status of Women Canada, Human Resources Development Canada, Statistics Canada, and Canada Mortgage and Housing Corporation). There are now five Metropolis-funded research centres in Canada (Atlantic, Montreal, Toronto, the Prairies, and Vancouver), and the Metropolis website (canada.metropolis.net) gives references to much of the research that has been generated from these five centres.

The Federation of Canadian Municipalities is currently calling for an intergovernmental approach to the management of ethnocultural diversity, including the involvement of the federal government. In June 2002 the federation encouraged its members, as well as the provincial and territorial associations and governments, to work with the federal government in order to support municipal committees on interracial relations, employment equity, training programs for intercultural sensitivity, and other initiatives in interracial relations (FCM 2002, 4). This would indeed be a change from current practice, involving a much stronger role for the federal government and therefore a shift in existing intergovernmental relations.

To summarize, the federal government is involved in the determination of the broad levels of immigration, in a few settlement programs, and in the development of a model to integrate immigrants (historically, a multiculturalism model but increasingly, one of universalism). Provincial governments are involved in settlement questions as well as in the models to manage diversity. Cities, too, are involved in settlement, and also in the implementation of specific models and various administrative and political mechanisms to deal concretely with various aspects of diversity. Clearly, because of their powers over matters closely linked to immigration issues (such as culture, housing, transit, police), cities and provinces have developed some relationships. The current fiscal imbalance, if not corrected, also means that the federal government will in future have to play a stronger role in many local areas, including ethnocultural diversity. In the following section we consider more closely some aspects linked to this intergovernmental context.

LOCAL GOVERNANCE AND THE CANADIAN INTERGOVERNMENTAL SYSTEM

If municipal interest in Montreal and Ottawa relates to demographic reality, this should lead to increasing municipal action relating to ethnic diversity and, indeed, to increasingly autonomous municipal action, because the large cities in Canada are considerably more ethnically diverse than the provincial populations. Bus since, as the preceding sections demonstrated, cities are already involved in this field, we must be cautious with such a statement and link the municipal activity in ethnic diversity to the general level of municipal capacity and organization. It is therefore necessary to look more broadly at the evolution of the place of municipal government in the Canadian intergovernmental system in order to understand the likely evolution of the capacity of municipalities, even those as large as Montreal and Ottawa, to create effective systems of governance of ethnocultural diversity.

First of all, playing this kind of governance role requires that municipalities have a stronger place in the Canadian intergovernmental context than that which currently exists (Cameron 2002). In fact, there is a contradiction between the discursive environment, which places the emphasis on the political role of municipalities, and the unchanged intergovernmental context of the actual Canadian political system. The provincial and federal governments have not yet symbolically or practically recognized the political and fiscal importance of cities.

Both Montreal and Ottawa, along with the Federation of Canadian Municipalities, the Canadian Association of Municipal Managers, and other cities, are asking for formal and official recognition of the political role they play and a renewal of the fiscal and political relations between the three levels of government. Montreal is one of the five Canadian cities (along with Vancouver, Calgary, Winnipeg, and Toronto) that have been meeting as the C5 group of mayors to lobby for a stronger role for municipal government. They have argued for more federal support for urban issues, and these arguments have had some weight.

They have not been alone in making these arguments; the TD Bank, the Liberal caucus, through its Task Force on Urban Issues, and a variety of university-based researchers have also called for greater federal activity on urban issues. The City of Toronto has played a particularly active role, adopting the document *Towards a New Relationship with Ontario and Canada*, developing a charter for Toronto and a model framework for a city charter, establishing a website as part of a national campaign (with Vancouver, Winnipeg, Saskatoon, Ottawa, and Halifax) entitled "Canada's Cities: Unleash Our Potential," and working with the Federation of Canadian Municipalities, both directly and through the FCM's Big City Mayors' Caucus (Toronto 2001). These bodies ask that the local level be recognized as a legitimate order of government, that it be autonomous, with broadly defined powers and larger fiscal resources, that it be consulted when affected by policies from other levels, and that decisions taken at the local level will not be unilaterally modified by other levels.

These changes are important if we want cities to become not only service providers but a truly political arena for their citizens (Tindal and Tindal 2000, 249). At present, it is not clear whether there will be any change, much less a major change, in intergovernmental relations or in the financial support given to municipal governments. There is a discursive will expressed by cities to take a more active role in diversity issues, but, concretely, things are moving more slowly. So there is a paradox: amalgamations and the downloading of various services give the impression that the local level is now extremely important and that citizens will at last be able to organize themselves and participate fully in the development of local public policies, but the financial resources to meet these challenges are inadequate (Fenn 2002; Kitchen 2002).

A reorganization of intergovernmental relations would accelerate the realization of these changes. It is as if cities are waiting for such a rearrangement before assuming their new political role completely. The image that citizens, elected representatives, and municipal employees have recently developed regarding the role of the local level must be translated by the other levels of government into political recognition as well as fiscal autonomy.

There are some encouraging signs, though. The last city contract signed between the Government of Quebec and the City of Montreal is particularly promising. It includes political recognition of the city, decentralization of some services, complete autonomy in some fields, formal dialogue between the two levels of government, future revision of the fiscal system, and the possibility of entering into agreements with the federal government. In British Columbia in 1996, a protocol of recognition was signed by the Union of British Columbia Municipalities and the province's minister of municipal affairs, involving partnership, information sharing, consultation on future legislative changes, joint council for reviewing legislation, policies, and programs, and other matters). Also, Alberta's *Municipal Government Act* of 1994 defines broad spheres for municipalities and gives them natural persons powers.

However, even if we can say that urban affairs in Canada are back on the political agenda (Andrew, Graham, and Phillips 2002), there is still a lack of a real intergovernmental will. This can be linked to three features of current Canadian federalism: the tendency towards centralization; fiscal federalism; and symmetrical federalism.

First, we have in Canada, unlike the United States, what we can call a "blurred" or mixed federalism – one that is not clearly defined. While the *Constitution Act, 1867*, established a separate list of powers for the federal government and the provinces, it gave very broad spending powers to the federal government, which has used them extensively to involve itself in provincial spheres of jurisdiction, such as welfare, social programs, education, culture, and health. Also, there has been a strong tendency, especially since 1982 and the new Canadian Constitution, towards centralizing of the political system into the hands of the federal government. So the provinces are not likely to accept without negotiations the involvement of the federal government in municipal affairs. Moreover, the federal government has a tendency to consider the other political levels as subnational ones rather than equal partners. This is very problematic if we want a trilateral political recognition of the local level.

This is linked to a financial element – the fiscal imbalance between the revenues of the federal government and the limited revenues of the provinces and cities, which are facing growing needs in public health, education, and such urban issues as transit, housing, the environment, and infrastructure. The provinces want to be able to levy more income taxes, with the federal government reducing its revenues, so that the former are not always in the position of having to ask Ottawa to spend in these areas. This is why a redefinition of the fiscal autonomy of the cities is closely linked to a redefinition of the fiscal relationship between the federal and provincial governments. The agreements signed in June 2005 between the Canadian government and the Ontario and Quebec governments regarding the sharing of the federal gas tax is promising, and it will be used to finance infrastructure and transit facilities in cities.

Canadian federalism evolved as a symmetrical political system rather than an asymmetrical one. Asymmetry means that various parts of a federation possess varying powers in relation to their different interests; it implies that federal policies may be different from one place to another. Quebec and also from time to time some western provinces and Newfoundland have asked for this kind of flexible federalism. But the federal government has a very different vision and sees Canada as a symmetrical federation, with each province having the same powers, and with federal policies and programs being similar from coast to coast (backup up with national objectives and means). This is very problematic with respect to urban and ethnic issues, since the needs and priorities of Montreal may be very different from those of Vancouver. Even if the government of Paul Martin repeatedly says that his approach is more flexible, a stronger involvement of the Canadian government in urban issues would necessitate a redefinition of its way of conceiving the federation. The agreement regarding the health-care system clearly demonstrates that this is possible.

So the challenge will be to keep a flexible approach that recognizes that all cities do not face the same problems and therefore do not need the same powers and the same level of political and fiscal autonomy. The greater empowerment of municipalities must be flexible. There must be a set of custom-built powers, responsibilities, and capacities that match a city's particular needs and aspirations – the policy must be sensitive to local variations: "The services which must logically belong under municipal jurisdiction are those which can vary in their provision and their standards from place to place" (Tindal and

Tindal 2000, 224). In the field of immigration and settlement, there must be national standards (especially regarding discrimination), but since immigration issues are closely linked to questions of identity and local matters, there are various ways to integrate immigrants, and the task of building models and defining mechanisms must be left to the different local communities.

CONCLUSION

This comparison between two of our cities shows that both are active in the management of ethnic diversity. Montreal is clearly more involved, while Ottawa has only very recently begun to take the matter into account. The dominant universalist discourse in Ottawa may help explain this difference. Now that Ottawa is using more multicultural references, major gaps appear between the discourse and the practical reality, which is far from what we observed in Montreal. We also saw that both cities use a combination of models. In this regard, some important variations may appear, even in Montreal, between the discourses and the politics put in place. As a result, the policies for the management of diversity that have been adopted by the different levels of government are sometimes complementary and sometimes contradictory. But these variations indeed demonstrate a level of autonomy for local action.

We need to recognize that municipalities are playing a role in the management of ethnocultural diversity and that their actions relate to models that differ in their objectives and their approaches. Municipal officials have to manage access to services, equipment, and facilities in order to ensure that they are inclusive of different ethnocultural minorities. They also must respond to the various needs expressed by ethnocultural communities and ethnic interest groups. In doing so, cities are not only service providers (which is their traditional role, and one defined in the nature of intergovernmental relations up to the present), but they are real political agents. Most importantly, we think that this field is a very good example of the changes currently transforming the distribution of federal-provincial-municipal responsibilities and the dynamics of intergovernmental relations in Canada.

NOTES

This paper is part of broader research which received financial support from the Social Sciences and Humanities Research Council of Canada and the Faculty of Graduate and Postdoctoral Studies, University of Ottawa. I would like to thank Caroline Andrew for helping me with the writing and content of many parts of the paper, as well as the referees for their very helpful comments.

1 Interview with a member of EDAC, 15 October 2002.
2 For a more detailed analysis of these models, see Benhabib 2002, Fenton 2003, Kelly 2002, Parekh 2000, Semprini 1997, and Constant 2000.

REFERENCES

Abu-Laban, Y. 1997. "Ethnic Politics in a Globalizing Metropolis: The Case of Vancouver." In *The Politics of the City: A Canadian Perspective*, ed. T.L. Thomas, 77–96. Toronto: ITP Nelson

Abu-Laban, B., and T.M. Derwing, eds. 1997. *Responding to Diversity in Metropolis: Building an Inclusive Research Agenda*. Edmonton: Prairie Centre of Excellence for Research on Immigration and Integration

Andrew, C., and M. Rajiva. 1996. "Qui peut exister? La construction des acteurs sur la scène politique municipale." In *Femmes francophones et pluralisme en milieu minoritaire*, ed. D. Adam. Ottawa: Presses de l'Université d'Ottawa

Andrew, C., K.A. Graham, and S.D. Phillips, eds. 2002. *Urban Affairs: Back on the Policy Agenda*. Montreal & Kingston: McGill-Queen's University Press

Benhabib, S. 2002. *The Claims of Culture: Equality and Diversity in the Global Era*. Princeton: Princeton University Press

Berthet, T., and C. Poirier. 2000. "Politiques locales d'intégration et immigrants aisés: une comparaison France-Québec." *Politique et sociétés* 19 (2–3): 181–213

Cameron, K. 2002. "Some Puppets, Some Shoestrings! The Changing Intergovernmental Context." In *Urban Affairs: Back on the Policy Agenda*, ed. C. Andrew, K.A. Graham, and S.D. Phillips. Montreal & Kingston: McGill-Queen's University Press

Canada. 1996. *1996 Census*. Ottawa: Statistics Canada

– 2001. *2001 Census*. Ottawa: Statistics Canada

Constant, F. 2000. *Le multiculturalisme*. Paris: Flammarion

Edgington, D.W., and T.A. Hutton. 2002. *Multiculturalism and Local Government in Greater Vancouver*. RIIM Working Paper no. 02-06, March. Vancouver: Vancouver Centre of Excellence

Edgington, D.W., et al. 2001. *Urban Governance, Multiculturalism, and Citizenship in Sydney and Vancouver*. RIIM Working Paper no. 01-05, January. Vancouver: Vancouver Centre of Excellence

Federation of Canadians Municipalities. 1986. *Improving Interracial Relations in Canadian Municipalities*. Ottawa: FCM

– 1987. *A Point of Departure: Municipal Administration and Community and Interracial Relations*. Interracial Relations 1. Ottawa: FCM

– 1988. *Adapting to Diversity: The Access of Multicultural Communities to Municipal Services*. Interracial Relations 2. Ottawa: FCM

– 1990. *Fill the Gap: Intercultural and Interracial Training in Municipal Administrations*. Interracial Relations 3. Ottawa: FCM

– 1991. *Take Down the Barriers: Equality in Employment.* Interracial Relations 4. Ottawa: FCM

– 1992. *Program for Innovative Employment: Recognition of Cultural Diversity*, Interracial Relations 5. Ottawa: FCM

– June 2002. *Policy Statement on Interracial Relations*, June. Ottawa: FCM

Fenn, W.M. 2002. "The Changing Role of the Municipal Sector." *Revue fiscale canadienne* 50 (1): 147–55

Fenton, S. 2003. *Ethnicity.* Cambridge: Polity Press

Germain, A., and F. Dansereau, eds. 2003. *Les pratiques municipales de gestion de la diversité à Montréal.* March. Montreal: INRS – Urbanisation, culture et société

Germain, A., and P. Harel. 1985. "L'autonomie des collectivités locales: entre la crise et le changement," *Revue internationale d'action communautaire* 13 (53): 35–45

Germain, A., and D. Rose. 2000. *Montreal: The Quest for a Metropolis.* Toronto: Wiley

Kelly, P., ed. 2002. *Multiculturalism Reconsidered: Culture and Equality and Its Critics.* Cambridge: Polity Press

Kingdon, J.W. 1995. *Agendas, Alternatives, and Public Policies.* New York: HarperCollins

Kitchen, H. 2002. "Canadian Municipalities: Fiscal Trends and Sustainability." *Canadian Tax Journal* 50 (1): 156–80

Liberal Party of Canada. Prime Minister's Caucus Task Force on Urban Issues. 2002. *Canada's Urban Strategy: A Vision for the Twenty-First Century.* Chair Judy Sgro. Interim Report. [Ottawa: The Task Force]

Milroy, B.M., and M. Wallace. 2002. *Ethnoracial Diversity and Planning Practices in the Greater Toronto Area.* Final Report. CERIS Working Paper no. 18. Toronto

Montreal. 2001. *Conseil Interculturel de Montréal.* Montreal

– 2002. *Thème 3: Métropole agréable à vivre, solidaire et inclusive.* Montreal: Sommet de Montréal

Ottawa. 2000. *Diversity Makes Sense.* Ottawa: Diversity and Community Access Project Team

– 2002a. *City of Ottawa Official Plan. Preliminary Draft.* Ottawa

– 2002b. *Ottawa 20/20. Human Services Plan: Priority on People. Draft.* Ottawa

– 2002c. *Terms of Reference.* Ottawa: Equity and Diversity Advisory Committee

Paré, S., W. Frohn, and M.-E. Laurin. 2002. "Diversification des populations dans la région de Montréal: de nouveaux défis de la gestion urbaine." *Canadian Public Administration* 45 (2): 195–216

Parekh, B. 2000. *Rethinking Multiculturalism: Cultural Diversity and Political Theory.* Cambridge: Harvard University Press

Poirier, C., and C. Andrew. 2003. "Décision et consultation au niveau local: dynamiques et tensions entre la démocratie représentative et la démocratie consultative à Ottawa." *Gestion: Revue internationale de gestion* 28 (3): 28–36

Quebec. Ministère des communautés culturelles et de l'immigration. 1990. *Au Québec pour bâtir ensemble: énoncé de politique en matière d'immigration et d'intégration.* Quebec: Gouvernement du Québec

– Ministère des relations avec les citoyens et de l'immigration. 2001. *Plan Stratégique 2002–2004.* Quebec: Gouvernement du Québec

– 2002. *Tableaux sur l'immigration au Québec, 1997–2001*. Quebec: Ministère des relations avec les citoyens et de l'immigration

Quesnel, L., and E. Tate. 1995. "Accessibility of Municipal Services for Ethnocultural Populations in Toronto and Montreal." *Canadian Public Administration* 38 (3): 325–51

Semprini, A. 1997. *Le multiculturalisme*. Paris: Presses universitaires de France

Siemiatycki, M., et al. 2001. *Integrating Community Diversity in Toronto: On Whose Terms?* CERIS Working Paper no. 14, March. Toronto

Tindal, C.R., and S.N. Tindal. 2000. *Local Government in Canada*. Scarborough: Nelson

Toronto. 2001. *Establishing a New Relationship with the Federal and Provincial Government: Progress Report*. Toronto staff report

Wallace, M., and F. Frisken. 2000. *City-Suburban Differences in Government Responses to Immigration in the Greater Toronto Area*. Toronto: Centre for Urban and Community Studies, University of Toronto

10

What Factors Shape Canadian Housing Policy? The Intergovernmental Role in Canada's Housing System

J. David Hulchanski

Ce chapitre fournit un aperçu de l'évolution de la politique du logement au Canada et propose un meilleur cadre conceptuel pour analyser les problèmes de logement, et il examine aussi le rôle que joue chaque niveau de gouvernement dans le système de logement au Canada. Le cadre conceptuel proposé repose sur trois idées importantes : (1) la nécessité de reconnaître que chaque pays met sur pied son propre système de logement – des institutions, des lois et des pratiques qui veillent (ou qui ne veillent pas) à ce qu'un nombre suffisant d'habitations de qualité soient construites, à ce qu'il y ait un système juste d'attribution des logements et à ce que le parc de logements soit bien entretenu; (2) la nécessité de comprendre la dynamique des questions juridictionnelles intergouvernementales en ce qui concerne le système de logement; (3) la nécessité de mieux comprendre pourquoi et comment certains groupes en bénéficient davantage. Cette analyse du système de logement du Canada identifie deux ensembles de tendances qui aident à définir les trajectoires probables des politiques du logement au niveau du gouvernement municipal, provincial et fédéral.

Housing policies provide a remarkable litmus test for the values of politicians at every level of office and of the varied communities that influence them. Often this test measures simply the warmth or coldness of heart of the more affluent and secure towards families of a lower socio-economic status.

John Bacher, 1993

This paper provides a brief overview of the nature of Canadian housing policy and the role played by government. It is not about Canada's current housing problems. Rather, it outlines an improved conceptual framework for thinking about Canada's housing problems and offers an explanation for the policy role played by the different levels of government.

Three main building blocks for such a conceptual framing are presented. The first is the need to recognize that each country develops a housing system – a method of ensuring (or not) that enough good-quality housing is built, that there is a fair housing allocation system, and that the stock of housing is properly maintained. Government plays the central role in creating, sustaining, and changing this system. It establishes and enforces the "rules of the game" through legislation that defines such things as banking and mortgage lending practices, tax and regulatory measures affecting building materials, professional practices (for example, real estate transactions), subsidy programs, and incentive patterns for average households. This system is so ingrained in the culture and so intertwined with related systems (such as tax measures and welfare state benefits) that it tends to be taken for granted, thereby potentially limiting the quality of the analysis and the range of policy options considered.

Understanding the dynamics of the jurisdictional issue in the housing system is the second building block. What role does each level of government play in the housing system? All countries are organized differently, with different levels of government having constitutionally defined roles and a set of practices that have evolved over time. Very similar Western nations have very dissimilar housing systems (Scanlan and Whitehead 2004; van Vliet 1990). In Canada it is the federal and municipal levels of government that have played the more important roles in shaping how Canadians are housed. Over the decades, no matter how the constitutional jurisdiction issue was defined or what any particular province thought about federal involvement in housing, it was the federal government that played the major role in shaping how Canada's housing stock was financed and allocated. With the introduction of land-use planning regulations by the mid-twentieth century, municipal governments began to play a major role in the nature of the form and density of the housing and residential districts in which Canadians live.

The third building block in understanding the dynamics in Canada's housing system is to understand why and how some groups and some housing forms/tenures benefit from public policy decisions more than others. To do this we need to situate housing within the context of the full range of social benefits that we call the "welfare state" and the housing-relevant sociopolitical dynamics that shape it. Analysts have for some time noted that Western welfare states tend to have a dual system of benefits (Esping-Anderson 1990; Myles 1988). The nature of the welfare state system of benefits is important in defining the nature of the housing system (Prince 1998). Canada has a housing system that allocates differential benefits for two groups of citizens on the basis of whether they are in the primary or secondary part of the housing system, as defined below.

CANADA'S HOUSING SYSTEM: POLICIES THAT PRIVILEGE OWNERSHIP

For some Canadians the term "housing policy" is likely to invoke images of public housing, government subsidies for low-income households, and programs aimed at helping Canada's many unhoused individuals and families. It is easy, though inaccurate, to view housing policy as having this limited scope. One reason is that 95 percent of Canadian households obtain their housing from the private market. Two-thirds of all households own the house in which they live. About one-third of all renters at any time are on their way to eventually buying a house. They are merely passing through the rental market. Only 5 percent of Canada's households live in non-market social housing (defined here as including government-owned public housing, non-profit housing, and non-profit housing co-operatives) – the smallest social housing sector of any Western nation except for the United States. In Western Europe, the percent of the housing stock in the social-housing sector is much higher: 35 percent in the Netherlands and 15 to 20 percent in France, the United Kingdom, Austria, Denmark, Finland, and Sweden (Scanlan and Whitehead 2004, table 2). These are societies that are similar in many respects to Canada, yet their housing systems are very different. Canada's housing system, in contrast to that of most Western nations, relies almost exclusively on the market mechanism for the provision, allocation, and maintenance of housing. This is a problem for households too poor to pay market rents for housing appropriate to their needs. These households generate a "social need" for housing rather than a "market demand" for it. A housing system based on the market mechanism cannot adequately – if at all – respond to social need. Given the significant role played by market dynamics, it is easy to assume that government housing policy plays a very small role in Canada. But this is not the case.

Many of the politicians, lobbyists, and average citizens who like to "fed bash" and complain about federal government intrusion in what they claim to be provincial jurisdiction are most likely to be homeowners. However, if it were not for federal government housing policies and programs, past and present, Canada's ownership rate would be much lower. Mortgage lending and insurance institutions are necessary. These were created by federal and provincial government statutes, regulations, and subsidies in the decade following the Second World War (Bacher 1993). Municipal governments provided the necessary serviced land and zoning regulations that permitted the construction of relatively cheap housing in postwar subdivisions – the sprawl onto new land around all cities, which rarely included provision for rental housing. Since the early 1970s a steady stream of house purchase assistance programs has been necessary simply to maintain Canada's ownership rate at about two-thirds.

It was not until a policy change in 1963 that the federal government, in a program requiring joint provincial funding, began to directly provide subsidized rental housing for low-income households. Specially created provincial housing corporations (for example, the Ontario Housing Corporation and the Alberta Housing Corporation) were established to own and manage the housing, under agreements with the federal government. By the mid-1970s, when this "public-housing" program was replaced with a more decentralized and community-based non-profit program, about 200,000 public-housing units had been built (which is about 2 percent of Canada's current housing stock). This was a rather modest program because of the broader policy objective of leaving as much of the housing system in the market sector as possible (Rose 1980).

The Canada Mortgage and Housing Corporation (CMHC), established in 1946, focused public funds almost exclusively on the ownership sector. Although federal legislation in 1949 permitted federal and provincial subsidies for public housing, only 12,000 units were built before the 1963 policy change. The CMHC focused mainly on making the amortized mortgage market work – both for house buyers and for private investors in rental housing. The federal Mortgage Insurance Fund (MIF) was introduced in 1954 to encourage banks to enter the then risky mortgage lending market. Managing the MIF remains today one of the major functions of the CMHC, a federal crown corporation. For about two decades, from the mid-1940s to the mid-1960s, most households obtained at least part of their mortgage loan directly from the federal government (joint public/private sector loans).

Most of the history of the role of Canadian government housing policy and programs is a history of efforts targeted at the house-ownership sector. Depending on when they first purchased a house, Canada's households would have taken advantage of any number of federal subsidy programs. These have included the Assisted Home Ownership Program, the Canadian Homeownership Stimulation Plan, the Registered Homeownership Savings Plan, and the Mortgage Rate Protection Program. In 1992, as the federal government was ending its social-housing programs for low-income households, it created the First Home Loan Insurance Program, which allows CMHC to insure mortgages up to 95 percent of the value of a house. This temporary program was made permanent in 1998 and is no longer limited to first-time buyers. It enables a 5 percent minimum down payment instead of the previous minimum of 10 percent. In addition, another temporary program, the 1992 Home Buyers' Plan, is now permanent. It permits first-time buyers, and anyone who has not been an owner for a specified number of years, to borrow up to $20,000 ($40,000 for a couple) from their Registered Retirement Savings Plan (RRSP), tax- and interest-free, in order to buy or build a house. It is no coincidence that these measures were introduced just before a federal election.

When an owner-occupied house is sold in Canada, if there is a capital gain, the owner pays no tax on it. This is because of effective lobbying when the capital gains tax was introduced in the early 1970s. Owner-occupied houses were exempted. The Department of Finance estimates that this is a $3.7 billion annual subsidy to owners – the amount that would be collected if the capital gain was taxed (Canada, Department of Finance 2004b, table 1). There is no equivalent tax benefit for either private-sector renters or rental-housing investors. This benefit to owners is twice the $1.8 billion annual subsidy bill (a direct budgetary expenditure) for all federally subsidized social-housing units ever built (the 550,000 social-housing units in the country; an average federal subsidy of $275 per unit per month).

Owning a house is a long-term investment that helps maintain a certain standard of living over the course of one's life. The 50 percent of Canadian owners who have paid off their mortgages spend only 11 percent of their income on housing and therefore have more funds available for other activities and investments. Moreover, a large, expensive house can be traded for a smaller, less expensive one to free up money, or a reverse mortgage can be negotiated, providing regular annuity payments to the owner. Lifelong renters who cannot afford to purchase a house do not have anything similar to draw on as they age.

It is important therefore, when considering housing policy and the jurisdictional role of the three levels of government, to place the policy discussion in context. Canada has a "housing system," not just particular housing policies and programs for poor people. Although many Canadians refer to the health-care *system* or the social-welfare *system*, few refer to the housing *system*. In most housing discussions in Canada, people generally refer to the housing *market* – which implies and has the image of a non-governmental activity; when they refer to housing policy, they mean a government activity focused on redistribution – helping households in need of adequate housing. But the housing market, in the ownership and the rental sectors, exists in its present form because of public policies and programs. Canada has its current housing system thanks to a long history of government activity and to the ongoing role of all levels of government in creating and maintaining Canada's particular approach to supplying, allocating, and maintaining the nation's housing stock. The focus of the government role in housing, since its first housing program in 1919 (which helped veterans buy houses), has been almost exclusively on the ownership sector. John Bacher aptly named his 1993 history of Canadian housing policy *Keeping to the Marketplace*. The ownership sector of Canada's housing system has always had a well-financed lobby, with sympathetic ministers and deputy ministers, and a majority of Canada's voters supporting it.

The point here is not that there is anything wrong with owner occupancy and government house-ownership policies; it is to highlight the extent to which this key characteristic of Canada's housing system is generally ignored in policy discussions and in intergovernmental considerations of who should do what to help improve the housing system. The availability and cost of residential land and the cost of housing in each market area are shaped by what happens in the dominant part of the housing system – the house-ownership sector. Yet policy discussions tend to be focused on low-income households and the unhoused, and which level of government ought to do something. With the ownership sector, this jurisdictional debate is usually absent, and all three levels jump at opportunities to assist owners.

During recent decades the growing gap between rich and poor Canadian households has increasingly manifested itself in the housing system. The social need for housing tends to be mainly among renters – tenants whose income (and lack of wealth) cannot generate effective market demand. Public-policy decisions since the mid-1980s have further privileged the ownership sector – even more so than past policies – and have helped exacerbate problems in the rental-housing sector, problems that include widespread homelessness.

As the most extreme manifestation of the housing and income inequity problem, homelessness in its contemporary version began to emerge in the 1980s – when the first significant cuts in social spending began and when baby boomers began to enter the housing market, forcing up prices. While homelessness is not only a housing problem, it is always a housing problem. The central observation about the diverse group of Canadians known as "the homeless" is that they are people who once had housing but are now unhoused. Canada's housing system once had room for virtually everyone; now it does not. Homeless-making processes are now a part of Canada's housing and social-welfare systems.

Homelessness does not occur by itself. It is not a "natural" phenomenon. It is the outcome of "normal" day-to-day societal practices. As Jahiel notes,

> The events that make people homeless are initiated and controlled by other people whom our society allows to engage in the various enterprises that contribute to the homelessness of others. The primary purpose of these enterprises is not to make people homeless but, rather, to achieve socially condoned aims such as making a living, becoming rich, obtaining a more desirable home, increasing the efficiency of the workplace, promoting the growth of cultural institutions, giving cities a competitive advantage, or helping local or federal governments to balance their budgets or limit their debts. Homelessness occurs as a side effect. (Jahiel 1992, 269)

Having no place to live means being excluded from all that is associated with having a home, a neighbourhood, and a set of established community networks. It means being exiled from the mainstream patterns of day-to-day life. Without a physical place to call "home" in the social, psychological, and emotional sense, the hour-to-hour struggle for physical survival replaces all other possible activities.

The "dehousing" processes operating in society are producing a diaspora of the excluded. Up to a quarter of the homeless people in some Canadian cities are Aboriginal, and about 15 percent of Toronto's hostel users are immigrants and refugees (Toronto 1999, 19). Race is still a barrier to equal treatment in Canada's housing and job markets. Families are now the fastest-growing group among the homeless. Some landlords refuse to rent apartments to families with children, to single mothers, or to people on social assistance (Dion 2001; Novac et al. 2002). Many community-based services that used to help these families have lost their government funding. Federal and provincial human rights codes are well-intentioned but often toothless documents with weak enforcement mechanisms. In addition, budget cuts have slowed progress in combatting discrimination.

While most Canadians have adequate housing, about 8 percent live in dwellings that require major repairs and about 5 percent live in housing that is overcrowded. When we disaggregate this information, we find that almost 20 percent of renters, compared with 10 percent of owners, live in housing that is in need of major repairs or is overcrowded. Although the average household spends 21 percent of its total income on housing, owners spend 18 percent, compared with 28 percent for tenants (Canada, Statistics Canada 2000).

The data on Canadian housing conditions reveal that Canadians are divided into two very different groups according to housing tenure. Owners are not only wealthier, but have twice the income of renters. Although there is only one housing market, Canada's housing system has two pools of housing consumers with dramatically different incomes and assets.

The problem has become much worse over recent decades. In the late 1960s, when a great deal of private rental housing was built, the income gap between owners and renters was about 20 percent (Hulchanski 1988). Between 1984 and 1999, the gap between the median income of owners and renters grew by 16 percent (see table 1). In 1984 owners had almost double the income of renters (192 percent). By 1999 the gap had increased to more than double (208 percent). This represents an average growth in the income gap between owners and renters of about 1 percent a year. During the same period, the wealth of owners (which, for most people, is mainly the mortgage-free portion of their house) increased from being twenty-nine times that of renters in 1984 to seventy times that of renters in 1999. Poverty and housing tenure are now much more closely connected (Hulchanski 2001).

An additional problem is that there has been a significant change affecting the feasibility of building rental housing in Canada. This relates to municipal zoning for rental housing. Before the late 1960s and early 1970s there was no condominium form of ownership housing in Canada (Hulchanski 1988). Residential land was zoned for either rental or ownership housing. All areas zoned for medium and high residential densities were by definition rental districts. Low-density zoning tended to be associated with owner-occupied housing (although some houses were rented and some had second suites). Since passage of the provincial legislation creating the condominium form of ownership in the early 1970s, rental housing providers have had to compete with condominium providers for zoned building sites. Since renters have about half the

Table 1: Comparison of Income and Wealth of Owner and Renter Households in Canada, 1984 and 1999

	Median income				Median net worth	
	Owners	Renters			Owners	Renters
1984[1]	$41,380	$21,554		1984[1]	$116,845	$3,985
1999	$43,478	$20,947		1999	$145,200	$2,060
change	$2,098	–$607		change	$28,355	–$1,925
% change	5%	–3%		% change	24%	–48%

[1] 1984 adjusted to 1999 dollars

Source: Canada, Statistics Canada, 1984, 1999

income of homeowners, condo developers can always outbid rental developers for residential sites.

As in the United States, though not in many other Western nations, there is a pervasive cultural and institutional bias against renting. This is a key characteristic of Canada's housing system. In his "history of renting in a country of owners," Krueckeberg puts the problem in the following terms:

> We are the inheritors of a nasty and pervasive property bias in our society with roots that run deep, just as other strong biases of gender, race, and nationality still do in spite of our efforts to outlaw them. Our institutions and practices continue to embody and perpetuate the property bias, particularly in the tax system – in the subsidies given to owners but denied to renters and in many of the property tax laws that deny that renters are stakeholders in their communities. The celebration of homeownership in the United States stigmatizes those who don't, can't, or won't buy property. What is needed, it seems, is a civil rights movement for renters. (Krueckeberg 1999:26)

Krueckeberg asks a question about the United States that more Canadians need to ask about the Canadian housing system: "Where are the institutions that promote and protect the economic and political interests of renters?"

As mentioned above, although many Canadians refer to the health-care system or the social-welfare system, they should also recognize that Canada has a housing system, not just a housing market. Owners are happy when they hear that house prices are going up; renters who can afford a house or a condominium watch mortgage interest rates carefully. Few people, however, pay close attention to the rental market and to the social need for housing. Canada's housing system is out of balance; it is discriminatory in the way it treats owners and renters; and it is a system in which the market mechanism of supply and demand works for the ownership sector but not for the rental sector. It has become an increasingly exclusive system, in the sense that some households are now actually excluded from access to housing. Governments – all three levels – are always making choices when it comes to decisions that affect the housing system. One important element of the policy debate over housing in Canada – especially the effort to create a more inclusive system (the demands from civil society to help low-income households and end homelessness, for example) – is the jurisdictional issue: Which level of government is or ought to be responsible for what part of the housing system?

INTERGOVERNMENTAL JURISDICTION: WHO IS RESPONSIBLE FOR HOUSING POLICY?

The short answer to the above question is that all levels of government have responsibility. They are all continually making decisions to take, or not to take, certain actions. There has never been any dispute over this fact. The dispute has been over jurisdictional issues.

FEDERAL-PROVINCIAL RELATIONS

There was a proposal – never implemented – that would have explicitly removed the federal government from housing policy and program making, though housing was never explicitly defined. In policy discussions, "housing" without a modifier tends to refer to social housing and other forms of housing assistance for low-income households – the expensive policy problems.

When the federal government tabled its proposals for constitutional change in September 1991, housing and "municipal/urban affairs" were two of six sectors offered up as exclusive provincial domains, because they were "more properly the responsibility of the provinces." The federal government, according to the proposal, was prepared "to recognize the exclusive jurisdiction of the provinces ... and to withdraw from these fields in a manner appropriate to each sector" (Canada 1991, 36–7). No explanation was offered for why these two, along with tourism, forestry, mining, and recreation, were considered to be "more properly" the responsibility of the provinces.

During the negotiations that led to the August 1992 constitutional agreement (Charlottetown Accord), the federal and provincial governments agreed that housing and municipal and urban affairs were among several areas over which "exclusive provincial jurisdiction ... should be recognized and clarified through an explicit constitutional amendment and the negotiation of federal-provincial agreements." This "should be accomplished," the agreement stated, "through justiciable intergovernmental agreements, designed to meet the specific circumstances of each province." Provincial governments had the option of taking cash transfers, taking tax points, or requiring the federal government to maintain its spending in the province (Canada 1992, s. 3).

Although this constitutional agreement was rejected by Canada's voters in a national referendum, the desire of the federal government (with its huge annual deficits at the time) to extricate itself from social housing subsidies continued into the 1990s. In the March 1996 federal budget, the government announced that it would transfer administration of federal social-housing programs to provinces and territories, ending fifty years of direct federal involvement in the administration of social-housing programs. As stated in the 1996 *Budget Plan*,

> CMHC will phase out its remaining role in social housing, except for housing on Indian reserves. The first step has already been taken – there has been no funding for new social housing units since 1993. To further clarify jurisdiction in the social housing field, the federal government is now prepared to offer provincial and territorial governments the opportunity to take over the management of existing social housing resources, provided that the federal subsidies on existing housing continue to be used for housing assistance for low-income households. This should result in simpler administration and improved service to Canadians. The issue of the role for third parties in the administration of the social housing stock will be discussed with the provinces and territories. (Canada, Department of Finance 1996, 43–4)

This was a unilateral policy decision, not the settlement of a legal or constitutional dispute over jurisdiction. It was also a financial decision – a means of saving money at the federal level. The federal government, though maintaining its involvement in the ownership sector and playing a major role in the housing system through CMHC, would not provide any new money for meeting housing needs. This policy decision handed responsibility down to the provinces, and some provinces handed it down to municipalities. The federal government would no longer be responsible for the stream of subsidies once the initial funding packages for the approximately 500,000 social-housing units expired.

What about the provincial and territorial role in social housing and related urban and social programs since 1993? Most of their policies and program changes also represent a withdrawal from helping those most in need. It is important, however, to place provincial and territorial budget cuts in housing, social spending, and urban affairs in the context of the federal government's downloading of the deficit onto provincial taxpayers. Provinces can either raise taxes to make up for the cuts in federal transfer payments (creating the conditions for a taxpayer revolt and boosting the popularity of politicians who promise tax cuts) or they can pass on the cuts to groups that have no electoral clout.

Federal cash transfers to the provinces and territories have been falling since the early 1980s. The share of federal expenditures transferred to the provinces and territories ranged from 3.6 to 4.2 percent of GDP in the early and mid-1980s. Since 1996 it has ranged from 2.3 to 2.8 percent of GDP (Canada, Department of Finance 2004a, table 8). In short, huge amounts of money that were once transferred to provinces and territories were unilaterally withdrawn. The money had previously been used for health, education, and welfare programs. Some federal funding, particular for health care, has since been restored.

Another way of looking at these federal budget cuts is to examine the share of total budget revenues that federal cash transfers represent. In Ontario, for example, during the first period (1980–86) an average of 17 percent of provincial revenues came in the form of federal cash transfers. During the second period (1987–95) this had fallen to an annual average of 13.4 percent. By the third period (1996–2001), only 9.3 percent of Ontario's budget revenues came from federal cash transfers. The amount has been increasing in recent years. By the 2003–04 fiscal year, the federal share had increased to 13.4 percent as a result of new federal-provincial spending agreements. This is still substantially less than the 1980s levels (Canada, Department of Finance 2004a, table 22).

This historic shift in transfer payments has made it more difficult for provinces and territories to replace federal cuts in social-housing spending should they wish to do so. Of course, most provinces have not wanted to engage in social-housing spending, except for Quebec and, until recently, British Columbia. From time to time, some provinces have played an active role in housing, but this has been an exception. Between 1985 and 1995, for example, the Province of Ontario played a significant role in adding to the social-housing stock of the province and assisting with housing needs in other ways (such as raising social assistance benefits and the minimum wage).

The federal government during the 1990s not only cut the transfer payments to provinces but also reduced its direct spending on housing, thereby saving the Treasury about $1.5 billion a year. The approximately $2 billion of federal money spent annually on housing (1 percent of total federal spending) pays for subsidies on about 550,000 social-housing units that were built before the 1993 termination of the federal role in subsidizing new social-housing units. Dismantling the social-housing supply program meant that provinces and municipalities had to bear the indirect costs of inadequate housing and homelessness. These include the costs of physical and mental health care, emergency shelters and services, and policing.

In contrast, eighteen years earlier, at the January 1973 Federal-Provincial Conference on Housing, the federal minister of urban affairs defended his government's position on provincial demands for block funding by arguing that housing and urban programs were "matters of national concern," that block funding would "clearly weaken the Federal Government's role in providing leadership and co-ordination in housing and urban programs across Canada," and that housing had "obvious social and economic impacts on the country" and was "relevant even to the question of national unity" (Canada, Ministry of State for Urban Affairs 1973, 8).

By the time the Liberals were back in power in 1993, they simply implemented the previous Conservative government's termination of the social-housing supply program. The 1996 decision made by Paul Martin, as finance minister, to download federal social housing is in sharp contrast to what, as opposition housing critic, he had recommended a few years earlier in his 1990 task force report on housing: "The federal government has abandoned its responsibilities with regards to housing problems ... The housing crisis is growing at an alarming rate and the government sits there and does nothing ... The federal government's role would be that of a partner working with other levels of government, and private and public housing groups. But leadership must come from one source; and a national vision requires some national direction" (Martin and Fontana 1990a).

The recommendations of the National Liberal Caucus Task Force on Housing, chaired by Paul Martin and Joe Fontana, who were in opposition at the time, provided a detailed and comprehensive set of housing recommendations (see table 2 for a summary). The report called for "the development of a national housing policy and related strategies" and named specific categories of housing programs that ought to be federally funded (Martin and Fontana 1990b). These could have provided the basis – a policy framework – for moving forward on addressing housing problems under a Liberal government. Yet during the 1990s the Liberal government failed to implement them. In fact, it did the opposite, attempting to exit altogether from helping Canadians in need of housing assistance. The federal government was indeed engaged in housing policymaking.

The main point here is that it is politics – policy decisions by the government of the day, under the specific realities of the times – and not any legal or constitutional constraints that define the federal role in housing, and the same is true of the provincial role. However, this is played out in the broader context of a historical continuity that privileges housing interventions in the ownership sector and interventions that conform with and are supportive of the market. By contract, the provision of social housing replaces the market (some households end up living in non-market housing), and any programs to help impoverished and homeless households are expensive. Housing is the single largest budget expenditure for most households. Programs that provide an adequate housing support, via whatever option, are simply very expensive.

There is no legal or constitutional impediment to federal or provincial governments engaging in any variety of housing policies and programs. The federal

Table 2: Liberal Task Force on Housing, May 1990:
Ten Key Recommendations[1]

All Canadians have the right to adequate housing	That the issue of housing rights be placed on the list of items to be discussed at the next First Ministers' Conference.
Restore cuts to transfer payments for provincial social assistance programs	That cuts in transfer payments to the provinces for social assistance be restored and that negotiations be initiated with the provinces to increase the shelter component of provincial social assistance allowances.
An income supplement for the working poor	That the federal and provincial governments establish a new social program providing an income supplement for workers whose earnings from employment leave them below the poverty line.
A national conference on homelessness be convened	That a national conference on the homeless be immediately convened to set real objectives and policy responses for the eradication of homelessness in Canada.
Eliminate all substandard on-reserve housing	That the federal government set the year 2000 as the target for the elimination of substandard on-reserve housing and allocate the necessary funds to accomplish this objective.
Restore funding for the federal Co-op Housing Program	That funding for the federal Co-operative Housing Program and the Rent Supplement Program be increased to allow for the construction of 5,000 new co-operative housing units annually.
Provide affordable housing for all Canadians with special needs	That the federal government ensure that an adequate supply of affordable housing units be made available for individuals with special needs.
Develop a new community housing investment mechanism	That the federal government immediately develop new community and housing investment mechanisms that facilitate the supply of affordable housing through public-private and nonprofit-private partnerships.
Review all forms of taxation on housing	That the federal government convene a special meeting with the Federation of Canadian Municipalities to review the full range of consequences of housing taxation at all three levels of government.
Develop a national housing policy	That the federal government convene at the earliest possible date a national housing forum to discuss the development of a national housing policy and related strategies, such as municipal infrastructure, aimed at alleviating the housing crisis in Canada.

[1]There were twenty-five recommendations in total.

Source: Martin and Fontana 1990b. See www.urbancentre.utoronto.ca/findingroom/

and provincial governments have historically engaged in many different programs, both unilateral and joint. The jurisdictional issue appears to be
significant only because politicians raise it when they do not want their level
of government to be responsible for addressing a particular housing problem.

THE MUNICIPAL GOVERNMENT ROLE

There is a constitutional barrier when it comes to a direct federal-municipal
relationship in a policy area. Municipalities can do only what their provinces
allow them to do. In practical terms, however, this has not been a barrier for
federal government involvement in local housing and related neighbourhood
issues. If federal money is made available to municipalities, it is politically
difficult for a provincial government to deny municipal government access to
that money. There is a long history of federal government programs that assist
municipalities on key housing and neighbourhood issues.

Even before the Ministry of State for Urban Affairs was established, the
federal government supplied "slum clearance" funding to municipalities under the 1944 *National Housing Act* (NHA), "urban redevelopment" funding
under the 1954 NHA, "urban renewal" funding under the 1964 NHA, and
"neighbourhood improvement" funding under the 1973 NHA. As a result of
the decision to build more public housing in 1964, the provinces created housing corporations to channel federal money to municipal housing corporations.
When the federal government wanted direct credit for its housing activities, it
changed from federally funded public housing, developed and administered
by the provinces, to non-profit housing under the 1973 amendments to the
NHA (Rose 1980). After 1973 the federal government directly funded (without provincial involvement) new social-housing projects built by non-profit
societies as well as non-profit housing corporations established by municipalities for that purpose. And when, as noted above, the federal government
did not want to fund any further new social housing, it unilaterally stopped all
such funding in 1993 (Hulchanski 2002).

There was also no constitutional problem with the federal government establishing a Ministry of State for Urban Affairs (MSUA), as it did in 1971.
MSUA dealt with "urban" issues, not "municipal government" issues. It was
an experiment in building a new kind of federal government institution for
policy development and for advising government on issues that cut across
many departmental and governmental jurisdictions. After the Second World
War, the federal government had a considerable impact on urban areas through
its involvement with airports, transportation, health care, postsecondary education, children's programs, social services, Aboriginal peoples, military
installations, the location of government facilities, employment and training
programs, research and innovation investments, regional economic development initiatives, and immigration policy (most immigrants and refugees settle

in the three largest metropolitan areas). These policies and programs were rarely coordinated and were not part of any explicit federal urban strategy or agenda (Oberlander and Fallick 1987).

During the 1960s it became clear that many federal programs were *de facto* urban programs, yet their urban impact was rarely mentioned or considered. MSUA had a mandate to coordinate and integrate federal initiatives and policy relating to urban regions. The ministry had two main functions: (1) the coordination of well-established federal activities in fields such as housing, transportation, and public works as they affected urban Canada; and (2) offering policy advice on federal urban priorities and initiatives. The ministry was to conduct research to create and sustain an effective information and analytic base for urban public policy, and to carry out interdepartmental and intergovernmental consultation, including consultation with those most directly affected – municipalities (Gertler 1987).

Many provinces, especially Quebec, were not happy about this federal initiative. They chose to view "urban affairs" as synonymous with "municipal affairs," which they saw as a provincial responsibility. Municipalities at that time were not very well organized and had no unified position or voice. This has changed recently because the Federation of Canadian Municipalities has become an increasingly active and effective national organization and lobbies on behalf of municipal governments.

In 1979 MSUA was abolished. Michael Pitfield, secretary to the cabinet at the time, provided the following explanation for the ministry's demise: "As the '70s came to an end, the Trudeau Government came to look upon MSUA first, as a front for a retreat to show the public federal sensitivity to provincial demands and, ultimately, as a piece of government apparatus to sacrifice in order to demonstrate federal sensitivity to popular concerns with 'Big Government.' As the 1979 general election came down upon it, the Trudeau Government declared victory and wound up the Ministry of State for Urban Affairs" (Pitfield 1987, 34). He added: "From my own perspective, it was wound up just as it was beginning to succeed" (ibid., 35).

From that point on, until very recently, the federal government showed no interest in formulating a national urban strategy, in understanding urban trends and the impact of federal policies on cities, or in providing resources in a coordinated fashion. In fact, beginning in the mid-1980s, as the federal government withdrew transfer payments from the provinces, the provinces in turn withdrew resources from municipalities and, in some cases, downloaded expensive functions to them. Recent federal initiatives affecting urban areas have tended to be ad hoc responses to immediate political pressures. As a result, urban social problems were compounded.

To do nothing – or at least initially to appear to be doing nothing – became increasingly difficult for the federal government by the end of the decade. With pressures building from civil society organizations and from municipalities themselves for federal assistance, the prime minister established a Caucus Task Force on Urban Issues. In its 2002 interim report, the task force noted the need for "coordination, collaboration, cohesiveness and commitment to a new approach to Canada's urban regions" (Liberal Party 2002, 2). This was similar to the Speech from the Throne thirty-two years earlier, which had drawn attention to the "new accumulation of problems" caused by rapid urbanization and the need to "foster coordination of the activities of all levels of government and contribute to sound urban growth and development" (Canada, House of Commons 1970). The task force's interim report opens with a now widely accepted assertion that Canadian cities are in crisis: "There is mounting evidence that our cities are ailing due to deteriorating infrastructure, declining air and water quality, traffic gridlock, homelessness, growing income polarization and marginalization, and budget crises. With few ways to generate revenue other than through property taxes, urban regions are finding it increasingly difficult to provide basic services and make repairs to infrastructure (Liberal Party 2002, 2). After much talk and many promises, the 2004 and 2005 federal budgets allocated some new funds for housing and municipal infrastructure. As in the past, the federal government is launching housing and urban affairs initiatives in the face of strong political pressures (and during a minority government) – without the jurisdictional debate getting in the way.

Is there anything special about municipal government's commitment to and action on housing issues? The answer, for the most part, has to be no. Voter turnout at municipal elections tends to be very low, with owners voting in greater numbers and demanding proper attention from city council on zoning matters. The "not in my back yard" (NIMBY) pressures on municipal politicians are great. It is very difficult to locate housing or housing-related services for low-income people in most municipalities. While they do not have a substantial tax base, municipalities do have resources, and city councils rarely vote on a consistent basis in favour of programs or initiatives that target the very poor in their communities.

THE DUALISM IN CANADA'S POSTWAR SOCIAL POLICIES

A number of questions flow from the history outlined above. Why did the federal Liberal Party have a policy in favour of funding numerous housing and urban programs when it was in office during most of the 1960s, 1970s, and early 1980s, but not during the 1990s? Why has it seemingly re-engaged in these issues by allocating funds for social housing and municipal infrastructure in the 2004 and 2005 budgets? Why did Paul Martin and Joe Fontana not implement their 1990 housing task force recommendations when their party was elected in 1993 and Martin became finance minister? Claiming that the government at certain times "lacks a political will" to take action and at other times "has the political will" to take action is not helpful. This is a descriptive statement, not an explanation.

The explanation must be set, as noted at the beginning of this paper, in the context of an understanding of how policies have evolved over several decades – there is indeed significant continuity – and all aspects of Canada's housing system, including the jurisdictional debates and the focus on market provision of housing, must be included in the analysis. There is a common theme to postwar Canadian housing. There is a dualism – a differential treatment of owners and renters, of those who are well off and those who are poor. There is simply no evidence that governments have ever intended to make progress towards a more inclusive and just housing system. This was not a policy objective, though it appears in political rhetoric around election time.

THE SOCIAL SECURITY AND THE SOCIAL ASSISTANCE WELFARE STATES

The term "welfare state" refers to the set of social practices and strategic accommodations designed to address specific problems of the day relating to both the production of goods and services and their distribution (Myles 1988, 74). Since the early 1990s, and in view of the large package of dynamics subsumed under the term "globalization," the welfare state has been undergoing a historic shift that we have yet to fully analyse and understand. Canada has (or perhaps had) what is usually described as a liberal welfare state, in which means-tested assistance, modest universal transfers, and modest social insurance plans predominate, and in which interference with the commodification of goods and services is minimized, the granting of social rights minimized, and a dualism between market and state allocation maintained (Esping-Anderson 1990, 26–7; O'Connor 1989; Myles 1988). The dualism relating to the allocation of benefits is helpful in understanding Canada's housing system. The dualism explains why there is political will to help one part of the housing system and not the other. It also explains why there was at least some effort to help households most in need of housing assistance during the 1960s and 1970s and why even this minimal government role was cut back in the 1980s and then eliminated in the 1990s.

Until the development of the postwar welfare state, government provision of help to those in need was based on a social assistance model, in which welfare assistance for certain categories of "worthy" poor was designed to allow individuals and families to subsist. After the 1940s the social security welfare state emerged alongside this social assistance welfare state. The social security welfare state was never an anti-poverty welfare state. It was designed to provide wage stabilization for the emerging middle class, not to engage in redistribution to assist the poor. In contrast to the means testing of the welfare state, there are two principles of distribution in the social security welfare state: universality and wage replacement. Universality means payments

become entitlements, rights of citizenship, or earned benefits. Wage replacement benefits were linked to past earnings and were at levels high enough to
maintain a continuity of living standard when the wage earner left the labour
market due to illness, unemployment, or disability. The aim of the social security
welfare state is "to smooth the flow of income over the ups and downs of the
economic life cycle of individuals and families" (Myles 1988, 86–7). Owners
certainly consider the non-taxation of capital gains on the sale of their houses to
be an entitlement (not a welfare-type subsidy). Few politicians in a country where
a vast majority of voters own the house in which they live (or hope to own it one
day) even mention this inequity in the treatment of owners versus renters.

The problem which the social security welfare state sought to address is
the maintenance of high and stable levels of mass consumption. This was part
of the more general Keynesian approach to management of the economy. The
big problem during the postwar years was not how to produce enough but how
to stabilize product markets. Systems of wage stabilization helped to solve
this problem. Since the end of the Second World War, the federal government's housing activities have been part of this process by focusing on
achieving high and relatively stable levels of housing starts. This contributed
to overall economic growth and provided many well-paying jobs. The federal
government successfully carried out this housing activity in a fashion that is
compatible with and assists (rather than replaces) housing, land, mortgage
lending, and real estate markets. This aspect of housing policy, part of the
social security welfare state, has nothing directly to do with assisting impoverished households obtain adequate housing – which is a function of the social
assistance part of the welfare state.

The most relevant feature of Canada's welfare state for assessing the dynamics of housing policy (who gets what, of what quality, and with what state
assistance) is the dualism in the provision of benefits. There is still the social
assistance welfare state that has continued to develop since the last century,
but in addition there is now the social security welfare state alongside it. There
is some overlap where benefits are universal – though most universal programs have been abolished. In general, however, a dualism existed and
continues to exist in many policy areas, including housing.

Dualism refers to the existence of two different benefit systems for two
different groups in society. In the case of housing, it exists for the two different housing tenures: owning and renting. One set of policies is based on
market-differentiated benefits, in which the state plays a key but often an indirect role in developing and maintaining benefits (for example, indirect
subsidies through tax exemptions, special regulations and so on). The other
set of policies is based on means-tested benefits through social assistance
programs (direct subsidies to individuals).

How can we best conceptualize Canada's housing system? The dualism
means that there are two separate parts to Canada's housing system, a primary

and a secondary one, each with its own distinct and unequal range of government activities and subsidies – and each, therefore, with separate policy trajectories. These two mirror the dualism in Canada's welfare state. The primary part of the housing system is a component of the social security welfare state, whereas the secondary part is a component of the social assistance welfare state. Table 3 provides a summary of the key features of Canada's dual housing system.

Table 3: Canada's Two-Part Housing System: Key Features

	Primary part[1] (about 80% of households)	*Secondary part[2]* (about 20% of households)
Type of welfare state	Social security welfare state: ensure high living and accumulation standards over the ups and downs of the economic cycle	Social assistance welfare state: ensure subsistence for the "deserving" poor, without competing with market mechanism
Method of distributing benefits	Universal benefits, distributed as entitlements, as "rights" "earned" by investors and owners	Selective discretionary benefits, distributed by means testing and targeting
Economic rationale	Ensure high and stable levels of consumption and accumulation (housing as a key sector of the economy)	Meet basic (minimum) housing needs of some of the "truly needy," while minimizing decomodification effects of programs
Political rationale	Political clout of middle class and of house-building, mortgage-financing, and real estate industries	A "stop and go" process of addressing housing needs, depending on political circumstances and strength of the beneficiary groups
Federal role based on constitutional considerations	Federal government will continue to be involved no matter what the constitutional arrangement; economic and political management issues are more important factors	Likely only if federal government seeks to enhance national unity by a strategy requiring higher federal profile on certain issues deemed to be of national significance

[1]Includes most homeowners, tenants at the higher end of the rental market, and some social-housing residents.
[2]Includes tenants at the lower end of the rental market, some rural and impoverished homeowners, and some social-housing residents.

The primary part consists of about 80 percent of households, including most owners and those tenants who live in the higher end of the private rental market. It also includes households that live in the co-operative housing sector and some but not all of those who live in non-profit and public housing. These households have secure tenure in good-quality housing appropriate to their needs and at a price they can afford. The secondary part consists of everyone else, including tenants in the lower half of the rental market (where housing quality is low), residents of poor-quality and poorly managed subsidized housing, and rural and impoverished owners. The division is in large part, though not totally, based on housing tenure (owning and renting). All three levels of government behave in a similar fashion. They privilege the ownership sector and provide good-quality social housing to a minority of those in need of adequate and affordable housing. They tend to ignore the needs of most low-income renter households.

The very nature of the type of welfare state that Canada has developed – and, in particular, the dualism in the distribution of state benefits – is the key factor in shaping Canada's housing policy and programs. It is this broader policy context in which decisions about housing policy and programs are made. The primary part of the housing system receives benefits mainly in the form of entitlements (universal rather than selective) as "natural" parts of the way the housing system operates. These include the government-created and managed mortgage lending system, the government mortgage insurance program, the special tax treatment of capital gains on owner-occupied housing, the occasional programs to assist with the initial down payment, and the generally superior community services and amenities in districts with higher-cost owner and tenant-occupied housing. Low-income households, if they happen to receive any benefits, generally do so on a selective means-tested basis aimed at meeting minimum needs. Households in the secondary part of the housing system have little political clout, and in the new economic realities that have emerged since the early 1990s ("globalization," more "flexible" labour markets, and the like) they may have even less. Thus, Canada's housing system, for purposes of analysing government activities, consists of two substantially separate and distinct housing subsystems. Each has its own distinct form of government involvement. Government reacts differently to housing problems based on which subsystem the problem is in.

TWO HOUSING POLICIES FOR CANADA'S TWO-PART HOUSING SYSTEM

Based on this analysis of the evolution of the government role in Canada's housing system, there are two sets of trends that help define likely policy trajectories, one for the primary part and another for the secondary part of Canada's housing system.

POLICY FOR THE PRIMARY PART OF THE HOUSING SYSTEM

For the primary part of the housing system, the federal and provincial governments will continue to play an interventionist role during difficult economic
times, whether or not exclusive jurisdiction is given, taken, or claimed by
either level. The house-building sector is a key part of the economy and, with
the support of middle-class owners, is able to mount an effective lobby. Federal government housing activity relating to the primary sector, whether direct
(budgetary spending programs) or indirect (tax expenditures), is rarely considered to be a subsidy or a drain on the economy or on the federal budget.
Rather, these actions are viewed as the proper responsibility of government in
difficult times, and the subsidies are considered incentives and entitlements –
as rights associated with investing in and owning housing.

For the federal government, it is a very practical economic and political
rationale, based on immediate short-term considerations that govern the decision either to take action or to refuse to take action. This is the historical
record, and there is no reason to project any change. Political philosophy and
constitutional and jurisdictional nuances matter little when the government is
confronted with political pressure capable of being mobilized because of problems in the primary part of the housing system. "Problems" here include any
range of policy decisions on issues that provide special treatment for the primary part of the housing system. An example is the introduction of the tax on
capital gains in 1972. One category of capital gain was exempted from the tax
– the capital gain on the sale of owner-occupied houses – even though it was
recognized that such an exemption was regressive among owners (the beneficiaries) and discriminatory in that it excluded one-third of households (renters)
(Powers 1992; Dowler 1983).

Another example is the federal government's decision, announced in the 1992
budget, to introduce the Home Buyers' Plan, which allows house buyers to use up
to $20,000 in tax-sheltered retirement savings as part of their down payment.
This was resisted by federal officials because it risked retirement savings, because it introduced an ad hoc benefit for some house buyers, and because there
was no evidence that such incentives do anything more than move demand for
new houses forward (that is, there is no long-term net gain for the economy). The
pressure "to do something" during a severe construction slump, however, became
so great that the federal government granted the demands of the house-building
and real estate lobbies. In his 1992 budget speech (1992,12–13), the finance minister admitted that the Home Buyers' Plan "responds to requests from industry
groups, provincial governments and individuals" and that it "will support strong
growth in the housing sector this year." In the same budget, however, social housing was further cut from the expected 12,400 units to about 8,000, and the co-op
housing program (about 3,500 units) was terminated. All social-housing supply
programs were terminated in the next budget.

The proposed constitutional agreement that was reached in August 1992 does not appear to affect the federal role in relation to the primary part of the housing system. It has been implemented, however, in relation to the secondary part of the housing system (the 1996 downloading of federal social housing to the provinces). It should be noted that the preamble to section 3 of that agreement, a section on roles and responsibilities, states that "when the federal spending power is used in areas of exclusive jurisdiction" it should, among other things, "contribute to the pursuit of national objectives" (Canada 1992). This implies that there would have been little or no change in the ability of the federal government to initiate its own housing measures even if the voters had approved the constitutional accord. Are there any federal policies or programs about which it cannot be claimed that they "contribute to the pursuit of national objectives"?

Housing plays such an important role in the economy that, during recessions in particular, both the federal and provincial governments have a consistent record of introducing short-term programs that most often are focused on assisting ownership and tenants in the high end of the rental market (the primary part of the housing system), particularly those who are able to buy a house. During the 1970s and 1980s there was a consistent pattern of introducing short-term private-sector subsidy programs (of which the early 1990s Home Buyers' Plan is an example, though it has become permanent). This type of federal housing program activity results from economic and housing market conditions and the stronger political clout of actors in the primary part of the housing system.

In the mid-1970s, in response to the recession, during which housing starts and rental starts fell sharply and vacancy rates fell to the 1–2 percent range in most major metropolitan areas, the 1974 and 1975 budgets introduced the following programs: the Multiple Unit Residential Building (MURB) tax incentive, the Registered Home Ownership Savings Plan (RHOSP), the Assisted Home Ownership Program (AHOP), and the Assisted Rental Program (ARP). The finance minister explained in his June 1975 budget that these measures were designed to "stimulate demand" and to "give an important stimulus to a sector of the economy which has not in recent months played its full role in providing jobs for Canadians." While these programs were introduced within the context of a government wanting to assert the federal role, the particular measures were directly the result of the economic conditions of the day as they affected the housing system. All these measures were targeted at the primary part of the housing system – ownership and the higher end of the rental sector.

A few years later, in response to housing-sector pressures created when mortgage interest rates hit their highest level in history (21 percent in August 1981), the 1981 and 1982 budgets announced a number of new federal housing initiatives that were designed to "spur recovery in the housing industry."

They included short-term subsidy programs for owners (the Canada Home Ownership Stimulation Program and the Canada Mortgage Renewal Plan) and for investors in the higher end of the private rental sector (the Canada Rental Supply Program). There was also a temporary increase in the allocations of social-housing units (2,500 more units in 1982 and another 2,500 in 1983). Thus, both parts of the housing system received some assistance at this time.

POLICY FOR THE SECONDARY PART OF THE HOUSING SYSTEM

Political philosophies, legal nuances in constitutions, and intergovernmental agreements do matter, or at least seem to, when it comes to the secondary part of the housing system. Housing subsidies for lower-income households are part of the social assistance welfare state, over which the provinces claim jurisdiction. They certainly want federal money, but they want to distribute it through programs of their own choosing.

Trends in the federal role in the secondary part of the housing system depend very much on the particular nature of the federal-provincial relations and disputes of the day. The constitutional and social policy philosophy of the federal political party in power is also very important, as is the effectiveness of national housing and social welfare organizations in mobilizing popular support for specific housing and urban policies and programs. The federal government will unilaterally do what it wants if it has the political will to do so. Jurisdictional issues are not in the way. But alleged jurisdictional issues are a problem if the federal government does not want to change its policy or engage in a particular program. The in-between measure is the joint-funding formula – an offer of federal money if it is matched by provincial governments. This is a good delaying (and even avoidance) tactic, and it allows the federal government to point the finger at the provinces when citizens complain that something should be done. The recent federal funding for some "affordable housing" (not necessarily social housing or housing targeted at the greatest need) is an example. After two years, very few units have been subsidized and very little money has been spent. Since the subsidy levels are relatively shallow, the money may not assist many people currently in the secondary part of the housing system.

The trend in federal housing and urban affairs activity in relation to the secondary part of the housing system is, therefore, difficult to predict. For the immediate future, current policies will likely continue, creating a growing division between the quality of the housing for those fortunate enough to be in the primary part of the housing system (the standards of which are among the highest in the world) and the households stuck in the secondary part. Growing homelessness in the 1990s did not result in governments doing anything that has resulted in fewer homeless people. The problem is larger today than five years ago when the federal government started its Supporting Communities

Partnership Program, which has sprinkled the country with some money for services for homeless people and with many press releases about this federal initiative. It will take a very serious deterioration in the quality of the existing aging rental stock (which has already begun to occur) and widespread discontent and effective organization by grassroots organizations for positive and effective federal action to be taken.

An emerging reality that has likely affected (and explains) the current federal government's decision to ignore the secondary part of the housing system relates to changes in the broader economic situation. Global economic trends and domestic corporate investment strategies (economic globalization) mean that there is no institutional or structural imperative to do much about the people in the secondary part of the housing system, other than to forestall embarrassment (too many homeless on the streets). A large unskilled pool of labour is no longer required as it once was.

Such a trajectory for federal housing policy also means growing regional disparities between the larger and economically stronger provinces and the rest of the country. Regional housing market situations combined with changes in provincial governments can result in provincial activism in social housing and urban affairs in the wealthier provinces, which only makes regional disparities even greater. Between 1985 and 1995, for example, Ontario produced about 50,000 housing units with its own funds, thereby removing that many Ontario households from the secondary part of the housing system. In addition, up to 1995, Ontario used its own funds to supplement the federal-provincial social-housing program to eliminate what it considered to be the more regressive regulations imposed by the Conservative government in the 1980s and early 1990s.

For the foreseeable future, there is likely to be more talk and promises and announcements (and re-announcements) of potential spending programs rather than any significant investment in assisting households that are in desperate need of adequate housing they can afford. While support for the primary part of Canada's housing system will continue, there is likely to be very little federal activity in the secondary part of the housing system. The budget compromise reached between the minority Liberal government and the New Democratic Party in 2005, even if fully spent as planned, will not make much of a dent in the social need for housing, nor will it do much to decrease homelessness. In the end, the debate over whether and how to address housing needs and homelessness is a political problem, and there is no scientific or objective way to arrive at an answer to a political problem. The nature of the problem is well understood, and the potential sets of programs are not complicated or even very expensive for a country with Canada's wealth. The question about serious and effective government action on current housing and urban problems is a question about political will. What pressure is there for government to address homelessness? Why worry about poor-quality housing for poor people, urban and rural? There seems to be no economic or significant political pressure to address problems in the secondary part of the housing system. It is, by definition, secondary – not primary. All three levels of government will continue to worry about problems as they arise among households in the primary part of the housing system. The major change affecting the "welfare state" and the sense of nationhood since the early 1990s may mean that the secondary part of the housing system does not matter at all.

REFERENCES

Bacher, J.C. 1993. *Keeping to the Marketplace: The Evolution of Canadian Housing Policy*. Montreal: McGill-Queen's University Press

Banting, K.G. 1990. "Social Housing in a Divided State." In *Housing the Homeless and Poor: New Partnerships among the Private, Public, and Third Sectors*, ed. G. Fallis and A. Murray, 115–63. Toronto: University of Toronto Press

Canada. 1991. *Shaping Canada's Future Together: Proposals*. Ottawa: Supply and Services Canada

– 1992. *Consensus Report on the Constitution: Charlottetown, August 28, 1992. Final Text*. Ottawa: Supply and Services Canada

– Canada Mortgage and Housing Corporation (CMHC). 1985a. *A National Direction for Housing Solutions*. Ottawa

– 1985b. *Consultation Paper on Housing*. Ottawa: CMHC

– Department of Finance. 1984. *A New Direction for Canada: An Agenda for Economic Renewal*. Ottawa, November

– 1996. *Budget Plan*. Ottawa, 6 March. Available at www.fin.gc.ca/budget96/bp/bp96e.pdf

– 2004a. *Fiscal Reference Tables*. Ottawa: Department of Finance

– 2004b. *Tax Expenditures and Evaluations*. Ottawa: Department of Finance

– House of Commons. 1970. *Debates*, 8 October

– Minister of Finance. 2001. "Budget Speech." Ottawa, 10 December

– Ministry of State for Urban Affairs. 1973. "Intergovernmental Operating Relations." Ottawa: Federal-Provincial Conference on Housing. Statement by the Minister. mimeo, 10 pages

– Statistics Canada. 1984, 1999. *Survey of Financial Security*. Ottawa: Statistics Canada

– 2000. *Survey of Household Spending*. Ottawa: Statistics Canada

– Task Force on Housing and Urban Development. 1969. *Report*. Ottawa: Queen's Printer

– Task Force on Program Review. 1985. *Housing Programs in Search of Balance*. Ottawa: The Task Force

Carver, H. 1948. *Houses for Canadians*. Toronto: University of Toronto Press

Dion, K. 2001. "Immigrants' Perceptions of Housing Discrimination in Toronto: The Housing New Canadians Project." *Journal of Social Issues* 53 (3): 523–39

Dowler, R.G. 1983. *Housing-Related Tax Expenditures: An Overview and Evaluation.* Major Report No. 22. Toronto: Centre for Urban and Community Studies, University of Toronto

Esping-Anderson, G. 1990. *The Three Worlds of Welfare Capitalism.* Princeton: Princeton University Press

Gertler, L. 1987. "Research Based Urban Policy." In *The Ministry of State for Urban Affairs,* ed. H.P. Oberlander and A.L. Fallick. Vancouver: Centre for Human Settlements, University of British Columbia

Hulchanski, J.D. 1988. "The Evolution of Property Rights and Housing Tenure in Post-War Canada: Implications for Housing Policy." *Urban Law and Policy* 9 (2): 135–56

– 2001. *A Tale of Two Canadas: Homeowners Getting Richer, Renters Getting Poorer, 1984 and 1999.* Research Bulletin no. 2. Toronto: Centre for Urban and Community Studies, University of Toronto

– 2002. *Housing Policy for Tomorrow's Cities.* Discussion Paper F27. Ottawa: Canadian Policy Research Networks (CPRN). www.cprn.org

Jahiel, R.I. 1992. "Homeless-Making Processes and the Homeless-Makers." In *Homelessness: A Prevention-Oriented Approach,* ed. R.I. Jahiel. Baltimore: Johns Hopkins University Press

Jenson, J. 1989. "'Different' But Not 'Exceptional': Canada's Permeable Fordism." *Canadian Review of Sociology and Anthropology* 26 (1): 69–94

Krueckeberg, D.A. 1999. "The Grapes of Rent: A History of Renting in a Country of Owners." *Housing Policy Debate* 10 (1): 9–30

Liberal Party of Canada. Prime Minister's Caucus Task Force on Urban Issues. 2002. *Canada's Urban Strategy: A Vision for the Twenty-First Century.* Chair, Judy Sgro. Interim Report. [Ottawa: The Task Force]

Martin, P., and J. Fontana. 1990a. "The Government Has Given Up on Housing." Liberal Task Force on Housing. Press release, 14 May

– 1990b. *Finding Room: Housing Solutions for the Future.* Ottawa: Liberal Task Force on Housing

Myles, J. 1988. "Decline or Impasse? The Current State of the Welfare State." *Studies in Political Economy* 26: 73–107

National Council of Welfare. 2002. *Welfare Incomes, 2000 and 2001.* Ottawa: National Council on Welfare

Novac, S., J. Darden, J.D. Hulchanski, and A. Seguin. 2002. *Housing Discrimination in Canada: The State of Knowledge.* Ottawa: Canada Mortgage and Housing Corporation

Novac, S., and M.A. Quance. 1998. *Back to Community: An Assessment of Supportive Housing in Toronto.* Toronto: Mayor's Homelessness Action Task Force

Oberlander, H.P., and A.L. Fallick, eds. 1987. *The Ministry of State for Urban Affairs.* Vancouver: Centre for Human Settlements, University of British Columbia

O'Connor, J.S. 1989. "Welfare Expenditure and Policy Orientation in Canada in Comparative Perspective." *Canadian Review of Sociology and Anthropology* 26 (1): 127–50

Pitfield, P.M. 1987. "The Origins of the Ministry of State." In *The Ministry of State for Urban Affairs,* ed. H.P. Oberlander and A.L. Fallick. Vancouver: Centre for Human Settlements, University of British Columbia

Powers, G. 1992. "A House Is Not a Tax Shelter." *Policy Options* 13 (7):30–4

Prince, M.J. 1998. "Holes in the Safety Net, Leaks in the Roof: Changes in Canadian Welfare Policy and Their Implications for Social Housing Programs." *Housing Policy Debate* 9 (4): 825–48.

Rose, Albert. 1980. *Canadian Housing Policies, 1935–1980.* Toronto: Butterworths

Scanlan, K., and C. Whitehead. 2004. *International Trends in Housing Tenure and Mortgage Finance.* London: Council of Mortgage Lenders

Toronto. Mayor's Homelessness Action Task Force. 1999. *Taking Responsibility for Homelessness: An Action Plan for Toronto.* Toronto: City of Toronto

van Vliet, W., ed. 1990. *The International Handbook of Housing Policy and Practices.* New York: Greenwood Press

V

Processes

11

Local Whole-of-Government Policymaking in Vancouver: Beavers, Cats, and the Mushy Middle Thesis

Patrick J. Smith and Kennedy Stewart

On a admis, il y a longtemps, que certaines questions concernant la politique urbaine tel que la réduction de la criminalité, le transport et les développements importants au niveau de l'infrastructure nécessitent une réponse de « l'ensemble du gouvernement » et donc la coopération des uns avec les autres du gouvernement fédéral et des gouvernements provinciaux et municipaux. Dans de tels cas, les municipalités sont souvent perçues comme des participants de moindre importance parce qu'elles possèdent moins d'autorité formelle. Dans ce contexte, il a parfois été écrit que les gouvernements municipaux sont soit des « castors » soit des « chats ». Les villes castors sont officiellement les créatures les plus faibles de la province et elles ont tendance à fuir les conflits interjuridictionnels. Les chats représentent les villes qui bénéficient d'une certaine autonomie gouvernementale et qui ont beaucoup plus de liberté en ce qui touche à l'élaboration de politiques. Utilisant des exemples de villes de la Colombie-Britannique, ce chapitre utilise ces métaphores pour classer de façon plus efficace l'habileté des gouvernements municipaux à influencer les programmes politiques et la formulation de politique au niveau de l'ensemble du gouvernement. Premièrement, les castors et les chats – donc tous les gouvernements municipaux – sont perçus comme étant assis au centre d'un continuum d'autorité formelle non-opposé à absolue et ces deux groupes d'animaux sont qualifiés soit de « forts » soit de « faibles » selon la force de leurs pouvoirs formels. Deuxièmement, et d'importance cruciale, l'idée d'agence est ajoutée au mélange pour mieux expliquer comment les castors arrivent parfois à influencer les réponses de l'ensemble du gouvernement en matière de politique même s'ils possèdent peu d'autorité formelle. En utilisant deux exemples provenant de la ville de Vancouver, on démontre que les vaillants castors, c'est-à-dire les conseillers et les maires, de nature batailleurs, peuvent obtenir ce qu'ils veulent même s'ils possèdent peu d'autorité.

INTRODUCTION

It has long been recognized that certain urban policy issues, such as crime reduction, transportation, and major infrastructure development, require a "whole-of-government" response involving the co-operation of municipal, provincial, and federal governments. In such instances, municipalities are often portrayed as minor players because of their weak formal authority. In the 1980s, when comparing this local/senior jurisdictional exchange, Victor Jones and Patrick Smith described local governments as being either "beavers" or "cats" (Jones 1986; Smith 1986). Building on the long-held view of Canadian local governments as "creatures of the province," or U.S. municipalities as "tenants at will," beavers were seen as formally weak creatures prone to danger avoidance and fleeing from interjurisdictional conflict, while "home-rule/charter city" cats were described as relatively autonomous units enjoying considerably more policymaking discretion (Jones 1986, 90).

Using examples from British Columbia, this paper builds on the Jones/Smith metaphor to more effectively classify local government's ability to affect whole-of-government agenda setting and policy formulation.[1] The first addition to the metaphor is that beavers and cats – and hence all local governments – are portrayed as sitting in the "mushy middle" of a none-versus-absolute formal authority continuum, with the two animal families being further described as "strong" or "weak," depending on the potency of their formal powers. Second, and more critically, the idea of agency is added to the mix to help explain how beaver cities can sometimes drive the whole-of-government policy responses despite a lack of formal authority. As demonstrated using two examples from the City of Vancouver, aggressive "eager beaver" councils and mayors can overcome formal limits to their authority to "get it done even when they are not in charge" (Fisher and Shar 1998).

BEAVERS, CATS, AND THE MUSHY MIDDLE THESIS

Whole-of-government responses to urban policy problems are common when cities are faced with issues too large to handle on their own (Australia 2004).[2] Roosevelt's Depression-era New Deal is a favourite historical example of a joined-up crisis response, though many contemporary cases of cooperation also exist. Those who write and teach about local government in North America will inevitably, and rightly, explain that from a traditional institutionalist perspective, local governments are weaker than national and provincial/state governments. Canadians describe how section 92(8) of the *Constitution Act, 1867*, gives provincial governments control over all municipal affairs – including local government structure and form. Americans recount how the U.S. Constitution's tenth amendment states that "powers not delegated to the United

States … are reserved to the states respectively, or to the people" (United States 1791). These clauses make clear that provincial/state governments are free to determine the discretionary power of these lower-tier bodies. As described by Jones and Smith, local governments can be either beavers (those with a strictly delimited range of authority) or cats (those with the freedom to expand into policy areas without the express permission of upper-tier jurisdictions).

Some U.S. states have sought to create cats by giving local bodies "greater leeway to undertake a variety of actions of their own without first having to obtain expressed state permission" (Ross and Levine 2001, 94). This idea first found formal expression in 1875 when Missouri amended its state constitution to allow "home rule" (Krane and Blair 1999). But despite a more than century-old movement for more independent municipalities, the United States is still much more a land of beavers. Some U.S. cats do exist, but because of the broad range of powers afforded local governments, depending on their size and home state, there is little agreement on which local governments fit into which category. For example, Mead found there were nineteen home rule states, twenty-six states with legislative home rule (where local governments exercise any powers granted to them or not prohibited by either the U.S. or the state constitution), and just five strictly Dillon's Rule state (Mead 1997). In contrast, Richardson et al. have identified forty Dillon's Rule states (2003).

Figure 1: The Mushy Middle Continuum

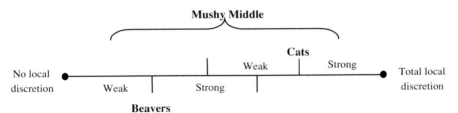

Disagreement about whether a municipality is a beaver or a cat indicates that further refinement is needed to classify local governments more accurately. In an effort to move towards a workable categorization scheme, figure 1 suggests that all local governments sit in the "mushy middle" of a continuum of formal local government authority that has "No local discretion" at one end and "Total local discretion" at the other. These two extremes were chosen to demonstrate that all local governments have at least some discretionary power but never total control – a view confirmed by many, including Richardson et al.: "No state reserves all power to itself, and none devolves all of its authority to localities. Virtually every local government possesses some degree of local autonomy and every state legislature retains some degree of control over local government."(2003, 51). The same is true in Canada, where local governments have usually been seen as beavers.

Although all local governments are located in the mushy middle, the "beavers and cats" metaphor is still a useful label when broadly describing in which of the two categories a particular local government may be classed. But it is probably even more helpful to acknowledge that some beavers and cats are "strong" and some "weak." A strong beaver, defined through formal restraints on its autonomy and the degree to which it controls its own economic, territorial, and political resources, will have a broader range of formal authority to set agendas, formulate policy, and influence decision making on matters that affect its citizens than a weak beaver does.[3] On the flip side, strong cats have fewer formal restrictions on their authority than weak cats. As shown in figure 1, some strong beavers may actually have as much or more formal ability to shape policy as weak cats – indicating that struggles for home rule/charter status may be less enabling than merely requesting a broader range of powers.

Using examples from British Columbia, the next section explores the role of local government in light of the above continuum. The final section, which takes examples from Vancouver to explore how informal and formal authority mix, paints an even more detailed expansion of the metaphor. In conclusion, the paper brings the discussion full circle by using lessons from these British Columbia cases to generalize about the role of local authorities in whole-of-government policymaking.

FROM BEAVERS TO CATS? EVALUATING RECENT LEGISLATIVE CHANGE IN BRITISH COLUMBIA

Many scholars of local government acknowledge that early Canadian local governments were endowed with very little formal policymaking authority, both before and immediately after Ontario's 1849 Baldwin Act (Tindal and Tindal 2000, 27). But as populations grew, so did their formal authority. To use the analogy from the last section, weak beavers grew into stronger beavers as their jurisdiction increased. However, a full species change has never been achieved, since permission from upper-tier masters has generally been perceived as being needed only to expand into new policy areas. But recent developments suggest that provinces may now be willing to allow beavers to transform into cats. For example, a recent B.C. minister in charge of municipal affairs stated that his recent round of legislation – British Columbia's Community Charter – was to "replace a provincial tradition of rigid rules and paternalism with flexibility and co-operation ... [and] encourage municipalities to be more self-reliant" – language that suggested radical change was on the horizon (British Columbia 2002, 3).

The promise of more empowered local governments has existed for some time. For example, the general trend of municipal legislation in British Columbia "has been to give as large as possible a measure of local and self-government autonomy to municipal corporations, and to facilitate the incorporation of municipalities wherever warranted by population and property" (Crawford 1954, 47–8). Having entered Confederation in 1871, the British Columbia provincial government passed initial general municipal legislation in 1873. This legislation allowed local governments to undertake a range of activities but did not include provisions for incurring debt or mandatory responsibilities (Bish 1987, 15). Later amendments allowed for municipal borrowing (1881), and the *Municipal Incorporation Act* and *Municipal Clauses Act* of 1896 provided a system similar to that of Ontario, without a county tier of government. These acts fleshed out the authority and responsibilities of B.C. local government – for example, "a requirement to make suitable provisions for the poor and destitute" – and set a basic framework for all municipalities (Tindal and Tindal 2000, 46).

The ability to opt in or out of a broad range of powers has allowed B.C. municipalities to develop at least into strong beavers, if not yet into cats. According to Robert Bish, the 1936 B.C. *Municipal Act* listed "266 voluntary functions" for local governments, and "few constraints have been exercised if a municipality had a good reason for wishing to undertake some new function … The range of functions municipalities perform has expanded greatly over time" (Bish 1987, 16–18). Smith and Stewart have traced this expansion of formalized powers into the 1990s and early 2000s, describing a number of initiatives designed to expand the roles and autonomy of local governments in British Columbia. Under several New Democratic administrations, local political parties were encouraged and a new *Local Government Act* was established. Additional action was intended on related accountability reforms, but it fell by the wayside when the NDP lost power in 2001 (Smith and Stewart 2005).

The most recent developments in the evolution of local government in British Columbia include a "community charter" initiative undertaken by the Liberal premier, Gordon Campbell, elected in 2001. This latest municipal legislation contains language with a promise of Canadian cats. One of the "first ninety days" commitments contained in the B.C. Liberal Party's New Era election platform document of 2001 was action on the creation of new municipal legislation – the *Community Charter Act*. Structurally and functionally little was to change under the Community Charter, but the legislation, as passed announced a number of financial and jurisdictional reforms – all of which, the province claimed, would free up the hands of local government. These included:

- *Natural person powers* B.C. municipalities were corporate entities, meaning that their powers were subject to some limitations on the making of agreements and providing assistance. Natural person powers do away with itemized corporate powers and increase the corporate capacity of the municipality in relation to already delegated powers.

- *Service powers*   Municipal councils may now provide any service they consider necessary, and bylaws are no longer required to establish or abolish services.
- *Agreements*   In terms of public-private partnerships, municipalities gain a simplified authority to grant an exclusive or limited franchise for transportation, water, or energy systems, and provincial approval for agreements between a municipality and a public authority in another province is eliminated.
- *Additional revenue sources*   The Community Charter "puts forward for discussion" (but does not yet commit the province to) a number of potential municipal revenue sources outside property taxes, including fuel tax, resort tax, local entertainment tax, parking stall tax, hotel room revenue tax, and road tolls.

In addition, the Community Charter claimed to go some length to clarifying the local-provincial relations by recognizing municipalities as "an order to government" and promising the following:

- *Consultation*   The provincial government agrees to consult with the Union of British Columbia Municipalities (UBCM) before changing local government enactments or reducing revenue transfers.
- *No forced amalgamations*   Amalgamations between two or more municipalities will not occur unless electors within the affected communities approve the merger.
- *Reduction of provincial approvals*   Under the Community Charter the number of routine provincial government approvals will be reduced. As well, the charter allows the province to reduce approvals further over time through regulations.

These legislative commitments suggested that the Campbell Liberals wished to increase administrative flexibility and, as much as possible, free local authorities from time-consuming provincial interference – a measure underscored by the move from corporate to natural person powers, reduced provincial oversight, and promises of consultation and increased revenue- generating capacity. This municipal legislative reform in British Columbia was posed as an attempt to increase efficiency through decentralization, based on limited financial and jurisdictional tinkering and no major structural or functional reforms. The language used by the Liberals suggested that all British Columbian beavers might become extinct.

Passed in March 2003, the *Community Charter Act* set out its purpose in language that was still echoing the earlier promise of transforming all B.C. municipal beavers into cats. Its purposes reflect a desire to clarify both the

municipal and the provincial components of the provincial-municipal relationship in British Columbia and, potentially, to add to local autonomy:

> The purposes of this Act are to provide municipalities and their councils with:
> (a) a legal framework for the powers, duties and functions that are necessary to
>   fulfill their purposes,
> (b) the authority and discretion to address existing and future community needs,
>   and
> (c) the flexibility to determine the public interest of their communities and to
>   respond to the different needs and changing circumstances of their commu-
>   nities. (British Columbia 2003a)

Walking the "cat" talk, however, has proved difficult in British Columbia.
The Community Charter reform package was much delayed – initially by provincial secrecy and then by local governmental ambivalence. For example,
the provincial government met with the UBCM at the union's annual conference in September 2002 with a plan to introduce the Community Charter bill
for legislative approval that autumn. However, the more that UBCM members
considered the draft charter, the more concerns they expressed. While the charter promised no provincial downloading onto municipalities without
consultation and equivalent fiscal compensation, no such consideration was
made when the province simply offloaded a responsibility or service, essentially dropping it entirely. This meant that municipalities have had to take a
range of actions in response. They have, for example, had to buy their community hospitals (as Kimberley did after provincial cuts forced its closure); to
hold referendums (as Delta did in the November 2002 municipal election to
get voter approval for a local tax increase to fund its hospital emergency ward
on a twenty-four-hour basis, rather than having it open only during the day
and early evening); and attempt to recall the local MLA (as Delta, among
other constituencies, has tried to do – unsuccessfully to date).

Further, despite the charter's talk of limiting interference by the senior provincial authority, if local governments decide to raise local taxes (for instance,
on businesses) rather than opting for the newly preferred user fees or public-
private partnerships, the province has reserved the right to impose limits on
property tax rates – in direct contradiction of the charter's "empowering local
autonomy" intent. And under a redefined provincial-municipal relationship,
the charter reminds local governments that apart from acknowledging and respecting each other's jurisdiction, the legislative intent is to "work towards
harmonization of Provincial and municipal enactments, policies and programs"
(British Columbia 2003a, s. 2(1b)).

This may work in many instances, but not where a local government wishes
to take a very divergent policy tack. Here, the intergovernmental game becomes more perilous for local authorities – a situation more akin to "beaver"

status. The battle between British Columbia's Ministry of Transportation and the District of West Vancouver over the route of the Vancouver to Whistler "Sea to Sky" highway is a good example of this (Smith and Stewart 2005). Having largely lost at the Federal Court of Canada (May 2005), West Vancouver has appealed the verdict. Also against local wishes, the province pushed an amalgamation into the Vancouver Island community of Courtney (*Courtney Comox Valley Echo* 2005). The City of Vancouver, of course, is the legislative exception, since it has its own Vancouver Charter. It has been allowed to "cherry pick" aspects of the Community Charter that it feels are of benefit (Smith and Stewart 2005).

Traditional beaver thinking has also crept back into the province's post-charter legislative agenda. For example, the *Significant Projects Streamlining Act*, passed in 2003, allows the provincial government to override any local governmental opposition to any project deemed of significant provincial interest (British Columbia 2003b). This Act conjures up images of previous actions by the province: the dismissal of school boards in the 1980s; the "over a weekend" order-in-council eliminating Greater Vancouver Regional District's authority to regulate the region's watershed when it tried to block provincial implementation of a natural gas pipeline through that watershed to Vancouver Island; and the elimination of regional planning (Oberlander and Smith 1993). The more recent (2001–5) overturning of a Delta bylaw, which limited the negative air-quality arising from large greenhouses by requiring them to use natural gas or propane rather than wood waste, also undermines the idea of a catlike transformation.[4]

It would appear, then, that the Liberal's first-term New Era (2001–5) served only to reinforce the beaver metaphor in British Columbia, though perhaps the beavers have become slightly stronger. Re-elected in May 2005, the Campbell Liberals restructured the local government ministry again in June – now as Community Services for a "Golden Decade," but with no promise of stronger municipal governments. Although the municipalities of the twenty-first century may have more powers then those of the nineteenth century, their policymaking powers remain significantly circumscribed by the provincial government.

BEYOND FORMAL CITY LIMITS: VANCOUVER'S EAGER BEAVERS

Despite the language used by various provincial governments, it would appear that British Columbia is largely a land of beavers. However, Robert Bish and others indicate that, in the past, local governments in British Columbia have rebelled and have pursued policy in spheres outside their formal range of authority – felinelike actions, which Bish considers to be of the open-ended, home-rule type (1987, 5–16). This raises the possibility that local mayors and councils may sometimes manage to circumvent formal limitations or – to continue the metaphor – that in some circumstances beavers may temporarily become "eager." The City of Vancouver provides two recent examples that help shed light on "eager beaver" local governments. While these cases do not represent a local governmental norm in British Columbia, they do illustrate some of what any B.C. municipality might need to do to be successful in whole-of-government policy settings.

URBAN DRUG POLICY: VANCOUVER'S SAFE INJECTION SITE

Insite, North America's first legal supervised heroin injection site (SIS), opened on Vancouver's Hastings Street in September 2003. Operated by the Vancouver Coastal Health Authority and the Portland Hotel Society (a Downtown Eastside advocacy non-governmental organization), it is based on a partnership with the City of Vancouver, the Vancouver Police Department, and the community. Insite was established as a scientific research project to assess whether such an operation could reduce the harm associated with heroin and other injected drugs (Vancouver Coastal Health 2005). The first of its kind in North America, Insite is modelled on similar European sites. It was developed by the City of Vancouver through study tours of the health-focused harm-reduction approach taken in EU cities such as Frankfurt and Amsterdam, in contrast to the American-led "war on drugs" approach to drug treatment in North America's cities (Thomson 2004).

Beginning in the 1990s, momentum for Insite stemmed from an overwhelming need to address a significant community problem. Between 1990 and 2000 more than twelve hundred people died from drug overdoses in Vancouver. These deaths were especially prominent in the city's Downtown Eastside (DTES) and were due to a variety of factors: changes in the local drug market, increased poverty, the decision to shut down large mental institutions, lack of affordable housing, and high unemployment. Open drug consumption in the DTES (already Canada's poorest neighbourhood) triggered a common urban problem of core decay – a phenomenon where small businesses and middle-class residents flee problem-ridden neighbourhoods. This core decay served to attract even more problem elements to the DTES, thus amplifying the open drug use and related criminal activity.

Heroin deaths in the DTES peaked in 1993, increasing from eighteen to two hundred in a single calendar year. A 1994 report by the chief coroner of British Columbia, Vince Cain, noted that this increase had occurred despite the Province of British Columbia pouring millions of dollars into related law enforcement and heath services in the area (Cain 1994). Most significantly, the Cain Report represented the first major attempt by a public official to get governments at all levels to see addictive drug use not as a criminal problem but as a health issue and to get them to view drug addicts not as criminals but akin to diabetics in need of health treatment.

A series of reports by other health officials made similar pleas, but they were mainly ignored by all levels of government, and the DTES continued to decline. In October 1997 the Vancouver Richmond Health Board announced a public-health emergency in Vancouver on the transmission of HIV among injection drug users. By 1999, 61 percent of Vancouver's drug-related arrests and 18 percent of the city's crimes against persons took place in the DTES, despite the fact that this area has only 3 percent of Vancouver's population. A 2004 Macleod Institute report corroborated the poor social conditions that prevailed in the DTES:

> In the decade leading up to the Vancouver Agreement, the city's downtown eastside (DTES) was falling into serious social and economic decay. The community had once been vibrant with retail, manufacturing and resource-based businesses operating out of Vancouver's original centre of commerce. When the venerable and long established Woodwards' store on Hastings closed in 1994, it significantly contributed to the decline of the DTES' commercial sector. In 1998, 27% of the stores along one major thoroughfare were vacant and two-thirds of the area's residents were living below the poverty line. (2004, 9)

Yet as the Macleod Institute noted, it would be erroneous to suggest that governments were ignoring these obvious problems. In fact, approximately $1 million was being spent per day by some twenty-five federal, provincial, and municipal departments (2004, 10). Not surprisingly, then, citizens grew frustrated at the apparent inability of governments to meet the health, social services, housing, and safety needs of the DTES community (McGirr 2005, 30).

These serious problems did not go unnoticed, especially by the community worst affected by this crisis. Feeling abandoned by all levels of government, in 1997 a large number of drug users, artists, health activists, and others from the Downtown Eastside came together to form the Vancouver Area Network of Drug Users (VANDU). Although individual members had already made efforts to establish consumer advocacy groups, peer support networks, and even an illegal safe injection site, they felt that as a collective they could force decision makers to adopt policies to rescue their community (Health Canada 2001). In the same year, the Non-Partisan Association (NPA) mayor of Vancouver, Phillip Owen, brought together business, government, non-profit organizations, and advocacy groups to create the Coalition for Crime Prevention and Drug Treatment, which discussed how to engage the community in addressing Vancouver's drug problem and drug-related crime (Health Canada 2001).

Initially, members of this coalition were far apart on how to solve the problem. VANDU and other DTES social service agencies lobbied for harm reduction, including the establishment of a safe injection site. Local businesses owners, some police, and politicians at all levels were opposed to safe injection sites. For example, Ujjal Dosanjh, who at the time was attorney general of the NDP government of British Columbia (and in 2005, as a member of the federal Liberal Party, was minister of health), stated: "You're basically saying, 'if you become an addict we will help you and give you drugs in a safe place.' Well, I'm sorry, that's absolutely the wrong message to send to anybody" (Steffenhagen 1999). Mayor Owen himself repeatedly stated that Vancouver would not put in safe injection sites until they were established in other Canadian cities, because "otherwise, we'll have 20,000 addicts here instead of 5,000" (Bula 2000).

However, with pressure from VANDU and other Downtown Eastside groups, Owen began to soften his stance towards a harm-reduction approach to addressing the ills related to injection drug use in the DTES, and he began to lobby other levels of government to establish such a program. As a result of this city-led pressure, in July 1999 all three levels of government signed a letter of commitment on a deal that eventually became known as the Vancouver Agreement. Officially ratified in February 2002, the Vancouver Agreement provides a framework for the three levels of government to work together in three broad areas: community health and safety; social and economic development; and community capacity building (Vancouver 2000).

Building on the success of the Vancouver Agreement, in 2000 Mayor Owen released a discussion paper describing a four-pillar approach to addressing the city's drug ills. As explained in *A Framework for Action,* the four pillars are harm reduction, prevention, treatment, and enforcement (Vancouver 2001). This framework marked a change in how the problem was viewed, moving the issue of drug addiction from the realm of purely criminal activity to mainly a health issue. It aroused considerable controversy and received a negative response from U.S. President George Bush's "drug czar" (Bula 2003).

In May 2001 the four-pillar approach was adopted as policy by the City of Vancouver. The most controversial aspect of the proposal was to develop a pilot project, since the safe injection site would be the first of its kind in North America. Although adopted by the City of Vancouver, many of the proposals required approval and funding – and even new legislation – by the provincial and federal governments. In November 2002 the federal minister of health, Allan Rock, agreed to fund a pilot safe injection site and create the necessary legal framework. But while praising Owen for his work on the issue, Rock stated that he would not ask any other Canadian cities to open safe injection sites. Rock's stance put Owen in a difficult political position, for he had always stated that he did not want Vancouver to be the only Canadian city with a safe injection site. Even this moderated stance proved unpopular within Owen's right-of-centre Non-Partisan Association party, which had backed him for mayor during previous elections (Bula 2001).

After some contemplation and additional study, Owen veered even more radically from his party's position: he decided to continue to champion the four-pillar approach even though Vancouver would have to go it alone and establish Canada's only safe injection site. His new stance riled many members of his political party. This rift came to a head in the spring of 2002 when NPA party executives informed Owen that he would have to stand for nomination for the 2002 municipal election – in effect, forcing him to reapply for a job he had held since 1993. Such a request had never been asked of an NPA incumbent mayor, and it signalled to Owen that he had lost the support of his party. After debating for a month whether he would run as an independent, he decided not to run at all, and he stepped aside for Jennifer Clarke – a councillor less committed to the full four-pillar approach (Bula 2002a). Far from having a smooth ride into her new job, Clarke was branded Lady Macbeth for what was portrayed in the media as stabbing the popular Owen in the back for her own political gain (*Vancouver Courier* 2005).

At the same time that Clarke replaced Owen as NPA mayoral candidate, former Vancouver coroner Larry Campbell was recruited by Vancouver's other major civic political party to run as its candidate for mayor. A perennial opposition party, the Coalition of Progressive Electors (COPE) was able to assemble a winning team around Larry Campbell, and for the first time in the 116-year history of the city, a single left-of-centre party won the mayoral position and a majority on Vancouver City Council. This victory can be attributed to infighting within the NPA, together with Larry Campbell's popularity (the CBC television series *DaVinci's Inquest* is based on Campbell's career) and the professionalization of COPE by political strategist Neil Monckton. Larry Campbell put the pledge to support the safe injection site and the residents of the Downtown Eastside at the centre of his election campaign, whereas Jennifer Clarke pledged to take the city back "one block at a time" (*Vancouver Sun* 2002).

During the November 2002 election, Campbell stated he would open the safe injection site by 1 January 2003. He took office in December 2002, but the complications of working with multiple agencies from three levels of government forced him to revise his timeline to 1 March 2003 (Bula 2002b). However, by April 2003 the site had still not been opened, owing to a lack of funding. Neither the province nor the federal government wanted to be on the hook for the multimillion-dollar pilot project, and the city simply could not afford to run the site all on its own (*Vancouver Sun* 2003). To add to Campbell's headaches, the coalition that initially supported the safe injection site began to unravel slightly, with one group starting its own unsanctioned safe injection site.

By June 2003, Campbell had managed to persuade Health Canada to back a three-year trial of the safe injection site in Vancouver's Downtown Eastside. In support, the federal government agreed to provide $1.5 million over four years to cover the cost of a scientific evaluation of the pilot, run by the Vancouver Coastal Health Authority, while the provincial government agreed to provide $1.2 million to renovate the site in which the project would be housed. Campbell still needed to secure $2 million per year to cover staffing and supply costs for the site, which he eventually secured from the provincial government (O'Brian and Bula 2003).

In September 2004, Insite released its first public report, in which it reported that there had been no deaths despite the fact that there were 107 overdoses between 10 March and 3 August 2004. The research team at the B.C. Centre for Excellence in HIV/AIDS claims that it is difficult to calculate how many lives have actually been saved, but the site serves 588 users per day and on some days as many as 850, showing that the need is great (Vancouver Agreement 2005). In April 2005 the Vancouver Agreement was renewed by the three levels of government. As McGirr has noted, "some key structural and procedural issues that remain to be addressed in the second term of the *Vancouver Agreement* include: how money is given out, labour intensity, implementation, communication, community involvement, and evaluation" (2005, 30). The ultimate test of success in this whole of government response to the drug crisis in Vancouver's DTES will be to see a degree of institutionalization of the Vancouver Agreement. At first renewal, however, it met the city's whole-of-government "priority challenge."

At his news conference announcing that he would not run again for mayor of Vancouver in November 2005, Larry Campbell described the establishment of Insite as one of his three main accomplishments. Despite not having the authority or the funding to move ahead with the project, he and his councillors had done so anyway. An obvious eager beaver, Campbell summed up his participation in this whole-of-government exercise in the DTES simply with the words "we changed federal health policy" (CKNW 2005). His other two accomplishments – the Olympic referendum and refurbishing a derelict department store in the DTES – are described in the next policy case.

URBAN HOUSING POLICY AND HOMELESSNESS: WOODWARD'S AND
THE OLYMPIC PLEBISCITE

The drug treatment issue demonstrates the capacity of a city to lead in a policy field where it has little or no jurisdiction. This second case illustrates the capacity of municipal politicians to use public support to leverage resources from senior governments. As explained below, Vancouver's eager beavers used a locally initiated non-binding referendum on Canada's bid for the 2010 Winter Olympics to fortify their plans for redeveloping the Downtown Eastside and reducing homelessness. Although they did not initially intend to use the Olympics to "blackmail" the provincial government, savvy local politicians soon recognized an opportunity to push their agenda on the provincial government and effectively did so to suit their own agenda.

In 1998 the Canadian Olympic Association selected Vancouver to represent Canada in the competition to host the 2010 Olympic Winter Games and the Paralympic Winter Games. In preparation for the July 2005 decision by the International Olympic Committee, the Vancouver bid committee put its best efforts into winning against Salzburg, Austria, and Pyeongchang, South Korea. As the decision date neared, discussion about the potential positive and negative effects of the games on Vancouver residents began to build. In March 2003 the Impact of the Olympics on Community Coalition (IOCC) called for a provincewide referendum on the issue. In September, Larry Campbell (who at the time was COPE's mayoral candidate) said no to a provincewide vote. But later, on a call-in radio show just before the 16 November 2002 civic election in which he and a majority of COPE councillors were swept to power, he said yes to a non-binding plebiscite administered by the City of Vancouver (McMartin 2002).

Both senior levels of government voiced concern. Referendums in other Olympic-hopeful cities had failed, and there were fears that a similar Vancouver vote might imperil the 2010 bid. At first the province suggested that even if the new COPE council rejected the games it could hold the city to a commitment made by the previous NPA administration. Liberal Premier Gordon Campbell openly opposed the referendum, though he later campaigned for the "yes" side (Palmer 2003). However, unlike the harm-reduction plan in the Vancouver Agreement, here the City of Vancouver had the capacity to control all cost issues internally and was able to move ahead – although negative pressure from business and media was intense. One of the first orders of business for Larry Campbell and his new COPE-majority council was to pass a motion for a non-binding plebiscite on the Olympic Games. On 10 December 2002 the city announced an "Olympic vote," to be held on 22 February 2003, in which Vancouver residents would be asked, "Do you support or do you oppose the City of Vancouver's participation in hosting the 2010 Olympic Winter Games and Paralympic Winter Games?"

Although the city set aside approximately $700,000 to advertise and administer the citywide vote, no monies were offered to the "yes" or "no" side. Thus, if Vancouver's Olympic bid was to avoid the fate of cities such as Berne, Switzerland, and Denver, Colorado, where "no" Olympic victories forced bid withdrawals, a strong "yes" contingent was needed to champion the cause. Many of the new COPE councillors were lukewarm or even hostile to the Olympics. For example, Mayor Campbell's strongest council ally, Jim Green – a former IOCC chair – was initially against the games. But as explained below, Green recognized that the provincial Liberals were desperate to win the bid because it tied in with their plans for reinvigorating the economy, so he moved to exploit this position to the benefit of the DTES community, in which he had been active for decades (Garr 2003).

A decade ago, the Woodward's shopping empire dissolved, leaving a large store building between Vancouver's downtown and the DTES. What to do with the building or the site had long bedevilled the city, the province, and private developers. In 2001, during the dying days of the NDP provincial government, former Vancouver city councillor (and then municipal affairs minister) Jenny Kwan "bought" the Woodward's building from a developer who had not been able to complete a plan acceptable to the city. By then the building had been the site of years of protest by DTES and housing activists, who wanted a public-housing component included in the plan for the site, rather than only higher-end stores and offices. The cost to the province was more than $20 million. Then, in the May 2001 provincial election, the NDP government was wiped out (77 seats to 2) by Gordon Campbell's right-wing Liberals.

Days before the Olympic vote, a spate of intergovernmental Olympic deals were announced. Woodward's was sold to the City of Vancouver for a fraction of its value ($5.5 million), with the province promising to fund at least a hundred social-housing units at a cost of up to $10 million – despite deep cuts to social spending across the rest of the province. The federal and provincial governments agreed to a $20 million "living legacy" fund for the Downtown Eastside. Finally, the province also agreed to turn some of Southeast False Creek's Olympic Village into social housing after the games were over (Howell 2003). Directly after these announcements, Jim Green signed on to the Olympic vote's "yes" team, as did Mayor Campbell shortly thereafter. When asked whether "his cool demeanor towards the Olympics was a deliberate strategy to see what he and his pals could squeeze out of Victoria," Green responded, "I don't see anything wrong with that interpretation" (Garr 2003).

On 22 February 2003, just days before the visit of the Olympic Selection Committee, 64 percent said "yes" in the Olympic vote. A surprising 50 percent of registered voters cast ballots – usually Vancouver electoral participation is closer to 30 percent. The Vancouver bid gained considerable momentum from the overwhelming public support, and in July 2003 the IOC announced that Vancouver had been successful. For the city, many of the benefits of its Olympic bid had already been secured by the eager beaver actions of a few savvy council members. In September 2004, Vancouver City Council chose Westbank Projects/Peterson Investment Group to be the developer for the Woodward's project, with Simon Fraser University announced as the project's major partner. So ending the long battle to regenerate an important segment of the DTES.

This case demonstrates that by arming themselves with previous electoral commitments, eager beavers can sometimes drive the intergovernmental agenda. Although this strategy is not without risk, the city saw a clear opportunity to advance its agenda. Local councillors determined that the provincial government was politically vulnerable and used the leverage of public opinion to produce a deal more in line with the city's interests. In this case, eager beavers advanced their agenda under conditions where less aggressive behaviour would have failed.

THE POTENTIAL OF EAGER BEAVERS IN WHOLE-OF-GOVERNMENT URBAN POLICYMAKING

The lessons from these two Vancouver cases for local decision makers when thinking about whole-of-government responses to their priority challenges are several:

- *Individuals can make a difference*   Policy champions are needed if local governments are to play the whole-of-government policy game successfully.
- *Political will is essential*   Even where stakes are higher, politics matters. Vancouver's response to developing a harm-reduction model on drug treatment was exactly the opposite of that of neighbouring Surrey, the region's second city. There, the main pillar in local policy is enforcement. In Vancouver there are four pillars.
- *Local political support is essential*   Although not everyone was on the same policy page regarding how to proceed, the new city council had armed itself with electoral support. This made it harder for senior governments to ignore it.
- *Local buy-in is even more important*   Despite millions of dollars in investment in Vancouver's DTES, the relative success of the SIS to date has depended more on local involvement – in the city and in the community.
- *Understanding the organizational cultures of other governmental levels is important*   It seemed clear at the beginning of the Vancouver Agreement development that each jurisdiction operated in some isolation. The renewal of the agreement in 2005 showed that considerable learning had taken place in the interim.
- *The policy goal itself is key*   The two cases – the drug crisis and homelessness – were recognized across the local political spectrum as priority challenges. The high standing of both issues helped engage the other levels of government in adapting existing public policy to find new solutions.

In the larger sense, the two examples from Vancouver also substantiate the claim that a more complete understanding of the local policymaking process can only be reached by moving beyond an examination of formal institutions. This extralegal or behavioural dimension of local governmental policy influence has been discussed by some U.S. authors as well. For example, describing what they call the Lexis-Nexis Fallacy, Krane and Blair suggest that an overreliance on legal sources, when assessing the capabilities of local governments to influence agendas and policy formulation, leads scholars to assume mistakenly "that the legal language of constitutions and statutes accurately reflects actual practice" (Krane and Blair 1999, 13–14). This strictly legal focus creates several important problems in trying to unravel the scope of local powers and local-senior intergovernmental relations. In the United States:

1   "[I]n actuality, the amount of discretionary authority available to [local governments] is often not explicit, and varies significantly from state to state" (Zimmerman 1995).

2   "[A] classifcation based solely on the availability of the charter option completely misses other important dimensions of local government authority" (Liner 1989; Gold 1989).

3   "[A] legalistic approach to local autonomy does not clearly distinguish between the activities of local governments, and local governments and policy makers" (Gargan 1997).

4   "[T]he traditional legal approach to home rule provides little, if any basis for the development of systematic knowledge about the discretionary authority of municipal government and the consequences of variation in that authority (i.e. what difference does home rule make?)"(Krane and Blair 1999).

The usefulness of the formal approach – or, as we have done, classifying local governments as beavers or cats or even as weak and strong beavers and cats – has its limits. This is especially true in understanding whole-of-government responses to local policy problems. Hanson describes the lack of information about informal interactions as a "blind spot." In the United States, says Hanson, "few scholars know much about the constitutional, political and fiscal ties that bind states and localities, and even fewer have much information about the complex interactions between state and local governments engaged in the delivery of public goods and services" (1998, 3).

For Krane, this continuing blind spot means that "without more comprehensive information about local government discretionary powers in all fifty states, any understanding of local governmental capacity in the United States will be limited" (Krane and Blair 1999). Ellis Katz concurs, stating that despite the constant reaffirmation of Dillon's Rule, "the political reality is that America's cities and towns enjoy a remarkable degree of autonomy and independence" (Katz 2003, 1). Finally, Victor Jones cautions that "the right of a legislature to create, modify or destroy is just that – a right; that is, it is only a legal authority to act. Even though the right may be plenary, it must be distinguished from power, or the ability of the authority to act in full or in part, to exercise unfettered choice, to act at any time, any place, or to any extent it chooses" (1986, 90). It would appear, then, that to classify the policymaking influence of local governments correctly, particularly on senior governmental agendas, some attention must be paid to "mushy middle" local governments that go beyond the law to enact policy – to lead when they are not in charge.

To this end, figure 2 provides a revised policymaking capacity continuum by which to classify all local governments. Following the previous model,

Figure 2: Revised Mushy Middle Continuum

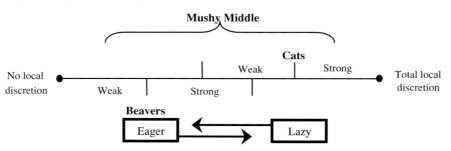

local governments can initially be classified as either beavers or cats, and then can be subdivided further as strong or weak, depending on their range of authority. As shown in figure 2, some "eager" local governments can increase their ability to influence their city's priority policy challenges in a number of ways around this whole-of-government thinking. Although not explored here, it is easy to imagine lazy cats achieving less than eager beavers, but it is easier still to imagine lazy beavers achieving very little at all. Thus, expanding the Jones/Smith metaphor to include a mushy middle does not only provide a new perspective on the ability of local governments to influence whole-of-government policy. It also makes it harder for municipal leaders to justify inaction, claiming that they are limited by formal constraints. As the examples from Vancouver demonstrate, local politicians are often as powerful as they wish to be – a valuable lesson for local and provincial politicians and the citizens who elect them.

NOTES

1 Agenda setting (where problems are identified) and policy formulation (where possible solutions are posed) are the first two stages of the policy cycle – followed by actual decision making, implementation, and evaluation (Howlett and Ramesh 2003).

2 This type of intergovernmental cooperation is similar to "horizontal management" (Bakvis and Juillet 2004; Hopkins, Couture, and Moore 2001) or "horizontality" (Hopkins, Couture, and Moore 2001).

3 Zimmerman suggests four components of local discretionary power: (1) structure; (2) functions; (3) finances; and (4) personnel (1995).

4 The Municipality of Delta had passed a bylaw to provide some local control of large (in this case, 18-acre) greenhouse operations, in particular their use of less-clean fuel sources for heating. The B.C. government intervened when a grower challenged the bylaw, citing Right to Farm legislation over the right of a municipal-

ity to legislate on local businesses. The province also argued that the local bylaw contradicted the provincial *Waste Management Act*, which exempts agricultural operations. Urban-rural issues of this sort are not new to Delta, a Vancouver suburb. In the late 1980s and 1990s, Delta held the longest land-use dispute hearing in Canadian history (over efforts to develop farmland for urban use). The debates over the so-called Spetifore lands near the Tsawassen ferry terminal to Vancouver Island led Bill Bennett's Social Credit government to abolish regional planning in 1983 when the Greater Vancouver Regional District initially prevented development plans by a Delta Social Credit supporter. The minister of agriculture and fisheries has since also precluded use of local bylaws to prevent/regulate coastal fish farms in British Columbia (Penner 2003).

REFERENCES

Atkins v. *Kansas,* [1903] USSC

Australia. 2004. *Connecting Government: Whole of Government Responses to Australia's Priority Challenges.* Canberra, Australia: Management Advisory Committee. www.apsc.gov.au/mac/connectinggovernment.pdf (accessed 25 July 2005)

Bakvis, H., and L. Juillet. 2004. *The Horizontal Challenge: Line Departments, Central Agencies Leadership,* Ottawa: Canadian School of Public Service

Bish, R. 1987. *Local Government in British Columbia.* Richmond: Union of British Columbia Municipalities

British Columbia. 2002. *The Community Charter: A New Legislative Framework for Local Government.* Victoria, B.C.: Ministry of Community, Aboriginal and Women's Services

– 2003a. *Community Charter Act.* www.legis.gov.bc.ca/37th4th/1st_read/ gov14-1-pt01.htm (accessed 15 June 2005)

– 2003b. *The Significant Projects Streamlining Act.* www.legis.gov.bc.ca/37th4th/ 1st_read/gov75-1.htm (accessed 15 June 2005)

Bula, F. 2000. "Comprehensive Health Services Aimed at Closing Drug 'Market': Ottawa, Victoria, and the City Get Together to Fund a New Health Centre in the Downtown Eastside." *Vancouver Sun,* 30 September

– 2001. "Safe-Injection Site a Go if B.C. Wants It, Rock Says: Health Minister Praises Vancouver Mayor for His Courage to Develop Drug Policy." *Vancouver Sun,* 15 November

– 2002a. "After the Split, Rebuilding a Tarnished Image: Drug Policy Played a Key Role in Owen's Departure." *Vancouver Sun,* 12 October

– 2002b. "First Safe Drug Site to Open by March, Mayor Says." *Vancouver Sun,* 18 December

– 2003. "Safe Injection Sites Will Draw Key Users: Study." *Vancouver Sun,* 4 January

Cain, J.V. 1994. Task Force into Illicit Narcotic Overdose Deaths in British Columbia. *Report.* Burnaby, B.C.: Office of the Chief Coroner

City of Clinton v. *Cedar Rapids and Missouri River R.R.Co.* (1868), 24 Iowa 455,475 [25 Iowa 163 at 170]

CKNW. 2005. Interview with Mayor Larry Campbell on the *Jennifer Mather Show*, 30 June

Community Communication Co. v. *Boulder,* [1982] USSC

Courtney Comox Valley Echo. 2005. City Desk interview, 8 July

Crawford, K.G. 1954. *Canadian Municipal Government.* Toronto: University of Toronto Press

Feldman, L., and K. Graham. 1979. *Bargaining for Cities: Municipalities and Intergovernmental Relations, an Assessment.* Montreal: Institute for Research on Public Policy

Fisher, R., and A. Shar. 1998. *Getting It Done: How to Lead When You're Not in Charge.* New York: Harper

Frisken, F. 1994. "Metropolitan Change and the Challenge to Public Policy." In *The Changing Canadian Metropolis: A Public Policy Perspective*, vol. 1, ed. Frisken. Berkeley: IGS Press, University of California

Gargan, J.J. 1997. "Local Government Governing Capacity: Challenges for the New Century." In *Handbook of Local Government Administration,* ed. Gargan, ch 22. New York: Marcel Dekker

Garr, A. 2003. "Woodward's Deal Buys Olympic Support." *Vancouver Courier*, 29 January

Gold, S.D. 1989. *Reforming State-Local Relations: A Practical Guide.* Washington, D.C.: National Congress of State Legislatures

Hanson, R.L., ed. 1998.*Governing Partners: State-Local Relations in the United States.* Boulder: Westview

Health Canada. 2001. *Responding to an Emergency: Education, Advocacy, and Community Care by a Peer-Driven Organization of Drug Users. A Case Study of Vancouver Area Network of Drug* Users (Vandu). Ottawa: Health Canada

Hopkins, M., C. Couture and E. Moore. 2001. *Moving from the Heroic to the Everyday: Lessons Learned from Leading Horizontal Projects.* Ottawa: Canadian Centre for Management Development

Howell, M. 2003a. "Games Watchdog Group Says Green Defection No Problem. *Vancouver Courier*, 9 February

– 2003b. "'Insite' Opening an International Media Event." *Vancouver Courier,* 17 September

Howlett, H., and M. Ramesh. 2003. *Studying Public Policy: Policy Cycles and Policy Subsystems.* 2nd edn. Toronto: Oxford University Press

Jones, V. 1986. "Beavers and Cats: Federal-Local Relations in the United States and Canada." In *Meech Lake: From Centre to Periphery,* ed. H.P. Oberlander and H. Symonds. Vancouver: Centre for Human Settlements, University of British Columbia

Katz, E. 2003. "Local Self-Government in the United States." Report for the U.S. Embassy, Thailand. www.usa.or.th/services/docs/work16.htm (accessed 19 March 2003)

Krane, D. 2001. *Local Government Autonomy and Discretion in the USA.* Washington, D.C.: National Academy of Public Administration

Krane, D., and R. Blair. 1999. *The Practice of Home Rule: Report for the Nebraska Commission on Local Government Innovation and Restructuring*. Omaha: Nebraska Commission on Local Government Innovation and Restructuring

Lee, J. 2003. "Green Likely to Back the Olympics: Social Housing Remains His Major Concern." *Vancouver Sun*, 30 January

Liebshutz, S.F., and J.F. Zimmerman. 1997. "Fiscal Dependence and Revenue Enhancement Opportunities for Local Governments in the United States." In *Future Challenges of Local Autonomy in Japan, Korea, and the United States: Shared Responsibilities between National and Sub-National Governments*, ed. F. Horie and M. Nishio. Tokyo: National Institute for Research Advancement

Liner, E.B. 1989. "Sorting Out State-Local Relations." In *A Decade of Devolution: Perspectives on State-Local Relations*, ed. E.B. Liner. Washington, D.C.: Urban Institute Press

McGirr, E. 2005. "Intergovernmental Policy-Making in Canada: The Role of Local Governments and the Vancouver Agreement." Honours thesis, Department of Political Science, Simon Fraser University

Macleod Institute. 2004. *In the Spirit of the Vancouver Agreement: A Governance Case Study*. www.wd.gc.ca/rpts/audit/va/default_e.asp

McMartin, P. 2002. "Olympic Vote Idea Just Grew and Grew." *Vancouver Sun*, 12 December

Mead, T. 1997. "Federalism and State Law: Legal Factors Constraining and Facilitating Local Initiatives." In *Handbook of Local Government Administration*, ed. J.J. Gargan. New York: Marcel Dekker

Oberlander, H.P., and P.J. Smith. 1993. "Governing Metropolitan Vancouver: Regional Intergovernmental Relations in British Columbia." In *Metropolitan Governance: America/Canadian Intergovernmental Perspectives,* ed. D. Rothblatt and A. Sancton, 329–73. Berkeley: Institute of Governmental Studies, University of California

O'Brian, A., and F. Bula 2003. "Injection Site Gets Go-Ahead." *Vancouver Sun,* 25 June

Palmer, V. 2003. "Oh No! There's Politics in Vote on Olympics. *Vancouver Sun*, 9 January

Penner, D. 2003. "Tomato King Cheers Right to Burn Wood: Court Overturns Bylaw That Restricted Growers' Fuel – Delta Bylaw 'Set Undue Restrictions.'" *Vancouver Sun*, 19 April

Richardson, J., et al. 2003. *Is Home Rule the Answer? Clarifying the Influence of Dillon's Rule on Growth Management*." Washington, D.C.: Brookings Institution

Ross, B., and M. Levine. 2001. *Urban Politics: Power in Metropolitan America*. 6th edn. Itasca, Ill.: F.E. Peacock

Smith, P. 1986. "Local-Federal Government Relations: Canadian Perspectives, American Comparisons." In *Meech Lake: From Centre to Periphery,* ed. H.P. Oberlander and H. Symonds. Vancouver: Centre for Human Settlements, University of British Columbia

Smith, P., and K. Stewart. 2005. "Local Government Reform in British Columbia, 1991–2005: One Oar in the Water." In *Municipal Reforms in Canada: Dimensions, Dynamics, Determinants*, ed. J. Garcea and E. Lesage Jr. Toronto: Oxford University Press

Southern Contractors Inc v. *Loudon County Board of Education*, [2001] USSC
State ex. rel St. Louis Housing Authority v. *Gaertner* 695 SW2d 460 Mo.(1985)
Steffenhagen, J. 1999. "Safe-Injection Sites Send the Wrong Message, Dosanjh says:
	Opposes Plan For." *Vancouver Sun*, 23 January
Thomson, J. 2004. "The Benefits of a Closed Political Opportunity Structure: Urban
	Social Movements, the Vancouver Local Government, and the Safe Injection Site
	Decision." MA thesis, Department of Political Science, Simon Fraser University
Tindal, R., and S.N. Tindal. 2000. *Local Government in Canada.* 5th edn. Toronto:
	Nelson
United States of America. 1791. *U.S. Constitution: Bill of Rights*
Vancouver. 2000. *Administrative Report.* RTS no. 01372, CC file no. 1367/4113. Van-
	couver: City of Vancouver, 28 March
– 2001. *A Framework for Action: A Four Pillar Approach to Vancouver's Drug Prob-
	lems.* Vancouver: City of Vancouver
Vancouver Agreement. 2005. www.vancouveragreement.ca (accessed 15 June 2005)
Vancouver Coastal Health. 2005. "Insite – North America's First Official Supervised
	Injection Site." www.vch.ca/sis (assessed 30 May 2005)
Vancouver Courier. 2005. "Et tu, Brute?" 9 February
Vancouver Sun. 2002. "'Not in My Back Yard' the Universal Cry: NIMBYism, in All
	Its Guises, Is the Incurable Disease of Civic Politics." 7 November
– 2003. "Lining Up the Dollars for the Safe-Injection Site." 7 April
– 2005. "Vancouver Agreement to Be Extended Five Years." 4 April
Wynn, G. 1992. "The Rise of Vancouver." In *Vancouver and Its Region*, ed. G. Wynn,
	and T. Oke. Vancouver: University of British Columbia Press
Zimmerman, J.F. 1995. *State-Local Relations: A Partnership Approach.* Westport,
	Conn.: Praeger

12

Rhetoric and Restraint: Municipal-Federal Relations in Canada's Largest Edge City

Tom Urbaniak

Ce chapitre examine les relations municipales-fédérales de la ville de Mississauga en Ontario au cours des dernières années. Les politiques concernant l'aéroport, la régénération du secteur riverain et le logement y sont soulignées. Cette ville a su exercer une certaine influence sur le gouvernement fédéral et a même parfois établi elle-même le programme politique, et ce sans médiation, ou très peu, de la part du provincial. Les gouvernements progressiste-conservateur de Brian Mulroney et de Kim Campbell ont été forcés de faire des concessions à la ville de Mississauga en ce qui concerne l'aéroport et ils ont essayé d'obtenir le soutien de la ville afin de se prémunir contre les autres lobbyistes. La ville de Mississauga était à la tête de la planification de la régénération des terres riveraines appartenant au fédéral. Les dirigeants de la ville de Mississauga et ceux du palier supérieur de la municipalité régional de Peel ne se battent pas avec la même ferveur lorsqu'il est question de redistribution sociale que lorsqu'il est question de développement économique. Toute description des relations municipales-fédérales doit tenir compte de la perspicacité des chefs et de leurs prévisions pragmatiques, surtout lorsqu'il s'agit d'un chef tel que la mairesse Hazel McCallion. Les prescriptions impartiales des économistes politiques ne correspondent pas toujours aux prévisions et aux motifs des chefs politiques municipaux.

"A new deal for cities," demands the *Toronto Star* in a year-long series of articles and editorials. In the same vein, the Federation of Canadian Municipalities' Big City Mayors' Caucus (FCM 2003) is calling for a new partnership with the Government of Canada. Given the considerable media coverage and expressions of concern from political, business, and social service leaders, it is difficult not to surmise that Canada's cities – or at least the large cities – have some very wide-ranging and well-developed demands, not only of provincial but also of federal policy.

But if cities in general, and not just advocates for the inner cities, are determined to secure a comprehensive partnership with Ottawa, we would probably
find that Mississauga, Ontario, is a leader in this campaign. With 680,000
people, it is Canada's sixth-largest city and the largest suburban municipality.
Mississauga's long-serving leader, Hazel McCallion,[1] enjoys extraordinary
popularity, has a high profile outside the city, plays an influential role in the
upper-tier Regional Municipality of Peel (population 1.1 million), and has a
reputation for being outspoken and often confrontational.

This paper argues that Mississauga does indeed exert some influence over
the federal government – sometimes in unlikely areas – and the Constitution
notwithstanding, it often successfully bypasses the province. Most of the advocacy, however, is carried out on a sector-by-sector basis with relatively
short-term objectives. Despite the mayor's occasionally highly charged public rhetoric, the city is not generally pursuing major changes to federal policies
that would serve redistributive rather than economic-development objectives.

Mississauga's and McCallion's approach to municipal-federal relations is
thus consistent, to some degree, with Paul Peterson's "city limits" thesis.
Peterson (1981) proposes that because of the structural constraints within which
cities must operate, including their inability to regulate directly the intermunicipal movement of goods and people, they are likely to concern themselves
primarily with "developmental" (economic productivity) objectives and much
less with social or progressive goals.

This is an incomplete explanation, however, because it fails to account adequately for the shrewd, pragmatic calculations that give primacy to the leader's
own prospects for influence. This paper therefore also invokes Richard
Neustadt's (1990) "self-help" thesis of leadership. What is advantageous politically does not always serve local economic objectives.

SURVEYING THE LANDSCAPE

Federal policy affects Mississauga and the Region of Peel significantly. Loans
and insured mortgages provided by the Central (now Canada) Mortgage and Housing Corporation arguably contributed to suburban development and sprawl (Sewell
1994). Immigration policies have altered the ethnic and racial composition of the
community and have contributed to the city's remarkable growth. Mississauga's
population is almost double what it was twenty years ago, though growth has
slowed recently as the municipality becomes built up. According to the 2001 census, 39 percent of Mississauga's residents are immigrants and more than 40 percent
are members of visible minority groups (Mississauga, PBD 2003).

National debates threaten occasionally to engulf local politicians. Take, for
instance, McCallion's 1995 statement that Bloc Québécois leader Lucien
Bouchard should be tried for treason (*Toronto Star* 1995) or her awkward

speech at a March 2003 peace rally, during which she told the crowd that they ought instead to be urging the federal government to solve domestic social issues such as homelessness (author's notes taken during the event). Even more controversial were the mayor's comments to a *National Post* columnist about federal immigration policies (Francis 2001). McCallion was quoted as complaining that one of the local hospitals was "loaded with people in their native costumes." Although insisting later that she had been referring only to illegal immigrants, she eventually did issue a grudging apology.

The most prominent intersection of federal and municipal responsibilities in Mississauga occurred in 1979 following the spectacular derailment of a Canadian Pacific train and the subsequent chlorine spill and fire. Almost 250,000 residents of Mississauga were relocated for up to five days, making this one of the world's largest peacetime evacuations. By most popular accounts, it was McCallion who was in control of the response. It was the dynamic municipal leader who determined, on the advice of the city's fire chief, when to evacuate and when to give the all-clear signal. It was her image more than anyone else's that was shown around the world (Cahill 1980). Later, some of the city's recommendations for more stringent federal regulations were echoed by the federally constituted Mississauga Railway Accident Inquiry and implemented. These included requiring detailed chemical cleanup plans, more sophisticated methods for measuring the amount of chlorine remaining in a boxcar, and that "all cars, whether dangerous-goods cars or not, should have roller bearings" (Grange 1980, 194).

Putting aside the exceptional circumstances of the great derailment and the mayor's occasional incendiary statements about federal policies and politicians, most federal-municipal relations in Mississauga have revolved around two themes: the use of federal property and requests for federal money, primarily for specific infrastructure initiatives. The controversy over the future of Pearson International Airport and the coordination of waterfront regeneration are cases in point. These can be contrasted with the less assertive municipal and mayoral advocacy of and activities on affordable housing.

THE CASE OF PEARSON INTERNATIONAL AIRPORT

Except for a tiny sliver in the City of Toronto, Canada's largest airport, Lester B. Pearson International, is situated within Mississauga. Big-picture students of intergovernmental relations would likely expect that municipal influence over such a major federal installation would be marginal. Indeed, even those who focus only on what is reported in the press, or on the actual influence the city exerts today, would reach the same conclusion. Alternatively, perhaps any meaningful opportunities for input from Mississauga emerged after 1996, thanks to the presence of two Mississauga residents on the board of the Greater Toronto Airports Authority (GTAA).[2] After all, the federal Environmental

Assessment Panel, which had endorsed many of the grievances of residents living close to the airport, had argued that a local airport authority would be much more accountable to citizens and their municipal governments (Canada, EAP 1992a, 81).

But a closer examination reveals that the city exerts less influence now, with the airport under the administration of a local airport authority, than it did when the facility was run directly by the federal Department of Transport. Especially intriguing are the not widely reported details of the city's behind-the-scenes manoeuvring during the 1989–93 period, when the Progressive Conservative federal government contracted out the construction of a new terminal and attempted, with the mayor's shrewd support, to privatize the operations and the major redevelopment of the two old terminals.

The privatization approach was favoured by Ottawa in lieu of devolution to a local airport authority, which seemed to be the preferred option else-where in the country and in the National Airports Policy of 1987 (Canada, Senate 1995a, 11 and II-7). Pearson Development Corporation, a private con-sortium, was awarded a fifty-seven-year lease and was contracted to effect major renovations. Finalized in the middle of the 1993 election campaign, the deal generated uproar from the opposition parties. The agreement subsequently was cancelled by a new Liberal government (ibid., appendix B).

The Conservatives' transactions were the subject of extensive hearings in 1995 by a special Senate committee. Two very different interpretations emerged. In its report, the Conservative majority on the committee argued that the whole process had respected the public interest and had been carried out, over several years, with integrity and objectivity. The Liberal minority report charged that there had been a one-track determination to privatize the facilities and to ensure that the beneficiaries would be friends of the govern-ment. (Mississauga-based developer Don Matthews, chair of the Matthews Group and a key player in Pearson Development Corporation, was a past presi-dent of the Progressive Conservative Party.)[3]

According to the Conservative senators, Ottawa did not have a fixed priva-tization agenda but was being deferential to Mississauga because that is the city in which the airport is situated, because the renovations were needed ur-gently (McCallion was calling Terminal 1 "a slum" and actually was sending in the Peel Health Department), and because the mayor had the ability to cre-ate obstacles. McCallion had earlier threatened Huang and Danczkay, the outfit contracted by Ottawa in 1987 to build and operate a new terminal (no. 3), that she would not provide municipal services (including water and sewage) if they refused to pay development charges. They relented (Canada, Senate 1995b, 25 July).

But in 1991, with the federal government's promised call for private-sector proposals having still failed to emerge, and with Toronto business leaders and the provincial government working hard to set up an "airport authority" as a proposed alternative to privatization, there was growing concern in Mississauga that Ottawa might waver from its course and allow the airport to be taken over by a Metro-dominated entity. Such a body, it was feared, would ignore Mississauga's requests for development charges, for building inspections (along with their associated fees), and for transportation infrastructure to connect the airport better with the rest of Mississauga rather than only with Metropolitan Toronto to the east. There was also concern that there would be attempts to divert the airport noise cones that affected Metro residents, deflecting them to Mississauga neighbourhoods (McCallion and Shaw interviews 2003).

McCallion thereafter became more aggressive in her efforts to thwart the Metro-dominated initiative. She showed up uninvited at a meeting of the would-be airport authority and senior federal and provincial officials – including ministers – to express concerns about the process. She began calling the Metro body "the illegal airport authority," and, most important, she proceeded to launch a rival airport authority (Canada, Senate 1995a, 44).

Thanks to McCallion, therefore, while the federal government was evaluating the privatization proposals, the competing airport authorities, neither of which had any formal authority, were bogged down through much of 1992 negotiating a *modus vivendi*. A task force of the chairmen of the Greater Toronto Area regions had to be set up to break the impasse. An arrangement that gave Peel the right to appoint (not just nominate) two of the fifteen members and that limited Metropolitan Toronto to two members was finally concluded late that year (Peel 1992), soon after which Mississauga resident Sid Valo became the chair.[4] The new set-up was endorsed by the Region of Peel Council and Mississauga City Council.

But Mississauga's endorsement was conditional – and the Peel council later was persuaded by Mississauga to support the city's qualified position. The city called on the new airport authority to oversee both Pearson and the Toronto Island airport, even though Toronto Island was being operated under a tripartite arrangement involving the City of Toronto, the Toronto Harbour Commissioners, and the federal government. This condition was cited by Transport Minister Jean Corbeil as the reason for not negotiating with the local airport authority but continuing instead with the privatization process (Canada, Senate 1995b, 19 September).

Mississauga was determined to extract guarantees from the federal government in exchange for supporting the latter's privatization initiatives. To force the issue, in June 1993 the city council passed a resolution saying it now was opposed to the new north-south runway, which had been proposed by Ottawa along with two new east-west runways. The stated motivation for Mississauga's resolution was the federal government's failure to meet eighteen conditions laid down by the city in a January 1992 resolution. This set the stage for negotiations between Mississauga and the federal government on an airport-operating agreement. The federal government agreed to establish a noise authority to monitor aircraft traffic, and it also agreed that the runway would not be used at night and not when the wind conditions allowed for the use of the other runways. But the majority of the city's runway conditions were in fact infrastructure and financial matters, not noise issues. The minister agreed, for example, to construct new access roads, making it easier to get inside the airport from Mississauga (Pecar 1993).

The day before the privatization deal was signed, the mayor and the transport minister were still in touch to ensure that the minister would honour his guarantee that Mississauga would not lose any federal revenue as a result of the privatization. The private consortium would pay property taxes, a significant portion of which would go to the school boards and the region. But in the absence of property taxes, Mississauga had been receiving the full share of the federal payments in lieu of taxation. The switch to property taxes would mean an annual loss to Mississauga of approximately $3.2 million. The federal government acceded to Mississauga's demand to make up the difference (*Mississauga News* 1993b).

The influence that Mississauga had, or was about to have, came to an end with the election in October 1993 of a new government, which was determined to pursue a very different course on the Pearson file than the one followed by the Conservatives. Even an attempt by Mississauga to appear conciliatory by dropping the Toronto Island condition did not so much as gain the mayor a sympathetic hearing from the minister (Petovello interview 2003).

The Greater Toronto Airports Authority's sixty-year ground lease, which commenced in December 1996, has exacerbated Mississauga's predicament. (The plural term "airports" is used even though the GTAA manages only Pearson.) Three of the board's fifteen members are nominees of the Region of Peel, but these directors (who are usually business executives) must be appointed formally by the GTAA board itself. They are required by the GTAA's bylaws to concern themselves solely with the airport's interests. This is not an obscure clause; it is top of mind for GTAA officials. In 1998 the GTAA board of directors rejected Peel nominee Lou Parsons on the grounds that he would be more loyal to Mississauga than to the airport. This rejection later was overturned by the courts (*Mississauga News* 1999). The board earlier had declined another nominee of the city and picked instead someone suggested by the Mississauga Board of Trade.

Meanwhile, the airport appeared to stall a long-planned and apparently badly needed western access road unless the city agreed to drop its eventually unsuccessful legal challenge to win the right to collect development charges on the airport's planned ten-year, $4.4 billion expansion program. The airport refused to discuss noise-management issues with the city on the grounds that the authority was being sued by one of the residents' associations. Meetings of the board of directors are closed to the public.[5]

The governance structure – in which the board is, in effect, accountable to itself – gives enormous authority to its president and CEO, until recently was Louis Turpen. He had previously been manager of the San Francisco Airport, where he had frequent confrontations with Mayor Dianne Feinstein and State Senator Quentin Kopp (*San Francisco Examiner* 1995). Typical of most Mississauga observers, the head of the Mississauga Board of Trade perceives Turpen as a "gunslinger" and has compared him to New York's legendary but unaccountable master builder, Robert Moses (Gordon interview 2002; Caro 1974). Turpen, for his part, did not hesitate to heap scorn publicly on his opponents.

Concerned perhaps that McCallion might still somehow get her loyalists onto the GTAA board, the sitting directors proceeded to rewrite the authority's bylaws to state that the regions *collectively* would nominate several candidates and that the GTAA board would "consider" whether to appoint any of them. These changes were approved by Transport Minister David Collenette, an action that McCallion attributes to Collenette having been "a weak minister" (McCallion interview 2003).

Even the coordination of routine functions appears to have been affected by the political wrangling between Mississauga and the GTAA. According to the former city manager, the GTAA has refused to submit to the municipal fire department any structural blueprints or information on the location of hazardous material, even after pledges by the city to designate key officials who would undergo the strictest security clearance. The GTAA has likewise refused to submit its projects to the city for building permits, a practice which the federal government followed when it had direct charge of the airport (O'Brien interview 2003).

WATERFRONT REGENERATION: THE CITY IN THE LEAD

Until the 1970s, policy and planning concerning harbours and waterfront land use on Mississauga's fifteen-kilometre-long Lake Ontario shoreline went largely uncoordinated among the many public bodies that had a stake and ownership. The federal government owned Port Credit Harbour and leased parcels of it to private parties without prior consultation with the municipality. The Government of Canada also retained ownership of a thirty-acre, largely derelict site in southeastern Mississauga, which had served as a military training area during the Second World War. The provincial government had acquired some land years earlier in anticipation of the South Peel Water and Sewage System, although some of it was leased to the municipality for park purposes. Ontario Hydro, a provincial Crown corporation, owned and operated the massive Lakeview Generating Station. In the late 1960s, the Credit Valley Conservation Authority (CVCA) began leasing or acquiring its own parcels of land as part of the initial steps towards a scheme for regeneration (CVCA and Crysler and Lathem 1972; CVCA 1983; Kennedy interview 2003).

When one public body acted, it usually did so with minimal consultation with the other public bodies, unless agreement with another was a legal necessity. Thus, for example, in the early 1950s the federal government built, with little warning, a huge $4.5 million structure on its harbour lands in Port Credit to accommodate industrial marine vessels, mainly those of Canada Steamship Lines.[6] When the federal government decided that a breakwater was needed just offshore near Port Credit, it decided in 1974 to partially sink a large rusty surplus freighter, the *Ridgetown*. Some residents objected at the time to what they considered an eyesore (Mississauga, with Hough, Stansbury, and Woodland 1987).

In 1974 the federal government's industrial harbour building lost all its tenants as large-vessel traffic ceased completely around Port Credit. A long-term lease (in effect until 2035) with a private entrepreneur, who agreed to convert the terminal into a recreational docking facility, was then negotiated. Again, there appears to have been no serious consultation with other levels of government (Blanchard interview 2003).

Indications of intensifying cooperation between local and federal officials appeared finally in the late 1970s and early 1980s, when the city and the CVCA persuaded the federal government to construct a $1.5 million breakwater in order to create dozens of new docking opportunities at the CVCA's new park, adjacent to the Lakeview Generating Station (Kennedy interview 2003). The federal government was also persuaded by the municipality to clean up the serious silt problem in Port Credit Harbour. The silt was proving to be an obstruction to the pleasure craft (Carr and Ruffini interview 2003) in what had become one of North America's largest freshwater recreational harbours Mississauga, PBD 1990; Crombie 1992, 279).

A more fundamental change took place in 1984. The federal government's lease with the Port Credit Yacht Club (one of the major tenants at Port Credit Harbour) was set to expire in five years. The yacht club was eyeing new facilities at Lakefront Promenade Park, beside the generating station. Meanwhile, the city learned that the private entrepreneur who was leasing the former Canada Steamship facility was developing a proposal to purchase the site outright and redevelop it. Given the potential controversy, the mayor and local bureaucrats decided that it was time for the city to have a plan (Mississauga, PBD 1990, 11).

The ensuing Port Credit Harbour Study was promoted by the mayor as a potential formula for recreational and economic expansion. It became a multi-year, increasingly more expansive planning and implementation process, involving the city, the provincial government, the federal government, the Region of Peel, and the CVCA (Port Credit Harbour 1985, 4). What is especially significant for our purposes, however, is that thenceforth the City of

Mississauga was always the leading – indeed, the dominant – public body in this multilevel, multilateral process. The steering committee for the Port Credit Harbour Study, which concerned itself mostly with federal land, was made up primarily of city staff, with only one person representing the federal government.

All the officials at the table were at liberty to comment on any aspect of the matters at hand, even if these lay outside their jurisdiction (Barron interview 2003). This appears to have been possible because all acknowledged the city's leading role, since it was the one municipality that would be affected directly. It was also understood from the early stages that the city would shoulder most of the costs. The parties likewise acknowledged that the city had more expertise in land-use planning than any of the other public bodies (Carr and Ruffini interview 2003; McCallion interview 2003).

Furthermore, as of the mid-1980s, federal policy has called for the divestiture of all small-craft harbours (Blenkarn 1987). By then, the Government of Canada had fewer than a dozen staff overseeing its more than four hundred small harbours in Ontario, western Canada, and northern Canada. The staff did not have the resources to take a detailed interest. "We tried to operate in a non-confrontational way with the municipalities," explained Duane Blanchard, regional director for small-craft harbours, Fisheries and Oceans Canada (Blanchard interview 2003). "We recognized [the municipalities] as partners. It made sense. We weren't trying to build a federal empire. We were trying to get this stuff managed as well as we could for as little as we could ... We let them be the lead." He added that the province has been involved in these municipal-federal relations only where it has a contractual interest in particular properties, although the federal government tried initially and unsuccessfully to divest all the small-craft harbours to the provincial government and to let it deal with the municipalities or other interested parties.

City politicians and bureaucrats who were involved in the Port Credit process recall that there was no organized public movement pushing for it (confirmed by Carr, Ruffini, and Kennedy interviews 2003). The impetus seemed to come from within the bureaucracy and was quickly endorsed by the mayor. Although she involved herself only at strategic moments, she remained abreast of developments to the point that the chief federal official involved attests that he constantly "felt" her presence (Blanchard interview 2003).

AFFORDABLE HOUSING: LESS ASSERTIVENESS

Mississauga is not a strictly affluent municipality. It has neighbourhoods where poverty is a serious and pervasive problem. The waiting list for the Region of Peel's non-profit housing corporation stands at almost 20,000. In 2000 the region opened a forty-bed homeless shelter in Mississauga, which immediately became filled to capacity. Between 1995 and 2002, only seventy-nine new rental spaces were created (sixty of which were considered high end) in the otherwise rapidly growing region. In 1999, 21.3 percent of children under fourteen were living in poverty in Mississauga (Layton 2000, 89–92; Peel 2002).

"Never one to shrink from a fight, Mayor McCallion has launched offensive measures on three fronts," argues Jack Layton in his recent book on homelessness. "She delivered blistering and very public criticisms of the federal government's abandonment of its affordable-housing mandate; she worked with her communities to establish emergency shelters; and she dispatched Peel Region housing agency head Keith Ward to help create the National Housing Policy Options Strategy of the FCM. A McCallion unleashed is a force that few voluntarily contend with. After all, as Toronto Life put it, 'Her Town, Her Rules.'" But in the very next paragraph Layton presents a somewhat more subdued picture: "Not that an explosion of affordable housing has begun in Peel Region. A summer 2000 policy and planning document put together for Peel Regional Council sets aside some modest funds for small affordable housing projects and supportive initiatives for the homeless, but, as so many other communities, Peel is waiting for Ottawa" (Layton 2000, 91–2).

Which scenario best describes the local stance: assertive, proactive, progressive, or reluctant, not particularly assertive, and waiting but not pushing too hard? A casual observer might conclude that the local elected officials are tireless crusaders for affordable housing. Seldom do a few days elapse without a stirring speech by the mayor urging Ottawa to do more. Moreover, the regional non-profit housing corporation, established in 1977, was the first in the Greater Toronto Area after Metropolitan Toronto's, and it is highly regarded in the human services sector.

Yet a closer examination reveals that the municipal politicians are far less assertive than is suggested by the public image they project. Mississauga council has, over the years, passed several resolutions that have specifically shunned an active role in promoting affordable housing. In 1995 the new Progressive Conservative provincial government pushed through legislation repealing the previous government's prescribed targets for ensuring affordable housing as part of the land-use planning process. After Bill 20 received royal assent, Mississauga council deleted the following statement in the updated draft official plan: "The City will provide opportunities to ensure that on a City-wide basis a minimum of 30% of new housing units will be affordable" (Mississauga PBD, n.d.).

The homelessness and affordability problems have figured prominently in the headlines in the Greater Toronto Area, especially since 1998, when Canada's Big City Mayors' Caucus (which includes Mississauga) declared the problem to be a "national emergency." Toronto Mayor Mel Lastman promptly appointed a Mayor's Task Force on Homelessness. The reverberations were felt in Peel (where housing is addressed at the regional level).

In 1999, following Toronto's report, the Region of Peel appointed its own Task Force on Homelessness, although this one consisted primarily of regional staff. Its recommendations called for a much expanded role for the region and both senior levels of government, including re-engagement by the federal government in housing at least to the extent of the 1980s (Peel 1999).

Although new emergency shelters were established, and although the region's housing staff are respected by their professional colleagues and by many advocates, most of the task force's recommendations for local initiatives have not been implemented. The region has not revised its strategic directions to place more emphasis on housing. Staff reports recommending new measures must therefore be justified by referring to the rather vague "Goal 3" in the strategic directions, which states that there will "be a strong and effective regional government," or the strategic direction calling on the region "to act as a leader and advocate on issues of Regional concern" (Ward et al. 2001).

In late 1999, federal Labour Minister Claudette Bradshaw announced the allocation of $753 million over three years to assist homeless Canadians and to prevent homelessness. In March 2000, regional staff reported to their political superiors: "[A] number of preliminary decisions may have already taken place regarding the allocation of $250 million. It also appears to staff funding may be directed towards 10 cities identified as facing acute homelessness. Peel Region was not included" (Peel 2000). Staff urged councillors to demand federal support. Although council concurred, it seems that very little behind-the-scenes lobbying had taken place before the regional public servants urged their political superiors to take up the mantle – and not much has happened since.

This apparent sluggishness does not characterize local advocacy on all social programs. There are some files on which the local politicians have been more assertive. For example, Regional Chair Emil Kolb pushed hard, and successfully, to launch a federal-municipal pilot project, the Sponsorship Breakdown Program. Under this plan, the federal government and Peel Region have agreed jointly to be assertive in recouping social service costs from sponsors of immigrants whose sponsoree becomes a burden on the welfare system. The region has also been sending a bill (which goes unpaid, of course), with accumulating interest, to the federal government for all social service costs incurred by refugees (Kolb and Maloney interview 2003).

Regional staff have been working on ideas for pilot projects related to social housing (Ward interview 2003), but the politicians appear not to have taken up the mantle in an assertive manner. When asked by the author on which issue she spends more time, housing or immigration, the mayor replied without hesitation that it is the latter (McCallion interview 2003).

MUNICIPAL ADVOCACY AND ECONOMIC DEVELOPMENT

In the above cases, we see the local leaders tenaciously pursuing federal policies and arrangements that generate local benefits without requiring new local social investments, or those that seek a competitive advantage over other cities, such as preventing what was perceived as an attempt by local Toronto interests to control the airport. But we see a reluctance to become actively engaged in redistributive issues.

This portrait is consistent with Paul Peterson's theory of urban political economy, developed in his 1981 book *City Limits*. To understand the overriding thrust behind local priorities, we must understand that "city politics is limited politics" (Peterson 1981, 4). Cities do not make war or peace. They cannot impose tariffs. They cannot prevent outsiders from entering their jurisdiction. They are thus forced to exist in an extremely volatile economic environment, where they can do little to shield themselves from competition with other cities. As a result, cities prefer "developmental" policies (which are likely to expand the local economy) over redistributive policies, such as housing and welfare services. To put it simply, a city with generous redistributive policies and without a much greater fiscal capacity than its neighbours is likely to be unattractive to wealthy taxpayers but attractive to needy citizens, who pay little in taxes to the municipality but require more services than their more affluent fellow citizens. According to Peterson, the nature of local leadership, the machinations of elites, and the relative strength of various interest groups are all shaped by and exist within this framework.

"Developmental" policies are not necessarily of the same ilk. They can include everything from downtown redevelopment to building a new zoo – anything that is likely to attract business and bolster the prosperity of the city, taken in the aggregate. Peterson observes that cities' propensity to favour developmental initiatives even spills over into intergovernmental relations. He finds, for example, that it is too simplistic to assert that local governments' failure to implement many of President Lyndon Johnson's "Great Society" initiatives can be attributed to the "complexity" of the programs. Economic-development-oriented programs (such as federal money to build roads and infrastructure) were implemented successfully, but many redistributive programs languished. In the former case, the federal government and local governments had congruent interests. In the latter they did not (Peterson 1981, 87–8).

On the Pearson Airport file, although Mississauga's mayor worked hard on behalf of the expansion and modernization of the old terminals, she was less enthusiastic about defending the neighbourhood interests articulated by organizations representing residents who would be affected by aircraft noise generated by the new runways. The mayor cited the economic benefit of having Canada's largest (and expanding) airport within Mississauga's boundaries.

It is almost certain that this benefit would far outweigh a possible decline in the property values of some residences, a decline that even the negative report of the federal Environmental Assessment Panel expected to be minor (Canada, EAP 1992a, ch. 4).

The residents argued that the 1978 official plan – based on the stated assumption (which was not challenged at the time by federal or provincial authorities) that there would be no new runways at Pearson – represented a "social contract" with the community. This interpretation was supported by the MP for Mississauga East (Canada, EAP 1992b, 271; Searle interview 2003). It was rejected by the city, however, which asserted that there were no legal guarantees to this effect from the federal government and that "the Doctrine of Paramountcy continues to rule" (Marc Neeb, Mississauga airport liaison officer, in Canada, EAP 1992b, 90).

To be sure, the mayor did manoeuvre in an attempt to ensure that any new airport authority would not be constituted so as to shift negative effects (such as noise) to Mississauga. But she always supported expansion. As she complained in 1995 to the Senate committee: "Here we sit with Canada's most important airport and no action [on expansion]." She also told the senators, "We have 101 Japanese companies in our city. We have 86 German companies, and we consult with each company as they move in as to why they chose Mississauga. I would say that eight times out of 10 it is the airport. Others are because our taxes are the lowest. I am sure you know that we are a debt-free city. I thought that Ottawa might like to know that especially" (Canada, Senate 1995b, issue 20, p. 10).

Consider also the only airport-related issue that the City of Mississauga has pursued aggressively since the Greater Toronto Airports Authority's ground lease took effect – namely, the unsuccessful judicial dispute that Mississauga launched against the GTAA to get the latter to pay development charges to the city on the planned $4.4 billion expansion. By failing to pay, the mayor charges, the GTAA has been turning the airport into "a city within a city" (McCallion interview 2003).

With regard to waterfront regeneration, the city became active even without previous public pressure to do so. In recent years, as regeneration has spread beyond the relatively contained Port Credit Harbour to include vast tracts of shoreline, the city has brushed off neighbourhood resistance to the prospect of increased traffic and disturbance, arguing that property values are likely to increase markedly (Kennedy interview 2003).

The local reluctance to be more assertive on housing is not surprising considering that the mayor of Mississauga appears to be almost as critical of the regional staff as she is of the federal government. In her interview with the author, Hazel McCallion called Peel's housing managers "empire builders." She argued that the region's housing stock should be contracted out to a private firm and that the federal government's housing strategy should be based entirely on rent subsidies and incentives to build private rental housing rather than public housing. Although she spoke passionately about the right of every Canadian to lodging, she conceded that she is reluctant to seek support for expanding the region's housing initiatives, because the matter ought to be strictly federal: "Otherwise, Milton [which borders Mississauga on the west] could get away with doing nothing and the problem would be shifted here" (McCallion interview 2003). According to the mayor, housing should be a federal and not a local matter precisely because it is a basic human right.

There is evidence that when a formerly dormant issue becomes entangled with the municipality's developmental interests it rises accordingly on the city's intergovernmental agenda. Until recently, public transit in Mississauga had been regarded as a social service, a method of transportation for those who cannot afford an automobile.[7] Even in the six years before the provincial government's downloading of transit costs, Mississauga's transit system had gone without any expansion, despite the rapid population growth (McCallion 2003a).

In recent years, however, with a marked increase in traffic gridlock, the municipality has come to see an effective public transit system as critical to the economy. "All levels of government need to deal with this pressing issue with speed if we are to maintain our competitive edge in the world arena," wrote the mayor in an article (2003a). McCallion has been calling loudly for more federal and provincial investment in transit, including dedicated gas taxes, which now appear to be in the offing. This, along with timely infrastructure funding and the uploading of housing responsibilities, are what she sees as the most important planks in a "new deal" for municipalities (McCallion 2003b).

THE "SELF-HELP" THESIS AND MUNICIPAL-FEDERAL RELATIONS

Peterson uses the term "able servant," as opposed to "inefficient slave," to describe local leaders who tenaciously pursue the economic productivity of their cities. Does this description apply to Hazel McCallion's relations with Ottawa, or does it omit some important dynamics of local leadership?

Peterson describes in detail only one "able servant," New Haven Mayor Richard Lee, who, with great "entrepreneurial skill," saw to the execution of a major program of downtown redevelopment that involved significant investment from other governments. Peterson claims that this program was indisputably an economic boon to the city because it made the downtown more accessible to automobiles (and to the shoppers who drive them) and because it encouraged middle- and upper-income residents to move into new high-rises in the core. Moreover, it supposedly did not cost the city a penny, since most of the money was extracted by the mayor from the federal government (Peterson 1981, ch. 7).

Whether or not Peterson's glowing evaluation of downtown redevelopment is accurate (the hollowing out of many American downtowns has been exacerbated by misguided redevelopment schemes), it must be acknowledged that there are very few economic development initiatives in which a municipality can participate directly that come free of charge to the city. Yet initiatives requiring local investment, if pursued, may well result in enormous stimulus to the local economy.

But what if local leaders have built a reputation on rigid fiscal conservatism, even if it sometimes defies the city's economic interest? What if a local leader must tread carefully to protect political credibility that is based on foundations that are not strictly economic? In short, does politics matter more than Peterson allows? Here we find the bifurcation between the dispassionate prescriptions of the political economists and the calculations (and motives) of local leaders.

The "self-help" or "prospective power" thesis is an apt moniker for the leadership analysis developed by Richard Neustadt in his famous study *Presidential Power and the Modern Presidents*. It is based on the assumption that an American president's starting position as a leader is weak because most of his powers are shared, *de facto* or *de jure*, with others. His effectiveness (measured in influence over the long term) is thus based not strictly on decisions examined in isolation but on what calculations he makes that might in future give him leverage over other matters or political actors.

Neustadt's framework requires heavy doses of pragmatism, caution, a willingness to forgo immediate success in anticipation of future gains, even on unrelated issues, and an approach that never strays too far from the grain of public sentiment (Neustadt 1990). By invoking the "self-help" thesis, we can gain a satisfying perspective on why an effective leader sometimes pulls back from acting in what appears to be the economic interest of the city. The level of risk may be acceptable to the city as a corporate entity, but the same level of risk may be unacceptable to a mayor concerned about other policies, about maintaining an air of strong, successful leadership, and about building a reservoir of influence for future decisions and controversies.

In her dealings with the federal government, Hazel McCallion has followed the self-help/prospective power principles very astutely. She has recognized that even issues over which her government has no formal authority whatsoever could affect her leadership adversely if they are not handled attentively and diligently and with an eye to the prevailing public mood. Her positions on airport issues have never diverged markedly from the grain of public opinion. For example, in the 1970s, as mayor of Streetsville and then as a councillor on Mississauga City Council, she opposed any expansion (Mississauga 1978, 38–42). In the 1990s, as mayor of Mississauga, her ambiguous position was generally to support (albeit with conditions) new runways that would cause airplanes to fly over neighbourhoods.

Without the aid of opinion polls or a formal network of advisers, McCallion had sensed that the mood of the municipality was far more complex than it had been in the 1970s. Whereas in the 1970s local economic expansion and residential development were almost synonymous, and whereas at the time a far greater proportion of the municipality's population lived in the eastern neighbourhoods (which were under the proposed flight paths), by the 1990s the population was much more dispersed, and many in Mississauga regarded Canada's largest airport as a major economic asset to the city. The Mississauga Board of Trade, which did not exist when the earlier controversy was raging, favoured airport expansion without conditions. Furthermore, the residents' movement of the 1970s was certainly more vociferous than its counterpart twenty years later. This probably was partly due to the fact that aircraft in the early 1970s were more noisy than in the early 1990s when "Chapter 2" jets were being phased out in favour of the quieter "Chapter 3" variety.

Although McCallion sometimes was criticized by leaders of the anti-airport-expansion residents' groups, she managed to contain the opposition and protect her local public stature through well-calculated public relations, such as re-fusing to attend certain airport functions or ribbon-cuttings because of the failure of the federal government (and later the Greater Toronto Airports Authority) to comply with the city's noise conditions. Far from enhancing the local economic balance sheet, these mayoral gestures alarmed the airport boosters in Toronto and even the board of trade in Mississauga (Stewart 1994), making them more wary of the city, and rendering them all the more determined to build in provisions to shield the new GTAA from any political influence. This may have harmed the mayor's prospects for affecting airport decisions, but it defused a potentially explosive local controversy that was threatening to erode what is arguably McCallion's most formidable political asset – the overwhelming popular support she receives from her constituents, making her the dominant figure at City Hall.

Although placating the residents in some respects, the mayor was also careful to ensure that they did not become emboldened. She resisted Transport Canada's attempt in early 1993 to establish its own community advisory committee with representatives of some of the vocal residents' groups (Ferenc 1993). When residents' angst over the runways grew louder, and when some groups demanded not only city support but also city funding to carry on their advocacy, McCallion created her own residents' advisory committee (as well as a business advisory committee) and tried to make it the focus for deliberations between the city and residents on the positions the city should take to the federal government. It appears that she and her council colleagues carefully controlled the information the committee received (Stewart 1993).

The battle for airport development charges can also be seen through a leadership lens and not simply in rational economic development terms. Consider, for example, that although the Mississauga Board of Trade was worried that appealing the initial ruling in favour of the GTAA would be futile and expensive (Gordon interview 2003), the city proceeded anyway. Although the city lost that battle and although its prospects for losing were always thought to be rather high (O'Brien interview 2003), it was by no means a futile fight from the mayor's point of view. Here was an issue around which the whole community could rally, including the business sector (at least initially) and the resident activists, who did not mind seeing the GTAA challenged. The case gave the mayor national attention and was seen as a very important test by the Federation of Canadian Municipalities. Even in defeat, therefore, the mayor's stature was enhanced.

Despite the obvious economic benefit of some of the waterfront projects and the federal-municipal agreements that have been finalized, here too we find a divergence between what is probably in the objective economic interest of the municipality and what is in the perceived rational interest of its leaders. At the very least, it casts some of Peterson's analysis in doubt by demonstrating that it is not often easy to discern what is in the economic interest of a city. For example, Mississauga has not done anything to plan for its waterfront plan's proposed sport-fishing hall of fame, art gallery, or marine museum (Mississauga, PBD 1990). Such initiatives might qualify for funding, not only as infrastructure projects but under existing federal cultural investment programs. However, as is conceded by the mayor and the local councillor, such investment has not been sought. Instead, the city applied for and will receive waterfront funding through the Canada-Ontario Infrastructure Program to renovate an existing library and improve a park some hundred metres north of the shoreline.[8]

Part of the explanation may lie in the city's very conservative fiscal policy, which is frequently promoted as an example of "good management" but is not necessarily congruent with a program of economic expansion. The policy is conservative, not only by virtue of tax freezes or decreases (between 1992 and 2002 there was no increase on the city portion of the property tax bill) but also in its aversion to what many may consider acceptable risks. The local councillor, Carmen Corbasson, says that the proposed Port Credit tourist facilities (like the hall of fame and museum) will be left to the initiative of citizens, and she does not regard it as her role to be a facilitator or initiator of such projects (Corbasson interview 2003). The mayor, for her part, maintains that even if there had been federal or provincial funding, the city would almost certainly have had to assume a significant portion of the operating expenses (McCallion interview 2003). This factor alone, she believes, is compelling enough to put these projects on the back burner. In defending the above assertion, the mayor points to the example of the city's $76 million Living Arts Centre, which opened in 1997 with $20 million from Mississauga's development charges fund and $13 million from each of the senior levels of government. But the centre has had significant unanticipated operating deficits and has become a burden on the city treasury.

In a similar vein, although many of Mississauga's and Peel's objectives in their relations with the federal government have focused on economic development rather than social policy, this may sometimes be a function of what the local leaders have calculated to be likely to produce some results (a small success that they can deliver to their constituents) rather than being the most advisable in principle (a noble cause for which the municipality would have little to show for its efforts). Former Member of Parliament Bob Horner recalls that after the 1984 election he was summoned to the mayor's office and presented with a checklist of the mayor's ten most important demands from the federal government. No one has kept a copy of this list, but Horner insists that all the items were relatively small and local – money for railway overpasses, improvements around the harbour, and so on (Horner interview 2003). These matters could be arranged, and most have been. A demand concerning social policy would probably not be something that could be worked out for the city or the region alone. Indeed, the Mississauga councillor who chairs Peel's housing committee asserts that the paucity of forceful advocacy by local politicians is attributable to exhaustion and frustration with a perceived lack of federal progress (Mullin interview 2003).

NEXT STEPS

As the case of Mississauga reveals, an urban agenda is not necessarily a municipal agenda. Progressive civic movements and advocates of more federal intervention and activism in social policy areas affecting urban residents may find that their local leaders will champion their policies only half-heartedly. Knowing this, how should their strategies be fashioned? Let us consider the following two options.

BYPASS THE LOCAL LEVEL

In Mississauga, some groups demanding redress from the senior levels of government have devoted considerable effort to getting the municipal government onside. This is attributable in part to the stature of the mayor. As one MP said at a public meeting at which the mayor was present, "Everyone who lives in Mississauga knows the prowess of Hazel McCallion. If she wanted to stop the runways and she put her mind to it, she could" (*Mississauga News* 1993a). As we have seen, however, the municipal government may be very reluctant to go beyond sympathetic public rhetoric in pursuing policies that have redistributive consequences. Even with federal support, such policies are likely to place an added burden on the local tax base and perhaps attract more needy residents to settle or remain in the city.

Although these economic considerations do weigh heavily on local policymakers, they are not always determinative. After all, the mayor has been publicly professing concern about the problem of homelessness, and this has helped draw attention to the issue, even if she has not always been working vigorously on the file behind the scenes. On the runway issue, the mayor did show some deference to the neighbourhood groups, even in the face of pressure from the board of trade and even in the absence of concrete evidence that their property values would decrease. Might it still be possible, therefore, to enlist strong, spirited, and persistent participation from the municipal government in support of a progressive urban agenda? This brings us to the second option.

CULTIVATE AN ETHOS OF CIVIC ENGAGEMENT

As the examples in this paper have shown, organized citizen pressure can sway the municipal government even to the point of defying the prescriptions of the economists. In a city whose leaders are astute at making calculations of prospective power – and at discerning the public pulse in order to make those calculations properly – efforts to alter the public pulse may bear fruit.

As mayor of the former town of Streetsville (1970–73), McCallion espoused a comprehensive progressive agenda based on protecting the environment pro-viding more public amenities, and promoting heritage conservation, among other objectives. Streetsville (population 7,000, and centred around a historic downtown) was home to an active well-informed citizenry, an attentive press, and vibrant civic organizations (Urbaniak 2002a).

The same cannot be said of Mississauga, a fact conceded even by McCallion (interview 2003). Voter turnout in municipal elections seldom exceeds 25 per-cent. Most residents' associations are moribund, tending to arise only to protest the occasional infill development project. There is no radio station focused on Mississauga, and the local cable television station serves all of Peel and part of the County of Dufferin. The Toronto media outlets do sometimes cover Mississauga issues, but seldom in depth. Despite the rapid population growth, the local press has been in decline for the past twenty years.

Perhaps, then, concerned citizens should focus initially on long-term mo-bilization strategies and on convincing the municipal government to nurture the conditions that make constructive civic participation a natural part of liv-ing in the community. Thus far, the municipality has been reluctant to do this (Urbaniak 2005, ch. 19). Moreover, although issuing statements of encour-agement, the city has decided against contributing any funds to the nascent Mississauga Community Foundation (Prentice interview 2003), which has been having trouble getting started. In many communities, such foundations play a critical role in studying and cultivating social capital.

Urban planning and design can also be faulted for Mississauga's civic stagnation. Streetsville was a compact, mixed-land-use community where people knew their neighbours. Much of Mississauga consists of sprawling subdivisions with few incentives for pedestrian circulation. There is usually a sharp division between residential and commercial areas, making it likely that people will use an automobile even for minor errands. Some reform may be possible on this front, however. In response perhaps to growing public unease and the apparently intensifying popular concern about the local environment, McCallion has been acknowledging recently that the city could have been planned better. She has been championing many principles of "Smart Growth" (see, for example, Central Ontario Smart Growth Panel 2003).

CONCLUSION

This paper has argued that the City of Mississauga does exert influence over some federal activities, though its objectives tend to be narrowly focused and developmental rather than redistributive. The combination of Paul Peterson's "city limits" thesis and Richard Neustadt's "self-help" thesis helps explain the city's positions.

The study of federal-municipal relations reveals more about these two levels of government than many social scientists have hitherto appreciated. It also prompts us to rethink some common assumptions. Are municipalities really the government's closest to the people? Are they the most sensitive to social needs? In what circumstances does Ottawa actually listen? Would cities be more sensitive if they had the money, or would other priorities get in the way? How do strong local leaders emerge in the absence of wide-ranging formal authority? Insofar as the large cities do pursue redistributive or socially progressive objectives in their intergovernmental dealings, are they acting in a manner that is not common among municipal governments?

To answer these questions, we need to bring the budding literature down from its sweeping characterizations to develop a series of case studies and comparative research enterprises that apply rigorous analysis to these issues. Whether or not a comprehensive "new deal" emerges, the questions raised by the intensifying rhetoric about cities should be a "big deal" to Canadian researchers.

NOTES

The author gratefully acknowledges John Stewart of the *Mississauga News* for his comments on an earlier draft of this paper and the Social Sciences and Humanities Research Council of Canada for its doctoral support.

1 McCallion has been mayor of Mississauga since 1978, and she has served in one local elected office or another without interruption for the past thirty-five years. In each municipal election from 1985 on, she has polled more than 90 percent. Since 1991, she has not mounted any re-election campaign.

2 Indeed, proponents of the airport authority claimed that the new set-up would somewhat alleviate the situation whereby "local municipalities have no local control of federally managed airports." See Peel 1992, UB-1(q).

3 Ibid. At one point the Liberal minority report even states, "The Prime Minister did not shrink from letting the Clerk of the Privy Council, Mr. Shortliffe, know that he wanted his friends *'to get a piece of the action'*" (II-116; emphasis in original).

4 Valo lasted as chair until shortly after the 1996 ground lease took effect. He was then offered a job as the airport's vice-president of legal services. He therefore resigned as chair to take the new position. Within a few months he had suddenly departed, without any explanation being offered by the GTAA.

5 A request by this researcher to sit in on a board meeting was denied.

6 There are differing accounts about the federal motives for proceeding with this particular project, though the author's interviewees who have first- or second-hand familiarity with this issue have suspected local favouritism of some kind. One version of events, articulated most assertively by former councillor Harold E. Kennedy, has it that the Liberal government of Louis St-Laurent believed that it could capture the Peel riding from the Conservatives, and that such an economic development project was part of the arsenal. Others, most notably former MP Don Blenkarn (a Conservative), assert that the Conservative MP Gordon Graydon was so well regarded on both sides of the House that he was successful in obtaining the project from a Liberal government.

7 The author served on the recent Citizens' Task Force on the Future of Mississauga. This statement was made on several occasions by city manager David O'Brien in his meetings with the task force.

8 The federal portion of the funding is subject to a favourable review under the *Canadian Environmental Assessment Act*. The Credit Valley Conservation Authority will also receive funding to assist with the regeneration of Rattray Marsh Conservation Area in Mississauga. The total funding for local waterfront projects to be given to the Waterfront Regeneration Trust to disburse among its partners is $4.6 million from both the federal and the provincial governments. See "Backgrounder," www.superbuild.gov.on.ca/userfiles/HTML/nts_2_25603_1.html.

REFERENCES

Blenkarn, Don. 1987. "M.P.'s Update" *Port Credit Beacon*, spring edition

Cahill, Jack. 1980. *Hotbox: The Mississauga Miracle*. Toronto: Paperjacks

Canada. Environmental Assessment Panel Reviewing Air Transportation Proposals in the Toronto Area (EAP). 1992a. *Air Traffic Management in Southern Ontario*. Interim Report. November. Ottawa: Federal Environmental Assessment Review Office

– 1992b. *Public Hearings* (transcribed by International Reporting Inc., 1991–92). 11 and 27 January. Ottawa: Federal Environmental Assessment Review Office

– Senate. 1995a. *Report of the Special Senate Committee on the Pearson Airport Agreements*. Ottawa

– 1995b. *Proceedings of the Special Senate Committee on the Pearson Airport Agreements*. Ottawa

Caro, Robert. 1974. *The Power Broker: Robert Moses and the Fall of New York*. New York: Knopf

Central Ontario Smart Growth Panel. 2003. *Shape the Future: Final Report of the Central Ontario Smart Growth Panel*. Toronto

Credit Valley Conservation Authority (CVCA). 1983. *Interim Watershed Plan*. Vol. 8, *Mississauga Waterfront Program*. Mississauga: CVCA

Credit Valley Conservation Authority and Crysler and Lathem, Engineers and Planners. 1972. *Mississauga Waterfront: A Plan for the Development of the Mississauga Waterfront Sector of the Metro Toronto Planning Area*. Toronto: Crysler and Lathem

Crombie, David. 1992. *Regeneration: Report of the Royal Commission on the Future of the Toronto Waterfront*. Ottawa: Minister of Supply and Services

Federation of Canadian Municipalities. 2003. "FCM Big City Mayors Call for Revenue Sharing with the Federal Government." Press release, 30 May

Feldman, Elliot J., and Jerome Milch. 1983. *The Politics of Canadian Airport Development: Lessons for Federalism*. Durham, N.C.: Duke University Press

Ferenc, Leslie. 1993. "City Won't Name Staff to Residents' Airport Group." *Toronto Star*, 25 February

Francis, Diane. 2001. "Cities Fight for Fair Refugee Policy." *National Post*, 15 May

Grange, S.G.M. 1980. *Report of the Mississauga Railway Accident Inquiry*. Ottawa: Supply and Services Canada

Layton, Jack. 2000. *Homelessness: The Making and Unmaking of a Crisis*. Toronto: Penguin

McCallion, Hazel. 2003a. "Transit and Transportation." *Mississauga Board of Trade Business Bulletin*, January

– 2003b. "Needed: A New Deal." *Mississauga Board of Trade Business Bulletin*, February

Mississauga. 1978. Minutes of Mississauga City Council, 9 November. Office of the City Clerk, Mississauga City Hall

– Planning and Building Division (PBD). 1990. *Vision 2020: A Draft Plan for the Mississauga Waterfront*. Mississauga: PBD

– 2003. *2001 Census Update No. 5: Immigration, Ethnic Origin, and Visible Minorities*. Newsletter, January. Mississauga: PBD

– [n.d.] Mississauga Official Planning files. Office of Mr William Waite, Manager of Long Range Planning. Mississauga: PBD

Mississauga, with Hough Stansbury, and Woodland Ltd. 1987. *Port Credit Harbour Study and Waterfront Concept*. City of Mississauga

Mississauga News. 1993a. "Mayor McCallion Takes a Licking from Runaway Foes."
  31 March
– 1993b. "Privatization Won't Cost Mississauga a Revenue, Corbeil Vows." 19 October
– 1999. "Judge Says Peel's Nominee Should Be on GTAA Board." 1 October
Neustadt, Richard E. 1990. *Presidential Power and the Modern Presidents: The Politics of Leadership from Roosevelt to Reagan.* New York: Macmillan
Pecar, Steve. 1993. "City Cuts Deal on Runways, Opponents Say It's a Betrayal.
  Mississauga News, 15 July
Peel. 1992. "Memo re the Regional Chairmen's Task Force Establishing a Local Airport Authority." 19 November. Raffaela Baratta (past co-chair, Council of Concerned
  Residents), personal papers
– 1999. *Final Report of the Peel Regional Task Force on Homelessness.* www.region
  .peel.on.ca/housing/homeless/report/index.htm
– 2000. "Peel Wants Its Share of New Federal Homeless Program Funds." Press re-
  lease, commissioner of housing, 30 March. www.region.peel.on.ca
– 2002. "Fact Sheet" (Peel Housing Facts). www.region.peel.on.ca/housing/reports/
  fact-mar28-02
Peterson, Paul. 1981. *City Limits.* Chicago: University of Chicago Press
Port Credit Harbour. Study Advisory Committee. 1985. "Minutes," 14 June. Port Credit
  Harbour file, box 6, Harold E. Kennedy Papers, 95.0015, Region of Peel Archives
San Francisco Examiner. 1995. "S.F. Airport Director Lou Turpen Is Leaving." 29 October
Sewell, John. 1994. *Houses and Homes: Housing for Canadians.* Toronto: Lorimer
Stewart, John. 1993. "Oops – Mail Snafu Delivers Airport Deal to Expansion Foes."
  Mississauga News, 3 October
– 1994. "Board of Trade Lobbying Hard for Airport Expansion." *Mississauga News,*
  13 January
Toronto Star. 1992. "How Will Local Leaders Vote on the Accord?" 22 October
– 1995. "Prosecute Bouchard for Treason, Mayor Urges." 24 April
Urbaniak, Tom. 2002a. *Farewell, Town of Streetsville: The Year Before Amalgamation.* Belleville, Ont.: Epic Press
– 2002b. "Councillors, Residents Concerned about Canada Brick Plans." *Streetsville/
  Meadowvale Booster,* 5 March
– 2005. "Beyond Regime Theory: Mayoral Leadership, Suburban Development, and
  the Politics of Mississauga, Ontario." Ph.D. thesis, University of Western Ontario
Ward, Keith, et al. 2001. *Community Supports Plan to Address Homelessness in the
  Region of Peel: Report to Regional Council.* 1 March

INTERVIEWS

Baratta, Raffaela, past co-chair, Council of Concerned Residents (opposing airport
  expansion), 6 December 2002
Barron, Vicki, former general manager, Credit Valley Conservation Authority, 3 March
  2003

Blanchard, Duane, regional director, Small Craft Harbours, Fisheries and Oceans Canada, 27 June 2003

Blenkarn, Donald, former Member of Parliament, Mississauga South, 14 April 2003

Carr, Bruce, director, planning and administration, Community Services, City of Mississauga, 21 March 2003 (interviewed with Lorenzo Ruffini)

Corbasson, Carmen, councillor, Ward 1, City of Mississauga and Region of Peel, 21 April 2003

Gordon, David A., managing director, Mississauga Board of Trade, 6 December 2002

Horner, Dr Robert, former Member of Parliament, Mississauga West, 24 March 2003

Kennedy, Harold E., former councillor, City of Mississauga, 11 April 2003

Kolb, Emil, chair of the Region of Peel, 18 July 2003 (interviewed with Roger Maloney)

Maloney, Roger, chief administrative officer, Region of Peel, 18 July 2003 (interviewed with Emil Kolb)

McCallion, Hazel, mayor of Mississauga, 22 April 2003

Mullin, Patricia, councillor and chair of the Region of Peel Housing Committee, 7 July 2003

O'Brien, David, city manager of Mississauga, 17 February 2003

Petovello, Larry, director of economic development, City of Mississauga, 10 January 2003

Prentice, Maja, councillor, Ward 3, City of Mississauga and Region of Peel, 10 February 2003

Ruffini, Lorenzo, project manager, Mississauga waterfront, 21 March 2003 (interviewed with Bruce Carr)

Searle, Ron, former mayor of Mississauga, 7 February 2003

Shaw, Steve, vice-president, corporate affairs and communications, Greater Toronto Airports Authority, 17 March 2003

Ward, Keith, director of housing, Region of Peel, 30 June 2003

13

Urban Asymmetry and Provincial Mediation of Federal-Municipal Relations in Newfoundland and Labrador

Christopher Dunn

En général, l'asymétrie fédérale est le traitement différentiel des provinces. Ce chapitre suggère que ceci vient peut-être du fait qu'Ottawa ne traite pas tous ses partenaires de la même façon au niveau infraprovincial. Le gouvernement fédéral entretient des relations spéciales avec les plus grands centres urbains et les plus grandes agglomérations du pays, des relations basées sur ce qu'on considère être leurs besoins et leur potentiel économique. Il en résulte donc une « asymétrie urbaine » Ces relations existent avec les villes et les régions métropolitaines, ainsi qu'avec d'autres groupes locaux ou régionaux tels que les universités, les agences de développement économique communautaire et d'autres organismes à vocation particulière. S'intéressant surtout à Terre-Neuve et au Labrador, ce chapitre suggère que la manière dont le gouvernement provincial sert de médiateur dans les relations entre Ottawa et les organisations infraprovinciales est une fonction du contexte général des relations municipales-provinciales-fédérales. Au niveau fédéral, les exigences de l'agenda des connaissances et de l'innovation ont entraîné un ensemble complexe d'associations avec des partenaires nationaux et infraprovinciaux, une baisse d'intérêt envers les programmes provinciaux-fédéraux traditionnels et une tolérance envers des résultats régionaux asymétriques. Une telle province, qui joue un rôle marginal dans les structures de technologie des communications et de l'information nationale et qui possède une infrastructure municipale peu solide tout en dirigeant dans une culture d'égalité régionale, ne peut pas accueillir cette tendance avec sérénité. Le gouvernement provincial a réagi en différenciant le secteur soumis à la médiation du secteur non-soumis à la médiation en ce qui a trait à l'administration locale et au développement économique communautaire. Cette province a tendance à se soumettre à la médiation et à s'investir dans les relations intergouvernementales qui affectent l'égalité régionale. Elle n'a pas tendance à s'investir dans les secteurs où l'aspect distributif n'existe pas.

There has of late been much discussion of a "new deal for cities and communities" – a new urban agenda being developed by the federal government. Much of the discussion surmises that new federal initiatives will likely be felt in such policy areas as transportation, infrastructure, housing, and Aboriginal services. This immediately raises the question of what role the provincial governments will play or attempt to play in this possible new arrangement. In Newfoundland and Labrador the province would mediate – and by that term we simply mean involve itself as a partner in intergovernmental decision making – much as it has in the past. Provincial mediation of federal-local relations tends to take place or be attempted in areas where the regional distribution of public-sector benefits is politically important. That is the main message of this paper and it will be one reviewed in the second part of the paper. First, however, it is necessary to establish the context.

The story of federal-provincial-municipal relations in Newfoundland and Labrador cannot be considered in isolation from developments in federal theory and practice on the national scene. What has transpired nationally is complex and interesting, and forms the substance of the first part of this paper. There has been a collapse of federal-provincial trust and the growth of direct federal relations with subprovincial partners. So the term "federal-provincial-municipal relations" has to be rethought, or viewed in a larger context. Municipal partners are only one kind of subprovincial partner with which Ottawa now wishes to establish relations.

SETTING THE CONTEXT IN FEDERAL THEORY AND PRACTICE

Near the end of the twentieth century there was an epic struggle in Canada between two opposing theories of federalism, symmetrical and asymmetrical federalism. Asymmetry lost. It lost for a variety of reasons. The main arguments against it were that it permitted a checkerboard pattern of public services, that it harmed national standards in federal-provincial programs, countenanced unequal citizenship, encouraged separation, and possessed no natural limit or boundary. In fact, treating provinces alike has been the dominant federal theory of the reigning federal Liberal Party since the mid-1960s, and it has managed to inculcate the provincial equality doctrine as part of the political culture, at least in English Canada.

Some would argue that federal-provincial relations were and still are predicated on asymmetrical principles. In 1997, for example, the federal minister of finance accepted the provinces' request that they be allowed the option of applying provincial tax directly on taxable income, rather than as a percentage of the basic federal tax, in order to facilitate province-specific social and economic objectives. Also in 1997, New Brunswick, Nova Scotia, and Newfoundland signed on with the federal government to harmonize their provincial sales taxes with the goods and services tax (GST), thus creating the harmonized sales tax (HST); there are separate provincial sales taxes and GST in all other provinces, save Alberta. Moreover, equalization is by definition a program that treats all provinces differently, based on their fiscal capacity.

However, these are revenue matters, which, by their nature, tend to asymmetry. In other areas, symmetry has been the norm. Ottawa under the Liberals has resisted suggested broad constitutional reforms with asymmetrical overtones. It resisted changes in the division of powers. It has not allowed provinces the opportunity, in the Social Union Framework Agreement, to opt out of new shared-cost programs with compensation. Prime Minister Martin is reluctant to engage in non-constitutional Senate reform, a reluctance stemming from the fact that asymmetry in senatorial representation per province would continue.

It is a profound irony, then, that the Liberal government has been pursuing a kind of asymmetry in its dealings with the municipalities and subnational bodies of the country. This "urban asymmetry" has effects not unlike those of the provincial asymmetry theory, namely, that provinces are in fact treated unequally. This is the context for provincial mediation of federal-municipal relations in Newfoundland and Labrador. What the province experiences is the tail end of a number of initiatives designed for larger and more urbanized provinces, a series of disaggregated federal initiatives with few overarching themes. This province does not mediate much, nor does it particularly care to, given the realities of the new urban asymmetry.

Of course, specifying what asymmetry means has not always been one of the easier tasks for academics and other observers of intergovernmental relations. Some, such as Peter Hogg, would (in effect) see it as differences in the constitutional status of the provinces, with special provisions, special status, or larger powers for one province (or more) that are unavailable to other provinces. These constitutional differences are more fundamental than mere differences in the ways the provinces entered Confederation and also more fundamental than language or denominational education provisions that apply unevenly to some provinces but not others (Hogg 2004, 108). On the other hand, some have looser criteria. David Milne, for instance, sees significant asymmetries in "formal differences in law among units [of a federal system] either with respect to jurisdictional powers and duties, the shape of central institutions, or the application of national laws or programs" (Milne 1991, 285). Jennifer Smith prefers to concentrate on the forms of equality and therefore on the inequalities or asymmetries that may flow from deviations from these "equalities." There is jurisdictional equality (member states being equal in matters of jurisdiction); representational equality (equal state or provincial representation in national institutions); and economic equality (efficient horizontal competition, with smaller units being able to compete on an equal footing with the larger units because of the intervention of the natural monitor, the central government, which by several mechanisms – such as equalization payments – engages in province building and the enhancement of each province's ability to compete with others) (Smith 1998, 1–26).

There is much of value in all these approaches, but mine is a little different. I define asymmetry as the different treatment of provinces in terms of funds, special attention, matters appearing on the federal agenda, and comprehensive planning. In this paper I shall suggest that, increasingly, this different treatment is the after-effect of Ottawa dealing unevenly with partners at the subprovincial level. What results is "urban asymmetry," meaning that the federal government has special relationships with larger urban centres and agglomerations across the country, based on what it considers to be their needs and economic potential. The relationships are not only with cities and metropolitan areas; they are also with other regional and local actors, including universities, community economic development agencies, special-purpose bodies, industry associations, and research institutes. An important implication of the term – indeed, it is implied in the expression itself – is that the federal government does not have to treat the actors equitably. It may even choose to deal with only a handful of them in certain provinces, just for special programs – ones that are often conceptualized in terms of the knowledge-based economy. Urban asymmetry has special implications both for smaller provinces and for the municipalities of smaller provinces. The Province of Newfoundland and Labrador stands as a good example of the effects of urban asymmetry, as we shall see.

WHAT IS THE REASON TO [RE]TURN TO URBAN ASYMMETRY?

We have come to the era of urban asymmetry by a complicated chain of events related to the growing estrangement of the senior levels of government. For the federal government, the golden age of federal-provincial relations has passed and will probably not return. This is because, first, the provinces have sought to constrain the federal *marge de manoevre* at every turn by a combination of constitutional and intergovernmental mechanisms; second, Ottawa has realized the fundamental incompatibility between its economic vision and those of some provinces; third, Ottawa has interpreted the impact of globalization as requiring flexible partnerships, including those with cities; fourth, the federal spending power is increasingly being used as an economic instrument rather than a primarily social one; and, most important, for our purposes, Ottawa has found in the urban governments and other local actors willing partners that do not have the jurisdictional worries of the provinces.

The defining element of the federal golden era would have to be the use of conditional grants under the aegis of the federal spending power. From the end of the Second World War to the mid-1960s, this grant mechanism provided a way of circumventing constitutional rigidities and allowing rapid expansion of state economic and social programs. As Donald Smiley explained at the time, "with all their defects, conditional grants have brought an invaluable element of adaptability to a federal structure which has proved remarkably resistant to change through constitutional amendments or evolving patterns of judicial review" (Smiley 1963, 72). However, adaptability became a secondary consideration after the 1960s, when a combination of dwindling federal fiscal leeway and provincial opposition made conditional grants unattractive to both orders of government.

The last three decades of the twentieth century saw the provinces united in a grand effort to rein in the federal Leviathan. This was expressed first by a series of constitutional packages and then by a series of non-constitutional frameworks, most of which would, among other things, have constrained the use of the federal spending power (Dunn 2002). The Social Union Framework Agreement committed the first ministers to joint planning and collaboration, a dispute-avoidance and resolution procedure, and advance notice and a decision rule regarding the use of the spending power. Nor has the advent of a new century muted the provincial voices calling for reformed federal decision making. At their Annual Premiers' Conference in July 2003, the premiers agreed to the establishment of a Council of the Federation, with as-yet vague powers other than to provide leadership and to act as an umbrella for provincial/territorial coordinating bodies (Annual Premiers' Conference 2003). However, big things are foreseen for the body, at least from the standpoint of its main progenitors – Premier Jean Charest of Quebec and his intergovernmental affairs minister, Benoît Pelletier. "Ultimately it would be a joint decision-making body, which would oversee areas of overlapping jurisdictions such as health, education, social policy, and interprovincial trade. Mr. Pelletier said it would be funded first by the provinces, which would appoint representatives, with the federal government signing on later" (Aubry 2003).

Ottawa has also realized the fundamental incompatibility between its economic vision and those of some provinces. Its philosophy is not unlike that enunciated by the Macdonald Commission's report, which noted that regional economic development was principally the purview of provincial and local governments: "The emphasis on place prosperity is both understandable and defensible when it comes from a provincial government. It should not, however, unduly concern the federal government. Commissioners believe that community preservation, to the extent that people want it, is ultimately the responsibility of citizens and of their local and provincial governments" (Canada 1985, 219). As Donald Savoie has noted, the continuation of federal regional development programs stems not from philosophical commitment, as it once did, but as compensation for Ottawa's central-Canada-centred industrial policy (Savoie 2003).

In fact, Newfoundland has continued the emphasis on place prosperity and community preservation. One such example was the Renewal Strategy for Jobs and Growth (2001), a high-profile economic plan begun by the Tobin and Tulk governments, which was the mainstay of the government of Roger Grimes. Although the conclusions of the final report of the task force on the Renewal Strategy mention the need for choices and government not being all things to all people, the opposite impression comes through when one examines the content of the report (Newfoundland and Labrador 2001). Regions are given the impression that they will be able to share equally – or at least fairly – in the economic recovery foreseen by the Renewal Strategy. This regional equality theme was an important thread in the government's policy documents, including the Throne Speech and Budget Speech of 2003.

This theme has also been an important thread in the policy documents of Danny Williams's Conservative government. The 2004 budget allocated $1.7 million for the establishment of a Rural Secretariat, whose overriding goal is "to strengthen our rural communities and develop strong regions." In 2005, announcing government policy, the minister of innovation, trade, and rural development said that the province's Comprehensive Regional Diversification Strategy "will put all [nine] regions of the province on a path to economic prosperity," and that specially tailored "short, medium and long-term strategies will be identified for each region that will generate new industry, small business and employment opportunities" (NLIS 2005).

Stronger regional economies were not the concern of the federal government, which has a competing agenda. The predominant concern of the Liberal government has been what might be called "the innovation agenda." This agenda sees the world more in terms of clusters and less in terms of provinces. There has been a series of Liberal government policy documents, such as the *Red Book* (1993), the *Jobs and Growth Agenda: Building a More Innovative Economy* (1994), the *Innovation Strategy* (2002), and a host of throne speeches and budget addresses, all of which have advocated an innovation agenda. The Atlantic Liberal Caucus, reflecting mainstream thought in the party, has spoken of the need for "knowledge-based industrial clusters" as the wave of the future: "Development of a strong knowledge-based economy is not a function of the establishment of one or more individual firms, however independently successful. The emerging body of experience internationally is that a strong knowledge-based economy depends on the existence of a group of institutions at different levels and stages of the innovation process, who interact to feed upon and spur each others' development" (Atlantic Liberal Caucus 1999, 10). These clusters consist of manufacturers and suppliers in various industrial sectors acting in concert with educational institutions, research institutes, financing bodies, and communications and transportation systems. (Counterintuitively, the Atlantic Caucus suggests considering the whole of the Atlantic area as a cluster.)

Ottawa has interpreted the impact of innovation in the context of a globalizing economy as requiring flexible partnerships, including those with cities.

Provinces, revealingly, receive comparatively little consideration. The federal government follows the "innovation systems approach," the central elements of which are "interaction, co-evolution, value flows, institutional adaptation, knowledge creation and sharing (science, technology, and innovation), networks, partnerships, alliances and institutional learning" (de la Mothe 2003, 179). It is significant that Paul Martin places special emphasis on cities as a focus of innovation. Even before becoming prime minister, he influenced the Canadian Advanced Technology Alliance to hold a series of TechAction town meetings to encourage cities such as St John's, Halifax, Montreal, Ottawa, Toronto, Markham, Richmond Hill, Calgary, and Vancouver to visualize their innovative potential in terms of leadership, capital, infrastructure, and people (de la Mothe 2003, 174). Martin's 2004 and 2005 budgets elaborated on these themes.

One way of forging these networks, alliances, and partnerships in pursuit of knowledge and innovation is to use the spending power of Parliament. The federal spending power is now seen as primarily an economic instrument rather than a social one. It is not just about conditional and unconditional grants, it will be remembered; it is also about grants to individuals, corporations, universities, and municipalities for purposes over which Parliament may not always have direct jurisdiction.

It is true that there have been such programs before. The difference now is the rapidity of their growth, their coherence and interrelatedness, and, in the eyes of the last two prime ministers, the manifest importance of the innovation vision which unifies these programs. The 2005 budget reveals that since 1997 the federal government has provided over $9 billion to foundations such as the Canada Foundation for Innovation, the Canada Millennium Scholarship Foundation, Canada Health Infoway Inc., Genome Canada, and the Canada Foundation for Sustainable Development Technology. The combined base budgets of the three granting councils – the Canadian Institute for Health Research (CIHR), the Natural Sciences and Engineering Research Council (NSERC), and the Social Sciences and Humanities Research Council (SSHRC) – now stand at $1.5 billion, double their level in 1997–98. The government's 2005 budget committed $810 million from 2005 to 2010 on research, innovation, and enabling technologies. The goods and services tax rebate implemented in the 2004 budget, the gas tax sharing finally announced in the 2005 budget, and the continuing Green Municipal Funds program will provide Canadian communities with over $9 billion between 2005 and 2010.

Ottawa has found in the subprovincial entities willing partners that do not have the jurisdictional worries of the provinces. Urban asymmetry not only has cities and towns involved; it also involves other regional and local actors: universities, research bodies, community economic development agencies, special-purpose bodies, industry associations, and so forth. Each side sees advantages. The federal government likes urban asymmetry because it has overtones of the cooperative federalism of the 1950s and 1960s; because it can tailor its programs as a response to the size of the jurisdiction because building the knowledge economy is a new form of nation building; and because it allows the federal government to have high visibility. The politics also are important. Urban asymmetry allows the federal Liberal cabinet to court votes where there are a lot of them; to pick "winners and losers" in a seemingly technical, unobtrusive fashion; and to establish a process that involves an immense information cost for critics who want to compare on a regional or provincial basis. For their part, the subnational entities get a federal partner with deep pockets, and one that is not concerned with spreading the money around and thus diluting its efficacy.

THE CONTEXT FOR PROVINCIAL MEDIATION: INNOVATION AMONGST DEPRIVATION

The context for provincial mediation is a complicated one. The Province of Newfoundland and Labrador is underdeveloped, heavily rural, and its provincial and municipal finances (with the exception of St John's and Mount Pearl) are both in trouble. In the case of St John's, the debt service ratio is 10 percent of revenues, compared with almost 25 percent for the province. In the innovation economy the province is a player on the margins. However, government has always been seen as an equalizer and an economic actor, for better or worse. Laissez-faire government is not a current alternative.

HISTORY AND DEMOGRAPHICS

Municipal characteristics   Newfoundland and Labrador is not heavily urbanized. In 2001 *The Canadian Encyclopedia* classified only 57.7 percent of the population as urban. While the Newfoundland and Labrador Statistics Agency does not give any official urban/rural designation, the statistics agency in the Department of Finance has a definition of urban/rural that it uses for census population estimates (see table 1). Those it classifies as "urban" include the major urban centres (the census metropolitan area and the census agglomerations) and the communities with a population of 5,000 and over. The remainder are "rural." Using the statistics agency's definition, only 52.6 percent of the population of 512,930 was urban in 2001.

There are only three cities: St John's, Mount Pearl, and Corner Brook. And there is one census metropolitan area (population 172,918) surrounding St John's. The cities of St John's and the neighbouring Mount Pearl, plus the town of Paradise, were home to about 133,744 people in 2001, while Corner Brook had around 20,000 people. There are also 158 towns, 134 communities, and more than 100 local service districts, the latter two usually representing groups of communities. Town and community councils provide

Table 1: Urban/Rural Population (Newfoundland and Labrador Statistics Agency definition) Census Metropolitan Area (CMA), Census Agglomerations (CA), and Communities of 5,000 and over, Newfoundland and Labrador 2001 Census

Area	Community	Population
St John's CMA		172,918
	Conception Bay South	19,772
	Portugal Cove–St Philip's	5,866
	Pouch Cove	1,669
	Flatrock	1,138
	Torbay	5,474
	Logy Bay–Middle Cove–Outer Cove	1,872
	Bauline	364
	Paradise	9,598
	St John's	99,182
	Mount Pearl	24,964
	Petty Harbour–Maddox Cove	949
	Bay Bulls	1,014
	Witless Bay	1,056
Corner Brook CA		25,747
	Steady Brook	394
	Massey Drive	770
	Corner Brook	20,103
	Humber Arm South	1,800
	Meadows	676
	Irishtown–Summerside	1,304
	Mount Moriah	700
Gander CA		11,254
	Division No. 6, Subd. E	182
	Gander	9,651
	Appleton	576
	Glenwood	845
Grand Falls–Windsor CA		18,981
	Division No. 6, Subd. C	328
	Northern Arm	375
	Grand Falls–Windsor	13,340
	Peterview	811
	Botwood	3,221
	Badger	906
Labrador City CA		9,638
	Labrador City	7,744
	Wabush	1,894
Communities with population 5,000 and over	Bay Roberts	5,237
	Clarenville	5,104
	Happy Valley–Goose Bay	7,969
	Marystown	5,908
	Stephenville	7,109
Total urban		269,865
Total rural		243,065
Total Province		512,930

Source: Canada 2001

few local services. The provincial Department of Municipal and Provincial Affairs leverages infrastructure funding, while health, education, and policing are financed and operated by the provincial government.

Population loss   Between between 1991 and 2001, the province's population, as counted in the census, dropped by 9.8 percent, from 568,475 to 512,930. Furthermore, the province's decrease in population since 1996 was the greatest in the country; by contrast, the populations of Nova Scotia, New Brunswick, and Saskatchewan declined by only about 1 percent or less between 1996 and 2001.[1] The 2003 provincial budget estimated that the population decline had cost the province almost $900 million since 1993–94, including an estimated $140 million in 2003–4.

Rural depopulation   The Community Accounts, a provincial statistical service, noted: "The decreases in population [between 1991 and 2001] are more pronounced in rural regions. The Northeast Avalon SSP [Strategic Social Plan] region has dropped the least by less than 1% while the Eastern, Cormack-Grenfell and Central regions have dropped by approximately 15% each" (Newfoundland and Labrador [2003]).

Dispersed population   Since the population of the province is highly dispersed and is composed of only a few major urban centres, the provision of infrastructure is important. Furthermore, it is imperative to have cost-sharing arrangements that are sensitive to the limited ability of most of the 291 incorporated municipalities to pay for the needed infrastructure.

Crumbling infrastructure   One has only to travel around the countryside to realize that municipal roads and provincial highways are not in good shape. In 2002, Transportation Minister Percy Barrett estimated that Newfoundland and Labrador roads would need almost $1 billion in work over a decade (Canadian Press Newswire 2002).

Lack of a strong tradition of organized local government   Newfoundland received responsible government in 1855, but the only incorporated municipality in the province for most of the following century was St John's (1888). It was followed by Windsor in 1942 and thereafter by close to nineteen municipalities before Confederation in 1949 (Newfoundland 1974, 25). This meant that there was little of attention given to the training of councillors or preparation for infrastructure development. As well, "many communities have chosen to remain free from local taxes, building codes and other regulations and forgo the benefits of incorporation, such as road repair, garbage collection and street lighting. At present, out of over 800 communities, less than half have any form of local government" (*The Canadian Encyclopedia* 2001).

Municipal debt The province does not release consolidated information on municipal finances, but it is common knowledge that the finances of smaller rural municipalities are in desperate shape. This is due to a combination of an aging population, a historical antipathy to municipal property taxation, and skimpy financial training for municipal councillors. Some indication of the seriousness of the situation is the fact that a total of $47 million has been allocated to fifty-eight municipalities under the Municipal Debt Relief Program program since 1997–98 (NLIS 2002). In 2004–5 alone, the program allocated $9 million to twenty-five municipalities (Byrne 2004).

Provincial Finance A fourth concern is the province's finances. Many see them as unsustainable. By the time the Williams government was elected in 2003, provincial governments had run deficits – even on a cash basis – in fifty-two of the fifty-five budgets. The Williams cabinet undertook a third-party review of the province's financial situation in 2003–4. The PricewaterhouseCoopers Special Review noted that in the absence of restraint measures: (1) the average deficit (then on a newly adopted accrual basis, at $827.2 million) would exceed $1 billion annually for the next four fiscal years (2004–5 to 2007–8); and (2) the debt of the province would increase to $15.8 billion from $11.6 billion by 2007–8.

In response to this appalling financial state of affairs, various measures have been taken: nineteen departments became fourteen in February 2004, and ten departments were restructured: municipal operating grants for fourteen municipalities were reduced by $5 million over three years; fees and licences on practically every source were raised; and as many as four thousand positions in the public service have been targeted for elimination. In 2005 the situation improved somewhat as a result of enriched equalization payments, higher offshore royalties, a lower than expected deficit ($473 million), and the impending multiyear Atlantic Accord revenue enrichments of more than $2 billion. But the latter amounted only to a fraction of the close to $12 billion accumulated debt.

STATUS IN THE INNOVATION ECONOMY

In the innovation economy, the province is a marginal player. Data collected by Wade Locke and Scott Lynch reveal that in 1999 the information and communications technology (ICT) industry in Canada was concentrated mostly in four provinces, where 93 percent of all Canada's ICT firms were located. Ontario was the clear leader with 46.3 percent, followed by Quebec with 22.4 percent, British Columbia with 12.4 percent, and Alberta with 11.9 percent. Newfoundland had only a 0.63 percent share, while Atlantic Canada had 3.56 percent (Locke and Lynch 2003, 169).

Despite lagging behind other provinces in ICT industries, Newfoundland and Labrador has a relatively respectable share of federal innovation funding.

Although it has a population of 1.7 percent of the national total, it went from 1.8 percent to 3.1 percent of total federal innovation funding between 1997–98 and 2001–2 from such bodies as the Industrial Research Assistance Program (IRAP), the National Research Council (NRC), NSERC, SSHRC, CIHR, the Canadian Foundation for Innovation (CFI), the Canada Research Chairs (CRC), and the Atlantic Innovation Found (AIF), which garnered the province a total of $200 million during those five years (Locke and Lynch 2003, 193–5).

The partnerships in which federal actors engage through the CFI and AIF, for example, are mainly with subprovincial actors and not with the province itself. In the AIF, projects funded are with the Canadian Centre for Fisheries Innovation, the Centre for Cold Ocean Resources Engineering, the College of the North Atlantic, Memorial University (several projects), Consilient Technologies Corp, Instrumar Limited, Newfoundland Genomics, Inc., and Northstar Technical, Inc.

It should be emphasized that the innovation agenda in the province, such as it is, is concentrated in the St John's region. Locke and Lynch note: "In 2000, there were 383 ICT firms in Newfoundland and Labrador. The largest concentration was in the St John's region, which accounted for 67 per cent of the ICT firms in Newfoundland and Labrador. However, the City of ST. John's was the base of operations for slightly more than 50% of Newfoundland and Labrador's ICT firms" (Locke and Lynch 2003, 170).

PROVINCIAL MEDIATION AS DISTRIBUTIVE JUSTICE

Faced with rural infrastructural decline and unequal regional economic modernization, the province's reaction in both municipal and economic matters has been to adopt the stance of equalizer; that is, it serves as the arbiter of distributive justice. It has interpreted distributive justice as necessitating a rural bias in economic development, a promise that all regions will share in the post-fisheries crisis economic recovery, equal regional opportunity, and equitable distribution of infrastructure. These themes could be seen in the Liberal government's final report on the Renewal Strategy for Jobs and Growth and in various Conservative government documents.

It must be noted that this is not just a comfortable philosophical position that the government has taken; it is dictated by the raw realities of provincial politics. The political culture of the province – the result of centuries of relative hardship – is one that fosters close attention to what the other person, other town, or other region is getting. To some extent, this is a characteristic of all local politics, but the degree of localism here is arguably of a greater degree than elsewhere. It is, after all, the way the people survived – and survived for centuries – even when settlement was banned. Sean Cadigan has termed "the moral economy" the tendency of rural Newfoundlanders to resist the open-access types of resource exploitation promoted by the provincial and federal governments and to promote instead a conservationist policy – often unsuccessfully – of local community preference (Cadigan 2003, 14–42). In the fishery itself, the problem of regional conflicts gave rise to "local values" used to generate "fair" solutions to the conflicts: the principle of adjacency to the resource, the concept of historical use of the resource, and dependence on the resource (Palmer 1995, 72). Localism affects economic policy, at least in part.

Localism drives politics. The provincial legislature, the forty-eight-member House of Assembly, is dominated by forty rural representatives. In spite of the province's slight urban population advantage, the cabinet is disproportionately rural. The cabinet, with fourteen members including the premier, has only six urban members (four of them from the St John's region) if one does not count the premier – an anomaly, since although he is the quintessential "townie," he represents Humber West on the west coast of the province. The declining rural population should result in declining numbers of rural constituencies, but the last electoral boundaries commission was appointed in 1993; Premier Grimes appointed a new commission in 2003, but the Williams government ended it (Westcott 2005). The reigning Conservatives, apparently invincible after their 2003 win and the triumph of the Atlantic Accord, are increasingly vulnerable to charges by both the Liberal opposition and some of their own backbenchers about insufficient attention to rural issues.

For municipalities, the implications are important. The province sees a vital future for rural Newfoundland and Labrador, and municipalities are key actors in assuring it. Since the turn of the century, Newfoundland municipalities have been seen not only as the deliverers of the usual array of local services but as economic actors as well. The new *Municipalities Act,* which came into effect in January 2000, specifically enables municipalities to undertake community economic development. For the purpose of economic development, they may now purchase facilities or businesses, or invest in a business. However, with some exceptions, municipalities are expected to act in concert with a web of other local or regional actors, especially the regional economic development boards and the regional development associations. The regional economic development boards, as the Renewal Strategy clarifies, will continue from an economic development perspective to be the core institutional mechanism to help communities and regions help themselves.

In the context of localism and regionalism, provincial mediation follows a logical road. There is a mediated sector and a non-mediated sector in local government matters and in community economic development matters. The province tends to involve itself – or sometimes tries to mediate – in intergovernmental relations that touch on matters affecting regional equality. It tends not to get involved in areas where the distributive aspect is muted (see table 2).

Table 2: Provincially Mediated and Non-mediated Programs

Areas where the province does mediate	Areas where the province does not mediate
Infrastructure funding	The Green Municipal Funds program
Regional economic development funding and operations	Federal innovation programs
Housing agreements	Cases where the municipalities act independently as federal clients
	Federal information infrastructure initiatives

THE MEDIATED SECTOR: INFRASTRUCTURE DEVELOPMENT

The first sector in which the province mediates is infrastructure development. There are two major programs that are involved: the Infrastructure Canada Program and the Canada Strategic Infrastructure Program. We shall cover both in depth. It should be noted in passing that there is a developing interprovincial forum for infrastructure renewal matters. In July 2002 the Canadian Society for Civil Engineering, the Canadian Council of Professional Engineers, the Canadian Public Works Association, and the National Research Council joined forces to develop the Civil Infrastructure Systems Technology Road Map. The result was a report that recommended a national round table on infrastructure and a national council of ministers responsible for local government infrastructure. Negotiations are underway to give effect to the recommendations. We shall not cover these, however, because of their distance from the paper's topic.

INFRASTRUCTURE CANADA PROGRAM

Canada

Resources for municipal infrastructure development come from various own-source and provincial transfers. With some important exceptions, such as highways and harbours, federal funds have not usually been part of the resource mix. However, the federal commitment to municipal infrastructure has been growing across the country, including in Newfoundland and Labrador.

The provincial government has been a partner in the process of rebuilding the province because, of course, infrastructure is an archetypal example of an area in which considerations of municipal and regional equity abound.

Nationally, there has been a variety of halting steps by Ottawa in this area. In 2000 the federal government, through its Infrastructure Canada Program (ICP), committed $2.65 billion over six years for provincial and municipal capital expenditures. The program was twofold: $600 million went to provincial highways through the Strategic Highway Infrastructure Program, and $2.05 billion was dedicated to municipal infrastructure (water, sewer, transportation, and housing). Almost all of the ICP funding has been committed; the federal government estimates that close to three thousand projects benefited from the program. Further rounds are being contemplated.

Also introduced in 2000 were two complementary federal programs amounting to $125 million: the Green Municipal Investment Fund and the Green Municipal Enabling Fund; both were to be managed by the Federation of Canadian Municipalities. The federal budget of 10 December 2001 doubled the amount to $250 million. Budget 2005 reported that the funds had been able to leverage more than $1 billion in municipal, provincial, and private-sector funding for environmentally sustainable infrastructure. It contributed an additional $300 million in 2004–5 to the Green Municipal Funds, as they are now known (Canada, Finance Canada 2005, 186).

Another program, the Municipal Rural Infrastructure Program, which was announced in 2003 and funded to the tune of $1 billion, is designed to aid smaller-scale municipal infrastructure programs. This has no official municipal component, despite the title. Negotiations are underway with provinces and territories to establish co-management agreements.

Newfoundland and Labrador

Provincially, the province has had a longer record of transportation infrastructure transfer funding because of its special historical circumstances. Some of this funding tangentially affects municipalities. Term 31 of the Terms of Union between Canada and Newfoundland committed Canada to take over the Newfoundland Railway and have it operated by Canadian National Railways. In the late 1980s the rail service was ended, and the federal government substituted federal highway funding as replacement. The Canada–Newfoundland Transportation Initiative, commonly referred to as the Roads for Rails Agreement, saw approximately $800 million in federal funding channelled to the province. This was supplemented by another federal-provincial cost-shared agreement, the $235 million Regional Trunk Roads Agreement signed in 1991, which covered feeder roads. Both agreements ended in 2003. An average of $60 million a year was spent over the life of the Roads for Rails Agreement.

Now the province has to rely on only $11.5 million over *four* years – its share of the $600 million Strategic Highway Infrastructure Program (Canadian Press Newswire 2002). In 2002, as noted above, Transportation Minister Percy Barrett said that Newfoundland and Labrador roads will need almost $1 billion in work over a decade.

Federal expenditures transferred under the Canada–Newfoundland Infrastructure Program (CNIP), as part of the Infrastructure Canada Program, affect municipalities more directly. Under an agreement signed in 2000, CNIP is administered provincially by the Department of Municipal and Provincial Affairs and federally by the Atlantic Canada Opportunities Agency, and is cost-shared with municipalities. Expenditures under CNIP are for water and sewers, and for the Disinfection Action Program, which sees to the installation, repair, and upgrading of municipal water disinfection systems. The sharing arrangement is one-third each for the federal, provincial, and municipal governments. Under CNIP, the governments will cost-share $153.738 million in such infrastructure over five years; the federal money allocated to the province over the life of the agreement is about $51.246 million (Newfoundland and Labrador 2001–2, 10). In the first three years of implementation, as table 3 shows, $38.2, $38.6, and $22.1 million were spent on this program. In various years, CNIP accounts for between 40 and 50 percent of the infrastructure spending of the Municipal and Provincial Affairs Department. (Other provincial infrastructure programs either do not qualify for or have been excluded from federal cost-sharing.)

The intergovernmental nature of the agreement means that each level will have a role to play in the nature of the projects; but the distributional aspect means the provincial voice will have the most effect. Municipalities propose most of the CNIP projects, through the he federal and provincial governments also are allowed to nominate projects, to a maximum of 20 percent of the total value of all approved projects. A full 60 percent of the total value of all approved projects must be invested in green municipal infrastructure, and a minimum 56 percent of total approved costs for all projects in this province must be allocated to projects proposed by rural municipalities.

A federal-provincial management committee has been struck. It consists of two federal and two provincial members, the two co-chairs being the vice-president of the Atlantic Canada Opportunities Agency (ACOA), headquartered in St John's, and a senior Municipal and Provincial Affairs official. Its task is to determine which projects will get chosen. Generally speaking, much weight is placed on the list of priorities that have been set by the province. A consultative committee on infrastructure provides quarterly input from local government on the implementation of the program; however, efforts to have the local governments actually sit as members on this committee have been rebuffed. The province and Ottawa are also negotiating a Municipal Rural Infrastructure Program co-management agreement.

Table 3: Municipal Infrastructure Funding, 2001–2004

Project type		Municipal capital works program		Canada/NL infrastructure program		Multi-year capital works program		Special assistance		Inuit peoples agreement		Total	
		no.	$	no.	$	no.	$	no.	$	no.	$	no.	$
Disinfection assistance program	2003–4	10	366,906	14	880,147	–	–	–	–	–	–	24	1,247,053
	2002–3	13	407,320	49	3,867,537	–	–	51	166,403	–	–	113	4,441,260
	2001–2	14	749,677	105	8,189,764	–	–	209	448,210	–	–	328	9,387,651
Water/sewer	2003–4	87	11,289,745	78	21,268,116	–	23,882,051	99	358,926	4	2,840,000	268	59,638,838
	2002–3	73	8,487,526	123	34,809,238	–	23,882,051	74	588,609	11	1,125,738	343	51,139,270
	2001–2	44	3,706,110	105	30,024,126	18	16,369,600	283	1,039,434	–	–	450	51,139,270
Paving and/or road reconstruction	2003–4	41	6,679,420	–	–	–	7,516,016	11	88,365	–	–	52	14,283,801
	2002–3	44	8,532,272	–	–	–	7,516,016	9	84,965	–	–	97	31,165,286
	2001–2	13	4,642,927	–	–	6	1,304,183	17	150,117	–	–	36	6,097,227
Solid waste management	2003–4	5	136,156	–	–	–	34,000	1	1,000	–	–	6	171,156
	2002–3	9	1,031,862	–	–	–	34,000	3	34,200	1	27,000	14	1,195,062
	2001–2	3	269,404	–	–	–	–	–	–	–	–	3	269,404
Recreation	2003–4	27	4,705,451	–	–	–	1,407,500	4	35,800	1	330,000	32	6,478,751
	2002–3	17	5,862,353	–	–	–	1,407,500	10	112,927	2	182,500	33	10,380,280
	2001–2	14	4,357,916	–	–	–	–	–	–	–	–	14	4,357,916
Buildings/ firefighting equipment	2003–4	19	4,934,425	–	–	–	3,996,046	56	395,355	4	1,727,500	79	11,053,326
	2002–3	9	2,996,880	–	–	–	3,996,046	76	581,460	19	1,904,600	110	17,471,080
	2001–2	21	1,471,500	–	–	2	61,542	100	547,756	–	–	123	2,080,798
TOTAL	2003–4	189	28,112,103	92	22,148,263	–	36,835,613[1]	171	879,446	9	4,897,500	461	92,872,925[2]
	2002–3	165	27,318,213	172	38,676,775	–	36,835,613[1]	223	1,508,564	33	3,239,838	444	107,649,003
	2001–2	109	15,197,534	210	38,213,890	26	17,735,325	609	2,185,517	–	–	954	73,332,266

[1] Notional funding allocation based on a three-year cost-share program
[2] Figures from unaudited internal database
Source: Newfoundland and Labrador 2001–4

CANADA STRATEGIC INFRASTRUCTURE FUND

Canada

Nationally, the December 2001 federal budget included an announcement of the Canada Strategic Infrastructure Fund (CSIF), which featured an additional $2 billion (over and above the $2.05 billion committed under the Infrastructure Canada Program.) CSIF was designed to fund large-scale infrastructure projects of a scope and capacity beyond existing programs. Urban transportation projects and sewage treatment systems, for example, were (implicitly) too large to be considered under the ICP (Brittain 2002, 522–75).

Unlike existing infrastructure programs, where funding is generally on a per capita formula and costs are generally shared in a tripartite fashion, CSIF aims to recognize the unique needs and capacity of different urban areas. CSIF encourages a variety of municipal-provincial-private partnerships in areas of major national and regional significance and with significant economic growth potential. Accordingly, money has been approved for such diverse projects as the following: $435 million for improvements to the GO Transit and York Region Transit networks; $160 million to Manitoba for expansion of the Red River Floodway; money for the Kicking Horse Canyon ten-mile (Park) Bridge; Charlottetown and Summerside wastewater treatment; and highway improvement projects in Nova Scotia, New Brunswick, Quebec, and Saskatchewan. It will provide money (with Quebec and private funding) to finish Autoroute 30 and bypass the Island of Montreal; provide $350 million (matched by the Ontario government and Toronto) to renew transit services of the Toronto Transit Commission; contribute to the Trans-Canada Highway System improvements in Saskatchewan ($65 million from CSIF and $12 million from the Strategic Highway Infrastructure Program); and provide $65 million for transportation infrastructure through the Corridors for Canada project in the Northwest Territories.

In the 2003 Speech from the Throne, the Government of Canada committed itself to an additional ten-year engagement in public infrastructure. However, the Budget Speech of 2003 specified that the additional investment for this ten-year period was only $3 billion nationwide and that this was to be for both strategic and municipal infrastructure. CSIF was to be allocated two-thirds of the new money, so it was now a $4 billion program.

The Martin government was more optimistic than its predecessor, however. Budget 2005 promised that "significant funding will flow towards infrastructure projects" through the CSIF and related programs, such as the Municipal Rural Infrastructure Fund and the Border Infrastructure Fund; and that future budgets would "renew and extend" these infrastructure programs as they expired. By these measures, the government aimed to ensure that the gas tax sharing revenue program announced in the budget would provide additional revenues for municipal governments rather than displacing other funding.

Newfoundland and Labrador

Provincially, CSIF has resulted in the planned clean-up of the infamous "bubble" (as it is known to locals) in St John's Harbour. However, the story is not so much in the plans for the clean-up as in the fact that, as a distributive matter, harbour clean-up has engaged the attention of the provincial government since 1997. Parenthetically, it is also about the inordinate length of time it took for the federal government to become engaged, and the lack of pressure from the provincial government for it to do so.

Millions of litres of untreated sewage flow into St John's Harbour each day. In 1997 an environmental study noted: "Every day 120 million liters of raw sewage and storm water runoff enters the Harbour. This inflow contributes an annual loading to the Harbour of 3,700 tonnes of biochemical oxygen demand (BOD) material, 4,200 tonnes of solids and 200 tonnes of phosphorus. Harbour water is further contaminated with bacterial and pathogens, as indicated by extremely high fecal coliform bacteria counts. The sewage, mainly of domestic origin, includes waste water from industry, commercial operations, and institutions" (St John's Harbour, ACAP 1997). The study went on to list the obvious harmful health effects. Although it did not say it directly, the situation had to some extent been caused by all three levels of government in the first place.

> The present system of urban trunk and relief sewers, that mostly follow the natural gravity gradients to the Harbour, is based on design work carried out in 1974 and adopted by all three levels of government. It was never intended to have untreated effluent flowing directly into the Harbour, as is presently occurring. It was intended to divert all wastewater to the Southside of the harbour and pump it through a tunnel in the Southside Hills to Gunner's Cover, St. John's Bay. Sewage treatment was then to be added at progressive levels into the future. The plan phase was abruptly halted in the early 1980s when Federal funding was suspended. Since then the unintercepted trunk sewers remained in limbo, pouring increasing amounts of raw sewage into the Harbour as population and development increased. (Ibid.)

The Sierra Legal Defence Fund's national sewage report card in 1999 ranked St John's Harbour as the dirtiest in Canada. In 2001 Colin Nickerson of the *Boston Globe* said that it was an example of "harbor pollution on a scale unseen outside the Third World." He noted, by contrast, that "not a single city in the United States deposits untreated waste directly into urban waterways, and most American harbors are dramatically cleaner than in decades past," and he added that "government support for large municipalities in the States is a lot more than it is in Canada" (Porter 2001).

The need to clean up the harbour had been studied since the 1970s, and municipal decision makers in the St John's area had a clear idea of what had to be done to fix the problem. However, little concrete action had been forthcoming from the provincial or federal governments. The provincial government faced the problem of consistency: almost all harbour communities released raw sewage into the ocean waters surrounding them and might put demands on the province to extend a treatment policy to them. The federal government was apparently seized with the need for cleaner harbours, but it lacked a national process with which to go about the task.

Two successive federal regimes have mandated time-consuming consultative efforts, which saw over a dozen years pass with no shovel yet in the soil for a central treatment plant. The Conservatives created the Atlantic Coastal Action Program (ACAP) in 1991 to establish remedial action plans for eleven coastal areas. Federal officials made it clear that any future federal funding was contingent on prior participation in the ACAP process. Accordingly, the St John's Harbour ACAP was established in 1992 as a non-profit organization of concerned citizens and representatives of three levels of government, to be engaged in a variety of planning, education, and action activities. Their actions resulted in the Comprehensive Environmental Management Plan – a master plan for the harbour environment – and a commitment from three area municipalities to share expenses. St John's and the other two municipalities then lobbied the province, which committed finances officially in 2000 and thereby put pressure on the federal government. (The province in fact had been asking the federal government to share in the costs of a clean-up effort since 1997.) St John's also put pressure directly on the federal government, taking advantage of the close relationship which Mayor Wells had with the Paul Martin, who was then minister of finance. The federal government finally decided on the CSIF mechanism as its instrument for large-scale sewage projects such as the one in St John's.

In November 2002 the federal government announced its intention to sign a formal agreement on the harbour clean-up. All the partners were on board: the federal and provincial governments and the three municipal governments (the cities of St John's and Mount Pearl and the town of Paradise). Together, they would commit $31 million to build a centralized treatment facility on the south side of St John's Harbour, together with infrastructure for sewage collection and the disposal of treated effluent. The facility will apparently be a world-class one (Canada, Infrastructure Canada 2002). The provincial and federal governments spent over $11 million in preparatory engineering work. Initially, the federal government felt that the management committee, which manages the contribution agreement, should merely be a federal-provincial one. However, the province was amenable to St John's involvement (especially since it is paying 87 percent of the municipal share). Accordingly, the management committee is a tripartite one, with three co-chairs: federal, provincial, and StJohn's.

THE MEDIATED SECTOR: REGIONAL ECONOMIC DEVELOPMENT

Regional economic development is an important area in which the province mediates with municipalities and other actors. As actors with an explicit, legislated economic development role since 2000, municipalities have come to be seen as viable partners for senior governments. However, it is useful to make some extensive comments about the regional economic development regime of the province, because it provides the focus for many of the activities of municipalities and their senior government partners. It also puts in relief the concern of the province for regional equality and the increasing indifference of federal authorities for this concern. Both Conservative and Liberal governments have supported balanced regional development for decades, and the efforts are becoming more intense, the structures to achieve it more intricately elaborated, and the political semaphore more insistent.

REGIONAL DEVELOPMENT ASSOCIATIONS

Historically, regional development associations (RDAs) were the chosen instrument for economic development. Originally generated in the late 1960s by citizen activists in the Great Northern Peninsula, the Eastport Peninsula, and Fogo Island, they became institutionalized as provincial instruments for regional development by 1972–74 (Newfoundland and Labrador 1995). They involved a decentralized, volunteer-driven approach. For various reasons, not the least being that they were implementation mechanisms instead of planners and developers, they came to be perceived as suboptimal instruments, especially in the context of the cod moratorium of the early 1990s and its associated effects.

REGIONAL ECONOMIC DEVELOPMENT BOARDS

Regional economic development boards (the REDB mechanism) succeeded RDAs as the main development instrument in 1996. REDBs are community-based volunteer boards. They consist of representatives of municipalities, business, labour, community development groups, education and training institutions, and other interests in the zone. They have five core functions, some of which call implicitly for municipal involvement: (1) to establish strategic plans in the zones; (2) to establish a window for businesses to seek various forms of funding and administrative support from government; (3) to provide capacity-building support to agencies at the subzonal level; (4) to aid implementation of the initiatives that are undertaken by the zonal boards; and (5) finally to establish community life, community education, and community empowerment.

Their evolution began with the province's Strategic Economic Plan: Change and Challenge, which was introduced in 1992. Some of its guiding principles were instrumental in setting the direction for regional economic development policy in the province for the next decade. These guiding principles included an emphasis on strategic industries, on a private-sector-led strategy, and on industries that were innovative and technologically progressive.

One guiding principle was never enunciated clearly, but it was apparent in the institutional design suggested by the plan's designers: equal regional opportunity. The Strategic Economic Plan suggested a system of seventeen economic zones. These zones were to work in cooperation with regional government offices throughout Newfoundland and Labrador, which would see to it that the zonal plans were incorporated into the work of government departments and agencies. This was the concept introduced for public discussion in 1992. The *Change and Challenge* report caught the public's attention. The emphasis on equal regional opportunity was practically guaranteed by the rural-based nature of two of the provincial bodies that had been influential in pushing for the plan in the first place: the Newfoundland and Labrador Rural Development Council (NLRDC) and the Newfoundland and Labrador Federation of Municipalities (NLFM). They continued to push for its implementation after the report had been tabled, maintaining that they wanted a more orderly approach to regional development. Whether or not regional equality was consistent with a strategy of innovation and private-sector leadership was never explicitly explained by the report or its supporters.

The province's reaction to the favourable reception to the plan was to strike a task force on community economic development, which produced a report called *Community Matters* (Newfoundland and Labrador 1995). Its mandate was to translate the strategic plan into the equality-premised institutional framework. The result was the regional economic development boards. The next stage was to establish an organizational structure and functions for the REDBs, working on a combination of guidance from previous reports and local common sense. The aim here was to assert local ownership of the boards, to establish methods of accountability, and to put in place an orderly process of succession. For the provincial government, the political aim was both to disentangle the province from messy local economic disputes and to be seen to be treating the regions equally.

The constraints that are faced by the REDBs should be noted. The zonal board is meant to be only a policy centre. The operational side is meant to be undertaken by other agencies, such as municipal economic boards, regional development associations, and educational institutions. The provincial funding mechanism for the REDBs' memorandums of understanding, in keeping with the regional equality theme, provides for equal core funding for all zonal boards, large or small. But it provides no programming monies, only a skeletal staff and an administrative budget for each zone; the staff and board are expected to leverage money for projects from outside.

As is the case with most reforms in public or quasi-public agencies, there comes a time to revisit the original design. The *Taking Stock* report (Baird Planning Associates 2001), a reassessment of of the REDBs, was a joint effort undertaken by the major federal and provincial funding agencies (ACOA and the Department of Industry, Trade, and Rural Development (DITRD) and by the REDBs themselves. It never occurred to the writers of the report that one level of government would shut the other level out of the loop. But that is what happened with the ending of the Comprehensive Economic Development Agreement (CEDA). As will be demonstrated, ACOA now considers that its role is to interact as it wants and with whom it wishes, including municipalities, without the province as an intermediary.

FEDERAL DISENGAGEMENT FROM REGIONAL DEVELOPMENT
COST-SHARED PROGRAMS?

Various federal-provincial cost-shared mechanisms have been used over the years to fund zonal activities. They have included the Canada/Newfoundland Strategic Regional Diversification Agreement (SRDA); the Fisheries Restructuring and Adjustment Measures – Economic Development Agreement (FRAM–ED); the Canada/Newfoundland Agreement on Economic Renewal (ERA); and the Labour Market Development Agreement (LMDA).

However, the major cost-shared mechanism has recently been CEDA, a five-year cost-shared program that ended on 31 March 2003. It provided 70-30 cost sharing of core funding for the REDBs. (A qualification to this, of course, is that the federal and provincial governments also provided assistance in kind by donating the work of their field staff: DITRD's field offices and ACOA development officers in St John's and in field offices around the province.) The future of CEDA-type instruments for development was put in doubt as early as 2001 by Robert Thibeault, the new minister for ACOA. He noted during a "familiarization" tour of Atlantic Canada projects that he supported "the philosophical change at ACOA to move away from tying money to federal-provincial programs in favour of partnering on individual projects, opening the doors for partnerships with the universities or private industry" (Barron 2001). The five-year $700 million Atlantic Investment Partnership (AIP) – which belies its name by having no (mandated) provincial partners – would, he said, be the vehicle that would supersede CEDA. What was not apparent at the time was whether REDBs would still be funded under the new arrangement.

The Grimes government reacted to this uncertainty by mentioning in the 2003 Throne Speech a new model of federal-provincial cooperation: a Canada–Newfoundland and Labrador Economic Development Board. While this was being organized, the province called on Ottawa to extend CEDA by one year, through to 31 March 2004, with a $20 million allocation to be cost-shared on the traditional 70-30 basis between the two governments. The provincial budget allocated $5.5 million of the provincial share. If Ottawa did not cooperate, the province would commit the money to economic development. The Throne Speech made it clear that the government considered that external and community-based economic development organizations that had been supported under CEDA were being put in danger.

There was profound federal disinterest in the type of traditional co-management style advocated by the Grimes government. Ultimately, the federal government continued to support the zonal boards through ACOA and the AIP. The notable change is that there is no CEDA management board any more and therefore no joint federal-provincial decision making.

THE WILLIAMS GOVERNMENT'S REGIONAL DIVERSIFICATION STRATEGY

After the Williams government was elected in 2003, it concluded that regional development needed to be conceived as a set of interlinked initiatives, with no necessary dependence on federal partnership. In March 2005 it announced the Comprehensive Regional Diversification Strategy, with the familiar theme of implied regional equality – the strategy would "put all regions of the province on a path to economic prosperity" (NLIS 2005). A new regional system would be superimposed on other provincial agencies and coordinated by the Rural Secretariat, a part of the Executive Council. There would be be nine Rural Secretariat regions, each containing two or three large communities and a network of smaller communities; each region would have a regional council; each would have a representative on the provincial council of the Rural Secretariat; and each would develop its own economic development strategy. This structure has been supplemented by new programs, including a $10 million SME Revolving Fund to finance small and medium-sized businesses, a $5 million Regional/Sectorial Diversification Fund to address funding gaps of REDBs and other community-based economic organizations, and an Innovation Strategy, developed in conjunction with regional development agencies, federal and provincial agencies, and technology industries and interests. Conspicuous by its absence is any mention of a significant federal role.

We witness here an attempt at provincial mediation that became ineffectual because of the national Knowledge and Innovation Strategy. Ultimately – after leaving open the possibility of leaving the field altogether – the federal government continued to support regional economic development in the province. However, it found it unnecessary to engage in the traditional federal-provincial co-management that had marked thirty years of development activity by the RDAs and the REDB/CEDA models. Instead, Ottawa would decide matters itself, its decisions increasingly being driven by its Atlantic Innovation approach; and the province itself would assume the responsibility for place prosperity, under a province-driven regional diversification strategy.

THE MEDIATED SECTOR: FEDERAL AND PROVINCIAL HOUSING INITIATIVES

One of the areas touted as part of the new federal "urban agenda" is housing policy. Housing, of course, is another area where the distributive aspect is important. The province has involved itself here in order to influence the distribution of devolved and cost-shared federal housing programs. Strictly speaking, it may be stretching matters to call this a "local issue," since municipalities other than St John's are not involved in housing policy, but certainly coordination with local governments takes place in housing matters. There are currently certain aspects of housing policy that involve the province. One is the Canada-Newfoundland and Labrador Social Housing Agreement; another is the Provincial Home Repair Program (PHRP); a third, not yet a done deal in this province, is the Affordable Housing Agreement.

The Social Housing Agreement was signed in 1998 between the province and the federal government. Also known as the Devolution Agreement, it was part of a nationwide effort by the federal authorities to disengage from social housing. By this agreement, the provincial government took over the social housing component of the Canada Mortgage and Housing Corporation (CMHC) programs and assumed responsibility for properties that had previously been run directly by CMHC. There is to be a gradual withdrawal of financial contributions by the federal authorities over thirty years, after which time the federal contributions will stop. In the 2003–4 fiscal year, the provincial budget provided for around $93 million to be spent through the Newfoundland and Labrador Housing Corporation (NLHC) for various social housing initiatives; of this amount, the federal government is to contribute $54.8 million in block funding support (NLIS 2003). NLHC also delivers the Provincial Home Repair Program, an $11.5 million combination grant/loan program to assist about 2,000 low-income households with home repairs, mainly in rural communities. The program is cost-shared with CMHC and dictates a minimum cost sharing by the province of 25 percent; currently the province provides around 55 percent of the cost.

The province announced its intention to enter into a cost-shared Affordable Housing Agreement with the federal government through CMHC in the 2003–4 fiscal year. In the federal budget of 2002, Ottawa had announced a $680 million Affordable Housing Initiative; in the 2003 budget, it announced $320 million in additional funds, bringing the total federal expenditure to $1 billion by the end of 2007–8. The Canada-Newfoundland and Labrador Affordable Housing Agreement was signed with Newfoundland early in 2004. The province foresaw $4 million being committed in the 2003–4 fiscal year under this new program. It is 50-50 cost-shared. Newfoundland and Labrador's first affordable rental-housing development, Brookside Estates, was constructed in Stephenville in 2004–5 under the agreement. There is no management committee as there is in other programs; the program is administered by the NLHC according to the provisions of the federal-provincial agreement.

There is no municipal role in social housing, apart from that provided by the City of St John's. St. John's has several hundred units managed by its Department of Buildings and Property Management, so it is a fairly big actor in the city. The city provides some social housing and some in-fill housing (the Riverhead Project and "Jelly-Bean Row" on Forest Road), but there is no role analogous to that played by certain Ontario municipalities.

THE NON-MEDIATED SECTOR: THE FEDERAL GOVERNMENT AND THE NEWFOUNDLAND AND LABRADOR FEDERATION OF MUNICIPALITIES

The province tends not to get involved in areas where the distributive aspect is muted. A large number of federal-municipal interactions are largely unmediated by the province simply because they are small scale, have no policy implications of note, or amount to a welcome savings of provincial and municipal tax dollars. They include economic development workshops, the Green Program, cases where the municipalities are applying for grants as independent economic actors, and federal information infrastructure initiatives.

One possible exception to this pattern involves the dynamics surrounding the gas tax. The province is currently (2005) negotiating a gas tax rebate agreement with the federal government. The province is interested in this because of the distributive aspects of the rebate program. However, it has given the Newfoundland and Labrador Federation of Municipalities (NLFM) "observer status" in the decision-making process surrounding the negotiations, to make sure that all parties' concerns are dealt with. To this end, it has signed a memorandum of understanding on a "partnership climate" with the NLFM.

There are a few things to notice about the developing role of the NLFM. One is that it is becoming a means by which the federal government can have direct access to municipal officials without being mediated by the provincial government. Another is that the NLFMis becoming an active deliverer of federal services, rather than just an interest group. Another is that its meetings have come to be forums for legitimation of municipal sector/federal government partnership.

ACOA/NLFM COMMUNITY ECONOMIC DEVELOPMENT WORKSHOP INITIATIVE[2]

Traditionally, Newfoundland municipal councils had limited legislative flexibility in shaping community economic development. They had the ability to formulate land-use policy, manipulate property and business taxes, establish business improvement areas, and have a community plan – although most of the content of such plans was established by regional planners in the Department of Municipal and Provincial Affairs (Pollett 1995, 4–5).

This situation changed with the introduction of the new *Municipalities Act*, effective January 2000, which specifically enabled municipalities to undertake community economic development (CED). They may now purchase facilities or businesses, or invest in a business, for the purpose of economic development. In practical terms, this means that 291 incorporated municipalities and a multiplicity of municipal councillors had to be brought up to speed on their new responsibilities. They had to be able to identify what economic tools they had at their disposal, how to go about investing in a local business, and what best practices were available for consideration.

Into the breach to strengthen municipal capacities came not the province, but the federal authorities. ACOA, created in 1987, was especially interested in establishing close relations with local actors. One of its identified strategic priorities was in fact community economic development: to help communities take responsibility for their own future. ACOA therefore reacted favourably when the NLFM approached it with a proposal to prepare municipalities to undertake CED and to use the existing REDB mechanism to fulfill their responsibilities. The possibility of establishing close relationships not only with the NLFM but with hundreds of municipal councils, with provincial knowledge but without the need for provincial approval, proved to be an inviting one. Thus was born the ACOA-NLFM Community Economic Development Workshop Initiative. The partners designed it originally as a multi-year, three-phased approach: first, an introduction to CED and to the REDBs and their strategic economic plans; second, the development of practical skills; and third, learning from relevant international "best practices." Each phase featured workshops designed and delivered by the executive of the NLFM and other municipal councillors, with the involvement of invited ACOA representatives. A fourth phase, with the intent of extending the municipal role in regional development, will complete the initiative. Two-thirds of the incorporated municipalities in Newfoundland and Labrador have taken part in the workshops.

THE NON-MEDIATED SECTOR: THE GREEN PROGRAM

Another partnership between the federal government and the NLFM involves the Green Program. As was noted earlier, the Federation of Canadian Municipalities (FCM) manages the Green Municipal Funds, a municipal infrastructure program for the federal authorities amounting to a quarter of a million dollars (previously called the Green Municipal Investment Fund and the Green Municipal Enabling Fund). The fund provides money for R&D and various pilot projects that show how to develop municipal services in environmentally friendly ways, and it also performs a lending function, lending at rates below the Bank of Canada lending rate. These are programs that are free of provincial involvement; there is no provincial role in committees that decide on priority spending in the Green Municipal Funds, and there is no structural link to existing federal-provincial funding.

In Newfoundland, this pattern also pertains, and there has been tentative use of the program, mostly at the behest of the FCM. The FCM had noticed that the province's municipalities had not used the program, and it approached the NLFM to discover why. The answer was simple: the program had been overwhelmingly urban – oriented towards larger municipalities – and the application process was too complicated and time-consuming for towns with just one clerk running things. The NLFM stepped in as an intermediary, and it now helps municipalities expedite the process. There have been applications from St John's and Gander for retro-fits of some of their municipal buildings. This arrangement is proceeding over and above the normal decision making on infrastructure programs. In mid-2005, St John's completed negotiations to borrow $20 million from the Green Funds as part of its borrowing requirements for the harbour clean-up. The difference between the funds' interest rates and commercial rates will have to be reinvested in water conservation projects.

One has only to read the minutes of the annual autumn convention and trade show of the NLFM to realize that some interesting dynamics are taking place. One is that the annual meetings of the NLFM serve as a forum for the legitimization of the federal role in municipal affairs in the province. Increasingly, the federal government is praised for its various efforts. This is now the case with ACOA. Its community education effort has paid handsome dividends in goodwill.

Another interesting development is that over the years there has been a subtle change in the image of municipal councils and councillors. No longer are they just the deliverers of services; they are *bona fide* democratic representatives. Resolutions of the annual meeting are taken seriously. Provincial and, increasingly, federal politicians are taken to task for their policies and feel compelled to respond to the NLFM for actions they are taking or are contemplating. To some extent, this role has devolved to them by default.

There are few upper-level representatives. There are only seven MPs. The provincial house was downsized under Clyde Wells, and there are fears that future reforms could result in an even smaller House of Assembly. It is a sign of the increasing legitimacy of local government that any minister, federal or provincial, who is identified as a target in an NLFM resolution usually responds, and in detail.

THE NON-MEDIATED SECTOR: MUNICIPALITIES AS FEDERAL CLIENTS

As previously noted, there are numerous federal-municipal interactions that go largely unmediated by the province simply because they are small scale, have no policy implications of note, or amount to savings of provincial and municipal tax dollars. Municipalities in this context are just one of a number of clients for federal programs. Other clients could include REDBs, Memorial University, private-sector businesses, and non-profit organizations.

Activities undertaken by the City of St John's reflect the variety of federal services that municipalities can access. The city is an avid applicant to ACOA. The new St John's Civic Centre received a $4 million contribution from ACOA. It received another contribution to help pay for an overpass to connect Mile One Stadium and the Delta Hotel; the $800,000 cost was half paid by ACOA. The city partners with the St John's Board of Trade for economic development materials, and it regularly applies to ACOA for funding to offset their cost. An extensive scenic walkway and beautification system organized by a body called the Grand Concourse Authority was begun by the Johnson Family Foundation, but the bulk of its funding involves a partnership that includes ACOA, Human Resources Development Canada (now Human Resources and Skills Development), and the city. ACOA now has an "urban file," a result of the profile given to urban issues in the 2003–5 federal Throne Speeches. Other federal departments and programs are also used by municipalities. The St John's Economic Development Department has a Canada Business Service Centre funded by Industry Canada situated in its satellite office in the downtown area.

St John's and other communities also make frequent use of the Community Investment Support Program (CISP) in International Trade Canada. CISP is the federal government's instrument to help Canadian communities attract, retain, and expand foreign direct investment. Partnership with local private-sector actors is encouraged. The program is cost-shared, with successful applicants eligible for federal support of up to 50 percent of the cost of suitable activities in two categories: for community training and for FDI targeting. The provincial government can be brought in as one of the cost-sharing partners, but this is not necessary. The program's great advantage is that its criteria are clear and the turnaround time on decisions is short (six to eight weeks, compared with an average of four to six mnths with ACOA). In the past, St John's has used such funding to develop an investment database for international site selection conferences. It has not availed itself of the 2005–6 program. However, others have, in the advanced category – for example, the towns of Wabush and Labrador City, and the Irish Loop Development Board.

Another department, Human Resources Development Canada (HRDC), was used for employment subsidies. HRDC was especially relevant for low-employment areas and municipalities that are not unionized. While St John's does not fit this profile, HRDC funding has been an integral and valued aspect of rural municipalities and REDBs.

In 2003 the Martin government split the controversy-prone HRDC into two departments: a new Human Resources and Skills Development HR&SD) for the labour market side, and a new Department of Social Development (DSD) for income security issues and programs. One of the HR&SD programs, the Labour Market Partnerships, encourages communities to create local employment and can, in theory, involve employers, employees or their associations, provincial, territorial, and municipal governments, non-governmental organizations, health and educational institutions, band and tribal councils, and individuals and groups; but in Newfoundland and Labrador the only body it has involved has been a provincial department, Human Resources, Labour, and Employment (NLIS 2004).

Occasionally, cities receive emergency funding. Relatively recent cases include the famous 9/11 plane landings in Newfoundland and the damage wrought in the fall of 2001 by tropical storm Gabrielle. In such cases the province does mediate and administrate, because federal legislation provides for it. In both of the above cases, the province paid St John's first and then recovered the costs from the federal program.

THE NON-MEDIATED SECTOR: FEDERAL INFORMATION INFRASTRUCTURE INITIATIVES

Another form of federal-municipal interaction occurs between Industry Canada and selected municipalities in an initiative known as the Smart Communities Program. Industry Canada, one of the federal "superministries" created in the early 1990s, launched the Smart Communities Program in 1999 as a three-year program to make Canada a world leader in the use of information and communication technologies. The Smart Communities Program is part of the Government of Canada's "Connecting Canadians" initiative, which aims to make Canada the most connected nation in the world.

The fashion in which the program was administered by Industry Canada demonstrates a federal intent to influence the information infrastructure policies at the municipal level of government. There was a national competition which ultimately selected a dozen world-class "smart communities" – one per province, one northern, and one Aboriginal. Five million dollars in program funding was awarded over three years to support each smart community. The chosen communities were designated "demonstration projects" because they were intended to share the lessons they learned with other communities.

The services provided by SmartLabrador, the project that won in Newfoundland and Labrador, were ambitious. They included telemedicine for all Labrador nursing stations and health centres, enhanced distance education, an online Labrador regional news network, government services online, a virtual museum, the Heritage Mall e-commerce project, and computer training to improve citizen access to information technologies. Twenty-two communities were involved and $12 million in leveraged services. The project partners included REDBs, municipalities, educational institutions, departments, and private-sector businesses. SmartLabrador was a joint project of the five REDBs, and the management team was made up of zone representatives and the other partners.

The competition was intense. In Newfoundland alone, half a dozen communities were involved. The experience was a mixed one for the participants. Labradorians were overjoyed, of course. However, the unsuccessful candidates were disconcerted by the amount of work that the whole application process had involved, and many felt that the money involved could have been spread around to more districts. In one notable case, participants in the Clarenville area's Discovery Project decided to proceed as if they *had* won and expended their smart services.

CONCLUSION

This paper has suggested that the mechanics of provincial mediation must be considered within the general context of federal-provincial-municipal relations. Federally, the imperatives of the knowledge and innovation agenda have resulted in a complicated set of partnerships with national and subprovincial partners, a declining concern for traditional federal-provincial programs, and a tolerance for asymmetrical regional outcomes. A province such as this one – a minor actor in the national ICT structure, possessing a threadbare municipal infrastructure and operating in a culture of regional equality – cannot greet this with equanimity.

We have established that there is a mediated sector and a non-mediated sector in local government matters and in community economic development matters. The province tends to mediate or involve itself (or sometimes tries to mediate) in intergovernmental relations that touch on matters affecting regional equality. These involve such concerns as infrastructure funding, regional economic development funding, and housing agreements. The province tends not to get involved in areas where the distributive aspect is muted – for example, in the Green Municipal Funds, in programs where municipalities act as federal clients, and in federal information infrastructure initiatives.

In some cases, the province is being edged out of federal-local relations. We saw that the provincial attempt at mediation in regional development became ineffectual because the national Knowledge and Innovation Strategy obviated the need for traditional federal-provincial co-management. Ottawa would decide matters itself, in the context of the Atlantic Innovation approach, and the province itself would assume the responsibility for place prosperity under a province-driven regional diversification strategy. In many cases, the province does not even get to the mediation stage. Federal green funds to bring municipalities on board for the Kyoto Protocol and federal programs to expand local readiness for foreign direct investment and internet connectivity did not have enough financial import or political salience to warrant provincial interest.

For the foreseeable future, the province will have to contend with the fact that Ottawa tends to see problems and policy in a broader economic perspective, especially that of cluster development. Ottawa wants to throw off what it sees as the shackles of decades of programs that concentrated on place prosperity and get on with the job of national prosperity. What is province such as Newfoundland and Labrador, which is concerned with place prosperity, to do?

One thing will be to avoid the advice of Jack Mintz, who sees problems that involve a federal role in municipal areas of responsibility, to be taxation without representation. He prefers clear jurisdictional lines and expanded municipal taxation power. "Municipal fiscal issues are a provincial, not federal, responsibility," he says. "Federal intrusion in municipal affairs only worsens political accountability by undermining provincial authority. Moreover, the provinces are in the better position to deal with municipal problems, since the federal government is unable to balance political interests when thousands of municipalities are involved" (Mintz 2002, 17). But this will not work in Newfoundland and Labrador in the foreseeable future. The province is too dependent on federal transfers, and the municipalities are too debt-ridden to insist on such constitutional and economic purity. As well, the Newfoundland public sees the problem as being too few federal dollars rather than too many.

However, this province, like others, is likely to react to perceived threats to its authority and to the balancing of municipal and regional interests. Ultimately, one can see some new protocols being drawn up through provincial intergovernmentalism, perhaps by the Council of the Federation. These would specify new measures for accountability, for fair shares, and for performance measurement in this new era of urban asymmetry. Failing that, ironically the most logical approach for the province would be to adopt an asymmetrical approach of its own. Newfoundland tends to benefit when the asymmetrical or co-management style of arrangement is followed. One can think of satisfactory past arrangements, such as the Canada-Newfoundland Offshore Petroleum Board and the Atlantic Accord. Future ventures might feature fisheries, regional economic development, culture – and, last but not least, municipal affairs.

NOTES

1 For statistical information, see Newfoundland and Labrador Community Accounts, a provincial statistical service, at www.communityaccounts.ca/SALandscape/section6.asp?section=f1#f1.
2 Much of the following depends on material gracefully supplied by Shirley Dawe of ACOA's St John's office, and Craig Pollett, executive director of the Newfoundland and Labrador Federation of Municipalities.

REFERENCES

Annual Premiers' Conference. 2003. "Premiers Announce Plan to Build a New Era of Contructive and Cooperative Federalism." Communiqué 850-092/006 of the 44th Annual Premiers' Conference, Charlottetown, PEI, 9–11 July. www.scics.gc.ca/cinfo03/850092006_e.html

Atlantic Liberal Caucus. 1999. *Atlantic Canada: Catching Tomorrow's Wave*, 30 September

Aubry, Jack. 2003. "Quebec Sends Unity Envoy." *National Post*, 28 April

Baird Planning Associates. 2001. *Taking Stock of the Regional Economic Development Process: Background and Overview, Recommendations and Action Plans*. St John's: BPA

Barron, Tracy. 2001. "Grander Schemes Ahead: New Federal Minister Says Current Loan Program Too Limiting." *Telegram* (St John's), 27 July

Brittain, Len S. 2002. "Financing Capital Expenditures." *Canadian Tax Journal* 50 (2): 552–75

Byrne, Jack. 2004. Testimony of Minister of Municipal and Provincial Affairs to the Social Services Committee of the Newfoundland and Labrador House of Assembly, 19 May

Cadigan, Sean. 2003. "The Moral Economy of Retrenchment and Regeneration in the History of Rural Newfoundland." In *Retrenchment and Regeneration in Rural Newfoundland*, ed. Reginald Byron. Toronto: University of Toronto Press

Canada. 1985. Royal Commission on the Economic Union and Development Prospects for Canada. *Report*. Vol. 3. Ottawa: Minister of Supply and Services

– 2001. *2001 Census*. Ottawa: Statistics Canada

– Finance Canada. 2005. *Budget 2005*. Ottawa: Department of Finance

– Infrastructure Canada. 2002. "Prime Minister Chrétien Confirms a $31-million Contribution to Clean Up St. John's Harbour." Press release, 4 November

The Canadian Encyclopedia. 2001. Toronto: McClelland & Stewart

Canadian Press Newswire. 2002. "Nfld. and Labrador Roads Need Over $1 billion – Transport Minister," 19 March

de la Mothe, John. 2003. "Ottawa's Imaginary Innovation Strategy: Progress or Drift?" In *How Ottawa Spends, 2003–2004: Regime Change and Policy Shift*, ed. G. Bruce Doern. Don Mills: Oxford University Press

Dunn, Christopher. 2002. "The Federal Spending Power." In *The Handbook of Canadian Public Administration*, ed. Dunn. Toronto: Oxford University Press

Hogg, Peter W. *2004 Constitutional Law of Canada*. Student edition. Toronto: Thomson Carswell

Locke, Wade, and Scott Lynch. 2003. *What Does Newfoundland and Labrador Need to Know about the Knowledge-Based Economy to Strengthen Its Place in Canada?* A research and analysis paper prepared for the Royal Commission on Renewing and Strengthening Our Place in Canada. St John's: The Commission.

Milne, David. 1991. "Equality or Asymmetry: Why Choose?" In *Options for a New Canada*, ed. Ronald M. Watts and Douglas M. Brown. Toronto: University of Toronto Press

Newfoundland. 1974. Royal Commission on Municipal Government in Newfoundland and Labrador. *Report*. St John's: The Commission

Newfoundland and Labrador. 1995. *Community Matters: The New Regional Economic Development*. Report of the Task Force on Community Economic Development in Newfoundland and Labrador. St John's: The Task Force

– 2001. *Securing Our Future Together: The Renewal Strategy for Jobs and Growth*. Final Report, March. St John's: Government of Newfoundland and Labrador

– [2003]. *From the Ground Up: Benchmarking the Vision and Values of Our Strategic Social Plan*. Phase 2 of the Social Audit. St John's: Government of Newfoundland and Labrador

– Department of Municipal and Provincial Affairs. 2001–2. *Annual Report, 2001–2*. Available at www.gov.nl.ca/mpa. See also the federal ICP site, "Partners: Canada–Newfoundland and Labrador Infrastructure Program," www.infrastructure.gc.ca/icp/partners/nf_ip_e.shtml

– 2002–4. *Annual Reports*. www.gov.nl.ca/mpa

– Newfoundland and Labrador Information Service (NLIS). 2002. "Minister Announces Continued Support for Debt Relief Program." Press release, 21 March

– 2003. "Investment in Social Housing Continues." Press release, 27 March

– 2004. "Government of Canada and Government of Newfoundland and Labrador Fund Employment Projects in St. John's." Press release, 3 September

– 2005. "Government Announces Regional Diversification Strategy." Press release, 18 March

Newfoundland and Labrador Progressive Conservative Party. 2003. "Shelley Says Ottawa Ignoring Newfoundland and Labrador's Crumbling Infrastructure." Press release, 27 February

Mintz, Jack. 2002. "Welcome to the Tea Party." *Canadian Business* 75 (7): 17

Palmer, Craig T. 1995. "The Troubled Fishery." In *Living on the Edge: The Great Northern Peninsula of Newfoundland*, ed. Lawrence T. Felt and Peter R. Sinclair. Social and Economic Papers no. 21. St John's: Institute of Social and Economic Research

Pollett, Craig. 1995. *A Role for Municipalities in Regional Economic Development in Newfoundland and Labrador*. Halifax: Master of Resource Economics thesis, Dalhousie University

Porter, Stephanie. 2001. "*Boston Globe* Runs Front-Page Article on 'Fount of Filth.'" *Express* (St John's), 4–10 July

St John's Harbour. Atlantic Coastal Action Program (ACAP) 1997. *Comprehensive Environmental Management Plan*. St John's: ACAP

Savoie, Donald. 2003. *Reviewing Canada's Regional Development Efforts*. Research and analysis paper commissioned by the Newfoundland and Labrador Royal Commission on Renewing and Strengthening Our Place in Canada. St John's: The Commission

Seidle, F. Leslie. 2002. *The Federal Role in Canadian Cities: Overview of Issues and Proposed Actions*. Discussion Paper F27. Family Network, Canadian Policy Research Networks

Smiley, Donald V. 1963. *Conditional Grants and Canadian Federalism*. Toronto: Canadian Tax Foundation

Smith, Jennifer. 1998. *The Meaning of Provincial Equality in Canadian Federalism*. Working Paper 1. Kingston: Institute of Intergovernmental Relations, Queen's University

Westcott, Craig. 2005. "Losing Their Vote." *Express* (St John's), 18–24 May

14

Federal-Municipal-Provincial Relations in Saskatchewan: Provincial Roles, Approaches, and Mechanisms

Joseph Garcea and Ken Pontikes

Ce chapitre fournit un cadre d'analyse pour étudier le rôle de médiation des gouvernements provinciaux dans le contexte de la gouvernance à niveaux multiples et analyse ensuite la médiation effectuée par le gouvernement de la Saskatchewan au cours des dernières années. Ce chapitre examine la nature et les facteurs déterminants des rôles joués par le gouvernement de la Saskatchewan en ce qui concerne la gestion des relations provinciales-municipales-fédérale, ainsi que les approches et les mécanismes utilisés dans chacun de ces rôles. Le gouvernement provincial joue cinq grands rôles différents : la surveillance, la défense des intérêts, la médiation, la réglementation et le partenariat. Il a tendance à utiliser principalement des approches discrètes, informelles, non intrusives, réactives et bilatérales lors de l'accomplissement de ses rôles. Le gouvernement provincial a également tendance à utiliser des mécanismes intergouvernementaux et des mécanismes intra-gouvernementaux dans la gestion des relations provinciales-municipales-fédérale. Finalement, les décisions prises concernant ces rôles et ces mécanismes ont été influencées par ses politiques, ses intérêts politiques et financiers, ses ressources politiques et financières et par la mesure dans laquelle il a adhéré à la doctrine de la « nouvelle gestion publique ». De plus amples recherches devront toutefois être effectuées sur la gouvernance à niveaux multiples et sur la formulation des politiques.

INTRODUCTION

The Canadian federal system produces many interesting and important intergovernmental relations among the various orders of government. Such relations have varying degrees of effect not only on the nature and scope of public policy but ultimately for the operation and unity of the political system. The literature on Canadian federalism devotes extensive systematic analysis to most, though by no means all, facets of intergovernmental relations. One facet, which to date has not received extensive and systematic analysis, is federal-municipal-provincial relations. This is particularly true of the roles performed by provincial governments in managing these relations and the approaches and organizational mechanisms they use in doing so. Until recently, attention devoted to federal-municipal-provincial relations in both the federalism literature and the local governance literature focused primarily on three general topics: (1) constitutional and jurisdictional issues related to municipal governance (L'Heureux 1986, 179–214; Kitchen and McMillan 1986, 215–62); (2) federal interest and involvement in municipal infrastructure and in economic and social development programs and projects through the use of either its constitutional powers or, more commonly, its power of the purse; and (3) the vigilance with which various provincial governments have guarded against federal involvement in these programs and projects (Graham, Philips, and Maslove 1998, 171–202; Tindal and Tindal 2000, 207–54). However, relatively little attention was devoted to the provincial role in managing federal-municipal-provincial relations and to the approaches and mechanisms used for that purpose (see, for example, Andrew, Graham, and Philips 2002; Seidle 2002; Hulchanski 2002). This is now changing. Major research projects, have been launched, such as the one (funded by the Social Sciences and Humanities Research Council) that focuses on multilevel governance both in Canada and elsewhere. The analysis of "marble cake federalism" and "multilevel governance" is now very much in vogue both in Canada and in other federations (White 2002; Mejer 2000).

The central objective of this chapter is to provide an overview of the nature and determinants of the roles that the Saskatchewan government has performed in managing federal-municipal-provincial relations and the approaches and mechanisms it has used in doing so. It is important to note that this is a general and largely descriptive overview of these roles, approaches, and mechanisms rather than a detailed analysis or evaluation of them. As noted in the concluding section of this paper, a detailed analysis or evaluation should be part of the future research agenda which we hope will be stimulated by the conceptual and empirical components of this paper.

This chapter consists of six major sections. The first provides an overview of a selected set of significant programs and projects that involve federal-municipal-provincial relations. The next three sections provide a conceptualization and an overview of the roles performed by the Saskatchewan government in managing federal-municipal-provincial relations and the approaches and mechanisms it uses in performing these roles. The fifth section gives an overview of the factors that shape the provincial government's decisions regarding these roles, approaches, and mechanisms. The sixth and concluding section provides a summary of the major findings and offers some suggestions for further research.

THE FOCUS OF FEDERAL-MUNICIPAL-PROVINCIAL RELATIONS

In Saskatchewan as in other provinces, federal-municipal-provincial relations are focused on a plethora of policies, programs, and projects. The appendix, "Federal-Municipal-Provincial Collaboration in Saskatchewan: A Sample of Notable Programs and Projects in 2003," provides an overview of several types of programs and projects in the municipal sector that have been the focus of federal-municipal-provincial relations in Saskatchewan in recent years. More specifically, it provides a description of the following: the nature of such programs and projects; which order of government took a lead role in initiating, developing, and implementing them; which order of government contributed to funding them; which order of government was primarily responsible for implementing them; and which provincial department performed a lead role in dealing with them.

From the information contained in the appendix, it is possible to make seven general observations regarding the nature of these programs and projects and the roles and responsibilities of the various orders of government. First, the programs and projects are undertaken in a wide range of policy sectors. This includes minority language, community planning, airports, facilities for movie production, infrastructure, agriculture, university research facilities, culture, heritage, disaster assistance, housing, regional intersectoral planning, environment, emergency preparedness, construction codes, northern development, rural roads for grain transportation, policing, inner-city neighbourhood planning and development, forestry, summer student employment, urban development, and Aboriginal heritage.

Looking at these through a jurisdictional lens, it is apparent that they impinge on areas of federal and provincial jurisdiction as well as being in areas of shared jurisdiction. Moreover, the various programs and projects tend to have what might be termed "plurijurisdictional" characteristics which render them difficult to place in one particular jurisdictional category. Despite their plurijurisdictional nature, it is noteworthy that jurisdictional disputes do not loom large in relation to any of them in Saskatchewan. Invariably they are initiated and implemented on a cordial partnership basis with the consent and support of the various orders of government. The reason for this is that Saskatchewan is one of those provinces which – unlike Quebec, for example – is not excessively jealous of its jurisdictional authority either as a matter of principle or as a matter of strategic positioning in federal-provincial negotiations. Often its financial needs do not afford it the luxury of being excessively jealous of its jurisdictional authority. In this respect, Saskatchewan has much in common with Manitoba and the Atlantic provinces, which find themselves in a comparable political and economic situation within the Canadian federation.

The Saskatchewan government's willingness to see the federal government become actively involved in programs and projects, not only in the municipal sector but also in other policy sectors, is evident in the principle of "constructive entanglement" among various orders of government, which was articulated by the former premier of Saskatchewan, Roy Romanow, during the negotiations surrounding the Social Union Framework Agreement (Marchildon 1999, 80). Saskatchewan premiers have rarely opposed this principle in a concerted manner. Traditionally, their preference has been to engage, rather than exclude, the federal government in programs and projects, especially where federal dollars have been either promised or anticipated. The federal-provincial negotiations on the Social Union Framework Agreement, in which Saskatchewan's premier performed a leadership role in mediating a consensus among nine provinces and the federal government, is a case in point (Marchildon and Cotter 2001).

Second, the vast majority of these programs and projects were initiated and developed by the federal government; only a few were initiated and developed by the provincial and municipal governments. The federal government has been proactive in initiating and developing programs and projects within the scope of the municipal sector that it deems to be of national importance. A notable example is the Green Municipal Funds program, designed to support the federal government's climate change initiative and the Kyoto commitment. The federal government's tendency to be proactive in such initiatives has been influenced by a desire to work in partnership with the municipal and provincial governments to advance both its own political and policy goals and to some extent also the policy goals of the provincial and municipal governments. The federal government's political goals include enhancing its legitimacy as an order of government and advancing the partisan political and electoral interests of its party.

Third, the roles performed by the federal, provincial, and municipal governments in the initiation, formulation, and implementation of programs and projects are not necessarily consistent with federal and provincial responsibilities under the constitution. For example, constitutionally, the development and enforcement of the construction codes are clearly the responsibility of provincial and municipal governments. Nevertheless, since 1937 the federal government has initiated and maintained a process of coordinating a national system of building fire, safety, and plumbing codes. This is a case where, at least to date, the provincial and municipal governments have found it prudent and advantageous from a programmatic, financial, and political standpoint to let the federal government assume a lead role and responsibility. Whether they will continue to feel this way in the future is open to question. The reason for this is that the provinces retain the right to adjust national codes to respond to local needs or interests, and at times they have done so. Still, the shared goal is to keep the variations to a minimum in the interest of national consistency. In contemplating any changes from the status quo, the various orders of government should be cognizant that construction and architectural firms prefer to deal with one set of codes. Moreover, the research and administrative costs for establishing codes is considerably less if the work is coordinated by one order of government.

Fourth, most of the programs and projects are jointly funded by the federal, provincial, and municipal governments and in some cases also by other governmental or non-governmental entities. However, in many instances, if not most, the federal government assumes either all or at least the largest portion of the financial responsibility. Indeed, there is only one initiative among those identified in the appendix that does not entail a substantial federal financial contribution – namely, funding for the operation of regional intersectoral committees. Although these committees include representation from the federal government, they are funded entirely by the provincial government through its interdepartmental Human Services Integration Forum.

Federal funding for various programs and projects is generally provided for specific periods of time. Moreover, there is a preference for project-based funding, particularly in view of the extensive use of Western Economic Diversification as the funding source. The mandate of this agency focuses on project-based funding for a limited time frame which may or may not be renewable, rather than on ongoing long-term funding. The other prevalent mode of federal funding is a program-based rather than a project-based arrangement. But even this tends to be provided for relatively short and fixed periods (for example, ten-year funding for infrastructure funding, three-year funding for a homelessness initiative, six-year funding for the Green Municipal Funds, and five-year funding for the Prairie Grain Roads Program). On more open-ended programs, the federal government usually retains some flexibility to control its spending commitment – for example, adjusting funding availability under the Joint Emergency Preparedness Program or unilaterally deciding on eligibility criteria under the Disaster Financial Assistance Arrangements. The federal government has also tried to retain some flexibility in the nature and scope of involvement in the management of various programs or projects. For example, it was initially an important partner in the creation of the Wanuskewin Heritage Park in Saskatoon, which focuses on First Nations peoples, and accepted a position on the park's board of directors that was guaranteed by the related provincial legislation. While the federal government has continued to support specific projects at the park, such as providing funding for infrastructure improvements, for many years now it has not responded to requests to name someone to sit on the board as its representative. Such a decision may be based on a belief that appointing representatives to such boards is not always advantageous. Although doing so allows the government to influence management decisions, it also leaves it open to criticism and to political or legal liabilities resulting from any management decisions that are made.

Fifth, the federal government has been very actively involved not only in the initiation, formulation, and prioritization of programs and projects, but also in the adjudication of proposals submitted pursuant to such programs and projects. This involvement is based on its desire to exert some oversight and control in order to ensure that its policy goals and political interests are advanced. Here, too, the federal government faces a dilemma in that although this involvement gives it greater control, it also leaves it open to some political and legal liabilities.

Sixth, in the recent past the federal government has not been very involved in either the implementation or the evaluation of specific programs and projects; both have been the responsibility of the provincial and municipal governments, as well as other local governmental and non-governmental entities. This is for practical and philosophical reasons. The major practical consideration is the reality that the federal government does not have the requisite administrative infrastructure at the local level to become actively involved in the implementation, evaluation, and termination of specific initiatives. The major philosophical consideration is that the federal government has been influenced by the new public management notion that governments should "steer and not row." Although it has wanted to ensure that it is involved in "steering programs" and projects at the initiation and formulation stages, it has wanted to limit its involvement in "rowing" at the implementation, evaluation, and termination stages. In the case of evaluation, what we have been witnessing in recent years is an attempt by the federal government to institutionalize program and project evaluation systems as part of a strategic effort to increase the level of accountability and responsibility. By limiting its involvement in the implementation and evaluation of programs and projects, the federal government is able to shelter itself somewhat from any criticisms and political and legal liabilities that emerge.

The provincial government has been influenced by similar practical and philosophical considerations regarding the nature and scope of its involvement in various programs and projects. In recent years, it has been looking at municipalities and various other local governmental and non-governmental agencies to implement and evaluate programs and projects. It justifies this approach on the grounds that it enhances its degree of flexibility and sensitivity in meeting local conditions, needs, and preferences.

Seventh, provincial involvement in these programs and projects is not restricted to the provincial department or agency responsible for municipal affairs. A wide array of provincial departments and agencies have a lead role in various programs and projects, depending on their precise programmatic focus. The number of provincial departments or agencies involved has grown over the years as a result of the expanding number of programs and projects that fit more logically in their respective mandates rather than in the mandate of the department responsible for municipal affairs. An important consequence of this fragmentation is that it creates coordination challenges not only in the provincial bureaucracy but also in the federal-municipal-provincial coordination bureaucracy. Another consequence is that in order to facilitate the coordination, various types of coordinating mechanisms have to be developed both at the provincial and at the intergovernmental level.

In summary, programs and projects involving federal-municipal-provincial relations are undertaken in a wide range of policy sectors, and the vast majority of them are initiated and developed by the federal government. The alignment of roles among the three orders of government in relation to these programs and projects are not necessarily consistent with the federal and provincial jurisdictional authority, and they generally involve joint funding by all three orders of government. Furthermore, the federal government tends to be involved in the initiation and formulation of these programs and projects and to some extent in the adjudication of proposals concerning them, but not in the implementation and evaluation of specific programs and projects. Finally, provincial involvement in such programs and projects includes many provincial departments and agencies rather than only the provincial department responsible for municipal affairs or the central agency responsible for intergovernmental relations.

PROVINCIAL ROLES IN MANAGING RELATIONS

The programs and projects identified in the appendix reveal that the Government of Saskatchewan performs at least five major types of roles in managing federal-municipal-provincial relations: a monitoring role, an advocacy role, a mediation role, a regulatory role, and a partnership role. The objective in this section is to provide a brief explanation of each of these roles and to give some examples of each.

MONITORING ROLE

The provincial government monitors the relations and any resulting initiatives between the federal and municipal governments in order to ascertain what implications they may have for its own policy goals, its political interests, and the broader public provincial interests. It is likely that most, if not all, federal-municipal relations are monitored by the provincial government. This is particularly true of those related to the initiation, development, funding, and implementation of any program or project that would involve those two orders of government. However, the focus here is on two particular instances of provincial monitoring: (1) when the provincial government is not involved in initiating, developing, funding, and implementing a program or project; (2) when the provincial government may be involved in initiating and developing a program or project but is not involved in funding or implementing it. In both cases, the provincial government is in effect monitoring from various distances what the other two orders of government are doing. A notable example is the various federal programs related to the federal government's "rural agenda" under the Federal Framework for Action in Rural Canada, which was established in 1998. While some of these programs entail direct provincial participation, others do not. An example of the former is the Prairie Grain Roads Program; examples of the latter are the Agricultural Rural Minority Language Community Planning Initiative and the Canadian Agricultural Rural Communities Initiative.

ADVOCACY ROLE

The provincial government, either on its own initiative or at the request of municipal governments, may perform an advocacy role on behalf of its municipal governments vis-à-vis the federal government. There are at least three notable examples of this. One is the initial lobbying for the Canada-Saskatchewan Infrastructure Program, which the provincial government performed not only in its own interest and on its own behalf but also in the interest and on behalf of the municipal associations and their members, all of whom were very anxious to access federal funds for their transportation infrastructure. Another notable example is the provincial government's support for rural municipalities when the Saskatchewan Association of Rural Municipalities (SARM) was calling for higher compensation for specific land claims. The province had no direct financial obligation with respect to this matter but reluctantly agreed to support the municipalities' arguments, albeit very cautiously. The reason for its caution was that it was trying to maintain a tricky balance of supporting the position of rural municipalities without being pressured by the federal and municipal governments to contribute to the compensation package. By performing this advocacy role, the provincial government was in effect performing a dual role on the issue of compensation for specific land claims because it was also performing a limited mediation role on this particular issue. Another example is the Prairie Grain Roads Program and its predecessor program, the Canada Agri-Infrastructure Program. The provincial government ended up getting a share of the federal funding under this program for secondary provincial highways. The program was the culmination of many years of support to municipalities claiming that the grain handling and transportation changes following the withdrawal of the Crow Freight Rate Benefit were adding significant direct costs to farmers and were increasing financial pressure on municipalities to rebuild and maintain their roads.

MEDIATION ROLE

The provincial government, either on its own initiative or at the request of the federal or the municipal governments, or both, may perform a mediating role between the two orders of government. There are numerous instances in which the provincial government has done so. In some instances it has been invited or implored to do so. In other cases, it has chosen to do so of its own accord because it feels that it is imperative to prevent or settle some disagreement between those two other orders of government. When it is invited to act as a mediator, the provincial government tries not to become embroiled in issues that it feels have problematical policy or political implications that it could avoid through non-involvement.

There have been several notable examples in the recent past of provincial mediation between the federal and municipal governments. One example is the mediation related to the Disaster Financial Assistance Arrangements. This program was initiated and developed by the federal government with little formal negotiations with either the provincial or municipal governments. After it created the program, the federal government made some unilateral adjustments to the program that were intended to contain its financial exposure. It was at this point that the Saskatchewan government, along with other provincial governments, became involved in mediating discussions between the federal government and municipal representatives in an effort to establish a more stable, predictable, and durable framework for the program to compensate municipalities for losses suffered as a result of natural disasters. It should be noted that in this case, and others like it, the provincial government was not mediating entirely as an objective and disinterested third party. After all, the level of compensation provided by the federal government has a direct bearing on how much of its own money the provincial government may have to devote for reconstruction in the aftermath of a disaster.

Other examples of provincial mediation include negotiations between the federal, municipal, and Aboriginal governments involving compensation to municipalities for Treaty Land Entitlement and the creation of urban reserves. In both of these cases the provincial government was very reluctant to perform a mediation role. Insofar as it has done so, its role has been very limited, informal, and low profile. In the case of compensation for Treaty Land Entitlement, the negotiations were primarily between the federal government, SARM (which was negotiating on behalf of rural municipalities), and the Federation of Saskatchewan Indian Nations (which was negotiating on behalf of its member bands, who were signatories to the Treaty Land Entitlement Agreement that was concluded during the early 1990s). The negotiations were conducted in a formal process known as the Treaty Land Entitlement Round Table. At issue was how much compensation would be provided to rural municipalities for property taxes that were lost as a result of having land converted to reserve status, on which property taxes per se could not be collected (Mortin 1995, 80). The provincial government tried to avoid becoming involved and performing any role in the negotiations, largely out of fear that it would be called upon by the various parties around the table to make some financial contribution towards a mutually acceptable financial arrangement. Nevertheless, it was ultimately persuaded to become involved when negotiations reached an impasse and SARM threatened to take the issue to the courts. In an effort to prevent a court challenge, the provincial government agreed to serve either as a mediator or as a facilitator between the municipal and federal government representatives.

While the provincial government performed this role in a very limited and informal manner, apparently it also performed a very limited advocacy role on behalf of SARM by encouraging the federal government to find a mutually acceptable solution. The provincial government was reluctant to perform such an advocacy role in a public manner because it was a very sensitive matter. At issue was not simply how much money municipal governments could exact from the federal government as compensation but how much of the money which the federal government had already committed to the First Nations bands, pursuant to the Treaty Land Entitlement Agreement, would have to be used for compensating municipalities for loss of taxes. The provincial government did not want to be seen as siding with the municipal governments and against the First Nations governments.

Similar dynamics were at work in the provincial government's involvement in the creation of some urban reserves during the past decade – a process in which the federal, municipal, and Aboriginal governments were directly involved. There was strong opposition from the municipal government of Fort Qu'Appelle and, more recently, of North Battleford. In both cases, the provincial government was very unwilling to become involved either in a formal and direct way or in an informal and indirect way. Both publicly and privately, the provincial government's preferred approach was to encourage and implore all parties to be sensible, pragmatic, and fair in their efforts to find a mutually acceptable solution. Its discussions tended to be low profile and informal, largely designed to persuade the federal, municipal, and Aboriginal governments that it would be preferable for them to resolve the matter among themselves without provincial government involvement (Barron and Garcea 1999, 42–5).

REGULATORY ROLE

Pursuant to its constitutional prerogative and political imperatives, the provincial government may establish a regulatory regime for its municipalities through statutory or non-statutory policy instruments. Such a regime might have an effect on program and project matters on which a municipality might negotiate and enter into agreements with the federal government and the means by which it might do so. In performing a regulatory role vis-à-vis municipal governments, the provincial government may also enter into written or unwritten agreements with either the federal government or any other governments for the purpose of clarifying what it does or does not deem acceptable in their relations with its municipal governments.

Historically, there have been both statutory and non-statutory limitations preventing municipal governments in Saskatchewan from entering into negotiations for the purpose of concluding agreements with other orders of government in Canada or abroad without formal provincial approval. However, in some cases the provincial government has given municipal governments the authority to enter into such negotiations and agreements. An example is municipal policing. Under the *Royal Canadian Mounted Police Act*, the federal government, through the solicitor general, may enter into agreements with any province to contract the RCMP to assist in the administration of justice – which is a provincial responsibility under section 92 of the *Constitution Act* – as well as to provide municipal policing services. Saskatchewan's *Police Act*, which creates the legal framework for policing in the province, specifies that municipalities are responsible for providing adequate law enforcement personnel and facilities needed to maintain a reasonable standard of law and order. Municipalities can meet their policing responsibilities by establishing their own police service – something that is required for all urban municipalities with a population greater than 20,000 – or by entering into agreements with the federal government either directly, as specified under the *Police Act*, or through the provincial government under specific or general agreements to have such service provided by the RCMP. The important point to note regarding this program is that provincial legislation specifically authorizes the municipalities to enter into negotiations and contracts with the federal government. In Saskatchewan, provincial statutes, as well as other types of policy instruments, are generally silent on such matters. Instead, the provincial government tends to rely on conventions, tacit understandings, and periodic ad hoc discussions with municipal associations or with individual municipal governments in establishing what it deems to be appropriate protocols to regulate the relations of municipal governments with the federal government.

PARTNERSHIP ROLE

In performing a partnership role, the provincial government operates as a more or less equal member of a tripartite intergovernmental partnership with the federal government and municipal governments. As a partner, the provincial government may perform any of the roles that are commonly attributed to members of various types of partnerships (Kernaghan 1993, 57–76; Kernaghan, Marson, and Borins 2000, 179–206). These include the following: consultative partnerships, in which all members engage in consultations related to matters of mutual interest or concern, including coordination, as is the case with regional intersectoral committees; contributory partnerships, which entail a sharing of financial support for certain activities or services, as is the case with major project initiatives such as the Canadian Light Source and the Canada-Saskatchewan Film, Video, Production, and Education Centre, which is better known as the Sound Stage (Saskatchewan, Executive Council 2001); operational partnerships, which entail a sharing of the core management and administrative tasks that must be performed (for example, municipal policing); collaborative partnerships, which entail a sharing of core governance, strategic planning, and various decision-making tasks, as well as financial responsibility between two or more governmental or non-governmental organizations (for example, the Canada-Saskatchewan Infrastructure Program). Within the context of any of those partnerships, the provincial government has considerable opportunities to influence the nature and scope of federal-municipal-provincial relations.

The decisions of the provincial government to participate or not to participate in various federal-municipal-provincial partnership initiatives and the way it does so are crucial in managing both trilevel federal-municipal-provincial relations and any bilevel federal-municipal relations that may emerge. The consent of the provincial government to participate in, to support, or at least not to object to or impede such federal-municipal intergovernmental partnerships is absolutely essential. Without it, the other two orders of government would run the risk of having their initiative contested in the political or judicial arena, especially in the case of initiatives that impinge on areas of provincial jurisdiction.

There are many examples in which Saskatchewan's provincial government performs a partnership role. Indeed, most programs and projects entail a provincial partnership role. Several notable examples of this role are identified in the appendix. While the provincial government's precise roles and responsibilities in these partnerships vary, they usually entail one of the following: initiating, developing, funding, and implementing programs and projects. For illustrative purposes, it is useful to note some features of the intergovernmental dynamics surrounding the creation and operation of one such partnership. The current Canada-Saskatchewan Infrastructure Program is an example of one in which the provincial government and the municipalities were of the same view that federal funding for infrastructure was justified and was essential to ease their financial burden. In 1999, a year before the federal government agreed to renew its involvement in a provincial-municipal infrastructure program, the Saskatchewan government announced that it would contribute $10 million for such a program for the year 1999–2000. In making this announcement, it expressed support for the municipal call for assistance from other orders of government and urged the federal government to come on board. The federal government did so in 2000, when it announced that it would enter into agreements with the provinces to finance a new national infrastructure program. As with the previous versions of the program, the federal government negotiated the formal agreements with the provincial and territorial governments. The municipalities were not directly involved in the negotiations and were not signatories to the agreements, notwithstanding the fact that they were expected to contribute to the cost-sharing formula for the portion of the program that would apply to them. The reason why the municipalities were not included in the negotiations was, first, that the federal government saw this program primarily as an employment-creation program and not a municipal program; and, second, all the provinces wished to have the flexibility to determine how much of the funding would be directed to municipal priorities and how much would go to other provincial priorities. In Saskatchewan, at least 80 percent of the federal-provincial funding was to be directed to municipal priorities, with municipalities supplementing this funding to reflect a one-third contribution. In other provinces, the municipal portion was not as high.

Finally, in some instances the provincial government chooses not to be a partner with the federal and municipal governments, but it agrees not to stand in the way of such arrangements. An example is the federal government's Summer Work Experience Program for secondary and postsecondary students. Municipalities are eligible to apply to this program for wage subsidies to hire students during the summer. The Saskatchewan government established its own separate student employment program, for which municipalities are not eligible. Despite requests by the federal government to coordinate the federal and provincial programs and render them more consistent, the provincial government chose to act separately. Moreover, it refused requests by municipal governments to make them eligible for subsidies under the provincial program. In refusing their request, the provincial government encouraged municipal governments to apply for federal wage subsidies. Its rationale for doing so was that if municipal governments accessed federal funds, it would leave more provincial money for subsidizing the wages of organizations that do not qualify for the federal program.

In summary, the provincial government performs at least five different types of roles in managing federal-municipal-provincial relations. These are not mutually exclusive roles and may be performed either concurrently or consecutively in conjunction with a single program or project initiative.

PROVINCIAL APPROACHES IN MANAGING RELATIONS

In examining the approaches which the Government of Saskatchewan used in performing various roles in the context of federal-municipal-provincial relations, the following typology will be useful. It consists of five sets of paired and differentiated approaches:

- bilateral approach v. trilateral approach (McRoberts 1985)
- reactive approach v. proactive approach

- non-intrusive approach v. intrusive approach
- informal approach v. formal approach
- low-profile approach v. high-profile approach.

In proffering some generalizations regarding the Saskatchewan government's various approaches in this matter, a caveat is in order. The following generalizations are based on general tendencies rather than on perfectly consistent behaviour by each of the provincial governments that have been in power in recent years. After all, as noted below, there are some exceptions to the generalizations. Moreover, these generalizations are based largely on our own observations rather than on those of government officials or other academic observers.

The first of these five generalizations is that the provincial government tends to rely much more on a bilateral approach than a trilateral approach in performing various roles, especially its advocacy and mediation roles; it prefers to deal with the federal and municipal governments separately, either concurrently or consecutively. The federal government also seems to prefer bilateral negotiations. The municipal governments are less supportive of this "dual bilateralism." While they value a certain degree of bilateralism when it suits their purposes (either for certain programs or projects or at some stage of a consultation or negotiation process), their preference is generally to be invited to sit at the same table as the federal and provincial governments. In short, except where it suits their purposes, municipalities prefer genuine trilateralism to dual bilateralism with the provincial government serving as the go-between.

Second, the provincial government tends to rely on a reactive rather than a proactive approach in performing its roles in federal-municipal-provincial relations; it tends to respond to federal initiatives related to the municipal sector rather than undertaking its own initiatives and constraining the federal government to respond to them. This approach is a function of two related factors: that the provincial government realizes that it has limited financial resources to undertake many of its own initiatives in the municipal sector; and that it is realistic regarding the extent to which – given its relatively limited financial and political clout within the federation – it can constrain the federal government to respond to its own initiatives.

Third, the provincial government's tendency is to adopt a non-intrusive rather than an intrusive approach in federal-municipal consultations and negotiations. This is particularly true when new initiatives are under consideration. The provincial government seems to be quite content to monitor such interactions from a distance and wait for an invitation from the federal government or municipal governments to become involved. The Saskatchewan government generally does not exhibit the characteristics sometimes ascribed to provincial governments in some other provinces as jealously guarding jurisdiction and being highly sensitive about bilateral federal-municipal consultations, negotiations, and agreements. This is not to suggest that the Saskatchewan government is not concerned at all. After all, like other provincial governments, it wants to ensure that the federal and municipal governments do not pursue initiatives that are either far removed from provincial priorities and might not advance the provincial interest, or which could impose financial obligations on it. Nevertheless, the Saskatchewan government has been willing to allow municipalities to engage in direct negotiations with the federal government for various programs and projects. Its reason for doing so is largely linked to its own financial and political interests. In the case of its financial interests, it hopes that municipal governments are successful in obtaining federal funding that would reduce the political and financial pressures for the province to fund their respective initiatives. In the case of its political interests, it hopes that by reducing its involvement it will limit the adverse effects of any political fallout. Of course, this is a tricky matter for the provincial government because non-involvement can also leave it open to criticism and the resulting political consequences.

Fourth, the provincial government tends to prefer informal rather than formal approaches in performing various roles. This is particularly true of its monitoring, regulatory, advocacy, and mediation roles. In performing these roles the provincial government tends to eschew formal and institutionalized processes in favour of informal and ad hoc arrangements. This is largely because of its limited financial and human resources to devote to an institutionalization of these processes, rather than because of any philosophical predisposition. Although in recent decades Saskatchewan has followed other provinces in establishing an intergovernmental relations bureaucracy, the result has been a smaller and less resourced bureaucratic infrastructure than that of larger and wealthier provinces, such as Quebec, Ontario, British Columbia, and Alberta (Leeson 1987).

Fifth, the provincial government tends to prefer to use a low-profile approach in performing its roles vis-à-vis the federal government. One gets the distinct impression that it does not like to be seen as taking a strong public stand on any proceedings between the federal and municipal governments. This is equally true during provincial elections and between elections. The Saskatchewan government does not conform to the characteristic ascribed to its counterparts in some other provinces, where "fed-bashing" is an integral part of the strategic political behaviour to curry support with the local electorate. There are exceptions, however, as evidenced by the position taken by the provincial government on the gun registry. On that issue, it sided with Saskatchewan's municipal leaders against the federal government, and it did so in a public manner. But even on that issue, it articulated its position in a more tempered and lower-profile manner than, for example, the Alberta government. Its decision to be less strident was undoubtedly influenced by the province's heavy reliance on the federal government for financial transfers

for its volatile farm economy, among other things. Clearly, its financial standing does not allow it to act like Alberta, even when it holds the same view as
Alberta.

In summary, this overview on the approaches used by Saskatchewan's provincial government in dealing with federal-municipal-provincial relations
reveals that it has tended to rely on bilateral, reactive, non-intrusive, informal, and low-profile approaches. It also reveals that there are some differences
in the approaches of the Saskatchewan government and those of larger and
wealthier provinces. More detailed comparative research on this matter is required to provide more reliable generalizations regarding the precise nature,
scope, and determinants of these differences.

MECHANISMS FOR MANAGING RELATIONS

In managing federal-municipal-provincial relations, governments rely on various types of organizational mechanisms. Two types are generally used in
Saskatchewan: intergovernmental mechanisms and provincial mechanisms.
Both types are created by the provincial government, either on its own or in
consultation with municipal and federal officials, in its efforts to facilitate the
management of federal-provincial-municipal relations.

INTERGOVERNMENTAL MECHANISMS

Intergovernmental mechanisms consist of various types of coordinating committees comprising representatives of the various orders of government that
are responsible for managing federal-municipal-provincial relations. There
are at least two major types of these mechanisms: sector-based mechanisms,
which are established to deal with a wide range of issues in the municipal
sector that impinge on federal-municipal-provincial relations; and program-
based or project-based mechanisms, which are established to deal with
intergovernmental relations in connection with individual programs and
projects. Each type can take one of two forms, depending on the number of
orders of government they involve: a bilevel form, when they involve representatives of any two of the three orders of government; and a trilevel form,
when they involve representatives of all three orders of government – federal,
provincial, and municipal. A quadralevel form can also exist when, in addition to representatives of the federal, provincial, and municipal governments,
they include representatives of Aboriginal governments.

Notable examples of the sector-based intergovernmental mechanisms are
two bilevel round tables that have been established to facilitate communication and negotiations between the provincial government and the municipal
associations to deal with various types of matters, including those that fall

within the scope of federal-municipal-provincial relations. One of these is the provincial-municipal round table, which consists of representatives of the provincial government, the Saskatchewan Urban Municipalities Association (SUMA), and the Saskatchewan Association of Rural Municipalities (SARM). The other is the northern provincial-municipal round table, which consists of representatives of the provincial government and Saskatchewan Association of Northern Communities (SANC). SUMA and SARM send only their executive members to their round table meetings, but the northern round table includes representatives from SANC's executive and also from each of the northern municipalities. The extent to which these bilevel round tables are used for dealing with policy and program issues involving the various orders of government is highly variable and depends on the willingness of the provincial and municipal representatives to attend the meetings in order to address issues of interest or importance to them. Political machinations and personal relations have a substantial effect both on the extent to which the round tables are used for managing relations and their efficacy in doing so. The use of these formal provincial-municipal mechanisms is supplemented by informal mechanisms – for example, the most senior elected officials or the most senior appointed officials from both orders of government meet periodically on an ad hoc basis to deal with issues of mutual interest. A notable example of such meetings is when provincial officials meet with the Local Governments Federation, which in addition to SUMA and SARM includes the Saskatchewan School Trustees Association (SSTA). Its principal focus is on financial issues related to the property tax base, which in Saskatchewan is shared by municipal governments and school boards (Norton 2005, 59–60).

Notable examples of program-based or project-based mechanisms include the various bilevel and trilevel committees involved in the development, funding, or implementation of some of the programs or projects identified in the appendix. This includes the committees established in conjunction with the Saskatchewan Northern Development Accord, the Canada-Saskatchewan Northern Development Agreement, the Regina Inner City Community Partnership, the National Homelessness Initiative, and the Supporting Communities Partnership Initiative. A notable feature of most of these types of committees is that in addition to representatives of the federal, provincial, and municipal orders of government they also involve some representatives of various Aboriginal governments and authorities, as well as various non-governmental community-based organizations that have a stake in various programs and projects.

Participation by representatives of Aboriginal governments on these committees is becoming increasingly common. This is because of the sizable Aboriginal population in Saskatchewan, especially in the north and in such major urban centres such as Saskatoon, Regina, Prince Albert, and North Battleford. Increasingly, all orders of government and the general public have begun to understand that the "Aboriginalization" of the province's population is a significant demographic phenomenon. Saskatchewan is a leader among the provinces in the proportion of Aboriginals as a percentage of the total population, and it is likely to continue to be so to an even greater extent in future. Indeed, census data reveal that only Manitoba's Aboriginal population of 13.6 percent is higher than Saskatchewan's, which is 13.5 percent. Moreover, all indications are that the proportion of Aboriginal people will increase substantially in future, for the recent population trends are expected not only to persist but to accelerate during the next half-century. Whereas Saskatchewan's Aboriginal population increased by 17 percent from 1996 to 2001, the non-Aboriginal population decreased by 3.7 percent. This growth rate has led to projections that by 2045 Aboriginals will constitute approximately 25 to 33 percent of the province's population and possibly an even higher proportion of the population in major urban centres such as Saskatoon (Lendsay, Painter, and Hower 1997, 61; Saskatchewan, Government Relations and Aboriginal Affairs 2004). The increasing size of the Aboriginal population, along with the increasing migration to urban communities throughout the province, has heightened the need for all orders of government to deal on a coordinated basis with issues such as literacy, employment, and social services for urban Aboriginals. In Saskatchewan there is a highly developed system of Aboriginal governance at the local, regional, and provincial level. It includes the various orders of Aboriginal government as well as parallel and separate administrative and program-delivery mechanisms. This complex panoply of Aboriginal governments and program delivery mechanisms makes it increasingly difficult for the federal, provincial, and municipal governments to establish either sectoral committees or program-based and project-based committees that do not include representatives of Aboriginal governments and communities.

PROVINCIAL MECHANISMS

During the past decade, the provincial mechanisms for managing federal-municipal-provincial relations have consisted of the provincial government's line departments and central agencies. In some cases a line department responsible for municipal affairs has taken the lead in managing such relations, and in other cases a central agency responsible for intergovernmental relations has taken the lead. A common practice is for a line department and a central agency to do so on a joint and coordinated basis. As explained below, the growing recognition of the need for a joint and coordinated approach ultimately led the Saskatchewan government to integrate the line department responsible for municipal affairs with the central agency responsible for intergovernmental relations.

The line departments that have had a central role in managing federal-municipal-provincial relations during approximately the past decade have been those responsible for municipal affairs, namely Municipal Government (1993–98), Municipal Affairs, Culture, and Housing (1998–2001), and Municipal Affairs and Housing (2001–2). The central agencies that have been involved in managing these relations during the same time include the Department of Intergovernmental Relations (pre-1996), the Department of Intergovernmental Affairs (1996–97), the Department of Intergovernmental and Aboriginal Affairs (1997–2002), the Department of Government Relations and Aboriginal Affairs (2002–4), and the Department of Government Relations (2004–5).

The year 2002 constitutes an important watershed in the provincial mechanisms which the provincial government uses for managing municipal affairs and federal-provincial-municipal relations. Between 2002 and 2004 responsibility for both of these functions was entrusted to a multifunctional central agency named Government Relations and Aboriginal Affairs (GRAA). GRAA was responsible for municipal affairs and also for various types of intergovernmental relations (provincial-municipal, provincial-federal, provincial-Aboriginal, and international). The rationale provided in the annual report for the reorganization was that the "new department will provide the opportunity to strengthen government-to-government relationships with municipal, provincial, federal and Aboriginal governments" (Saskatchewan, Intergovernmental and Aboriginal Affairs 2002, 3).

In the fall of 2004, GRAA was split into two separate departments: Government Relations (GR), which continued to be responsible for both municipal affairs and three major sets of intergovernmental relations (interprovincial, federal-provincial, and international); and First Nations and Métis Relations (FNMR), which assumed responsibility for Aboriginal relations, including the provincial government's relations with First Nations and Métis governments in the province and also its relations with the federal and municipal governments related to First Nations and Métis governance. Ironically, the splitting of GRAA into GR and FNMR has meant that gains in intradepartmental coordination involving municipal governments were offset by the loss of intradepartmental coordination involving First Nations and Métis Relations. Those responsible for the departmental reconfiguration were undoubtedly aware of this trade-off but felt that, on balance, hiving off First Nations and Métis Relations was beneficial in narrowing and focusing the mandate of both departments. The belief was that the restructuring would give "greater attention to the government's approach to Aboriginal issues" (Saskatchewan 2004). The adverse effect of separating FNMR from GRAA was not as great as it might have been, largely because the personal and professional ties formed among officials who had worked in a single department for two years continued and facilitated coordination after they were reorganized into two departments.

The policy rationale for integrating municipal affairs into GRAA in 2002 and subsequently into GR in 2004 was that there was an increasing overlap of policy and program issues involving municipal governments and other orders of government (provincial, Aboriginal, and federal) within the province and the federation. In part, however, the integration also attests to an evolution that has been occurring during the past decade in the provincial government's perspective of municipal governments in Saskatchewan. Whereas in the more distant past the provincial government viewed and treated municipal governments as its local administrative units, in recent years it has been viewing and treating them more as relatively autonomous governments. The result is that it has been moving towards a more efficacious "government to government" relationship with them. Precisely how successful this has been is a point of considerable debate among municipal and provincial officials.

For purposes of federal-municipal-provincial relations within the multilevel governance framework, the main advantage envisioned in agglomerating the province's municipal affairs bureaucracy and its intergovernmental relations bureaucracy within one department is increased efficiency and effectiveness. The hope is that the agglomeration will create the organizational proximity needed to ensure that the management of federal-municipal-provincial relations receives greater and quicker attention by provincial experts in intergovernmental relations than was possible under the previous organizational framework. It is also hoped that making one minister and one deputy minister responsible for both municipal affairs and intergovernmental relations will reduce the number of senior provincial officials who, at least initially, would have to be involved in identifying, assessing, and reconciling organizational interests and imperatives related to federal-municipal-provincial relations. The reason for this is that the new organizational structure brings many aspects of federal-municipal-provincial relations squarely within the aegis of one senior cabinet minister and one deputy minister, who are in charge of what is arguably the most important central agency responsible for dealing with issues of multilevel governance not only in the municipal sector but also in other policy sectors. It is still too early to tell whether the benefits envisioned are being realized. The most that can be said at this point is that there are no visible signs that it has created any major problems. Although the new structure has considerable potential to be more efficient and effective in theory, in practice its efficacy for the management of federal-municipal-provincial relations will depend very much on the interests and abilities of the senior elected and appointed provincial officials in that department.

Finally, it should be noted that although the various types of provincial and intergovernmental mechanisms identified above perform important functions in provincial-municipal relations, there is a widespread sentiment among various governmental stakeholders that all of them could be improved to render them more efficacious in dealing with various aspects of federal-municipal-provincial relations.

DETERMINANTS OF PROVINCIAL ROLES, APPROACHES, AND MECHANISMS

Many factors affect the decisions of Saskatchewan's provincial government regarding the roles it performs in federal-municipal-provincial relations and the approaches and mechanisms it uses in performing them. The most significant of these are the following: the provincial government's policy, financial, and political goals; the political and financial resources that it has in advancing these interests; and the normative frameworks related to governance and public management that influence the thinking of its elected and appointed officials.

POLICY, FINANCIAL, AND POLITICAL GOALS

The policy, financial, and political goals of the Saskatchewan government all figure prominently in its decisions regarding what roles it will perform within the context of federal-municipal-provincial relations and what approaches and mechanism it will use in doing so. Its policy goals are related primarily to its own policy agenda and secondarily to items on the policy agendas of the federal and municipal governments that are consonant with its own. Its financial goals are essentially to maximize the level of provincial contributions to various programs and projects by the other two orders of government and to minimize the level of its own contributions whenever possible. Its political goals are to maximize not only its electoral support but also its legitimacy as an order of government vis-à-vis the other orders of government, both of which are essential factors for holding and exercising power. The provincial government's decisions regarding what roles to perform and how to perform them entail complex calculations regarding whether these roles will have a positive or an adverse effect on each of the aforementioned goals. Invariably, the government is willing to perform roles that are likely to contribute to advancing its goals, and it is reluctant to perform those that are likely to have an adverse effect on any of its goals. Its calculations regarding its political goals are heavily influenced by the fact that the municipal sector in Saskatchewan exerts considerable influence on public policy debates and in elections. The major reason for this, of course, is that it has a large membership consisting of community leaders who exercise substantial influence in shaping policy and political debates within their own communities.

FINANCIAL AND POLITICAL RESOURCES

Although the provincial government's goals and interests have been influential in its decisions regarding what roles to perform as well as the approaches and mechanisms to use in performing them, such decisions have also been heavily influenced by the financial and political resources that it has had at its disposal. Although its financial and political resources permit the Saskatchewan government to perform certain roles and to do so in strategic ways, they also have a constraining effect on what it can do because its resources are relatively limited compared with those of some of its larger and more powerful provincial counterparts. After all, in terms of both its financial resources and its political resources, Saskatchewan is not one of the "big four" provinces (Ontario, Quebec, British Columbia, and Alberta).

Saskatchewan has a much smaller budget and less flexibility in what it can do than any of the big four. Its limited financial resources constrain what it can do on its own, as well as what it can do in partnership with the federal and/or municipal governments. This problem is compounded by the fact that its economy is subject to relatively volatile swings, based on the vagaries of the farm economy and natural resources prices, which affect, among other things, whether it receives equalization payments from the federal government. Its financial capacity and the periodic fluctuations in its farm economy affect the number and type of programs and projects with which it can become involved, especially if they require it to make long-term financial commitments. Its limited financial resources constrain it to be more sensitive to the preferences of the federal government regarding matters such as the choice of programs and projects, the roles and responsibilities of the various orders of government, and the approaches and mechanisms it uses in managing federal-municipal-provincial relations.

Saskatchewan is also not one of the big four in terms of political power. Its relatively small population and small number of federal electoral seats limit its political clout within the federation. This limitation is compounded by the fact that the provincial electorate in Saskatchewan, unlike that in some other small provinces, does not generally engage in strategic voting to curry favour with the party forming the government. The only exception in recent elections was the strong albeit short-lived support for the Mulroney government, which expressed its gratitude just before the 1986 provincial election by providing a $1 billion farm aid package that benefited a large number of farmers living in various rural and even urban municipalities.

The political clout of the provincial government is also limited with respect to the municipal governments. Despite its constitutionally based jurisdictional primacy over them, the provincial government is not entirely free to do as it wishes vis-à-vis the municipal governments. They are powerful and capable governmental actors in their own right. Consequently, within the context of federal-municipal-provincial relations generally, the provincial government has to take into consideration their policy preferences and policy goals when choosing what roles it performs and the approaches and mechanisms it uses. This is true whether the muncipality is large or small. That is because the vast majority of municipalities in Saskatchewan consist of very small communities where people know their municipal politicians personally and feel a closer relationship with them than with more distant provincial and federal cabinet ministers. Moreover, municipal politicians are usually able to frame policy issues, including those that are addressed in an intergovernmental context, in ways that resonate with the perceptions and preferences of residents living in their communities. During as well as between elections, municipal efforts at "province-bashing" can be as effective as provincial efforts at "fed-bashing."

PUBLIC MANAGEMENT PHILOSOPHY

Another major factor that has had a significant effect on the roles that the provincial government performs in the context of federal-municipal-provincial relations, as well as in other aspects of municipal governance, is the "new public management" philosophy (Tindal and Tindal 2000, 284–94). This is especially true of the part of this philosophy that embodies the following tenets of neoliberalism and neoconservatism: more "limited government" in terms of state involvement in market and non-market matters; "steering rather than rowing" as a governance style; "subsidiarity" in developing and implementing programs and projects; "alternative modes of service delivery" in the production and delivery of various services, including increasing the number and types of "public-private partnerships" for that purpose; and maximizing reliance on "user pay" whenever feasible in funding various programs, projects, and services (Kernaghan, Marson, and Borins 2000).

The Saskatchewan government has not been immune to the effects of some of these tenets. It has followed the example of other governments in limiting the nature and scope of its involvement in various programs and projects and relying increasingly on the municipal governments and the voluntary sector to fill the void either on their own or in partnership with itself and other orders of government. Of course, from the perspective of municipal governments and voluntary sector organizations, this is tantamount to downloading rather than partnering, and they believe it is triggered largely by the concern of the provincial government to deal with its deficit and debt rather than thinking it the optimal way to administer such matters (Colligan-Yano and Norton 1996, 115–42). Regardless of what triggered it, the era of the "partnering state" has taken root in Saskatchewan, where it resonates relatively well with the political culture that has always valued the idea of federal and provincial governments helping local governments and local communities help themselves as they see fit. This is precisely the purpose of the provincial government's Voluntary Sector Initiative (Saskatchewan 2003). It is also the purpose of the regional intersectoral committees highlighted in the appendix. The Saskatchewan government has been a leader in establishing this particular type of intersectoral coordinating mechanism, whose principal function is twofold: to coordinate policies and programs among public, private, and non-profit sectors involved in human services within a given region; and, in some instances, to serve as peer review committees to evaluate program applications for project funding from various agencies within the region.

In recent years the provincial government has become increasingly disposed to use comparable adjudication committees when making project-funding decisions. In the Canada-Saskatchewan Infrastructure Program, a committee of municipal representatives provides peer review of the funding applications and makes recommendations – which are generally accepted by the federal and provincial governments – on how the limited funds will be allocated to the large number of competing municipal applicants. The underlying strategy of this process is to contain the criticism and disappointment from unsuccessful applicants by pointing to the peer review process. This approach mutes the municipal lobbying organizations – SUMA, SARM, and SANC – which have to support the decisions from the review process and are forced to take a public role in justifying why some municipalities' applications are successful and those of others are not.

SUMMARY AND FURTHER RESEARCH

To reiterate, the central objective of this paper has been to provide a general and preliminary overview of the nature and determinants of the roles which the Saskatchewan government has performed in recent years in managing federal-municipal-provincial relations and the approaches and mechanisms it has used in doing so. This concluding section will summarize the major findings and highlight some areas for further research.

The key findings can be summarized as follows. First, the provincial government performs five major types of role within the context of federal-municipal-provincial relations: monitoring, advocacy, mediation, regulatory, and partnership. Second, the provincial government tends to use bilateral, reactive, non-intrusive, informal, and low-profile approaches in performing its roles. Third, the provincial government tends to use both intergovernmental and provincial mechanisms in managing federal-municipal-provincial relations. The intergovernmental mechanisms generally take the form of bilevel rather than trilevel intergovernmental committees involving representatives of the municipal governments and the federal government. The provincial mechanisms involve both line departments and central agencies, which have been consolidated in recent years to facilitate the management of federal-municipal-provincial relations. Fourth, the provincial government's decisions regarding the roles it performs and the approaches and mechanisms it uses have been influenced by three sets of factors: its policy, financial, and political interests; its financial and political resources; and the extent to which it has subscribed to the tenets of the "new public management" philosophy.

Although this paper has provided some interesting and important insights into Saskatchewan's management of federal-municipal-provincial relations, much remains to be analysed at both the conceptual and the empirical level. At the conceptual level, more work is required in conceptualizing the types of roles performed by the provincial government, the approaches and mechanisms it uses in performing them, and the factors that shape its decisions regarding each of these matters. For that purpose the concepts and models in the extant literature on intergovernmental and interorganizational management and coordination should be consulted (for example, Stein 1989; Rogers and Whetten 1982).

At the empirical level, more descriptive and evaluative work is required on various matters dealt with in this paper. For that purpose detailed case studies should be conducted that focus on the provincial government's management of federal-municipal-provincial relations in conjunction with each major program and project identified in the appendix. Case studies should also be conducted of comparable programs and projects that are prominent on the public policy agenda today and will likely continue to be so – for example, those that deal with immigration and urban Aboriginals. In analysing programs and projects related to urban Aboriginals, the focus should be expanded beyond the trilevel relations involving the federal, municipal, and provincial governments to include the Aboriginal governments.

Furthermore, in conducting the cases studies, attention should be devoted not only to the roles the provincial government performs in managing these relations and the approaches and mechanism it uses for that purpose, but also to at least three other important matters. The first of these is the nature of the bureaucratic politics within the provincial government that affect its management of these relations. Reliance on the bureaucratic politics model, rather than on the unitary actor model, in analysing the provincial government's decisions regarding these relations will produce fuller and more accurate explanations of the causal factors. Second, it is important that the case studies also focus on the effect of the provincial government's management of federal-municipal-provincial relations – how the ways in which it manages them affect not only the nature of intergovernmental dynamics and coordination but also the effective and efficient formulation and implementation of programs and projects. A third important matter that should be the focus of such case studies is the views of federal, provincial, and municipal governmental officials regarding various aspects of federal-municipal-provincial relations in Saskatchewan.

Finally, at the empirical level comparable and ideally comparative case studies should be conducted of federal-municipal-provincial relations in other provinces. The overarching objective of all these case studies should be to find means of improving intergovernmental relations and management in ways that will enhance economic and social development and ultimately the quality of life in local communities.

APPENDIX

Federal-Municipal-Provincial Collaboration in Saskatchewan: A Sample of Notable Programs and Projects in 2003

Program	Description	Policy/program initiation and development	Funding agent(s)	Application adjudicator(s)	Administration and delivery	Lead provincial department
Agriculture Rural Minority Language Community Planning Initiative (2003–4)	The purpose of this program is to assist agricultural rural minority-language communities to produce community development plans. The emphasis is on economic diversification and job creation. Municipal governments, among others, are eligible to apply for funding.	Federal government (Agriculture and Agri-Food Canada and Canadian Heritage)	F	F	O	Provincial Secretary
Airport Capital Assistance Program (1995 to present)	Municipally owned airports can apply for capital funding to undertake safety improvements, asset protection, and operating-cost reduction. This program was created as part of the federal government's National Airports Policy. While Transport Canada fully funds the program in Saskatchewan, it is administered through the provincial Department of Highways and Transportation.	Federal government (Transport Canada)	F	F	P, M	Highways and Trans-portation
Canada-Saskatchewan Infrastructure Program (2000–1 to 2006–7)	At least 80% of the projects approved under this program are sponsored by municipalities. The first priority is for "green infra-structure" (approximately 50% of funding). While the federal government agreed to another version of this program in 2000, the Saskatchewan government initiated a $10 million one-year provincial-municipal infrastructure program in 1999–2000. Besides assisting municipalities with urgent infrastructure needs, this program demonstrated to the federal government that the pro-vincial and municipal governments place priority on addressing these needs and want federal involvement in a new program.	Federal government (Western Economic Diversification Canada)	F, P, M,O	F, P, M	P, M, O	Government Relations & Aboriginal Affairs

F – federal government and agencies; P – provincial government and agencies; M – municipal government and agencies; O – public, private, and third-sector organizations

Program	Description	Policy/program initiation and development	Funding agent(s)	Application adjudicator(s)	Administration and delivery	Lead provincial department
Canada-Saskatchewan Film, Video, and Educational Centre (i.e., Sound Stage)	Federal, provincial, and municipal governments in partnership with the film industry have jointly funded the construction of an $11.9 million, 7,600 m^2 film and video production and training facility in Regina. Opened in 2002, the facility preserved portions of an historic building owned by the Government of Saskatchewan.	Provincial government (Saskatchewan Property Management Corporation)	F, P, M, O	O	O	Saskatchewan Property Management Corporation
Canadian Agricultural Rural Communities Initiative (2000–1 to 2002–3)	The objective of this program was to enhance the viability of rural communities, with an emphasis on those affected by fundamental changes to the agricultural sector. Eligible recipients of federal funding included rural organizations, municipalities, Aboriginal groups, community-based groups, and educational institutions.	Federal government (Agriculture and Agri-Food Canada)	F, M, O	F	M, O	Monitored by Agriculture and Rural Revitalization
Canadian Light Source	The Canadian Light Source, located at the University of Saskatchewan in Saskatoon, is Canada's first synchrotron facility. The federal, Saskatchewan, and Saskatoon governments, as well as universities and industry, are funding the capital costs of the project.	University of Saskatchewan	F, P, M, O	F, P, M, O	O	Industry and Resources
Cultural Capitals of Canada	This program provides annual awards to municipalities to recognize an ongoing commitment to the arts and culture. Municipalities apply to the federal government for the awards and include as part of their application a proposal for celebrating and further developing their community's artistic and cultural identity.[1]	Federal government (Canadian Heritage)	F	F	F	Monitored by Culture, Youth, and Recreation

... *continued*

Program	Description	Policy/program initiation and development	Funding agent(s)	Application adjudicator(s)	Administration and delivery	Lead provincial department
Communities of Tomorrow Partnership [Centre for Sustainable Infrastructure Research] (2003)	Announced in May 2003, this partnership involves the establishment of a scientific centre in Regina that will undertake research into new technologies pertaining to the impact of urban infrastructure on the environment (e.g., water quality and waste water treatment). The centre will be established through a $15 million contribution from the federal government and $5 million each from the Government of Saskatchewan, City of Regina, and University of Regina. The National Reseach Council will operate the centre.	Federal government (National Research Council)	F, P, M ,O	F, P	F	Industry and Resources
Cultural Spaces Canada (2001–2 to 2003–4)[2]	This program funds the construction, adaptive use, or renovation of arts and heritage facilities and the acquisition, purchase of specialized equipment, and production of feasibility studies. Its purpose is to improve the physical conditions for artistic creativity and to increase and improve accessibility to the performing arts, media, and visual arts and to museums and heritage facilities.	Federal government (Canadian Heritage)	F	F	P, M, O	Monitored by Culture, Youth, and Recreation
Disaster Financial Assistance Arrangements (1970 to present)	Under these arrangements, the federal government provides financial assistance to provincial governments, municipalities, and private interests that have suffered uninsurable damage to property due to natural disasters (e.g., floods, ice and wind storms).	Federal government (Office of Infrastructure Protection and Emergency Preparedness)	F, P, M, O	F	M, O	Corrections and Public Safety
Green Municipal Funds (2000–7)	The federal government created an endowment in 2000 to encourage municipalities to pursue environmental innovation and to participate in reducing greenhouse gas emissions. (Subsequently, this program became part of the federal government's plan to implement the Kyoto Accord.) The program is managed by the Federation of Canadian Municipalities and consists of two components: Green Municipal Enabling Fund (providing grants for technical, environmental, and/or economic feasibility studies) and Green Municipal Investment Fund (providing interest-bearing loans and loan guarantees for environmental projects).	Federal government (Natural Resources Canada and Environment Canada)	F	F, P, M, O	M	Environment

Program	Description	Policy/program initiation and development	Funding agent(s)	Application adjudicator(s)	Administration and delivery	Lead provincial department
Joint Emergency Preparedness Program (ongoing, subject to budgetary approval)	This program provides federal funding to enhance Canada's national emergency response capability. "Earmarked funds" are assigned to each province and territory. The provinces and territories support the evaluation and prioritization of applications but do not make the final decisions on approval (since these depend on national, not regional, priorities and needs). Funding is channeled through the provinces and territories.	Federal government (Office of Critical Infrastructure Protection and Emergency Preparedness)	F	F	P, M, O	Corrections and Public Safety
Model Construction Codes (1937 to present)	The federal government coordinates and facilitates national consensus on the development and updating of national construction codes (e.g., National Building Code, National Fire Code, National Plumbing Code). The purpose of these model codes is to provide the basis for countrywide consistency in standards enforced under provincial and territorial legislation and implemented by municipalities.	Federal government (National Research Council)	F	F, P, O	P, M	Corrections and Public Safety
National Homelessness Initiative and Supporting Communities Partnership Initiative[3]	Announced in 1999, the National Homelessness Initiative involves $753 million of federal funding over three years to existing and new programs to address homelessness issues in Canada. A key element of this funding is the $305 million Supporting Communities Partnership Initiative, which supports local community-based efforts to find local solutions to these issues. It brings together all levels of government as well as non-profit, labour, and community-based organizations.	Federal government (Canada Mortgage and Housing Corporation; Human Resources Development Canada)	F, P, M, O	F	P, M, O	Community Resources and Employment
Northern Development Agreement/ Accord (2002 to present)	In 2002 the federal and provincial governments signed the Saskatchewan Northern Development Accord and a $20 million Canada-Saskatchewan Northern Development Agreement. These apply to the area known as the Northern Administration District of Saskatchewan. The accord is a memorandum of understanding	Provincial government (Northern Affairs) and federal government (Western Economic Diversification)	F, P	F, P, M, O (municipal involvement through Northern Development Board)	F, P, M, O	Northern Affairs

... continued

Program	Description	Policy/program initiation and development	Funding agent(s)	Application adjudicator(s)	Administration and delivery	Lead provincial department
	concerning the development of a strategic framework to guide federal and provincial governments and northern communities to improve the living conditions and enhance the economic opportunities of northerners. The accord calls for the federal and provincial governments to seek advice and recommendations and to work with the Northern Development Board, which consists of representatives from the Prince Albert Grand Council, Meadow Lake Tribal Council, Métis Nation–Saskatchewan, Saskatchewan Association of Northern (Municipal) Communities, and the Athabasca First Nation Chiefs. The agreement is administered by a management committee consisting of representatives from the federal and provincial governments and from the Northern Development Board.					
Prairie Grain Roads Program (2001–2 to 2005–6)	Federal cost-shared funding is provided to upgrade municipal grain roads and provincial secondary highways that are deteriorating or have become unsafe due to changing transportation policies and the restructuring of grain-handling systems. Eligible applicants include municipalities, the provincial government, and municipal organizations (SUMA and SARM).	Federal government (Prairie Farm Rehabilitation Administration)	F, P, M	F, P, M	P, M	Highways and Transportation
Municipal Policing (1928 to present)	Under contract with the provincial government, the Royal Canadian Mounted Police serves as Saskatchewan's provincial police. The provincial government requires municipalities with populations greater than 20,000 to have their own municipal police service. Other municipalities enter into agreements – either indirectly through the provincial government or directly – to have the RCMP provide municipal policing.	Provincial government (Saskatchewan Justice)	F, P, M	F, P	P, M	Justice

Program	Description	Policy/program initiation and development	Funding agent(s)	Application adjudicator(s)	Administration and delivery	Lead provincial department
Regina Inner-City Community Partnership	A federal-city government initiative to support a consultation process on local priorities within an inner-city community in Regina. The goal is to develop and implement a continuum of activities that will enhance the social and economic components of the neighbourhood. The partnership will bring together the three orders of government, relevant non-governmental organizations, and inner-city residents.	Municipal government (City of Regina)	F, M	F, M, O	P, M, O	Community Resources and Employment
Regional Intersectoral Committees	Established in 1994, the Human Services Integration Forum is a multidepartmental provincial government structure to promote and implement interagency collaboration and integrated planning and delivery of human services. The forum has facilitated the development and provides financial and coordinative support to nine regional intersectoral committees located throughout the province. Each committee consists of representatives from provincial and federal government departments, health districts, school divisions, postsecondary institutions, housing authorities, municipalities, police services, tribal councils, Métis organizations, and some community-based organizations. These committees support community-based planning, sharing of strategies, interagency collaboration and sharing of resources, and coordinated and integrated action for human services. They facilitate community involvement in consultation processes supporting the National Children's Agenda and the provincial government's early childhood development and the School PLUS initiatives.	Provincial government (Human Services Integration Forum supported by eight departments: Learning; Justice; Health; Community Resources and Employment; Corrections and Public Safety; Culture, Youth, and Recreation; Government Relations and Aboriginal Affairs; and Executive Council)	P	P	F, P, M, O	Human Services Integration Forum
Rural Community Forest Project (1994 to present)	Villages and towns in Manitoba, Saskatchewan, and Alberta with populations of less than 5,000 are eligible under this program to receive certain fruit-bearing tree	Federal government (Prairie Farm Rehabilitation Administration)	F, P, M	F	F, P, M	Saskatchewan Environment

... continued

Program	Description	Policy/program initiation and development	Funding agent(s)	Application adjudicator(s)	Administration and delivery	Lead provincial department
	species to enhance the quality of life in these communities and to provide habitat for wildlife. The trees and shrubs must be planted on municipal land. The Saskatchewan government participates in the program by funding the provision of plastic mulch for weed control.					
Summer Work Experience (ongoing as budgetary resources are available)	Municipal governments are eligible to apply for wage subsidies to hire secondary and post-secondary students in career-related summer jobs. The provincial government has a separate student employment program (Centennial Student Employment Program), but municipalities are not eligible.	Federal government (Human Resources Development Canada)	F	F	M, O	Monitored by Public Service Commmission and by Culture, Youth, and Recreation
Urban Development Agreements	These agreements involve the federal, provincial and municipal governments. They provide instruments for coordinating the action among orders of government and for providing the seamless delivery of programs and services. They encourage the development of strategic alliances to enhance the economic activity in the seven major cities in western Canada.[4]	Federal government (Western Economic Diversification Canada)	F, P, M	F, P, M	F, P, M	Government Relations
Wanuskewin Heritage Park	This national historic site, located north of Saskatoon, was the hunting and occasional wintering ground frequented by several Indian tribes of the northern plains for more than 6,000 years. It provides not only historical preservation and interpretation but also a place of spiritual importance for the descendants of the Northern Plains Indians. The park was developed through a partnership involving federal, provincial, municipal, First Nations, university, and other sectors. The Wanuskewin Heritage Park Corporation consists of representatives from Wanuskewin Indian Heritage Inc., the Federation of Saskatchewan Indian Nations, the City of Saskatoon, the Governments of Canada and Saskatchewan, the University of Saskatchewan, the Meewasin Valley Authority, and the Friends of Wanuskewin.	Provincial government (Culture, Youth, and Recreation)	F, P, M, O	F, P, M, O	O	Culture, Youth, and Recreation

NOTES

1 By the end of 2003 Saskatchewan communities had not received funding under this program. In 2003 the City of Regina submitted an application but was unsuccessful. Upon resubmitting its application in 2005, however, it was successful in being designated a "cultural capital" of Canada.
2 While Saskatchewan municipalities are eligible for funding, this program has provided support indirectly by funding projects with municipal involvement in a larger organizational structure (e.g., Wanuskewin Heritage Park, Moose Jaw Cultural Centre).
3 Most of the funding for projects has been dispersed to community-based organizations. Municipalities have been involved in the development of "community homelessness plans." These plans have been prepared by steering committees with representatives from federal, provincial, and municipal governments, as well as representatives from local social and private agencies and Aboriginal organizations.
4 Whereas urban development agreements for Edmonton, Winnipeg and Vancouver were signed several years earlier, the ones for Saskatoon and Regina were not signed by federal, provincial, and municipal representatives until May 2005. These agreements were signed as a result of the Martin government's attempts to find ways of enhancing its support among voters either to prevent any confidence votes in the House of Commons or at least to position itself for the next election in case it lost such a vote. For its part, the provincial government had already committed its portion of the funding for the initiative in its March 2005 budget. The Saskatoon and Regina agreements were identical in the amount of money ($5 million from the federal government and $2.5 million each from the provincial and municipal governments for a total of $10 million) and in the time frame (five years) and the six priorities for action which they included:

- community-based approaches to affordable housing, homelessness, and the renewal of older neighbourhoods;
- developing cultural and recreational opportunities to enhance the quality of life;
- supporting environmental protection and climate change solutions;
- enhancing Aboriginal participation in the economy;
- promoting innovative initiatives for a positive business climate and enhanced competitiveness; and
- addressing strategic infrastructure necessary for continued physical, social and economic development.

The lead federal and provincial agencies responsible for negotiating and administering the agreements were the federal department of Western Economic Diversification Canada and Saskatchewan's Department of Government Relations.

The authors wish to thank the anonymous reviewers for their valuable observations and suggestions.

REFERENCES

Andrew, C., K.A. Graham, and S.D. Philips, eds. 2002. *Urban Affairs: Back on the Policy Agenda*. Montreal: McGill-Queen's University Press

Barron, Laurie F., and Joseph Garcea, eds. 1999. "The Genesis of Urban Reserves and the Role of Governmental Self-Interest." In *Urban Indian Reserves: Forging New Relations in Saskatchewan*, eds. Barron and Garcea, 22–52. Saskatoon: Purich Publishing

Canada. 2005a. "Tri-partite Agreement to Invest $10 million into City of Saskatoon." News release, 13 May

– 2005b. "Tri-partite Agreement to Invest $10 million into City of Regina." News release, 13 May

Colligan-Yano, Fiona, and Mervyn Norton. 1996. *The Urban Age: Building a Place for Urban Government in Saskatchewan*. Regina: Saskatchewan Urban Municipalities Association

Graham, Katherine A., Susan D. Philips, and Allan A. Maslove. 1998. *Urban Governance in Canada: Representation, Resources, and Restructuring*. Toronto: Harcourt Brace

Hulchanski, J. David. 2002. *Housing Policy for Tomorrow's Cities*. Discussion Paper F27. Ottawa: Canadian Policy Research Networks (CPRN). www.cprn.org

Kernaghan, Kenneth. 1993. "Partnership and Public Administration: Conceptual and Practical Considerations." *Canadian Public Administration* 36 (1): 57–76

Kernaghan, Kenneth, Brian Marson, and Sandford Borins. 2000. *The New Public Organization*. Toronto: Institute of Public Administration of Canada

Kitchen, Harry M., and Melville L. McMillan. 1986. "Local Government and Canadian Federalism." In *Intergovernmental Relations*, R. Simeon, research coordinator, 215–61. Toronto: University of Toronto Press

Leeson, Howard. 1987. "The Intergovernmental Affairs Function in Saskatchewan, 1960–1983." *Canadian Public Administration* 30 (3)

Lendsay, Kelly, Marvin Painter, and Eric Howe. 1997. "Impact of the Changing Aboriginal Population on the Saskatchewan Economy: 1995–2045." In Federation of Saskatchewan Indian Nations, *Saskatchewan and Aboriginal Peoples in the 21st Century: Social, Economic, and Political Changes and Challenges*. Regina: Printwest Publishing Services

L'Heureux, Jacques. 1986. "Municipalities and the Divisions of Powers." In Intergovernmental Relations, R. Simeon, research coordinator, 179–214. Toronto: University of Toronto Press

McRoberts, Kenneth. 1985. "Unilateralism, Bilateralism, and Multilateralism." In *Intergovernmental Relations*, R. Simeon, research coordinator, 71–129. Toronto: University of Toronto Press

Marchildon, Gregory P. 1999. "Constructive Entanglement: Intergovernmental Collaboration in Canadian Social Policy." In *Collaborative Government: Is There a Canadian Way?* ed. Susan Delacourt and Donald G. Leniham, eds. 72–80. Toronto: IPAC

Marchildon, Gregory P., and Brent Cotter. 2001. "Saskatchewan and the Social Union Framework." In *Saskatchewan Politics: Into the Twenty-First Century,* ed. Howard Leeson, 367–80. Canadian Research Plains

Mejer, Kenneth J. 2000. "The Marble Cake: Introducing Federalism to the Government Growth Equation." *Publius: The Journal of Federalism* 30 (2)

Mortin, Jenni. 1995. *The Building of a Province: The Saskatchewan Association of Rural Municipalities.* Regina: PrintWest

Norton, Mervyn. 2005. *The Urban Age: Bridging to Our Future as Urban Government in Saskatchewan.* Regina: Saskatchewan Urban Municipalities Association

Rogers, David L., and David A. Whetten, eds. 1982. *Interorganizational Coordination: Theory, Research, and Implementation.* Ames: Iowa State University Press

Saskatchewan. 2003. *The Premier's Voluntary Sector Initiative: A Framework for Partnership between the Government of Saskatchewan and Saskatchewan's Voluntary Sector.* Regina

– 2004. "New Department of First Nations and Métis Relations." News release, Executive Council- 62, 1 October

– Executive Council. 2001. "Canada/Saskatchewan Film, Video, Production, and Education Centre Announced." News release, Federal/Provincial-808, 15 October

– Government Relations and Aboriginal Affairs. 2004. *Demographic Data, Aboriginal People in Saskatchewan, 2001. Updated – January 1, 2004.* www.fnmr.gov.sk.ca/html/mor/demographics/index.htm

– Intergovernmental and Aboriginal Affairs. 2002. *Annual Report 2001–2002.* www.gr.gov.sk.ca/PDFs/annual_reports/IAA_2002.pdf

– Task Force on Municipal Legislative Renewal. 2000a. *Options 2000: A Framework for Municipal Renewal (Urban and Rural Sectors).* www.communilink.sk.ca/municipal_task_force

– 2000b. *Options 2000: A Framework for Municipal Renewal (Northern Sector).* www.communilink.sk.ca/municipal_task_force

Seidle, Leslie F. 2002. *The Federal Role in Canadian Cities: Overview of Issues and Proposed Actions.* Discussion Paper F27. Ottawa: Family Network, Canadian Policy Reseach Networks (CPRN). www.cprn.org

Stein, Michael B. 1989. *Canadian Constitutional Renewal, 1968–1981: A Case Study in Integrative Bargaining.* Kingston: Institute of Intergovernmental Relations, Queen's University

Tindal, Richard, and Susan Nobes Tindal. 2000. *Local Government in Canada,* Scarborough: Nelson Canada

White, Graham. 2002. "Treaty Federalism in Northern Canada: Aboriginal-Government Land Claims Boards." *Publius: The Journal of Federalism* 32 (3): 89–114

VI

Chronology

15

Chronology of Events
January – December 2004

Aron Seal and Stephanie Quesnelle

An index of these events begins on page 405.

6 January *BSE*	The United States Department of Agriculture confirms that a Washington State cow found in December 2003 to be infected with BSE was originally exported from Canada. Genetic tests show the cow to have originated in Leduc, Alberta. Further tests are needed to determine how the cow became infected with the disease. This is the second case of mad cow disease involving Canada in less than a year; a northern Alberta cow infected with the disease was discovered in May 2004.
8 January *Softwood Lumber*	Provincial governments reject an American proposal to resolve the softwood lumber dispute. The offer would have given Canadian lumber producers duty-free access to 31.5 percent of the U.S. market. The provinces want a larger quota and explicit details on what reforms are needed for full access to the American market to be restored. Federal International Trade Minister Jim Peterson insists that negotiations with the United States will continue in pursuit of an acceptable agreement.
9 January *BSE*	Agriculture Minister Bob Speller announces a $92 million increase in federal funding for BSE testing. The funding should allow for the testing of as many as 30,000

animals per year, up from 5,500 in 2003. Speller's plan comes in response to recently released U.S. Department of Agriculture DNA evidence, which established Alberta as the origin of an American cow that was found in December 2003 to be infected with BSE. Critics, however, note that the number of cattle tested will remain less than one percent of the 3.5 million slaughtered in Canada each year.

10–11 January
British Columbia

The first meeting of the Citizens' Assembly on Electoral Reform is held. The assembly, composed of 160 randomly selected citizens, will spend eleven months considering various reforms of the province's democratic process. All of the assembly's recommendations will be put to referendum on 17 May 2005.

13 January
Canada–U.S.
Relations

The first official meeting between Prime Minister Paul Martin and U.S. President George W. Bush takes place at the Summit of the Americas in Monterrey, Mexico. Bush agrees to allow Canadian companies to bid for Iraqi reconstruction projects, to favour an integrated North American approach in dealing with BSE, and to consult Canada before deporting any Canadians to third countries (in reference to the Maher Arar affair). The talks produce little, however, with respect to softwood lumber.

14 January
Aboriginal Peoples

The Quebec government negotiates a peaceful ending to a thirty-six-hour standoff in Kanesatake. Dissidents had been holding sixty non-Kanesatake police officers hostage without food in their police station. The outside officers, recruited from other First Nations to help quell a growing crime problem on the reserve, were seen by protesters as a hostile takeover of the reserve's police. The protesters agree to lay down their arms in exchange for the safe evacuation and departure of the outside officers. Critics argue that the Quebec government gave in to the protesters' demands, undermining the authority of Grand Chief James Gabriel and his efforts to restore law and order on the reserve.

15 January
Alberta

A nine-member provincial government task force begins touring the province soliciting popular opinion on Alberta's place in Canada. The task force has been labelled the "firewall committee" by opposition parties, a reference to a plan endorsed by the Alberta Residents League that calls on the provincial government to opt out of the *Canada Health Act* and establish its own public pension plan, police, and tax collection. Task force chairman Ian McClelland insists that the committee will not consider any calls for Alberta's separation from Canada.

19 January *Aboriginal Peoples*	Quebec Public Security Minister Jacques Chagnon establishes a new policing plan for the Kanesatake native reserve which partners the band's police forces with the RCMP and the Sureté du Québec. Kanesatake leaders, however, are not included in negotiation of the arrangement. Grand Chief James Gabriel questions whether the plan will do more than the existing anti-drug partnerships with the RCMP. Gabriel's opponents argue that the provincial and federal police are no more welcome than the officers that had been held hostage the previous week.
22–23 January *Municipalities*	The mayors of Canada's largest cities come together at a summit hosted by Toronto Mayor David Miller. The mayors agree to collectively push for, among other objectives, full GST exemption for all municipal spending, a share of federal gasoline tax revenues, and a formal agreement relating to municipal relations with other levels of government.
27 January *Child Care*	The Quebec Court of Appeal, in a unanimous and strongly worded decision, rules that the federal government's national parental leave program infringes on provincial jurisdiction. The ruling calls for the option of provincial opt-out with funding for independent parental leave plans. The federal government will appeal the decision to the Supreme Court.
28 January *Aboriginal Peoples*	The ten commissioners for the Assembly of First Nations Renewal Commission are formally appointed by Assembly Grand Chief Phil Fontaine. Commissioners were chosen to represent the diverse regions, circumstances, and interests of First Nations across the country. The federally funded commission was created to produce recommendations for reforming the structure of the assembly.

28 January
Security

A public inquiry is launched into the reasons for the September 2002 deportation to Syria of Maher Arar, a Canadian citizen. American officials arrested Arar while he was changing planes in New York en route home from a vacation in Tunisia. He was subsequently deported on suspicion of connections to al-Qaeda. The mandate of the inquiry will be to investigate the involvement of Canadian officials and institutions in Arar's deportation and to make recommendations towards improving Canada's treatment of similar security investigations. American officials claim that Canadian information was part of the basis for Arar's deportation.

29 January
Health Care

The inaugural meeting of the National Health Council is held in Toronto. Composed of twenty-six members from both federal and provincial governments, the council is mandated with monitoring and reporting on the implementation of the 2003 First Ministers' Accord on Health Care Renewal, most notably with respect to provisions concerning accountability and transparency. Included in this mandate is the monitoring of provincial spending of federal transfers. Some provinces see the council as federal interference in provincial jurisdiction; Alberta has refused to take part in the council in any capacity, while Quebec, which has its own health council, is participating only as an observer.

29 January
Same-Sex Rights

Broadening a reference filed in 2003, the federal government asks the Supreme Court to rule on whether the traditional definition of marriage is consistent with the *Canadian Charter of Rights and Freedoms*. The original reference asked the court only to review questions relating to the framing of a law affirming the right to same-sex marriage, not the question of same-sex marriage itself. Though a hearing on the original reference had been scheduled for 16 April, the addition of the new question is expected to delay proceedings until after the expected spring election.

30 January
Energy

A federal environmental review panel is created to review the Mackenzie Gas Project. The project, a joint undertaking of the Aboriginal Pipeline Group and private corporations, will be studied for possible effects on the environment and wildlife in the Northwest Territories. Two Inuvialuit members will sit on the panel to represent Aboriginal interests.

30 January
First Ministers

Prime Minister Paul Martin meets with the premiers in Ottawa. He confirms that $2 billion of the 2003–4 federal surplus will be transferred to the provinces for health care spending as per a Jean Chrétien promise. Martin further pledges to increase provincial involvement in international relations. Premiers remain concerned, however, about the lack of long-term funding increase guarantees from the federal government.

2 February
Throne Speech

The federal government promises billions of dollars in new social spending and transfers in the Speech from the Throne. Proposals include $7 billion in GST rebates for municipalities and $3.5 billion over ten years to clean contaminated federal environmental sites. Also discussed are commitments to reduced hospital waiting lists, education and skills development for Aboriginals, expansion of the Urban Aboriginal Strategy, meeting Kyoto Accord objectives, and the creation of a national security policy. Critics see the speech as a collection of pre-election campaign promises, many of which impinge on provincial jurisdiction. They also note that western alienation received no mention.

4–5 February
Democratic Reform

Prime Minister Paul Martin releases *Ethics, Responsibility, Accountability: An Action Plan for Democratic Reform*. The plan brings together many promises Martin made during the 2003 Liberal leadership campaign. The proposals include more free votes, increased MP influence over legislation, annual review of cabinet ministers, and committee review of senior federal appointments. However, Liberal House Leader Jacques Saada announces the following day that there will be no free vote on gun registry spending estimates, despite suggestions to the contrary by Roger Gallaway, his parliamentary secretary. Budgetary questions, says Saada, are matters of confidence that cannot be put to free votes. Opposition parties, arguing that free votes on budget issues would reduce waste and mismanagement, accuse the government of evading the principles of the action plan.

9 February
Quebec

Claude Ryan dies at age seventy-nine. Ryan led the Quebec Liberal Party from 1978 to 1983, playing an integral role in the victory of the No side in the 1980 sovereignty referendum.

10 February
*Sponsorship
Program*

A scathing auditor general's audit of the federal sponsorship program is released. Words such as "appalling" and "scandalous" are used to describe numerous alleged cases of fraud and money laundering by institutions such as the RCMP, Via Rail, and Canada Post. The program, designed in principle to increase the public visibility of the federal government in the wake of the 1995 referendum, paid over $100 million to individuals and groups with links to the Liberal Party as well as large sums for events and advertising of questionable value. Prime Minister Paul Martin responds by announcing a public inquiry into the handling of the program and by recalling Alfonso Gagliano, who was minister of public works at the time of the alleged scandal, from his current position as ambassador to Denmark.

12 February
Atlantic Canada

The Council of Atlantic Premiers meets in Corner Brook, Newfoundland and Labrador. The premiers create an Atlantic Canada Action Team to promote Atlantic Canadian food products, particularly beef. They reiterate calls on the federal government for a long-term health-care funding increase and a more equitable equalization calculation structure.

17 February
Alberta

The Speech from the Throne includes plans for a provincial trade and policy office in Washington, D.C. The office will seek to promote Albertan interests, particularly with respect to agriculture and natural resource development. Alberta Economic Development Minister Mark Norris hopes the federal government will agree to house the office in the Canadian Embassy to reduce costs. No provinces currently have trade offices in Washington. Also discussed in the speech is the creation of a committee of federal, provincial, municipal, and non-governmental leaders to evaluate the sustainability of Alberta's water supply.

17 February
British Columbia

The Liberals table the first balanced budget of their tenure, projecting a $100 million surplus for the coming fiscal year. Announcements of new spending include $1.04 million over three years for health care, $313 million over three years for education, and $1.3 billion over three years for transportation infrastructure. The government further announces a lower than expected deficit for the third quarter of the 2003–4 fiscal year, savings the government intends to devote primarily to Olympic preparations, health care, and education. Critics view the elimination of the budget deficit as the government solving a self-created problem, given the large tax cuts implemented by the Liberals at the beginning of their term.

17 February
Energy

A Royal Society of Canada report on British Columbia offshore oil drilling is released. The study, commissioned by the federal government, concludes that there are no gaps in scientific knowledge that prevent the lifting of federal and provincial moratoria on offshore exploration. It stops short, however, of directly calling for a lifting of the bans. Federal cabinet ministers are divided over whether the ban should be lifted.

19 February
Health Care

Premier Ralph Klein, angered by a continuing impasse in federal-provincial health-care reform discussions, threatens to push forward with market-based health-care reforms despite *Canada Health Act* regulations. The value of his plans, he argues, would exceed the associated penalties. It is the first time a premier has openly suggested opting out of the Act.

20 February
Equalization

Finance ministers from equalization-recipient provinces leave a meeting with federal Finance Minister Ralph Goodale very dissatisfied. Agreement is not reached on reforms to methods of equalization calculation that would increase payment amounts; under the status quo, a weakened Ontario economy will result in a $3 billion reduction in total equalization payments for the coming year. The provincial ministers further fail to obtain a federal commitment on permanent increases in health-care funding. They warn that they will not cooperate with the federal government on municipal funding increases if the federal government does not cooperate with respect to health care.

23–24 February
Council of the Federation

The inaugural meeting of the Council of the Federation is held. The council was founded in 2003 to promote inter-provincial-territorial cooperation, closer ties between council members, recognition of Canadian diversity, and leadership on issues important to Canadians. Accomplishments from the meeting include the release of a work plan aimed at reducing internal barriers to trade, the creation of an agreement founding the Secretariat on Information and Cooperation on Fiscal Imbalance, and the establishment of the Council of the Federation Award for Literacy to recognize workplace literacy programs and strategies. The premiers further establish priorities for future cooperation on issues relating to health care, equalization, emergency responses, and youth involvement in government. Not all discussions are positive, however; the premiers offer dire predictions on the sustainability of national health care, fearing the end of the current system by 2010 if funding levels do not increase.

6–7 March
Political Parties

Deep internal tensions in the Liberal Party are exposed as two Paul Martin supporters defeat Jean Chrétien loyalists to win riding nominations for the upcoming federal election. Sheila Copps loses to Tony Valeri in Hamilton East–Stoney Creek, and Carolyn Parrish defeats Steve Mahoney in Mississauga-Erindale. Both races were marked by mudslinging and allegations of fraud.

8 March
Finance

The Conference Board of Canada releases an update of a 2002 report that confirms the continuing fiscal imbalance between the federal and provincial/territorial governments. The report projects steady increases in the federal surplus and the collective provincial/territorial deficit through 2020. Health-care costs, borne primarily by the provinces, are projected to be the single largest cause of expenditure growth in Canada. Provincial finance ministers see the findings as evidence of the need for reforms to health-care funding and equalization.

19 March
Same-Sex Rights

The Quebec Court of Appeal, in rejecting an appeal to a September 2002 Superior Court ruling, makes Quebec the third province in Canada to legally recognize same-sex marriages. The Superior Court ruling granted same-sex couples the right to marry pending a two-year moratorium to allow for the possibility of an appeal. The appeal, filed by the Catholic Civil Rights League, is rejected on the basis of changing attitudes towards the definition of marriage. The court ruling explicitly states that licences for same-sex marriages can be issued immediately.

20 March
Political Parties

Stephen Harper, with 56 percent of first-ballot votes, wins the leadership of the Conservative Party of Canada, defeating former Ontario Health Minister Tony Clement and former Magna International CEO Belinda Stronach. He is supported by a majority of delegates from all regions except Quebec and Atlantic Canada. Harper was pivotal in negotiating the merger of his Canadian Alliance with the Progressive Conservatives to form the new Conservative Party. He had run for the leadership on his record as Alliance leader and his success in uniting the country's right. Detractors fear that under Harper the Conservatives will be unable to establish strong support in central and eastern Canada.

22 March
BSE

Prime Minister Paul Martin announces nearly $1 billion in new aid for Canadian farmers. Most funding will go to cattle farmers affected by BSE, the rest being directed to specific issues such as drought and pests as well as to offsetting shortfalls in funding for existing farming programs. Martin dismisses suggestions that the timing of the announcement reflects plans for a spring election.

23 March
Finance

The federal government, facing lower than expected growth and fallout from the sponsorship scandal, releases a cautious budget for 2004 that follows through on previous commitments but establishes few new ones. A promised $2 billion one-time health-care transfer to the provinces is included, as well as a municipal GST exemption worth $7 billion over ten years. Also covered are military tax exemptions, postsecondary education financing, and infrastructure investment. Critics of the budget include Assembly of First Nations Grand Chief Phil Fontaine, who fears that the lack of new funding for Aboriginal concerns may reflect low Liberal commitment to First Nations. Provincial leaders note the lack of permanent health-care funding increases or equalization reforms.

24 March
Alberta

Ralph Klein's government tables its eleventh consecutive balanced budget. Highlights include $1 billion in debt reduction, $142 million on corporate tax cuts, an 8.4 percent increase in health-care spending, a 5.7 percent increase in education spending, and $900 million in new provincial building project expenditures. Budget figures are based on the expectation of 3.6 percent economic growth and an $11 per barrel decrease in oil prices. Opposition parties accuse the government of deliberately underestimating revenue so as to facilitate election period spending.

30 March
Public Transit

The federal, Ontario, and Toronto governments announce a $1.05 billion funding agreement for the Toronto Transit Commission (TTC). The money, to be received over five years, will be spent primarily replacing old subway cars, streetcars, and buses. Toronto Mayor David Miller says the agreement reflects the increased commitment to municipalities by the federal and provincial governments. Some, however, feel the funding is not enough to bring the TTC into good repair.

30 March
Quebec

Finance Minister Yves Séguin tables a balanced budget for the 2004–5 fiscal year. Included are $200 million in tax cuts, $547 for the establishment of a child assistance program, $243 million in supplements for low-income earners, a 5.1 percent increase in health care spending, and a 2.7 percent increase in education spending. Opposition parties note that $880 million in government assets needed to be sold to balance the budget, as well as the fact that tax relief amounts do not offset levies introduced by the government at the beginning of its tenure.

5 April
Energy

The final report of the Canada–U.S. task force investigating the August 2003 Great Lakes power outage is released. The report concludes that the blackout, which affected nearly 50 million people in Ontario and eight U.S. states, could have been prevented through stronger regulatory rules on energy suppliers and more effective enforcement of existing standards. Responding to the task force's analysis, Natural Resources Minister John Efford emphasizes the need for the federal government to work with the provinces to implement the recommendations of the report, noting that while the federal government and the National

Energy Board manage energy exports, the provinces are responsible for power supply regulation.

6 April
Aboriginal Peoples

The Government of Newfoundland and Labrador vows to end the slaughter of Red Wine River caribou by Quebec Innu hunters. The Innu are protesting the unwillingness of the Newfoundland and Labrador government to recognize their Labrador territory land claim, and they assert that the protest hunt will continue until negotiations are held. Red Wine River caribou are classified as endangered both provincially and federally, with the smallest herd numbering fewer than a hundred animals. The Innu Nation of Labrador's call for its Quebec counterpart to stop the hunt has also been ignored.

16 April
Health Care

Prime Minister Paul Martin, in a Toronto speech, outlines his government's plan to "fix health care for a generation." He promises reforms that include the hiring of more doctors and nurses, reducing waiting times and lists, better home care, and the creation of a pharmacare program covering catastrophic drug costs. He assures provincial leaders of his commitment to achieving a long-term funding agreement towards the pursuit of these objectives, conditional on the provinces' commitment to the pursuit of a sustainable, universal health-care system. The premiers offer cautious approval of Martin's plan but warn the federal government not to impinge on provincial jurisdiction. Alberta Premier Ralph Klein remains committed to his government's planned reforms, including user fees, privatization, and extra services for wealthy patients.

19 April
Aboriginal Peoples

More than seventy Aboriginal leaders meet with Prime Minister Paul Martin and numerous MPs at a summit in Ottawa. Both sides, in describing the results of the meeting, use words such as "extraordinary". Martin promises a new era of collaboration with Aboriginal leaders, including a restructuring of the Department of Indian Affairs and an updating of the *Indian Act*. He calls these reforms steps towards an eventual goal of Aboriginal self-government.

19 April
BSE

U.S. officials expand the list of cuts of Canadian beef exportable to American markets. A case of mad cow disease found on an Alberta farm in May 2003 led the United States to close its border to Canadian beef exports; prior to this announcement, the only reopening of the U.S. markets to Canadian beef, in August 2003, was limited to selected boneless cuts. Canadian cattle producers will now be able to export to the United States a wider list of beef products, including ground beef and bone-in cuts. Canadian officials are encouraged by the announcement but will continue to push for a complete lifting of restrictions on beef exports.

23 April
Ontario

Speaking in Markham, Ontario, Premier Dalton McGuinty proposes wide-ranging bilateral provincial-federal agreements on issues such as health-care funding and immigration should negotiations with other provinces not prove effective. McGuinty hopes for a leadership role for Ontario in achieving consensus between the provinces and Ottawa, given the positional proximity of the province with the federal government compared with other provinces. He emphasizes the importance of immediate long-term solutions. McGuinty's address follows Premier Jean Charest's comment the previous day that "pan-Canadian" health-care agreements are not necessary for reform.

29–30 April
Sport

A Canadian policy against doping in sport is adopted at a federal, provincial, and territorial conference of ministers responsible for sport, recreation, and fitness. The policy, which reaffirms Canada's commitment to international leadership in combatting drug use in sport, will ensure Canadian compliance with the World Anti-Doping Code, set to come into effect in 2004. The ministers further discuss possible measures to increase participation in and funding for physical activity.

30 April
Canada–U.S.
Relations

Paul Martin makes his first official visit to the White House. He obtains a commitment from President George W. Bush that the United States will drop its ban on Canadian exports of live cattle "as soon as possible," though no exact date is given. The two also discuss such issues as the ongoing softwood lumber conflict, continental security, and Canadian contributions to the reconstruction of Iraq. The tone of Martin's meetings with American officials is described as positive, particularly given the coldness of relations between Bush and the former prime minister, Jean Chrétien.

4 May
Fisheries

Federal Fisheries Minister Geoff Regan announces a limited reopening of cod fishing in the Gulf of St Lawrence. Newfoundland and Quebec fishermen will be allowed to fish 6,500 tonnes of cod in designated areas of the gulf. The announcement is welcomed by fishermen and their unions, many of whom were left unemployed by the cod moratorium imposed in April 2004. Scientists are outraged, however, given the continued scarcity of cod in the gulf. Noting the likelihood of an upcoming federal election, they deem that the reopening is compromising science in favour of political gain.

6 May
Fisheries

Federal officers cite a Portuguese ship for illegally fishing the protected American plaice flounder off the Grand Banks of Newfoundland. The move is touted by Prime Minister Paul Martin as a first step in a Canadian crackdown on the fishing of low-stock fish by foreign vessels. Newfoundlanders have been calling for such a crackdown for many years. Since international treaties allow prosecution of vessels in international waters only by their home countries, however, the owners of the ship cannot be brought to justice without Portuguese cooperation; as a result, critics call the ship's indictment little more than unenforceable rhetoric and electioneering.

10–11 May
Sponsorship Program

Charles Guité, former head of the federal sponsorship program, and Jean Brault, founder and head of Groupaction, are charged with six fraud-related counts by the RCMP. Both plead not guilty and are released on bail. The following day, the Liberals use their committee majority to suspend the parliamentary inquiry into the scandal. They seek to review the accumulated testimony and write an interim report. The suspension of proceedings will become a formal end to the probe if, as anticipated, an election is called before the committee reconvenes. Opposition MPs are furious, calling the suspension an attempt to hide the scandal's exposure in a pre-election period. They note that more than ninety potential witnesses have yet to pass before the committee.

12 May *Nova Scotia*	The federal and Nova Scotia governments announce a $400 million plan to attempt to clean the tar ponds of Sydney, Nova Scotia. The ponds, which contain a million tonnes of tar left over from the production of coke during the twentieth century, are filled with toxic material and have been linked to health problems, including cancer and liver disease. Although more than $100 million has already been ineffectually invested in the cleaning of the ponds, officials insist this effort will be successful.
15 May *Political Parties*	The Bloc Québécois is the first party to officially unveil its platform for the upcoming election. The party focuses on five issues: democracy, sustainable development, demographic shifts, services for Quebecers, and the internationalization of Quebec's voice. Though the platform contains no direct discussion of sovereignty, Bloc leader Gilles Duceppe insists that the goal of an independent Quebec remains the ultimate objective of the party.
18 May *Ontario*	The 2005 provincial budget is tabled in the Ontario legislature. It introduces an Ontario health premium, a levy deducted from wages by employers towards improvements in health care. Including revenue generated from the premium as well as other sources such as increased alcohol and tobacco taxes, the government expects to invest $4.8 billion in new health-care funding over the next four years. Opposition parties criticize the government for breaking its election promise not to raise taxes. They note that the new premium, despite not being formally called a tax, bears all the characteristics of taxation. Other budget highlights include a $2.1 billion increase in education funding and a two-thirds reduction in the provincial deficit.
20 May *Gun Control*	Deputy Prime Minister Anne McLellan announces plans to reform the federal gun registry. If re-elected, the Liberal government will eliminate fees for registering firearms and cap the program's expenses at $25 million per year. McLellan further outlines proposed stiffer penalties for firearms-related crimes. Critics deride the proposals, saying the government would be better off scrapping the registry entirely.

20 May
Political Parties

The Green Party of Canada unveils its platform for the upcoming federal election. Issues discussed include increases in gasoline taxes, rebates on the purchase of fuel-efficient vehicles, and promises to not run deficits without a referendum-approved mandate. Leader Jim Harris, noting the consistent 5 percent party support recorded in polls, boldly predicts that the party will receive one million votes and be represented in the next parliament.

21 May
Municipalities

Eighty-nine formerly independent municipalities are granted the right to hold referendums on megacity demerger. To force a referendum, 10 percent of eligible voters in each former municipality must sign a register over the course of two days. Voters in the former municipalities are angered by the undemocratic manner in which the megacities were created; the former Parti Québécois provincial government had ignored all demonstrations and indications of public will in pursuing its amalgamations. Referendums will take place on 20 June.

23 May
Federal Election

Prime Minister Paul Martin asks Governor General Adrienne Clarkson to dissolve Parliament and officially calls an election for 28 June. Martin defines the election as a choice between visions of Canada, taking direct aim at the Conservatives by calling on Canadians to reject proposals that replicate American values. He highlights the accomplishments achieved over three terms of Liberal government, including seven balanced budgets and $52 billion in debt repayment.

The opposition parties are equally quick out of the gates. Conservative leader Stephen Harper accuses the Liberals of running on a "campaign of fear" against his party to hide their failures while in government, particularly the sponsorship scandal. New Democratic Party leader Jack Layton contrasts the ideological distinctiveness of his party's platform with the similarity of the Liberals and Conservatives. The Bloc Québécois, downplaying sovereignty, calls on Quebecers to allow it to defend, in Parliament, Quebec values such as justice and tolerance.

25 May *Health Care*	In a campaign speech in Cobourg, Ontario, Prime Minister Paul Martin outlines his party's plans to improve health care if re-elected. Calling health his party's top priority, he commits $9 billion for reducing waiting times, hiring more doctors and nurses, and creating a national home-care program. He asserts that his plan can be achieved without increased taxes or premiums. Conservative leader Stephen Harper, speaking in Fredericton, New Brunswick, responds by noting that funding problems were created by Liberal governments in the first place. He further questions the source of the funds, noting that Finance Minister Ralph Goodale was unable to provide funding increases in the federal budget not two months earlier.
26 May *Aboriginal Peoples*	Inuit vote to accept a historic land claim agreement to gain limited self-government over a 15,800 km territory in Northern Labrador. The Inuit will be granted outright ownership of the land, natural resource rights, law-making abilities, and control over education and social services. The provincial and federal governments must now ratify the agreement.
26 May *Political Parties*	The New Democratic Party unveils its election platform. Its promises include $29 billion in new health-care funding over five years, an additional $9.9 billion for the national child benefit, and an increase in the basic personal tax exemption to $15,000. He insists that an NDP government would consistently balance its budget, imposing tax increases on high-income earners and corporations as well as implementing of an inheritance tax to finance his proposals.
28 May *Political Parties*	At a meeting of the Federation of Canadian Municipalities, Prime Minster Paul Martin announces his party's proposed New Deal for Cities. The plan includes a 5 percent share of federal gas taxes, worth $2 billion, and $1.5 billion in subsidies for housing growth. Responding to criticisms, Martin insists that the money will come without conditions. Many mayors are disappointed that full funding under the plan will come only in five years.
2 June *Ontario*	Fulfilling an election promise, Premier Dalton McGuinty introduces a bill to the legislature to set fixed dates for

provincial elections. Under the proposal, Ontarians will vote on the first Thursday in October every four years, starting on 4 October 2007. Following British Columbia, Ontario will become the second province to implement fixed election dates. The plan seeks to reduce voter apathy and increase electoral turnout.

3 June
Political Parties

The Liberal Party officially unveils its election platform, building on previous announcements made regarding health care and federal-municipal relations. The party promises $28 billion in new spending over five years while consistently maintaining balanced budgets. Proposals include a national child-care plan based on the Quebec $7-a-day model, expansion of the Canadian Armed Forces, and increased promotion of wind power as an alternative energy source.

5 June
Political Parties

The Conservative Party is the last of the major parties to unveil its election platform. The party proposes $58 billion over five years in tax cuts and spending increases, notably with respect to health care and the military. Though his promises cost twice as much as those proposed by the Liberals, leader Stephen Harper insists his plan is feasible without running a deficit.

14–15 June
Federal Election

The two leaders' debates take place in Ottawa. In the French-language debate, Bloc Québécois leader Gilles Duceppe launches stinging attacks on both the Conservatives and the Liberals. Insisting as he has over the course of the campaign that the focus of the election should not be sovereignty, Duceppe instigates a heated exchange with Prime Minister Paul Martin regarding the sponsorship scandal and then challenges Conservative leader Stephen Harper on his party's stance with respect to Iraq, social issues, and development. Duceppe blames the Conservatives' inability to make electoral inroads in Quebec on their party's ideological disjuncture with Quebec's interests. Recognizing the gains being made by the Bloc in the polls, both Martin and Harper attempt to paint the party as an irrelevant protest movement.

In the English-language debate, the three opposition leaders repeatedly attack Martin on his government's record, most notably with respect to the sponsorship scandal. Harper criticizes Martin for having called an election before the release of the results into the scandal's investigation, despite promises not to do so, and calls the Liberal platform a campaign of fear designed to hide the party's record in government. Harper takes heat of his own, however, from the other three leaders on his party's stance on moral issues. New Democratic Party leader Jack Layton attacks Harper on his promises to allow free votes should questions of abortion or gay marriage be brought before Parliament, and Martin presses the Conservative leader to tell Canadians whether he would use the notwithstanding clause to overrule court rulings in favour of gay marriage.

17 June
Aboriginal Peoples

The Saskatchewan government suspends all subsidies to the Métis Nation of Saskatchewan (MNS) following allegations of electoral irregularities. The MNS election of 26 May was marred by claims of voters turned away at polling stations and missing ballot boxes. Some fear that funding suspensions will inhibit dialogue between the MNS and governments without strengthening the nation's electoral structures.

18 June
Alberta

In a defining moment of the election campaign, Prime Minister Paul Martin calls on Premier Ralph Klein to announce his proposed health-care reforms before the 28 June federal election. Klein intends to outline his sought reforms publicly on 30 June, two days after the election. Martin accuses Klein of wanting to wait for the election results in the hope of a Conservative win, and he muses that Stephen Harper would allow Klein to violate the main tenets of the *Canada Health Act*. Klein responds by accusing Martin of fear-mongering; Harper insists he would expect Klein to uphold the principles of medicare if he becomes prime minister. Martin's accusation will be a cloud over Harper for the duration of the election.

20 June
Municipalities

Thirty-two municipalities win the right to demerge from megacities in the Province of Quebec. Referendums on demergers were held in eighty nine former municipalities across the province; to demerge, municipalities needed to obtain a majority of votes cast as well as a 3 percent voter turnout. Municipal mergers had taken place in 2002 under the Parti Québécois government; the Liberal Party had

platformed in 2003 on allowing municipalities the opportunity to regain their independence. The new cities will
become officially demerged on 1 January 2006.

21 June
Aboriginal Peoples

The Commission on First Nations and Métis Peoples and
Justice Reform releases its final report, *Legacy of Hope:
An Agenda for Chance*. Created in 2001 following the
surfacing of allegations of systemic discrimination in Saskatchewan's policing in 2000, the commission looks to
examine the relationship between the provincial justice
system and First Nations peoples and to find ways to incorporate Aboriginal culture into judicial structures.
Included among the report's 122 recommendations are an
expansion of the Aboriginal court worker program, creation of an Aboriginal advisory committee to advise the
government, and prioritized use of alternative punishments
to jail. Saskatchewan Justice Minister Frank Quennell says
his government will "wholeheartedly endorse and adopt"
the broad themes of the report.

21 June
Security

The public inquiry into the deportation of Maher Arar
begins in Ottawa. The inquiry seeks to establish the involvement of Canadian authorities in Arar's deportation
to Syria in September 2002 by the United States on the
suspicion of al-Qaeda connections. Arar denies having any
connections to terrorism. The federal government insists
that Canadian officials did not suggest Arar's deportation
to American authorities.

28 June
Federal Election

The results of the federal election give the Liberal Party a
fourth consecutive term in office, albeit in a minority government. Paul Martin's Liberals obtain 135 of a possible
308 seats, with the Conservatives taking 99, the Bloc
Québécois taking 54, the New Democratic Party taking
19, and one independent victory. Though the Liberals do
not preserve their majority, the results are surprising in
view of recent polls that had put the Liberals and Conservatives in a virtual dead heat. Martin calls his party's
loss of 42 seats a reflection of the need for his government to do better, but he insists that he will succeed in
making his minority government work. Though disap-
pointed, Conservative leader Stephen Harper promises to
hold the Liberals accountable after having increased his

party's size as the official opposition. Bloc Québécois leader Gilles Duceppe calls his party's showing a victory for Quebecers, while NDP leader Jack Layton is proud of his party's gains despite predictions of an even stronger showing. The Green Party makes a positive showing as well, receiving 4 percent of the popular vote and qualifying for federal funding as an official party.

30 June
Health Care

Alongside announcements of $700 million in new health-case funding, Premier Ralph Klein tables the Graydon Report on Health Care Funding, a set of recommendations made by a 2002 provincial health-care task force under Conservative MLA Gordon Graydon. The report calls for an increased private share of health-care expenses through the implementation of a health-care deductible and of increased health-care premiums. The premier was criticized for waiting until after the end of the federal election to release the report, a delay believed to have contributed to the decline in support for the Conservatives. Klein further alludes to plans for more radical change to health care in the province should his government win re-election in the fall, expressing a willingness to forge ahead even if his plans contravene the *Canada Health Act.*

7–9 July
Western Canada

The Annual Western Premiers' Conference is held in Inuvik, Northwest Territories. Unanimous support is expressed for the principles of the *Canada Health Act,* but the premiers insist that more money and flexibility is needed from the federal government to sustain the current system. The premiers foresee a window of eighteen months in which a new health-care agreement can be negotiated before another federal election can be expected. The Western Energy Alliance is created by the leaders to cooperate in developing and promoting the energy sector in the region. The premiers further call on the federal government to push for a reopening of the U.S. border for exports of Canadian beef and to create a comprehensive BSE recovery plan.

12 July
Alberta

Premier Ralph Klein announces a $3 billion addition to a debt-retirement account that will allow the province to pay off its provincial debt fully. Obligations will be repaid from the account as they mature in order to avoid penalties. The province will become the only one in Canada to be entirely debt-free.

13 July
Ontario

An inquiry begins into the 1995 shooting of Dudley George at Ipperwash Provincial Park. The long-awaited of hearings will investigate the death of George at the hands of the Ontario Provincial Police during a standoff over native claims to the land. The inquiry seeks to understand the decisions taken by the police and the provincial government leading to the shooting in the hope of preventing similar violence in similar clashes.

13–15 July
Telecommunications

The Canadian Radio and Telecommunications Commission refuses to renew the licence of CHOI-FM, a Quebec City "shock" radio station. The decision comes following continued complaints citing offensiveness and vulgarity despite warnings to clean up the station's broadcast content. CHOI becomes the sixth station, all Quebec-based, to be removed from the airwaves by the agency. Defenders of the station decry the decision as federal censorship and an attack on freedom of expression in Quebec.

Two days later, the CRTC approves nine new specialty channels for broadcast on Canadian cable television. Included is al-Jazeera, an Arab-language news station with a history of anti-Semitism. Despite the imposition of stringent content regulations, the station's approval dismays many Jewish communities. Members of Italian communities decry the exclusion of RAI International, an Italian-language specialty channel, from the newly approved stations. The decisions lead to controversy surrounding the proper role of the regulatory body.

14 July
Same-Sex Rights

A Yukon Supreme Court ruling changes the territory's common-law definition of marriage to include same-sex unions. Yukon joins Ontario, Quebec, and British Columbia among the jurisdictions allowing gay marriage.

20 July
Federal Politics

Prime Minister Paul Martin unveils a thirty-nine-person cabinet. Many top positions are left unchanged, including that of Ralph Goodale as minister of finance, Anne McLellan as deputy prime minister and minister of public safety, Irwin Cotler as justice minister, and Reginald Alcock as president of the Treasury Board. Eight first-time ministers are appointed, including Ken Dryden (Social Development), Ujjal Dosanjh (Health), Tony Valeri (house leader), and David Emerson (Industry). Shifted ministers include Pierre Pettigrew (from Health to Foreign Affairs), Lucienne Robillard (from Industry to Intergovernmental Affairs and president of the Privy Council), and Liza Frulla (from Social Development to Heritage). Four former cabinet ministers are excluded, including David Anderson and Denis Coderre. Sixteen of the ministers come from Ontario, eight from Quebec, six from Atlantic Canada, five from British Columbia, three from the Prairies, and one from the Northwest Territories.

22 July
Federal Politics

Stephen Harper unveils a forty-person shadow cabinet. Many top faces are parliamentary veterans, including Peter MacKay (deputy leader), Stockwell Day (foreign affairs critic), Monte Solberg (finance critic), and John Reynolds (house leader). Newcomers include Belinda Stronach (trade critic), Jim Prentice (Indian affairs critic), Peter Van Loen (social resources critic), and Steven Fletcher (health critic). Numerous former shadow ministers who made hard-line comments against gay rights and abortion during the election campaign, including Randy White, Cheryl Gallant, and Rob Merrifield, are notably absent. The shadow cabinet includes thirty-two men and eight women. Twenty-six shadow ministers are from western Canada, nine from Ontario, three from Atlantic Canada, and two from Quebec.

28-30 July
Council of the Federation

The premiers meet in Niagara-on-the-Lake. The primary focus of discussions is health care; looking towards their September meeting with the prime minister, the leaders remain committed to achieving a long-term federal-provincial health-care funding and renewal agreement. In an unprecedented proposal, they call for a national pharmacare program managed by the federal government with Quebec opt-out; such a plan, they note, would free up provincial health-care funds and avoid any need for privatization. Though the proposal would cost the federal government billions, pharmacare has been a federal Liberal platform issue since 1997. Other discussions between the premiers include the implementation of the Workplan on Internal Trade and of the National Diamond Strategy, the furthering of environmental initiatives, promotion of literacy, and interprovincial emergency assistance.

3 August
BSE

An auditor-general's report reveals that the Canada-Alberta BSE Recovery Program has provided more benefit to large meat-packing firms than to farmers. The plan, created following the May 2003 discovery of mad cow disease in Alberta and jointly funded by the federal and provincial governments, paid assistance to producers only for a short period and only on the slaughter of animals, causing a flood of supply which depressed the price of raw cattle by more than 60 percent. Alberta provincial officials claim they recognized the flaws in the federal program but were forced to accept it, given the urgency of the crisis.

11 August
Alberta

The provincial government committee for the re-evaluation of Alberta's place in Canada, led by Ian McClelland, releases its final report, *Strengthening Alberta's Role in Confederation*. The committee had been referred to as the "firewall committee" by opposition parties. The report dismisses calls for radical change such as separation, independent tax collection, and opting out of the Canada Pension Plan, but it endorses reforms to transfer payments, policing, and intergovernmental communications towards increased provincial autonomy. It further emphasizes the need to push for Senate reform by all possible means.

12 August
Health Care

Prime Minister Paul Martin responds to the Council of the Federation's proposal for a national pharmacare program. He calls the plan out of line with the priorities of Canadians, emphasizing home care and shorter waiting lists. Martin extends his government's support only for universal coverage of "catastrophic" drug costs. The premiers caution the prime minister not to dismiss the plan before its formal presentation at the forthcoming First Ministers' Meeting in September.

13 August
Sponsorship Program

André Ouellet resigns as president of Canada Post. The resignation comes as Revenue Minister John McCallum is considering Ouellet's dismissal following allegations of excessive spending and questionable hiring practises. Though Ouellet insists on his innocence, he asserts that political pressures relating to the continued sponsorship fallout would have inevitably led to his dismissal.

23 August
Municipalities

The Ontario government signs an agreement with the Association of Municipalities of Ontario binding the province to consultation with the association when proposing changes that would affect municipal budgets. Premier Dalton McGuinty hails the agreement as "historic," calling it recognition of municipalities as a full-fledged level of government. Toronto Mayor David Miller is infuriated, however, threatening to pull his city out of the association if the deal prevents his city from negotiating directly with Queen's Park. McGuinty responds by insisting that big cities will continue to have direct relations with the province.

24 August
Justice

Justice Louise Charron and Justice Rosalie Abella, both of the Ontario Court of Appeal, are nominated to fill vacancies on the Supreme Court of Canada. Despite allegations of making selections based on criteria such as gender and support for same-sex marriage, Justice Minister Irwin Cotler insists both choices were made purely on merit. While the selections will be subjected to committee review, the committee will have no veto power. Cabinet will approve the selections following the committee's review.

29 August
Sport

Canada finishes with twelve medals in the Athens Summer Olympics, tied with Bulgaria for nineteenth place overall. Canadian athletes bring home three gold medals, six silver, and three bronze. The Canadian Olympic Committee decries the poor showing as a reflection of the need for increased funding, and Jacques Rogge, International Olympic Committee president, promises to visit federal officials to petition for greater support. Minister of State for Sport Stephen Owen, however, insists that no new money will be forthcoming.

30 August
Quebec

A motion to force a leadership review in the Parti Québécois fails. Party leader Bernard Landry had faced heavy internal party criticism, with many in his party claiming he has been ineffective in promoting the sovereigntist cause. Some, including the former premier

Jacques Parizeau, have called for the party to run in the next provincial election on a platform of sovereignty declaration if elected as the government. Landry's detractors threaten to challenge him again if he does not advance the cause of the party substantially within one year.

1–2 September *Council of the* *Federation*	The premiers meet once again in preparation of their upcoming 13–16 September meeting with the prime minister. Seeking to avoid having federal officials unilaterally set the terms of the meeting, they compose a draft agenda and urge the prime minister to respect it. They reiterate their calls for a national pharmacare program, emphasizing the importance of such a program by quoting the Liberal Party platform from the June federal election. Federal officials continue to insist that universal drug coverage is both not a top priority and not the extent of election promises.
7 September *Sponsorship* *Program*	A long-awaited public inquiry begins into the management of the federal sponsorship program. The inquiry, led by Quebec Justice John Gomery, seeks to evaluate why the program was created, how it was managed, what the money was spent on, and how similar scandals can be avoided in future. The inquiry follows a parliamentary public accounts committee investigation into the program that was abruptly ended just before the June federal election. Hundreds of witnesses, both from government and from outside government, are expected to be called to testify before the Gomery Commission.
10 September *BSE*	Federal Agriculture Minister Andy Mitchell unveils a $488 million aid package for cattle farmers. The plan's objectives are to increase domestic slaughter capacity and expansion of foreign markets as well as to provide assistance to farmers until long-term structural market changes are achieved. The Alberta government will further contribute $230 million in new funds to help achieve the program's goals.
13–16 September *First Ministers*	A historic First Ministers' Meeting is held in Ottawa. The events begin with a meeting between the first ministers and Aboriginal leaders in the hope of improving health provision for First Nations people. They agree to develop

a blueprint plan for the improvement of Aboriginal health care for review within one year. They create the Aboriginal Health Transition Fund for the development of specialized health-care delivery mechanisms for Aboriginals, the Aboriginal Health Human Resources Initiative to encourage the training of Aboriginal health-care providers, and various targeted programs to address specific health-care issues in Aboriginal communities. The ministers further agree to hold a First Ministers' Meeting in the near future specifically dedicated to Aboriginal affairs.

The following days are dedicated to general discussion of health care. In an unprecedented fashion, many of the sessions are televised live. After three days of difficult negotiations, a $41.2 billion, ten-year deal is struck between the first ministers to increase federal transfers to the provinces for health-care delivery. Funding will be allocated through increases in the Canada Health Transfer, the Wait Times Reduction Fund, and federal investments in medical equipment and Aboriginal health. The Health Council of Canada is created to oversee and report on health-care provision and standards. Though the deal is widely applauded, some critics are dismayed that change within the plan comes almost exclusively through funding increases, doing little to address structural problems in health-care provision.

A separate agreement is made for the Province of Quebec. Among other distinctions from the main plan, Quebec is granted the right to set its own objectives and priorities with respect to issues such as waiting times, home care, and acute care. The province is further exempted from oversight by the Health Council of Canada. The side agreement, entitled Asymmetric Federalism That Respects Quebec's Jurisdiction, is touted by Prime Minister Paul Martin as a means of strengthening the Canadian federation, but it is criticized by some as preferential treatment for Quebec.

16 September
Same-Sex Rights

A court ruling makes Manitoba the fifth Canadian jurisdiction to recognize and license same-sex marriages, joining Ontario, Quebec, British Columbia, and Yukon. The Manitoba case is the first provincial same-sex marriage court challenge that the federal government has not opposed.

16 September *Sport*	The National Hockey League imposes a lockout on its players. The league's collective bargaining agreement expired at 10 p.m. the previous day; league players and owners are deeply divided in negotiations for a new agreement. Team owners, claiming large consistent losses, are demanding a cap on player salaries, while players refuse to accept any such measure. Neither side is optimistic about the possibility of a quick resolution to the dispute.
18 September *Municipalities*	The mayors of Canada's largest cities, meeting at a summit in Toronto, soften their demands for funding through federal fuel taxes. The mayors call for an immediate 2.5 cent municipal share of federal fuel taxes rising to 5 cents by 2007 (down from earlier calls for an immediate 5 cent share). Federal Minister of State for Infrastructure and Communities John Godfrey rejects the mayor's calls, however, saying that federal commitments to fuel tax redistribution amount only to half the amount demanded by the mayors. Speaking at the summit, Ontario Premier Dalton McGuinty commits the provincial government to reviewing the *City of Toronto Act* towards giving Toronto more independence in managing municipal affairs. Both provincial and city governments will participate in the review.
19 September *Ontario*	John Tory is elected leader of the Progressive Conservative Party of Ontario. Tory, seen as a more centrist choice than his opponents Jim Flaherty and Frank Klees, is expected to move the party away from the hard-right policies of Mike Harris and the Common Sense Revolution. Tory previously served as chief executive of Rogers Cable and ran unsuccessfully in the 2003 Toronto mayoral election.
24 September *Same-Sex Rights*	The Nova Scotia Supreme Court rules that banning same-sex marriage is unconstitutional. Nova Scotia thus becomes the sixth Canadian jurisdiction to recognize and license gay marriages. Provincial Justice Minister Michael Baker calls opposing same-sex marriage futile, given the precedents set by rulings in other provinces.
30 September *Governor General*	Adrienne Clarkson's term as governor general is extended to September 2005. Both Prime Minister Paul Martin and Opposition Leader Stephen Harper express their support

for Clarkson's ability and impartiality in overseeing the newly elected minority government. Critics, however, are dismayed by the reappointment, given Clarkson's history of lavish spending.

5 October
Throne Speech

The minority Liberal government narrowly averts the defeat of the Speech from the Throne that opens the thirty-eighth Parliament of Canada. Priorities expressed in the speech include debt repayment, equalization reform, health standards under the Health Council of Canada, fuel tax sharing with municipalities, Kyoto Accord implementation, and consideration of democratic reform. The Bloc Québécois and the Conservatives threaten to vote against the speech unless amendments to it are made in accordance with their requests. An agreement is ultimately reached with the Bloc, under which a proposed amendment is changed to remove a reference to Quebec Premier Jean Charest and to replace the term "fiscal imbalance" with "financial pressures some call the fiscal imbalance." The support of the Bloc gives the Liberals the majority it needs to ensure passage of the speech. A Conservative amendment is later accepted by the Liberals to make support for the speech unanimous across the parties.

16–17 October
Health Care

The Annual Conference of Federal-Provincial-Territorial Ministers of Health is held in Vancouver. Following a reaffirmation of the commitment of governments to the principles emerging from the Special Meeting of First Ministers and Aboriginal Leaders to improve Aboriginal health, the ministers devote their attention to implementation of the first ministers' Ten-Year Plan to Strengthen Health Care. Beyond reaffirming the commitment to improve waiting times and access as per the plan, they set up a ministerial task force on pharmaceuticals and agree to work towards the establishment of a set of health goals and targets. Other initiatives emerging from the meeting include the Canadian Health Technology Strategy for the effective use of technology in health-care provision.

26 October
Equalization

An agreement is reached between the first ministers to reform the Equalization and Territorial Financing Formula programs. The proposed changes will increase payments by $33 billion over ten years, including an immediate $13 billion increase and a 3.5 percent growth rate thereafter. A panel review of equalization payment allocation is further launched to examine inequities in current methods of funding distribution and to make recommendations. Support for the proposals is not unanimous, however. Newfoundland and Labrador Premier Danny Williams boycotted the meeting because of the conditions that Prime Minister Paul Martin seeks to place on his province's share of oil and gas royalties.

27–29 October
Northern Canada

The Northern Development Ministers' Forum is held in Chibougamau, Quebec. Topics discussed by the ministers include updating the forum's 2004–6 Action Plan, northern recruitment and retention, and transportation infrastructure. The ministers approve *Focus North*, an information package designed to promote the importance of Canada's North. Although Minister of Indian and Northern Affairs Andy Scott is not in attendance, the ministers are satisfied with the achievements of the meeting and look forward to meeting with Scott and receiving his support for the discussed principles and initiatives.

1 November
Aboriginal Peoples

A report commissioned by the Saskatchewan government on the integrity of the May 2004 Métis Nation of Saskatchewan (MNS) presidential election is released. The report confirms allegations of ineptitude and organized efforts to subvert the democratic process. In response to the report, the province announces its intention to cut off all intergovernmental relations with the MNS pending a new presidential election with independent scrutiny. The province will also continue to freeze just over $400,000 in provincial MNS funding, which was withheld during the investigation. Dwayne Roth, winner of the May election, views the government's actions as attempts to undermine Métis hunting rights and land claims. MNS presidential challengers, however, applaud the findings of the report.

2 November
Child Care

The Federal-Provincial-Territorial Meeting of Ministers Responsible for Social Services takes place in Ottawa in pursuit of a national early learning and child-care system. Agreement is reached on the fundamental principles of the plan, including quality, universal inclusiveness, accessibility, and a developmental focus. The ministers hope to finalize the agreement in early 2005. The federal government has pledged $5 billion in transfers to the provinces over five years to fund the plan, contingent on agreement and on provincial compliance with the program principles. Claude Béchard, Quebec family welfare minister, insists that federal monies be transferred unconditionally.

5 November
Same-Sex Rights

A family court judge in Saskatchewan rules in support of government recognition of same-sex marriage, declaring that refusal of marriage licences to same-sex couples is a violation of the *Charter of Rights and Freedoms*. Saskatchewan joins five other provinces and one territory in granting same-sex marriages. Neither the provincial nor the federal government has challenged the court application.

12 November
Education

Canadian Parents for French, a volunteer network of French-language education advocates, releases a national study entitled *The State of French Second Language Instruction*. The report finds that only one in ten students continues French-language studies through to grade 12. Enrolment in French-language programs is shown to be declining in all provinces except Prince Edward Island. The federal government has established the goal of doubling the number of bilingual young Canadians by 2013, and $350 million over four years was committed to the cause in 2003, but only Ontario has reached a funding agreement with Ottawa on the issue.

16 November
Finance

The federal government, in an economic and fiscal update, announces a projected surplus of $8.9 billion for the 2004–5 fiscal year – more than double the $4 billion surplus originally forecast by the government. The update forecasts total federal surpluses of $61 billion over the next five years, as well as further savings of $12 billion through bureaucratic expenditure reviews. The government will set aside $18 billion of projected funds to debt repayment and $13.5 billion as an "economic prudence" reserve in case of unexpected shocks, leaving the remaining funds for program spending. To the dismay of critics, significant tax cuts are ruled out by the government as a possible destination for surpluses. Critics further decry the continued unexpectedly high surpluses of the federal government, alleging intentional underestimation.

18 November
Political Parties

Missisauga-Erindale MP Carolyn Parrish is removed from the federal Liberal caucus by Prime Minister Paul Martin. The dismissal is the result of a year-long series of inflammatory public comments and actions by the MP, notably attacks on American policy and on the Iraq war. Parrish had further undermined the prime minister's leadership by affirming publicly in an interview that she "wouldn't shed a tear" if the Liberals lost the next election and Martin was forced to resign. The loss of Parrish reduces the Liberal minority government to 134 seats. The Conservatives hold 99 seats, the Bloc Québécois holds 54, and the NDP holds 19.

22 November
Alberta

Ralph Klein is elected premier of Alberta for the fourth consecutive time. Klein's Progressive Conservatives win 61 legislature seats, down 13 from the party's total on entering the election. The provincial Liberals take 17 seats, the NDP wins 4, and the Alberta Alliance Party finishes with one. The PC campaign was low key, focusing primarily on the government's record and on the continued prosperity of the province rather than on concrete promises. Opposition parties view the reduced Conservative majority as evidence of a desire for change in the province. Klein has said that this will be his last election campaign.

Alongside the general provincial election, a vote is held to elect senators-in-waiting for the province. Consistent with calls for Senate reform, including election of representatives, the vote is seen as a popular recommendation for filling three vacant Alberta Senate seats. Prime Minister Paul Martin has previously stated his intention to disregard the results of the election in choosing Senate nominees. Two previous elections of senators-in-waiting have been held in the province, with only one senator-in-waiting, Stan Waters, ultimately receiving nomination to the Senate.

22 November
Immigration

Federal Ethics Commissioner Bernard Shapiro launches an investigation into the circumstances surrounding the granting to Alina Balaican of a ministerial permit to stay in Canada by federal Immigration Minister Judy Sgro. Federal opposition MPs allege the permit was granted in recognition of the involvement of Balaican and her husband in Sgro's re-election campaign in Toronto. Sgro insists the permit was granted on humanitarian grounds.

30 November –
1 December
Canada–U.S.
Relations

U.S. President George W. Bush makes his first official visit to Canada. Although Bush had previously attended two summits in Canada, he had not previously made an official visit. A planned May 2003 visit had been cancelled following former Prime Minister Jean Chrétien's decision not to support the U.S.-led invasion of Iraq. Prime Minister Paul Martin meets Bush in Ottawa on 30 November to discuss issues including joint security, foreign policy, and beef exports, with Bush pledging on the final issue to act to expedite the reopening of American borders to Canadian cattle. In a public address the following day in Halifax, Bush outlines his government's foreign policy intentions and asks for Canadian support in the "war on terror" and on ballistic missile defence.

6 December
Aboriginal Peoples

The Government of Newfoundland and Labrador ratifies the Labrador Inuit Land Claims Agreement. The agreement grants the Inuit numerous community government rights as well as ownership of 15,800 square kilometres of land. The Labrador Inuit Association approved the agreement in May; only federal approval remains before the agreement becomes law. The Métis people of Labrador, however, stage a protest on the steps of the provincial assembly building, fearing that the agreement will hinder their attempts to reach a land claims agreement.

9 December
Same-Sex Rights

Ruling on a series of non-binding federal government questions, the Supreme Court defends the federal government as the sole arbiter of marriage rights in Canada. The ruling, in affirming marriage to be within federal jurisdiction, prevents provincial governments from using the notwithstanding clause in response to proposed federal same-sex marriage legislation. Alberta Premier Ralph Klein had previously threatened to use the clause should the federal government implement legislation redefining marriage to include same-sex couples. The ruling also defends the right of religious institutions opposed to same-sex marriage to refuse to perform them. The Supreme Court declines, however, to answer the question of whether restricting marriage to opposite-sex couples is unconstitutional.

21 December *Aboriginal Peoples*	Closing arguments conclude in the Samson Cree First Nation court case. The band is suing the federal government for $1.4 billion, alleging fifty years of mismanagement of oil and gas revenues. The trial has been one of the longest Aboriginal lawsuits in Canadian history, including 365 days of trial. It has also been one of the most expensive, the combined spending of the two sides exceeding $100 million. The case's ruling is expected to set a new precedent for the way in which Aboriginal oil and gas assets are treated in Canada. Lawyers for the band are already claiming partial victory; in a 17 December interim ruling, Justice Max Teitelbaum ordered that of $360 million in oil revenues, which the federal government had been holding in a trust fund, be returned to the Cree.
21 December *Same-Sex Rights*	The Supreme Court of Newfoundland and Labrador rules that the exclusion of same-sex couples from marriage is unconstitutional. Through the ruling, Newfoundland and Labrador becomes the seventh province in Canada to recognize same-sex marriage. Provincial government officials will not challenge the ruling.
23 December *Newfoundland and Labrador*	Following fruitless negotiations with Finance Minister Ralph Goodale on the issue of offshore oil and gas royalties, Premier Danny Williams orders the removal of all Canadian flags from provincial government buildings. Williams seeks the exemption of such royalties from calculations of equalization payments as per a promise made by Paul Martin during the June election campaign. According to Williams, offers presented by the federal government provide only partial exemptions of offshore oil and gas royalties from equalization calculations. Prime Minister Paul Martin calls the flag removals disrespectful, blasting the premier for using a national symbol as a tool in political negotiations.

26 December   An Indian Ocean earthquake measuring 9.0 on the Rich-
Natural Disasters ter scale triggers a violent tsunami that hits more than a
                 dozen countries in South and Southeast Asia. More than
                 140,000 deaths are reported. The Government of Canada
                 commits $425 million over five years towards humanitar-
                 ian aid, rehabilitation, and reconstruction in the most
                 affected countries, particularly Indonesia and Sri Lanka.
                 A further $20 million is donated by provincial and territo-
                 rial governments, and more than $230 million is donated
                 by non-governmental organizations, employee unions, and
                 the private sector.

30 December   Reports of a second Canadian case of mad cow disease
BSE   are released by the Canadian Food Inspection Agency.
                 Cattle industry officials, though dismayed, are not sur-
                 prised by the finding, given the increased testing
                 implemented following the initial Canadian BSE case in
                 May 2003. Representatives from both the Canadian and
                 the American government insist that the case will not af-
                 fect the planned timetable for the reopening of the
                 American border to Canadian cattle exports. The previ-
                 ous day, American officials had announced 7 March 2005
                 as a target date for allowing imports into the United States
                 of Canadian cattle under the age of thirty months.

Chronology 2004: Index

Queen's Policy Studies
Recent Publications

The Queen's Policy Studies Series is dedicated to the exploration of major policy issues that confront governments in Canada and other western nations. McGill-Queen's University Press is the exclusive world representative and distributor of books in the series.

School of Policy Studies

Global Networks and Local Linkages: The Paradox of Cluster Development in an Open Economy, David A. Wolfe and Matthew Lucas (eds.), 2005
Paper ISBN 1-55339-047-4 Cloth ISBN 1-55339-048-2

Choice of Force: Special Operations for Canada, David Last and Bernd Horn (eds.), 2005
Paper ISBN 1-55339-044-X Cloth ISBN 1-55339-045-8

Force of Choice: Perspectives on Special Operations, Bernd Horn, J. Paul de B. Taillon, and David Last (eds.), 2004   Paper ISBN 1-55339-042-3 Cloth ISBN 1-55339-043-1

New Missions, Old Problems, Douglas L. Bland, David Last, Franklin Pinch, and Alan Okros (eds.), 2004   Paper ISBN 1-55339-034-2 Cloth ISBN 1-55339-035-0

The North American Democratic Peace: Absence of War and Security Institution-Building in Canada-US Relations, 1867-1958, Stéphane Roussel, 2004
Paper ISBN 0-88911-937-6 Cloth ISBN 0-88911-932-2

Implementing Primary Care Reform: Barriers and Facilitators, Ruth Wilson, S.E.D. Shortt and John Dorland (eds.), 2004   Paper ISBN 1-55339-040-7 Cloth ISBN 1-55339-041-5

Social and Cultural Change, David Last, Franklin Pinch, Douglas L. Bland, and Alan Okros (eds.), 2004   Paper ISBN 1-55339-032-6 Cloth ISBN 1-55339-033-4

Clusters in a Cold Climate: Innovation Dynamics in a Diverse Economy, David A. Wolfe and Matthew Lucas (eds.), 2004   Paper ISBN 1-55339-038-5 Cloth ISBN 1-55339-039-3

Canada Without Armed Forces? Douglas L. Bland (ed.), 2004
Paper ISBN 1-55339-036-9 Cloth ISBN 1-55339-037-7

Campaigns for International Security: Canada's Defence Policy at the Turn of the Century, Douglas L. Bland and Sean M. Maloney, 2004
Paper ISBN 0-88911-962-7 Cloth ISBN 0-88911-964-3

Understanding Innovation in Canadian Industry, Fred Gault (ed.), 2003
Paper ISBN 1-55339-030-X Cloth ISBN 1-55339-031-8

Delicate Dances: Public Policy and the Nonprofit Sector, Kathy L. Brock (ed.), 2003
Paper ISBN 0-88911-953-8 Cloth ISBN 0-88911-955-4

Beyond the National Divide: Regional Dimensions of Industrial Relations, Mark Thompson, Joseph B. Rose and Anthony E. Smith (eds.), 2003
Paper ISBN 0-88911-963-5 Cloth ISBN 0-88911-965-1

The Nonprofit Sector in Interesting Times: Case Studies in a Changing Sector, Kathy L. Brock and Keith G. Banting (eds.), 2003
Paper ISBN 0-88911-941-4 Cloth ISBN 0-88911-943-0

Institute of Intergovernmental Relations
Recent Publications

Available from McGill-Queen's University Press:

Canadian Fiscal Federalism: What Works, What Might Work Better, Harvey Lazar (ed.), 2005
Paper ISBN 1-55339-012-1 Cloth ISBN 1-55339-013-X

Canada: The State of the Federation 2003, vol. 17, *Reconfiguring Aboriginal-State Relations,*
Michael Murphy (ed.), 2005   Paper ISBN 1-55339-010-5 Cloth ISBN 1-55339-011-3

Money, Politics and Health Care: Reconstructing the Federal-Provincial Partnership,
Harvey Lazar and France St-Hilaire (eds.), 2004
Paper ISBN 0-88645-200-7 Cloth ISBN 0-88645-208-2

Canada: The State of the Federation 2002, vol. 16, *Reconsidering the Institutions of
Canadian Federalism,* J. Peter Meekison, Hamish Telford and Harvey Lazar (eds.), 2004
Paper ISBN 1-55339-009-1 Cloth ISBN 1-55339-008-3

*Federalism and Labour Market Policy: Comparing Different Governance and Employment
Strategies,* Alain Noël (ed.), 2004   Paper ISBN 1-55339-006-7 Cloth ISBN 1-55339-007-5

The Impact of Global and Regional Integration on Federal Systems: A Comparative Analysis,
Harvey Lazar, Hamish Telford and Ronald L. Watts (eds.), 2003
Paper ISBN 1-55339-002-4 Cloth ISBN 1-55339-003-2

Canada: The State of the Federation 2001, vol. 15, *Canadian Political Culture(s) in
Transition,* Hamish Telford and Harvey Lazar (eds.), 2002
Paper ISBN 0-88911-863-9 Cloth ISBN 0-88911-851-5

Federalism, Democracy and Disability Policy in Canada, Alan Puttee (ed.), 2002
Paper ISBN 0-88911-855-8 Cloth ISBN 1-55339-001-6, ISBN 0-88911-845-0 (set)

Comparaison des régimes fédéraux, 2ᵉ éd., Ronald L. Watts, 2002   ISBN 1-55339-005-9

Health Policy and Federalism: A Comparative Perspective on Multi-Level Governance,
Keith G. Banting and Stan Corbett (eds.), 2002
Paper ISBN 0-88911-859-0 Cloth ISBN 1-55339-000-8

Comparing Federal Systems, 2nd ed., Ronald L. Watts, 1999   ISBN 0-88911-835-3

**The following publications are available from the Institute of Intergovernmental
Relations, Queen's University, Kingston, Ontario K7L 3N6
Tel: (613) 533-2080 / Fax: (613) 533-6868; E-mail: iigr@qsilver.queensu.ca**

First Nations and the Canadian State: In Search of Coexistence, Alan C. Cairns,
2002 Kenneth R. MacGregor Lecturer, 2005   ISBN 1-55339-014-8

Political Science and Federalism: Seven Decades of Scholarly Engagement, Richard Simeon,
2000 Kenneth R. MacGregor Lecturer, 2002   ISBN 1-55339-004-0

The Spending Power in Federal Systems: A Comparative Study, Ronald L. Watts, 1999
ISBN 0-88911-829-9

Étude comparative du pouvoir de dépenser dans d'autres régimes fédéraux, Ronald L. Watts,
1999   ISBN 0-88911-831-0

Working Paper Series

2005

1. *International Law and the Right of Indigenous Self-Determination: Should International Norms be Replicated in the Canadian Context?* by Jennifer E. Dalton

2. *Intergovernmental Fiscal Relations and the Soft Budget Constraint Problem* by Marianne Vigneault

3. *Property Taxation: Issues in Implementation* by Harry Kitchen

4. *The Impact of the Centralization of Revenues and Expenditures on Growth, Regional Inequality and Inequality* by Stuart Landon and Bradford G. Reid

5. *Autonomy or Dependence: Intergovernmental Financial Relations in Eleven Countries* by Ronald Watts

6. *An International Equalization Program (IEP): Rationales, Issues, and Options* by Richard C. Zuker

7. *Demographic Change and Federal Systems: Some Preliminary Results for Germany* by Helmut Seitz, Dirk Freigang, and Gerhard Kempkes

8. *Accords and Discords: The Politics of Asymmetric Federalism and Intergovernmental Relations* by Kathy Brock

2005 Special Series on Asymmetric Federalism

(Posted on our website at http://www.iigr.ca under Research, then Browse Publications)

1. *Asymmetry in Canada, Past and Present* by David Milne

2. *Public Opinion On Asymmetrical Federalism: Growing Openness or Continuing Ambiguity?* by F. Leslie Seidle and Gina Bishop

3. *Some Asymmetries are More Legitimate than Others – And Subsidiarity Solves Most Things Anyway* by Gordon Gibson

4. *A Comparative Perspective on Asymmetry in Federations* by Ronald L. Watts

5. *Equality or Asymmetry? Alberta at the Crossroads* by F.L.(Ted) Morton

6. *The Case of Asymmetry in Canadian Federalism* by Jennifer Smith

7. *Speaking of Asymmetry. Canada and the 'Belgian Model'* by Andé Lecours

8. *The Historical and Legal Origins of Asymmetrical Federalism in Canada's Founding Debates: A Brief Interpretive Note* by Guy Laforest

9. *Beyond Recognition and Asymmetry* by Jocelyn Maclure

10. *The Scope and Limits of Asymmetry in Recent Social Policy Agreements* by Peter Graefe

11. *German Federalism – Still a Model of Symmetry?* by Saskia Jung

12. *Western Asymmetry* by Roger Gibbins

13. *Survivance versus Ambivalence: The Federal Dilemma in Canada* by Hamish Telford

14. *Asymmetrical Federalism: Magic Wand or "Bait and Switch"* by Hon. John Roberts

15a. *Asymmetrical Federalism: A Win-Win Formula!* by Benoît Pelletier

15b. *Le Fédéralisme Asymétrique: Une Formule Gagnante Pour Tous!* by Benoît Pelletier

16. *Who's Afraid of Asymmetric Federalism? – A Summary Discussion* by Douglas Brown

17. *Federal Asymmetry and Intergovernmental Relations in Spain* by Robert Agranoff

For a complete list of Working Papers, see the Institute of Intergovernmental Relations web site at: www.iigr.ca. Working Papers can be downloaded from the web site under the pull down menu "pubications, working papers."